To my family.

Additional resources for Marketing: An Introduction, Fourth Edition:

Easy to use online teaching material for this book is available at

www.gillmacmillan.ie

To access this teaching resource on our secure website:

1. Go to www.gillmacmillan.ie.
2. Log on using your username and password. If you don't have a password, register online and we will email your new password to you.

Contents

Preface

Marketing involves understanding needs. This book seeks to serve the needs of students of marketing by providing an introduction to marketing theory, illustrated, where possible, with examples of marketing practice. This fourth edition provides updated perspectives on theory and practice, especially where these relate to marketing in Ireland.

Marketing continues to evolve: it is a dynamic discipline, and this book provides some insights into the ideas and concepts that have shaped, and continue to influence, it. As with the study of business in general, it is important to learn from marketing examples, which are all around us; so this book includes a significant number of case vignettes in each chapter. In addition, each part is followed by a number of more extensive case studies; these relate to the material covered in the preceding part and provide the reader with added insights and opportunities for analysis and discussion.

The book is written from an explanatory viewpoint. Topics are introduced and explained, hopefully in a clear and concise way. The emphasis throughout is on putting the customer at the centre of the business; this is the basis for making marketing decisions. The student of marketing should also appreciate the importance of monitoring forces in the environment that affect the firm. In Ireland we are fortunate that the news media and specialist business media provide extensive coverage of business and marketing-related topics, and many of the examples in the book have been obtained from these sources. This should also be an encouragement to students to look for such examples to increase their understanding of the business environment. While Irish examples dominate the book, it would be myopic to concentrate on them alone, and several international examples are also used.

Technology, in many forms, will continue to be an influential force on marketers, and firms will therefore be concerned with such issues as electronic commerce, the internet, and digital television, all of which, together with other technological developments, are discussed. In addition to its role in business, the internet will also be an important source of information for students. This will make it easier for them to keep in touch with developments in marketing and to find illustrative examples.

The book is divided into five parts, designed to follow on logically from each other. Each part is completed by a case study or case studies, designed to integrate and build on the material covered in the preceding section.

Part 1 is completed with the Nicholas Mosse case study, written by Hilda Burton. This case highlights the role of marketing in the establishment and development of the business.

Part 2 concentrates on the market. The forces in the marketing environment are described, and an introduction to the theories of buyer behaviour is given. The marketing research process is also introduced in a separate chapter. The important process of segmentation, targeting and positioning is described, and students are given examples to illustrate the link between them. Two cases studies, one on the Love Irish Food initiative and the other on Roma Pasta complete this section. The Love Irish Foods case highlights how the marketers involved responded to a challenging environment, while the Roma case provides an opportunity to develop a questionnaire for use in a consumer survey.

Part 3 concentrates on the elements of the marketing mix, what are traditionally referred to as the 'four Ps'. The nature of the product is explained, and considerable attention is paid to branding, packaging, and new-product development. The chapter on pricing examines the decisions to be made in pricing products and services; pricing methods are described, and market influences that affect price are examined. Rather than use the term 'promotion', the chapter on marketing communication presents a broad profile of the components of this dynamic aspect of marketing practice. The communication model is explained, and the nature of advertising, public relations, sales promotion, personal selling and sponsorship is described and discussed. The chapter on marketing channels is also broader than the more traditional 'place' description. Issues in channel management, including distribution, logistics, transport, wholesaling, retailing, and franchising, are explained. Part 3 is completed with case studies on Jacob Fruitfield and Donegal Catch. An updated Jacob Fruitfield case study traces some of the challenges this firm's brands have faced in recent years and how it responded to them. The Donegal Catch case study is an award-winning example of how advertising can be used to build a brand successfully.

Part 4 comprises four short chapters on marketing applications. These seek to introduce marketing practice in the context of services, international markets, business-to-business markets, and non-profit organisations. Each chapter demonstrates how the principles of marketing are equally relevant, regardless of application, but also why adaptation may sometimes be required. This section of the text is completed with an updated Jameson Irish Whiskey case study. This elaborates on how one of Ireland's most successful brands has gone from strength to strength in the international marketplace.

Part 5 consists of a single chapter on marketing strategy and planning, which integrates the components of the previous chapters and emphasises the importance of planning for the business. This part is completed with the Newbridge Silverware case study. Newbridge has been a very successful company in the past decade and this updated case study examines some of the strategic issues that it has faced.

At the end of each chapter, there are recommendations for further reading, selected to provide the reader with more detailed coverage of the material introduced in the chapter.

Acknowledgments

I would like to acknowledge the assistance I have received in writing the fourth edition of this book. I am particularly grateful to my colleagues Hilda Burton, who contributed the Nicholas Mosse case study. I would also like to thank: William Doyle, Managing Director, Newbridge Silverware; Michael Carey, Chief Executive, Jacob Fruitfield; Mark Saunders, Marketing Manager, Roma Foods; and Peter O'Connell, International Sales and Marketing Director, Irish Distillers Limited for their co-operation in the development of the case studies on their respective companies/brands. I am also grateful to the Institute of Advertising Practitioners of Ireland for permission to use the Donegal Catch case study.

I would like to thank Marion O'Brien, Aoife O'Kelly and Catherine Gough of Gill & Macmillan for their help and support. I would also like to thank Claire Rourke for her editing skills. As with the two previous editions, any defects or omissions remain very much my own.

PART 1

Marketing: The Customer and the Business

1
Putting the Customer at the Centre

arketing is a subject that should be interpreted rather broadly. It is widely associated with business practice, but it should not be defined in a purely business context. In the business context it can be described as an outlook or way of thinking that puts the customer at the centre. It is based on understanding the needs of customers and serving those needs, competitively, at a profit.

There have been many definitions. Kotler and Armstrong (2010) state that:

> Broadly defined, marketing is a social and managerial process by which individuals and organisations obtain what they need and want by creating and exchanging value with others. In a narrower business context, marketing involves building profitable, value laden exchange relationships with customers.

In 2004, for example, the American Marketing Association modified its definition of marketing to read:

> Marketing is an organisational function and a set of processes for creating, communicating and delivering value to customers and for managing customer relationships in ways that benefit the organisation and its stakeholders.

The Kotler and Armstrong definition is broad and is capable of being interpreted in a number of contexts, for example, personal (think of marketing yourself at a job interview), commercial (marketing consumer products), or non-commercial (a charity seeking to fundraise). The American Marketing Association definition can be described as narrow or managerial; in other words it defines marketing in a way that is useful to managers in business or organisations.

Marketing theory tends to be derived largely from business, Kotler and Levy (1969) considered that 'the business heritage of marketing provides a useful set of concepts for guiding all organisations'. The student of marketing should also consider other views and perspectives on the subject. A philosophy describes a way of thinking and there has been much debate among marketing academics and practitioners about the mission and role of marketing in business and society for example, whether marketing is an art or a science. Some theorists, for example Brown (1993) and Firat (1991), have observed that marketing emerged in the modernist era (an encompassing label for a wide variety of cultural movements that began in the mid-18th century). In the business context, modernism was reflected in scientific approaches to research and the mass production of consumer goods.

Another perspective is the post-modernist view; this questions the benefits of progress and challenges the idea that scientific method is the sole source of knowledge. Post-modernist theorists consider that value is created not in production (the modernist view) but in consumption. Brown (1993) states that 'the urge to consume is a characteristic symptom, perhaps *the* characteristic symptom, of the postmodern condition'.

Considering different perspectives is important as we begin to try and understand the meaning of marketing. In this book marketing is considered largely in the business context; however it will seek to reflect the contributions and perspectives of a variety of theorists.

The definitions considered above emphasise the importance of the customer. Understanding the customer, and especially understanding that customer needs can change, is fundamental to good marketing practice. This is well illustrated in the case of one of Ireland's oldest brands, Flahavan's.

FLAHAVAN'S AND THE RENAISSANCE OF PORRIDGE

When high-profile celebrities such as Demi Moore, Naomi Campbell and Bill Gates went public about their love of porridge in recent years, it was part of what John Noonan, sales and marketing director at Flahavan's called a 'porridge renaissance'. Within a few years the oat-based breakfast cereal had shaken off its old-fashioned image and gained appeal among a new generation of younger consumers.

Embracing this movement Flahavan's, which can trace its history back to an oats mill in Kilmacthomas, County Waterford, in the late 1700s and remains a family-owned company, repositioned itself with a strong brand focus, market segmentation, and the introduction of a new range of 18 products in drums, sachets, and pots. In addition, real fruit porridge and a selection of oat biscuit snacks were also introduced.

Traditionally, the porridge market had been quite homogenous, there was one main type and brands such as Flahavan's and rival Odlum's were sold in basically the same format—a bag. There was very little segmentation, and porridge struggled to compete with an ever expanding range of breakfast cereals from marketers such as Kellogg's and Nestlé.

A decision taken by the federal Food and Drug Administration in the United States in 1998 was to have a dramatic effect. The FDA allowed producers of porridge to make health claims based on the fact that porridge contains soluble fibre which is good for the digestive system and can reduce cholesterol. As a result, porridge received much favourable press coverage and began to feature in various health trends, including the Atkin's diet. Other trends evolved, including those that focused on the glycemic index or the benefits of eating whole grains.

Flahavan's carried out market research which found that consumers who were not buying porridge cited lack of convenience as one of the main reasons. The company responded by introducing a Quick Oats range, this is microwaveable and comes in individual tubs or in sachets.

In addition to product development, advertising and public relations were used to communicate the brand's benefits. Consumers were interested in the health benefits of porridge, so public relations proved effective when trying to achieve press coverage.

Launching new products that consumers had not seen before, such as the microwaveable range, also provided public relations opportunities. Another PR initiative was the teaming up with a well-known chef, Kevin Dundon, for an all-Ireland porridge promotion, including a porridge-making competition.

Television and radio advertising concentrated on the theme that the brand 'Sets you up for life', and highlighted the health and convenience of the products. Research among younger consumers, for example, revealed that the pots and sachets were often taken to work, so this theme was developed in some of the adverts. Other themes included the family aspect, with the Flahavan's 'family' or range of products being emphasised.

EXPORTS

Exporting has always been important for Irish food and drink marketers, providing opportunities for expansion outside what can be a small domestic market. Flahavan's developed an export strategy which proved successful and the company was named Irish Exporter of the Year in 2009. By 2010 exports accounted for 20 per cent of sales. Flahavan's entered the UK market in 2003; research there revealed that consumers would not respond to the marketing approach that had been used in Ireland. In Ireland the brand was well known and provoked an emotional response among consumers. In Britain it was necessary to concentrate on more functional aspects such as taste, convenience, and ease of preparation. As a result marketing activities concentrated on in-store promotion and events. The brand is stocked in Tesco, Asda, Sainsbury's, Waitrose and Wholefoods. In addition to the UK, Flahavan's is also sold in France, the Middle East, and Spain. In 2010 the company was researching the US market as its next export opportunity. The oatmeal market in the US was estimated to be worth €1.2 billion. One of Flahavan's rivals, Odlum's had marketed a range of porridge oats in the United States under the McCann's brand, but had sold this brand to an American company in 2006.

RESULTS

In 2009 Flahavan's reported a 65 per cent increase in market share and a 15 per cent increase in profits, a significant achievement in what was a recessionary environment. Flahavan's success was also recognised by the Marketing Institute, a representative body for marketers in Ireland, when John Noonan was named Marketer of the Year in 2009.

Sources: Catherine O'Mahony, 'Flahavan's wins Marketer of the Year with Impressive focus on growth', *Sunday Business Post*, 15 November 2009; Sorcha Corcoran, 'Progressive Oats', *Marketing Age*, Vol 4, Issue 1, 2010; www.flahavans.ie, www.odlums.ie.

The Flahavan's example illustrates many aspects of good marketing practice in business. The firm understands consumer needs and how these can change. It has responded to changes in the marketing environment and it has successfully developed a strategy involving product and brand development, advertising, promotion, distribution, and a successful launch into international markets. These aspects of marketing will be elaborated on in subsequent chapters.

In his book *Crowning the Customer*, Feargal Quinn, one of Ireland's leading marketing practitioners, outlined his view of marketing. He developed what he described as the 'boomerang' approach: quite simply, keep customers happy and they will keep coming back. The policy certainly worked for him, and his Superquinn chain of supermarkets was an acknowledged provider of high levels of customer service and innovation. It was also a consistently profitable company.

Firms like Flahavan's and Superquinn, demonstrate how understanding customer needs and serving those needs at a profit, is core to understanding the meaning of marketing in a business context.

THE NATURE OF MARKETING

Marketing should permeate the whole operation of the company as it seeks to determine what to produce and how and where to sell it. It is a process that begins before the product or service begins and continues after it has been sold.

The Flahavan's example indicates that there are many dimensions to marketing; for example, product development and advertising. In order to understand and clarify these dimensions, we need to appreciate the underlying concepts that are at the core of marketing. Kotler and Armstrong (2010), for example, have given us a useful model of the core concepts (fig.1.1) which will be examined in the next section.

NEEDS, WANTS, AND DEMANDS

Marketing begins with an understanding of human needs. *Needs* describe a state of felt deprivation. According to one theorist, Abraham Maslow (1943), human beings are constantly needing individuals. At a basic level we need air, food and drink, sex and shelter to survive; these are described as innate or primary needs. We may also need to feel secure,

Figure 1.1: Core marketing concepts

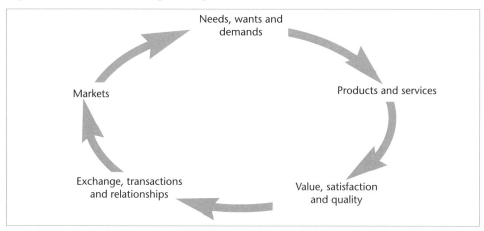

Source: Kotler *et al.*, 2010.

to belong, to acquire knowledge, to have power, and to be able to express ourselves. These needs are considered to be acquired, because they are influenced by our culture or environment. They are referred to as secondary needs.

All needs are motivational: in other words, if we feel the need for something we experience tension, and we will be driven towards reducing the tension by satisfying that need. At a basic level, if we are hungry we will reduce the tension we feeel by eating. This could involve any number of possibilities, from preparing something at home to dining out in a restaurant. What we eat may depend on secondary needs: for example, we may eat with friends in a restaurant, making it a social occasion, or we may go to a fashionable café where we like to be seen and where we hope we will meet others.

Wants describes the form taken by human needs as influenced by culture and the individual's personality. We need clothing, but we don't all wear the same style of clothes. Individuals may want to follow a particular style or fashion or express themselves in what they wear.

Demand exists when people have the purchasing power to satisfy their needs. Few people will have the income to satisfy all their needs, so they will make trade-offs, buying products and services that give them the greatest amount of satisfaction they can get for their money. Understanding how these trade-offs are made is important for marketers; it also emphasises the significance of customers' needs in marketing theory.

Most marketing practitioners are concerned to generate and satisfy the demand for their products or services. Company growth, development and profitability are usually dependent on achieving sales growth. There may, however, be circumstances when the marketer wants to dampen and control demand; this has been referred to as *de-marketing* (Lawther, Hastings and Lowry, 1997). In the health area, for example, advertising campaigns have been conducted to discourage people from seeking drug prescriptions for minor ailments; similarly, they have also attempted to discourage people from using casualty departments in hospitals.

Sometimes the need isn't just that of the customer as the example of Berney Brothers saddles illustrates.

BERNEY BROTHERS SADDLES

In 1880, Peter Berney founded a small saddlery in Kilcullen, County Kildare. Fourth and fifth generations of his family continue to design and make saddles which have gained a reputation for quality and durability among equestrian sports people. The company produces saddles for hunting, racing, dressage, cross-country, and show jumping. These can be considered as segments which are based on different user needs. The saddle design has, therefore, to take into account not just comfort and durability but also the context in which the saddle will be used. A jockey in a steeplechase, for example, will require a smaller lightweight saddle compared to a show jumper who will need a saddle that allows for changing leg position depending on whether jumping or landing. The saddle has also to take account the needs of the horse, in terms of comfort and fit. The saddle should not restrict the horse's movement, or cause pinching or discomfort. Custom-made saddles for individual horses and riders are often produced.

Source: www.berneysaddlery.com.

The difference between needs and wants

The terms *needs* and *wants* should not be used interchangeably. Every person has needs; some of these are innate. Wants are for specific products or services that will satisfy a need. If we are hungry, therefore—an innate need—we may want a bar of chocolate, a sandwich, or a four-course meal. Wants will depend on a combination of individual characteristics, and social and environmental influences.

An often-heard criticism of marketing is that 'marketers create needs to make money.' In reality, marketers cannot create needs. They can and do seek to influence wants. A hungry consumer can be influenced in what they choose to eat. The marketer did not, however, make the consumer hungry. We are familiar with advertising for food and drink products that promise different taste sensations, speedy preparation, or thirst-quenching properties. These are attempts by the marketers of these products to encourage consumers to differentiate between alternatives, to satisfy a need by wanting a specific product or brand.

Products

Usually the term *product* is used to describe what is being exchanged by the marketer with the market. A product is anything that can be offered to satisfy a need or a want. It can include physical things, such as cans of Coca-Cola or bottles of washing-up liquid; these are described as tangible. Something is tangible if we can see, touch, hear, smell or taste it. Products can also be intangible, such as the experience of visiting a theme park or seeking financial advice from a bank. Intangibility describes experiences, feelings, or emotions.

Marketers therefore use the term *product* in a very wide sense. In between these categories there are many products that have a combination of tangible and intangible features.

As we saw with the Flahavan's case, porridge is a tangible product, providing tangible benefits—satisfying hunger. It also satisfies intangible benefits in terms of how people feel about it; the popularity of the brand, for example, suggests that some consumers have an emotional reaction to it.

Kotler and Levy (1969) contended that marketing is a pervasive social activity that goes considerably beyond selling tangible products, such as toothpaste or soap. They suggested that the term *product* could be used to describe physical products, services, people, organisations, and ideas. The following are some examples of each type of product:

Physical products: Crisps; beer; detergent; fertiliser.
Services: Holidays; insurance; a haircut; advice.
People: Politicians; journalists; actors.
Organisations: Irish Farmers' Association; political parties; charities.
Ideas: Energy conservation; anti-litter campaigns; environmental awareness.

VALUE AND SATISFACTION

Whatever the nature of the product, it must be valued and must give satisfaction if it is to be demanded. Value and satisfaction can mean different things to different people, once again demonstrating the importance of understanding buyers' behaviour. To one consumer a product or service offering particular features and priced at a particular level may represent value and satisfaction; to another consumer it may not. Marketers must therefore understand the nature of the value and satisfaction consumers are looking for and tailor their products or product variations accordingly.

Customer value can be illustrated simply as:

$$customer\ value = \frac{what\ the\ customer\ gets}{what\ the\ customer\ pays}$$

The customer may do this calculation mentally, making a quick assessment of the value they get from the products and services they are buying or are considering buying. They may also carry out a more detailed value analysis, assessing and evaluating all the factors that contribute to overall value. Value analysis is common in organisational buying, where buyers may assess value using mathematical models or formulas.

Customer value reflects a wide variety of factors, depending on the nature of the product. For consumers they could include:

- the availability of information on the product to help the consumer make a decision
- the convenience of retail outlets
- how the consumer was treated by sales or customer service personnel
- ease of payment
- delivery
- operating instructions
- the performance and durability of the product
- the functions of the product
- maintenance cost.

For businesses, value would also be assessed on a variety of factors. These might include:

- the length of customer lead time (the time it takes from the order to receiving the product)
- variation from promised delivery times
- the condition of the product on arrival
- sales calls and order initiation requirements
- credit, billing and payment procedures
- the effectiveness of after-sales support
- the manual and instructions accompanying the product
- the performance, fit and function of the product
- the frequency and duration of downtime
- maintenance cost and difficulty.

Value may also refer to how the consumer feels about the product or brand. Fournier (1998) for example, explored the relationship between consumers and their brands. She presented a social relationship model of consumer–brand relationships; in other words, she argued that people can develop relationship bonds with brands, and therefore understanding how this happens can illuminate our understanding of brand loyalty and brand personality.

The implications of this for the marketer are the need to understand how customers measure value, and how the marketer can maximise value for the customer. The designing, manufacturing, marketing and support processes that the firm engages in will be the main sources of value for the customer. Firms therefore engage in what we can describe as a *value-adding* process. From the buying of raw material to production, branding, distribution, image-making—in fact all the activities of the firm—we see the value-adding process in action.

Marketing involves adding value. The activities of marketers, such as researching new features and benefits, branding, and advertising, involve adding value. This book examines the different ways in which marketers add value.

EXCHANGE, TRANSACTIONS, AND RELATIONSHIPS

Marketing is an exchange process. Typically, we exchange money for products and services. However, not all exchange involves money. We can exchange anything that has value: for example, organisations such as the Samaritans do not charge for their service, which involve the exchange of time, advice, and counselling.

Bagozzi (1975) considers that there are three types of exchange: restricted, generalised, and complex. *Restricted exchange* refers to two-party reciprocal relationships, for example retailer–consumer. *Generalised exchange* involves univocal reciprocal relationships among at least three actors. This can be illustrated with an example. The National Tidy Towns competition is sponsored by the SuperValu retail chain. The Tidy Towns organisation negotiated sponsorship with SuperValu; it also liaises with local communities and encourages participation. If people from these communities patronise SuperValu outlets as a result, this would be a generalised exchange. The third type of exchange suggested is *complex exchange*, which refers to a system of mutual relations among at least three parties.

A typical example of complex exchange would be manufacturer–retailer–consumer.

Transactions are a trading of values between two parties. While most transactions involve some form of monetary payment, this is not always the case. Bringing glass bottles to a bottle bank for recycling is a transaction, but it does not involve any monetary exchange between the consumer and the marketer. Transactions may also involve the customer trading in an older product in part-exchange for a newer one; this is common in the car market and has been used in electrical goods retailing. The important point is that in any exchange, a value is placed on what is being exchanged.

The notion of exchange has been developed into the concept of *relationship marketing*. Relationship marketing implies that the firm attempts to build relationships between itself and its customers, suppliers, and distributors—in other words, with any individual or firm it exchanges or wishes to exchange with. The central idea is that these interactions should be viewed as relationships involving the exchange of value.

The concept of relationship marketing helps illustrate the nature of value. In the case of the marketer–retailer exchange, for example, the relationship does not simply involve physical distribution but also involves other factors, such as market development, co-operation in marketing and distribution campaigns, and mutual problem-solving. If the marketer and retailer view their arrangements as a relationship that can be developed to be mutually beneficial, it is more probable that improved performance and profitability will follow. If the relationship is viewed as confrontational, this may be less probable.

The development of relationship marketing theory gathered pace in the 1990s. The creation, development and quality of relationships are at the core of marketing. This was well illustrated by the academic Christian Grönroos (1994) when he argued that relationship marketing was in effect a 'paradigm shift' in marketing theory. By this he meant that relationship marketing had led to a fundamental shift in the theory underlying marketing.

The theory of relationship marketing is a useful framework for understanding the concepts underlying marketing theory. It is also fundamental to the development of marketing practice. The marketer can apply the principles of relationship marketing in dealing with suppliers, channel members, and customers. The concept of 'customer', therefore, applies not just to the final customer or consumer but to the other individuals or firms that the marketer deals with.

The marketer–customer relationship is a core aspect of relationship marketing. Viewing the customer as an individual with whom the firm wishes to develop a relationship encourages businesses to look beyond mere transactions. The customer is someone whose needs the firm seeks to serve again and again.

THE MARKET

The *market* describes the actual and potential buyers for the product. In this book we examine markets such as the consumer market, the business-to-business market, and international markets. These are descriptions of different types of market, but all markets have one thing in common: they involve relationships. Whether marketer–consumer, consumer–consumer, or business–business, markets represent a set of relationships.

Market profiling is an important aspect of marketing. Markets exhibit different characteristics and trends, and comprehending and monitoring these is a central aspect of marketing. Understanding the customer is guided by universal principles, but the customer must also be understood in the context of their environment.

All markets are different. Chapter 3 describes the environmental forces that affect Irish marketers; chapter 12 describes how international environments can be different and where marketing activities and practice may need to be modified.

Earlier we saw how Flahavan's responded to change and engaged in product development. Another firm that has successfully contended with change is the the Galway-based footwear brand, Dubarry, that has maintained healthy profits by diversifying its business and engaging in manufacturing abroad.

DUBARRY OF IRELAND

Dubarry, the Irish footwear and clothing maker, has defied a difficult business environment with an international expansion focused on high-end retailers in several countries. The Galway firm made its first delivery to Harrods department store in London in 2009 and is striking deals with other key retailers and distributors. Dubarry is best known for its deck shoes, but marketing director Michael Walsh said that the company has reinvented itself with a move into 'country living' footwear, clothing, and luggage.

Dubarry was a traditional manufacturer of footwear, but increased competition from low-wage countries meant that it found it very difficult to compete. In the 1980s the company diversified into marine footwear, and started to make a specialist range of deck shoes that was very successful in international markets. The brand proved popular not just among sailors but was also adopted as a fashion item by Irish teenagers and young adults, the shoes coming to be described as 'Dubes'.

Dubarry had employed about 250 people in Ballinasloe in the early 1990s, but by 2010 this had reduced to about 55 staff—including research and design employees. All its manufacturing is carried out overseas. The winding-down of manufacturing in Galway in 2004 caused anger locally, but Walsh said the business had seen the benefits of the reorganisation. 'We were the last remaining footwear manufacturer in Ireland,' said Walsh. 'All of our components were coming in from overseas and being put together in Galway. We were paying top dollar for everything and freighting it into Ireland. The realisation dawned that footwear production had no future in Ireland.'

The vast majority of its products are made in Portugal, although it also started working with Chinese firms in 2005. It retains five production staff in Ballinasloe, who can do small product runs and work on prototypes or repairs if required.

In 2008, sales of Dubarry's country living goods outstripped its traditional marine-related business for the first time. The product range includes leather boots, costing upwards of €300, bags for about €400, and jackets that range from €500 to €600. Ironically, Walsh said that sales were holding up partly because the goods were at the premium end of the market. 'People can't get rid of their boats or the horses during a downturn. They are fairly committed to them,' he said.

The firm's overseas revenues also exceeded its Irish figures for the first time in 2008. The company estimated revenues of €15 million in 2009, close to the €15.5 million it recorded in the 12 months to the end of September 2008. It had revenues of €17 million the previous year, which included a gain of about €2 million from the sale of land. The company has been strongly profitable, making €2 million before tax in 2008 and €3 million in 2007.

The company's strategy of bringing products directly to consumers at outdoor-related shows and events proved successful. It has built a trade show stand and exhibited at events such as the Dublin Horse Show, the Chelsea Flower Show and Crufts dog show. Other important events include the Burghley Horse Trials in England, as well as events in Germany and the Hamptons in New York. The Rolex horse trials in Kentucky are also a key event for the firm.

'We have gone out and created demand for ourselves,' said Walsh. 'Our UK operation does 60 shows a year. We go directly to events to meet the end-users of our products. Because we are dealing directly with the public, we get a very quick reaction to products.' The move into non-marine products was helped by one Dubarry customer in particular—a sailor who also had an interest in hunting, from whom they developed the idea of spreading their footwear range. 'We have a sailing boot that was fully waterproof and breathable, so we made up a prototype with an outdoor sole and went after that market,' Walsh said.

The company's 'Dubes' had an established place in the market and sold well, particularly during the back-to-school season, said Walsh. 'They are fashionable, but they are not high fashion. They are not all the rage today and gone tomorrow.'

Sources: www.dubarry.com; Gavin Daly, 'Dubarry Steps out in profitable style', *Sunday Business Post*, 6 September 2009.

THE EVOLUTION OF MARKETING

While there have probably always been marketers—though they may not have been described as such—the origin of contemporary marketing can be traced back to the industrial revolution. The development of the factory system and the introduction of new forms of transport made selling products to a wider market more feasible. A central aspect of the factory system was large-scale, efficient production. This enabled companies to mass-produce products at attractive prices. The coming of the railways and improvements in shipping technology made the expansion of distribution networks possible. The development of advertising was also stimulated by the industrial revolution, as manufacturers needed to inform new and growing markets about their products.

Marketing evolved as a body of knowledge to meet a need. The growth in markets presented many challenges. Firms needed to plan, organise, develop, communicate and control in an integrated way. Over time, marketing theory developed and was refined to meet these needs—and it continues to develop. Needs change, markets change, and marketing theory is constantly subject to updating and addition. As a discipline, marketing is dynamic, it does not stand still.

With regard to guiding policies, the management of marketing is influenced by five alternative concepts: the production concept, the product concept, the selling concept, the marketing concept, and the social marketing concept.

The production concept

While the factory system did lead to the production and wider availability of products, in many cases it was company managers who decided what to produce; customers were not necessarily consulted. This meant that customers had no say in the process.

Firms that concentrate on production and distribution efficiency demonstrate the production concept. This holds that consumers favour products that are widely available and affordable. This approach is appropriate as long as what is produced is what the customer wants. If the customer wants something else and the firm cannot provide it, they may not buy, or may buy something else. In the air transport market, Ryanair could be considered to follow this approach. The company concentrates on producing a low-cost service. Unlike many of its competitors, it does not offer added benefits, such as in-flight meals or frequent-traveller schemes. The production concept works for this company: it serves a need for low-cost travel, and there is a sufficiently large market with that need.

The production concept may not work in markets where buyers require a high degree of customisation or additional benefits. If a business requires specialist financial advice, for example, it will not be able to buy a mass-produced service.

The product concept

The product concept holds that consumers favour products that offer the highest quality and the greatest number of performance and innovative features. As a result, manufacturers may spend considerable time and effort improving products by adding new features or benefits. This can also be important in maintaining market share or in reacting to competitors; but improvements must be valued by the market.

As we saw earlier, consumers will make trade-offs. They may like products with many features and high performance levels, but such products may cost more, and the consumer may not be able to afford them. In the search to improve products or add new features, manufacturers or service providers should not lose sight of customers' needs. The launch of compact discs, for example, led to a significant decline in the sale of records. While there is still a small specialist market for records, producers knew that no amount of improvement or added features could save the product. These producers had to view their businesses not as record providers but as audio product providers. Needs changed, and firms in the industry had to react.

It can be shortsighted, however, to follow the product concept too closely, as it can lead to 'marketing myopia'. This implies that the business is concentrating too much on the product and not enough on market needs. The concept of marketing myopia was well illustrated by Theodore Levitt (1960), who used the example of railway companies in the United States, which defined themselves as being in the railway business. The problems with this definition became apparent when competition from road and air became more intense. Levitt argued that the railway companies should have defined themselves as being in the transport business. It would have been myopic for record producers, for example, to ignore the new CD technology and persist with the production of records. What is produced is ultimately determined by customers' needs. If those needs change, businesses have to adapt.

The selling concept

Often people use the terms *selling* and *marketing* as though they mean the same thing. Selling is a function of marketing. Firms seek to sell products and services to make a profit; what they sell should be what the customer wants.

The danger with the selling concept is that the firm concentrates on selling rather than on matching products with needs. It is possible to sell people products they don't need or want. This is not what marketing is about, nor indeed is it what good salesmanship is about. It is myopic to concentrate on getting the sale without worrying about the customer's needs or post-sales satisfaction.

The marketing concept and the social marketing concept

The marketing concept is based on understanding customers' needs and providing competitive products or services to meet those needs, at a profit. Marketing is therefore concerned with understanding the customer, being competitive, and making a profit.

The social marketing concept introduces the idea of being responsive to the well-being of society in general. We can elaborate on both these concepts by examining the role of marketing in the firm and in society.

Marketing plays a number of roles, both internal and external to the firm. It is inseparable from the creation and development of enterprises, whether profit-making or non-profit-making. Whether researching an idea, testing a concept, or launching a product on the market, marketing activities come into play. Marketing plays a role in the initial research and creation of a product; it also sustains and is used to develop the product over its lifetime. Marketing has helped to create many of the products and services we take for granted. It has also helped to create successful products that have become what could be described as consumer icons. Think of products such as Coca-Cola, the Volkswagen 'Beetle', or Nike sports wear: without marketing, would they enjoy the success they have experienced?

Marketing also plays a role in society. It facilitates exchange, leads to the development of products and markets, provides jobs, and is a body of knowledge that enables products, services, places and ideas to be taken from initial thoughts to commercial and profitable reality.

Taking all this into account, what actually makes a marketing-oriented organisation? It is really a combination of factors, but the following list probably sums it up. A marketing-oriented organisation:

- is customer-driven
- is centred on satisfying customers' needs
- has a competitive advantage
- is capable of change
- is responsive to the customer's needs before, during and after the sale of the product
- is profit-driven (whether in financial or non-financial terms)
- is responsive to society's well-being.

According to Quinn (1996), there are three essential questions to be answered: how to get every member of your team working to meet customers' needs (team members also include customers themselves); how to create a bigger and better marketing department than the competition; and how to reward customer loyalty, as opposed to creating it. Superquinn seems to have managed to answer these questions: the business has grown, profits have increased, and the chain is widely recognised as providing high standards of customer service.

Centred on customers' needs

Being centred on customers' needs implies knowing what those needs are and attempting to serve them better than your competitors. Marketing research plays a role in finding out about customers' needs and monitoring how they change. Research will certainly be useful;

it will also be useful to apply common sense. There really is no great mystery to understanding the customer: what is often more mysterious is the ability of firms, with all their resources, to get it wrong.

There have always been businesses that have remained close to their customers and that have always concentrated on customers' needs. In the case of Kelly's Resort Hotel, this focus involved adapting over time to suit changing needs. This company has been putting marketing theory into practice for several generations.

KELLY'S RESORT HOTEL: LOOKING AFTER THE CUSTOMER SINCE 1895

Started as a tea-room to cater for Sunday beach goers, Kelly's Resort Hotel in Rosslare has grown over four generations of the Kelly family to become one of the best-known family hotels in Ireland.

The coming of the railway at the turn of the century was a spur to development. Guests could travel from all parts of the country to the hotel. The changing needs of guests over time meant that the company had to react: guests required more than accommodation, food, and beverage service. The hotel was the first in Ireland to build an indoor swimming pool and tennis courts, and it established a strong reputation for its amenities. In addition to providing a high standard of facilities, the hotel also catered for special-interest segments and offered courses in sport, health and beauty, wine tasting, interior design, and gardening

According to Linda Byron, a senior specialist at the Irish Management Institute, Kelly's is 'an Irish company that excels at looking after their customers and reaping the benefits'. The benefits are expressed in customer satisfaction and profitability. Sometimes up to 90 per cent of rooms are occupied by guests who have been to the hotel before. The organisational culture puts customers ahead of short-term profit, strong leadership is provided by the management, and there are good internal communications. The benefits are also expressed in a string of awards, including several National Hygiene Awards and the Egon Ronay Hotel of the Year award in 1995.

In 2010, a year that proved difficult for Irish tourism because of recession, Kelly's reported a very good summer season. General manager Bill Kelly said they had 95 per cent occupancy for June, July, and August helped by the best summer weather for many years.

Sources: *Sunday Business Post*, 10 September 1994; *Irish Independent*, 2 March 1996; *Sunday Business Post*, 23 March 1997; *Irish Times*, 22 May 2010; *Irish Times*, 28 August 2010.

Competitive advantage

Having a competitive advantage means that the business has something with which to differentiate its product or service from that of its competitors. Products or services must have *unique selling propositions* (USPs), otherwise customers may not be able to tell them apart. A competitive advantage is therefore a prerequisite of successful marketing. If the product or service is no better than that of competitors on criteria such as quality, price, availability, choice, or image, what is there to market?

Competitive advantage needs to be sustained: successful products and brands need to be kept up to date, and any new market potential needs to be examined. Consider the case of Tayto crisps, a successful brand in Ireland since the 1950s, and which was sold for €62 million in 2006.

Marketing has helped this brand become the market leader. Its competitive advantage derives from a number of sources. The product satisfies a need in the market and has been successful in responding and adapting to environmental forces, such as changing views on health and life-style. (In chapter 3 we consider the forces in the marketing environment that can present opportunities and threats for the marketer; these forces will affect the company's competitive advantage.) The Tayto product is aimed at defined market segments, and the brand positioning has been carefully developed. (In chapter 5 we will explore the nature of market segmentation, targeting, and positioning; these play an important role in achieving competitive advantage.) The product, pricing, promotional and distribution strategies employed by the company have also proved effective. (In chapters 7–10 we will examine how these four factors, collectively known as the *marketing mix*, can contribute to competitive advantage.)

Achieving competitive advantage is therefore a significant goal for any business. It is necessary for survival, and marketing will also have to play a role in helping this brand deal with some new competitive challenges.

TAYTO: IRELAND'S FAVOURITE CRISP

Tayto was established by Joe Murphy in 1954. He was fond of eating crisps but found the products available on the market at the time rather dull. He started the business in premises off Moore Street in Dublin and had one van and eight employees. One of its earliest successes was the invention of the cheese and onion flavoured crisp. The company expanded quickly and in 1964 a majority stake was purchased by Beatrice Foods, a large American company. They invested in the business and by 1970 the company had 300 employees and a large production facility in Coolock. In 1972 the King crisp company was acquired and in 1981 the Smith's food company, which had a range of crisps among its product portfolio, was added. Tayto was the first company in Ireland to manufacture extruded snack products. Joe Murphy was considered to have considerable marketing flair and was one of the first sponsors of a Radio Éireann programme when this became possible in the 1950s.

In 1999, Tayto was acquired by Cantrell and Cochrane (C & C). Tayto's position as market leader remained unchallenged until the arrival of Walkers crisps on the Irish market on St Patrick's Day in 2000. By 2005 it had taken a 20 per cent market share. In 2005, Tayto was still market leader, but its share had dropped to 30 per cent. King crisps had almost 11 per cent of the overall crisp market. The remainder of the market share was held by other brands such as Pringles and McCoys and by own-label products. Walkers is owned by PepsiCo and was market leader in the UK market.

Walkers' success was attributed in part to an advertising campaign featuring the former England soccer player Gary Lineker. PepsiCo, subsequently adapted these advertisements for the Irish market to feature Irish soccer players Roy Keane and Robbie Keane. Gaelic footballers Darragh Ó Sé of Kerry and Ciarán Whelan of Dublin were used in later advertising campaigns.

Tayto responded to Walkers by increasing its advertising and promotion. It also invested in new product development and in 2004 launched its 'Honest' range of low-fat/low-salt crisps and popcorn. The objective of the product was to target consumers who wanted a healthier product. By 2005, Honest crisps had a 3.5 per cent share of the total crisp market, while Honest popcorn had 16 per cent of the popcorn market. Ultimately, however, C&C was unable to recover market share and began to consider its options.

In April 2006, C&C announced it was carrying out a strategic review of the future of the Tayto brand; this followed the company's decisions to shut the manufacturing plant in Coolock in October 2005 and subcontract production of Tayto crisps to Largo Foods. Largo were also involved in the crisp and snack business and manufactured the Perri and Hunky Dory brands. In 2005 the Tayto brand had sales of €47.3 million and made a profit of €5.8 million. The outcome of the strategic review was a decision to sell the brand to Largo Foods for €62.3 million in July 2006.

Largo were quick to invest in marketing and promotion, running new advertising and promotion campaigns based on the character of Mr Tayto, a character that had appeared on the brand packaging for decades. These proved successful and in 2008, two years after the acquisition, Largo reported a market share increase in the crisps and snacks market, its total market share was 47 per cent, this was a significant achievement in a market where several large global firms such as Proctor & Gamble (Pringles), PepsiCo (Walkers) and United Biscuits (KP Hula Hoops) are key competitors.

The general election of 2007 had provided the ideal platform as Mr Tayto gate-crashed the election with a series of policies, including peace and reconciliation: 'It's time the Northside and the Southside learned to live together.' In 2008 Mr Tayto embraced the digital age as he launched a nationwide search for a wife using Facebook and Bebo and irresistible lonely hearts small ads: 'Are you a lovely girl? Potato-shaped individual would like to meet thick-ankled lovelies with marriage in mind. Must enjoy the finer things in life like a spin in a Massey Ferguson, crisp sandwiches and a good old knees-up. If your turn-ons include wellies, snacks and a bloke in a hat, I'm your only man.'

The 2009 campaign was based on Mr Tayto's autobiography, a lavishly produced, full-colour book telling the hilarious story of the life and times of the character, retailing in book shops at €6 and supported by an €800,000 media campaign. It became a bestseller.

In a commentary on Tayto's marketing, John Fanning, Chairman of McConnell's Advertising observed, 'A recent collection of essays from the prestigious Kellogg School of Management at Northwestern University stated in its introduction that "in an era of extreme advertising clutter and consumer avoidance, perhaps no other recent concept has captured more interest from marketers than engagement … Engagement embodies a heightened sense of involvement, of being connected with something". The Tayto campaign strategy fulfils this objective, completely inverting traditional thinking by substituting the standard "and now a word from our sponsor" with the audacious request that you fork out €6 to read what is in effect a 114-page advertisement for the brand.'

Sources: *Irish Times*, 13 October 2001; Barry O'Halloran, 'Crisp exchange sees UK brand take market share', *Irish Times*, 11 February 2005; *Checkout*, September 2005; Gabrielle Monaghan, 'Strategic Review for Tayto', *Irish Times*, 14 April 2006; Emmet Oliver, 'C&C sells Tayto to Largo for €62.3 million', *Irish Times*, 6 July 2006; Ciarán Hancock, 'Largo set for profit despite flat sales, *Irish Times*, 9 December 2009; John Fanning, 'How the man in the jacket gets under the nation's skin', *Irish Times*, 28 December 2009.

Capable of change

The Tayto example demonstrates the need for change. The launch of a new snack product was successful; over time, the product was developed, and its market positioning was changed. Marketers need to be able to adapt to changes in the environment; this ability to change will be necessary to sustain competitive advantage. Change in response to environmental forces both internal and external to the firm will be necessary. These forces are considered in more detail in chapter 3; for the moment, change can be illustrated by examining one force that has affected marketing in many ways: technology.

Technology is a source of competitive advantage, not simply by adding value to the consumer with improved products and services but also through its role in the practice of marketing. Technology is also a threat: it can become obsolete, quickly rendering the firm's products, services and management practices uncompetitive. The 1990s saw increased attention paid to what was referred to as 'electronic commerce'—this describes sharing business information, maintaining business relationships and conducting business transactions by means of telecommunications networks (Zwass, 1996). The applications of electronic commerce in marketing are widespread. It was argued that they would have the most impact in developing and maintaining customer relationships, direct marketing, finding new segments or markets, and linking the core business processes (Harrington and Reed, 1996). Obviously, the staff of a company need to know how to use this technology, which has implications for recruitment and the development of skills.

Information technology in particular has been very influential. The marketer's ability to gather information about customers and markets, generate databases, create management information systems, and interact with other firms has developed significantly since the 1980s. Specific marketing practices such as direct marketing, database marketing and telemarketing have all grown as a result. *Electronic data interchange* (EDI) has had particular application in marketing channels. (These marketing applications will be explored in chapters 9 and 10.)

In the late 1990s many organisations began to develop sites on the worldwide web and use of the internet increased. The internet enabled companies to communicate with existing and potential customers and also enabled them to offer new services.

Many commentators in the late 1990s were enthusiastic about the internet and its potential as a global business medium. Use of the internet would be most significant in business-to-customer communications and transactions. There also existed the *extranet—* inter-organisational networks, for example between a marketer and a retailer. This would have significant applications in business-to-business marketing (see chapter 13). *Intranets* are networks within an organisation, for example between departments in a large organisation. An intranet would therefore be useful for internal marketing applications (see chapter 3).

As mentioned in the Tayto case example, marketers have also started to use social networking sites, such as Bebo and Facebook, which enable people who have shared interests, opinions, or activities, to interact over the internet. The Tayto example suggests that people may engage with advertising on social networking sites. Other brands such as Pat the Baker have also experimented with this idea as the following example shows.

SOCIAL NETWORKS AND MARKETING

Pat the Baker is not what most people would regard as a Web 2.0 company, but in September 2008 the bakery firm launched a campaign on Bebo to complement its ongoing press, radio, and television campaigns. The Pat the Baker Bebo profile generated more than 3,000 friends. Brand manager Oliver Durkin said the Bebo campaign cost 1.2 per cent of the bread maker's overall marketing budget and its impact on the brand's visibility has been a 'phenomenal success'.

'It takes a lot of time,' said Durkin. 'You can hire out other companies to do it, but I don't think it works. I do it with four staff. We all take turns. We are on it 24/7. We respond to every single request and comment personally.' More than 4,000 users have downloaded the company colours to their own profile pages and the bread maker is releasing seasonal skins for Christmas, St Patrick's Day, and the summer to keep members interested. Even though the bulk of Bebo's users are under 25, Durkin is confident that Pat the Baker is targeting the right audience. The bakery used Bebo for a competition where members of the public were invited to record and submit video versions of the 52-year-old Pat the Baker jingle. The winner received a €10,000 prize, and visitors to Bebo can see clips of the current entries and find out how to submit their own.

'The quality and the level of entries is astounding. I thought it would be more kids in the bedroom. We have immediately had content generated by our very talented customers,' said Durkin. One of the more popular submissions is by Dublin dance music act Robotnik, which released its take on the Pat the Baker theme song as a Christmas single.

'It is so rewarding, from a brand manager's point of view, being at a gig where somebody plays your song and 3,000 people go mental,' said Durkin about a recent Robotnik's gig. The company is also giving away Pat the Baker T-shirts to Bebo members who send in a picture of their 'mammy, granny or a borrowed little old lady holding a Pat the Baker product'.

Blogs and social networking sites can be a great way for businesses to get their message out or they can be tremendous time sinks. Either way, they are as popular as ever with web surfers here—something many Irish businesses overlook.

No Nonsense Car Insurance, a trading name of FBD Insurance, tested a widget that Facebook members can install on their page. Users receive a €20 discount on their next year's premium or a €40 donation to their chosen charity for every person who takes out an insurance policy as a result. 'If it [the widget] works it will certainly be extended to FBD,' said Brendan Hughes, e-commerce manager for FBD Insurance.

'Irish businesses don't know where [blogging] fits within their marketing and communications mix and they don't understand the potential,' said Hughes, who is also Chairman of the Irish Internet Association's Social Media working group. 'Blogging is not advertising and it is not traditional PR. It is more akin to having conversations with customers—albeit informal and public conversations—and this is a new concept.'

Hughes wrote a post for the No Nonsense Car Insurance blog about how to drive during a flood. Web surfers concerned about driving under such conditions visited the company's site after this blog post appeared in their search results. These niche posts will never attract huge audiences but they will lure people relevant to a company's product or service.

Every year, public relations firm Edelman conducts a survey in 18 countries to determine the level of trust people place in organisations, institutions, the media, and various other groups. The 2008 Irish Trust Barometer found radio is a well-regarded source of information, with 59 per cent of respondents trusting the medium. Newspaper articles on individual companies ranked at 55 per cent, while 27 per cent of those surveyed trusted a company's own communications. Only 14 per cent of those surveyed said they used and trusted blogs as a source of information.

The survey also looked at whom people trust most to act as a spokesperson, with 57 per cent citing a doctor, healthcare specialist or NGO representative. Only 7 per cent said they'd trust a blogger to act as a spokesperson. This figure is down 5 per cent on 2007, suggesting fewer people believe what they read online.

'There are lots of opportunities for bloggers to offer an alternative source of information or a more in-depth resource,' said Piaras Kelly, Edelman's main Irish blogger. 'While bloggers will never rank as the most trusted source of information for the general public, what you will find is that a number of bloggers have built audiences that regard them as more informed sources of information on certain topics.' The readers of blogs often leave comments supporting or disagreeing with the poster or even providing further information to support their arguments. While there is no measurable bottom line to any of this—and some comments can even be unhelpful—Hughes argued that business bloggers needed to think of their readers as potential advocates. 'Advocacy ultimately leads to the bottom line,' he said. 'Consider social media not as a money maker but as a relationship builder. You won't make money through your social media activity, but because of it. There does need to be a return on investment, but how the return is measured needs to change to reflect this new way of connecting with customers.'

Social networking sites, like blogs, can also be an effective market research tool for businesses. Computer manufacturer Dell operates ideastorm.com as an online community for people to share ideas. It credits the suggestions of an Irish user on the site for the camera upgrades to the Latitude range of laptops. Similarly, public relations firm Slattery Communications launched an application on Facebook which enables marketing and advertising professionals to post ideas and comment on each other's suggestions. Those suggesting ideas have just a few lines to outline their concept, a medium of delivery, and the specific benefit of the suggestion.

Businesses should also consider Twitter, which is a form of micro-blogging. A possible use is for firms who have to provide regularly updated information to customers. Posters write a comment in less than 140 characters. This is then delivered to the mobiles or e-mails of 'followers'. Setanta Sport uses the service to update its followers about the latest sporting news.

Source: Bryan Collins, 'New way to hit target', *Sunday Business Post*, 7 December 2008.

Responsive before, during, and after

Marketing is concerned with developing a relationship with the customer. This relationship begins before the product or service is sold; it may involve significant interaction during the sale, and it continues after the sale has been made. Marketers need to be just as concerned about post-purchase satisfaction as with the factors that precede the sale. Factors such as creating awareness or sales technique are important aspects of pre-sales activity; but marketing does not end there.

The development of relationships is at the heart of the theory of relationship marketing. Firms must manage a number of relationships. The marketer–customer relationship is the obvious one, but there also exist marketer–supplier, marketer–intermediary and marketer–marketer relationships. Whatever the nature of the relationship, it should be managed in such a way that it develops and will last.

In chapter 6 the factors that influence behaviour before, during and after the purchase are examined. It would be myopic for marketers to concentrate only on the actual purchase. There are many pre-purchase influences in the buyer's environment; equally, post-purchase factors such as satisfaction must also be considered.

Profit-driven

Profit, for most firms, is the reward for entrepreneurial effort and is required by investors and shareholders in the business. It is also required to ensure the continued survival of most businesses. For some organisations, profit may not be measured in purely financial terms. There are many non-profit organisations that measure success in more intangible ways. Charities and cultural organisations, for example, do not exist to make profits for shareholders: their success may be measured in aid provided, support given, or heritage protected. Marketing principles are equally relevant to these organisations, for they are also involved in exchanging something of value.

Responsive to society's well-being

Marketing activities are carried out within society. They should not do anything to damage that society. This demonstrates the importance of ethical marketing practice.

Ethics is defined as generally accepted views of what is right and wrong. Ethical practice requires the firm to be socially responsible. Marketers have to serve the needs of society, and activities that do not do so can hardly be described as customer-centred. There is certainly a paradox if marketing appears to be unethical when its objectives are concerned with responding to consumers' needs.

Carrigan and Attalla (2001) examined whether ethics had an impact on consumers' behaviour. They proposed that there were four types of consumer, based on levels of ethical awareness and behaviour (see fig. 1.2).

Given the nature of marketing practice and activities, it is not surprising that ethical issues have emerged. Typical issues include misleading advertising, dubious pricing practices, and sales approaches being made under the guise of market research. Relative to the consumer, the marketer is usually in a more powerful position. This means that if the business loses sight of the core marketing principle of serving the customer, the customer may be compromised.

Marketing is not a regulated profession in the same way that pharmacy or medicine are. But codes of ethics do exist in specific areas of marketing practice, such as market research and advertising. The Marketing Institute of Ireland also has a code of practice, which outlines the professional responsibility and conduct required of its members. This code provides a useful overview of the responsibilities, conduct, and values that should be a feature of good marketing practice.

There are also various laws and regulations that govern the way in which business is done (some of these and their implications are considered in chapter 3). These are part of the environmental forces that affect marketers. Very often it is the way in which business is done that comes in for criticism.

Figure 1.2: Ethical awareness and behaviour

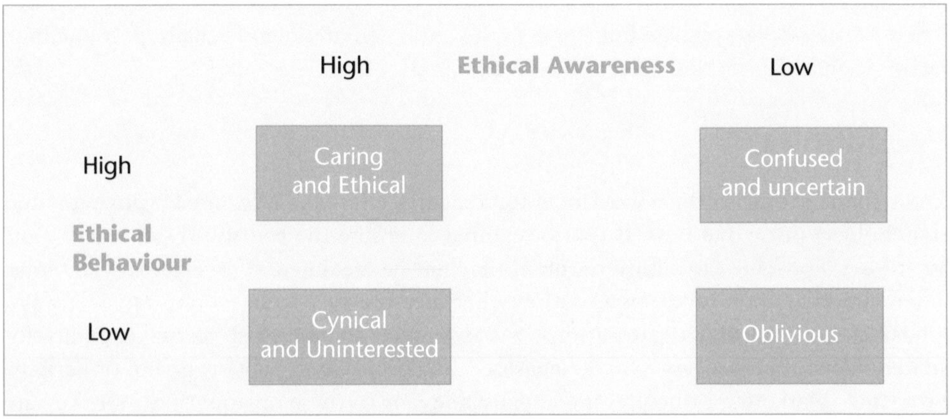

CODE OF PRACTICE OF THE MARKETING INSTITUTE

The code states that professional marketing executives have a responsibility to their employers or clients, to customers, to colleagues, to the marketing profession, and to the public in general.

It describes the importance of professional conduct, obliging members to conduct themselves at all times as people of integrity and to observe the principles of the code. In this way the reputation of members of the institute, the institute itself and of marketing in general will be enhanced.

The code describes the nature of professional conduct with regard to the instruction of others, injury to other members, honesty, professional competence, conflict of interest, confidentiality, and the securing and developing of business. It also obliges members to be aware of and to comply with other relevant codes of practice in advertising, sales promotion, market research, public relations, and direct marketing.

The institute can investigate and take action against members where breaches of the code have occurred.

Source: Marketing Institute of Ireland.

Given the complexities of business, the ethical issues and dilemmas raised can also be complex. By putting the customer first, however, it is less likely that a firm or its employees would engage in unethical practice. Firms should have a code of ethics, which would communicate what its priorities, values and expectations are. The code should be published and should send a clear signal to everyone in the firm that ethics are a priority. In the words of one commentator (Tierney, 1992), 'people weigh the ethical implications of their decisions not only by their personal values but also by the working environment created by the leadership'.

Codes of ethics will be useful only to the extent that people can understand them. Some firms have therefore invested in training programmes. These can involve examining organisational values, presenting people with ethical dilemmas, analysing ethical issues, and weighing up the consequences of particular actions. Codes and training are important, but they also need to be implemented and adhered to. The values incorporated in the code can be incorporated in the firm's performance appraisal system. This would imply that the firm's marketing personnel, for example, would be evaluated not just on criteria such as sales or profitability but also on the ethical performance of their role.

Carrigan and Attalla (2001) found that while consumers remain largely uninformed about ethical behaviour by firms, they are willing to purchase ethically but do not want to be inconvenienced in doing so. Very often, price, quality and value outweigh ethical criteria in consumer purchase behaviour. Carrigan and Attalla suggest that, in order to be persuaded to buy, consumers need to be convinced that their purchase behaviour can make a difference in ethical terms.

There is some evidence that marketers who highlighted their ethical principles enjoyed positive results. The increase in sales of Fairtrade products in Ireland is an example.

FAIRTRADE

In 2009 sales of Fairtrade products in Ireland were €118 million, an increase of 27 per cent on the previous year. One of the contributors to this growth was Cadbury Ireland which completed the conversion of its Dairy Milk and Dairy Milk Buttons products to Fairtrade certified raw materials. Nestlé had also converted its KitKat raw materials to Fairtrade and worldwide sales of Fairtrade products increased by 37 per cent to $1.1 billion.

Fairtrade products ensure that growers and producers, who are mostly located in poorer countries, have received a fair price for their output. In addition, Fairtrade ensures that a percentage of sales is used for development and educational projects in the producer's area.

In Ireland, Fairtrade products are sold in most supermarket chains. In 2006 Marks and Spencer switched its entire range of coffee to Fairtrade and planned to do the same for its tea. The Thomas Read group, which operated a number of bars, sourced all its coffee from Fairtrade, while O'Brien's Irish sandwich bars changed its tea products to Fairtrade in March 2006.

Research carried out by Fairtrade in Ireland revealed that 44 per cent of adults recognised the Fairtrade logo.

In October 2005, Nestlé launched the Nescafé Partners' Blend, which carried the Fairtrade mark. This indicated that the coffee had been bought from democratic smallholder organisations and traded according to agreed Fairtrade standards. The coffee came from five co-operatives of small producers in El Salvador and Ethiopia. Given that coffee is a commodity product, many producers had been experiencing difficulties because of price volatility. In addition to coffee, Fairtrade products  include tea, chocolate, sugar, bananas and other fresh fruit, juices, honey, cakes, preserves, nut oil, wine, roses and footballs.

Sources: Gabrielle Monaghan, 'Irish Fairtrade sales jump 30% to €6.5 million', *Irish Times*, 29 June 2006; www.fairtrade.org.uk.

A study by Low and Davenport (2005) highlighted some of the reasons for the success of Fairtrade. They pointed out that the Fairtrade distribution system had shifted from one that relied on alternative distribution channels to one that is increasingly reliant on the commercial mainstream. They concluded that the marketing of Fairtrade through mainstream distribution channels has been the major success and the major challenge for the fair trade movement over the past decade. Success has come through increased sales but challenges are apparent if commercial businesses are able to appropriate and control the Fairtrade brand. The researchers pointed out that the marketing of Fairtrade has shifted from being about international trade reform to one about 'shopping for a better world'.

MARKETING PRACTICE IN IRELAND

We have examined the nature of marketing and looked at how it has evolved as a theory. It is also useful to consider how marketing practice have evolved in Ireland.

As in other countries, marketing as a specific function began to appear in Irish companies in the 1950s. The following table presents a chronology of some of the important developments since then. Marketing was not a completely new idea: there were many firms that had always been marketing-oriented; what was new for most firms was the establishment of a specific marketing function. This was spurred on by the post-war development of domestic and international markets.

Table 1.1: Some important developments in marketing in Ireland

1952	Córas Tráchtála is established.
1962	Marketing Institute of Ireland is established.
1965	Sectoral Committee on Industrial Organisation criticises marketing practice Anglo-Irish Free Trade Area Agreement opens the way for increased competition
1968	Federation of Irish Industry expresses concern about lack of prominence of marketing.
1973	Ireland joins the European Economic Community, implying more competition
1982	Telesis Report on Industrial Policy considers marketing to be a major weakness in Irish companies.
1984	Ireland and Marketing report leads to debate about the state of marketing practice.
1987	First Minister of State for Trade and Marketing is appointed.
1992	Culliton Report suggests specific marketing initiatives.
1997	Research by the Marketing Institute demonstrates that marketing will become more influential in Irish companies.
2000	International Superbrands Organisation establishes a council in Ireland.
2004	The Enterprise Strategy Group recommends the development of international marketing and sales expertise to bring enterprise in Ireland closer to customer needs.
2010	The report Innovation Ireland, prepared for the Irish government, makes a number of recommendations about the role of marketing in fostering innovation and product development in Ireland.

In 1952 Córas Tráchtála, which had been established to promote the export of Irish products, employed American consultants to assess the export potential of some firms. They concluded that the firms should not try exporting, because they had not got quality products and had no inclination to take risks. The report also identified marketing as a weakness in the companies they studied (Ward, 1987).

In 1962 the Marketing Institute of Ireland was founded as a representative body for marketing practitioners. Its role involved representing, lobbying, and developing marketing practice. A significant aspect was education and training; this was particularly necessary in the 1960s and 1970s, when many managers had no formal marketing training or education. In 1965 the Sectoral Committee on Industrial Organisation confirmed this when it reported that there were management deficiencies in many firms, inadequate training, inadequate marketing, and poor marketing arrangements.

Also in 1965 the Anglo-Irish Free Trade Area Agreement was signed. As a result, Irish firms had to deal with increased competition. Many were unable to cope.

Marketing was still a serious weakness. In 1968 the Federation of Irish Industry was expressing concern that marketing had not been given the prominence it deserved.

Ireland joined the European Economic Community in 1973. This resulted in more competition in the home market, and also opened up greater export possibilities. In the 1970s and 1980s exports rose rapidly and firms came to appreciate the role of marketing and the need to keep in touch with the consumer, especially in markets both physically and culturally removed from the home market. They were reminded of this in the Telesis Report on Industrial Policy (Telesis Consultancy Group, 1982), which identified marketing as a central weakness in Irish firms.

A government report, *Ireland and Marketing* (Consultative Committe on Marketing, 1984), criticised poor marketing performance by companies and stated, that Ireland needed to market its products more effectively for economic growth and survival. The report stated that the failure of firms to adopt a clearly stated, strategic marketing orientation was a fundamental weakness in marketing practice. Following the publication of this report there was much discussion on the nature and role of marketing in Irish business (Condon, 1985; Cook, 1987). This was important, as it drew companies' attention to the importance of marketing and the role it should play in the firm. Interesting analogies were drawn; one leading academic asked the question, 'Where are our marketing samurai?' which reflected something of the state of marketing practice at the time and the need for change (Cunningham, 1987).

In 1987 the government appointed the first Minister of State for Trade and Marketing. This was a recognition of the important role played by marketing. The Culliton Report (1992) emphasised the importance of developing marketing skills in Irish business and suggested that specific marketing initiatives be taken in the food sector.

In 1997 the Marketing Institute of Ireland commissioned research into companies' attitudes to marketing. This showed that more than 80 per cent of companies had a more progressive attitude towards marketing than had been the case five years earlier.

In 2000, the International Superbrands Organisation—a representative body of marketing academics and professionals from the United States, Europe and Asia Pacific—established a council in Ireland (Butler, 2001). This was an indication that Ireland already possessed brands that had enjoyed success in global markets and had brands that were capable of future development.

Reporting to the government in 2004, the Enterprise Strategy Group recommended that the Irish enterprise community must develop, and be supported in growing, its capabilities in market intelligence, international sales, promotion, sales and strategic management. They recommended that Enterprise Ireland develop a more focused approach to export intelligence and promotional activities. They also recommended the establishment of a five-year programme to place 1,000 graduates and internationally experienced professionals in Irish firms to augment the stock of national sales and marketing talent.

In 2010 the Innovation Ireland report, a wide-ranging report on stimulating innovation in Ireland, recommended that the country should build on its existing IDA international marketing campaign to attract international entrepreneurs to Ireland; it also recommended that a single brand identity, based on innovation in Ireland, should be developed. The report considered that Ireland should be marketed internationally as an international marketing services centre. Other recommendations were made in relation to education, state support, and new product development.

A chronology of the development of marketing gives some idea of what has happened over time. It also emphasises the need for firms to keep abreast of change. Customers' needs can change, and firms must be able to change in response. Marketing is therefore a discipline that requires flexibility and adaptability, not least when it comes to planning for the future.

The Flahavan's and Kelly's Hotel approach to business has not been replicated by all firms in Ireland. As various reports and commentaries have shown, Ireland has been slow to develop marketing practice. There are a number of reasons for this. Protectionism tended to result in a market with few competitors and limited consumer choice. Industrially there may have been an overreliance on foreign direct investment and a slow development of indigenous industry.

Many foreign-owned companies established factories in Ireland but carried out their marketing activities elsewhere. As a result, there were few opportunities for managers to develop their marketing skills. Marketing education and training did become a strong feature of the third-level educational system and other relevant educators, such as the Marketing Institute and the Irish Management Institute, particularly since the 1980s. Firms in the 1960s and 1970s would not have experienced the benefit of this to the same extent as their counterparts in the 1990s and 2000s. In the years ahead, what are the likely challenges that marketers will face?

MARKETING CHALLENGES

The future is always uncertain. Ireland entered the new century as part of a growing and strengthening European Union. The opportunities to develop markets within and outside the European Union are substantial. There are also competitive threats; firms that cannot change and adapt will face difficulties. Those that maintain close links with their customers and markets should be better prepared for the challenges that will emerge.

It has been argued that in the 1980s and early 1990s marketing lost some of its strength by overt functionalism and a concentration on the tactical rather than the strategic (Doyle, 1995). While it is important that marketing functions such as promotions and distribution are carried out effectively, it is equally important to consider the strategic perspective. Doyle proposed an approach to marketing management based on internal and external networks. He argued that a marketing approach based on what he considered to be the core processes of innovation, operations, and customer support is necessary for marketing to remain at the core of the business. It is easy for businesses to lose sight of the core policy of marketing and to concentrate on functions or particular aspects of the business. New technological developments, for example, may mesmerise, but firms should be careful to avoid falling into a situation where they cannot see the wood for the trees.

The management of marketing will change. The marketing policy will not change, however. Customers will still be at the centre of the business. The way in which those customers are served, the products or services they buy, and how the firm may communicate or deliver to them may change. Marketers will therefore need to keep abreast of environmental developments. Technological change may be particularly important; the guiding principle, however, will remain the same.

In chapter 3 we will consider some of the issues in the business environment with which marketers will have to contend.

MARKETING AND ENTERPRISE

The interface between marketing and entrepreneurship is significant. Marketing plays a crucial role in the creation and development of enterprise. All aspects of marketing practice have one common denominator: they are all part of the value-adding process, whereby firms add value to serve the needs of consumers.

This value-adding process essentially describes what the business does. It therefore includes the development of new and improved products, entrepreneurship, and innovation. Marketing practice also involves the creation and development of specialist marketing enterprises that service other firms, for example advertising agencies and market research companies. Marketing and marketing practice can therefore provide opportunities for new business ventures. (The critical role of marketing in enterprise development is further explored in chapter 2.)

THE NATURE OF MARKETING MANAGEMENT

Marketing management is concerned with how the different elements of marketing are organised, planned, and controlled. It describes what the businessperson or marketing personnel actually do. These activities can range from carrying out marketing research, developing communication campaigns and selling to the development of marketing strategies to take the firm successfully into the future.

This book introduces the principal elements of marketing in relation to the decisions the marketer has to make. These decisions are based on an understanding of the concepts underlying marketing, which ultimately revolve around understanding the customer. The marketer will therefore need to appreciate the forces at work in the marketing environment and understand the nature of consumer behaviour. Marketing research will be vital in doing this.

Decisions will be made on segmenting markets, on selecting particular segments, and on how best to position products. Marketing planning prepares the business for the challenges in the market. Management of the marketing mix, which includes four elements—the product, price, promotion, and place—is a significant aspect of the marketer's role. Marketing practice may need to be adapted to suit what the marketer is marketing. The nature of services marketing, business-to-business marketing, international marketing and marketing for non-profit organisations is also important.

In exploring the nature of marketing management it is useful to examine the relationships between marketing, customer service, and quality. The three are interrelated concepts, as fig. 1.3 demonstrates.

Marketing, customer service and total quality management therefore have one crucial factor in common: understanding the needs of the customer. In the following section the broad nature of customer service and total quality management is described.

Figure 1.3: The relationship between marketing, customer service, and quality

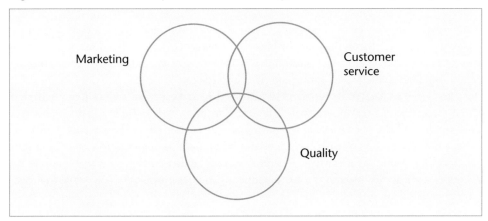

CUSTOMER SERVICE

Customer service has been defined as all the features, acts and information that augment the customer's ability to realise the potential value of a core product or service (Davidow and Uttal, 1989). Customer service is therefore a vital competitive tool that can be used to differentiate a business from its competitors.

Customer service requires successfully matching customers' needs with the company's abilities. This requires segmentation of customers' service needs. In the case of airlines, for example, the service needs of frequent business travellers may be very different from those of the infrequent flier looking for special offers. The airline needs to determine the needs of each segment and match these needs with the required level of service. Customer service strategy also requires that the business maintains a customer-service focus, not losing sight of the importance of the customer. In more recent times, increased prices for many products and services were not always accompanied by increased levels of customer service, suggesting that this was an area where improvement was required.

QUALITY

Quality is defined as fully satisfying agreed customer requirements at the lowest internal price. Quality theory owes its origins to several researchers and management writers, most notably, Deming (1986), Juran (1989), and Ishikawa (1985). The Japanese led the way in the 1970s and 1980s. Japanese products made huge inroads in many markets. The main strategy of the Japanese was quality and price competition. Consumers certainly approved and, in many product categories from cameras to cars, responded with increased demand for Japanese products.

Many companies were unable to withstand the challenge; the survivors realised that they would have to compete on quality. Quality management grew from this need. It describes an approach to business which looks critically at the products and services a company produces in relation to the processes it takes to create them and the people who do the work to make certain that outputs fully satisfy agreed customer requirements (Bank, 1992).

Marketing, customer service, and quality: the implications for marketing management

Marketing, customer service and quality have a common theme: an understanding of the customer. In fig. 1.3 this is illustrated where the three sets intersect. In addition, marketing intersects with customer service, customer service with quality, and quality with marketing. Marketing managers need to appreciate these interfaces.

This brings us back to the concept of relationship marketing, which brings together all three elements (Christopher, Payne, and Ballantyne, 1992). Relationship marketing encompasses all the activities before, during and after the sale of the product. Customer service helps create bonds with customers and other markets or groups to ensure long-term relationships of mutual advantage. The provision of quality customer service involves the marketer understanding what the customer needs and determining how to serve that need with a value-added product.

In his book, Feargal Quinn (1991) emphasises the importance of listening to the customer—a fairly common-sense approach to understanding customers' needs but one that not every firm follows. He also considers it important to create more customer complaints, which may not at first glance appear to be an ideal tactic. However, customers' complaints provide an opportunity to learn. If the customer has taken the trouble to complain, it is in the business's interest to react; if they don't, or do so badly, the customer is unlikely to return. A complaint may ultimately turn into a dissatisfied customer only if you let it. It is therefore important that complaints are welcomed and acted upon. The potential for negative word-of-mouth reputation from customers who have complained and were treated badly, or indeed customers who did not complain because they felt it was pointless, is significant.

It is important to note that good service for customers is not about surface-level or cosmetic issues: it must emanate from a core strategy. This must be supported internally in the firm, which demonstrates the need for integrated systems so that all departments are aware of and have access to the information required to deliver good service (Knutton, 1996).

JUMPING ON BANDWAGONS

One of the difficulties inherent in a discipline such as marketing, where new ideas and concepts are evolving rapidly, is determining the appropriateness of these for the company and its customers. There are dangers inherent in merely being a follower rather than assessing the relevance of particular actions for the company and its customers. In the rush to apply the principles of relationship marketing, for example, or to design customer loyalty schemes or develop a website, companies should be careful not to lose sight of the customer's needs. Levitt (1975) warned of avoiding marketing mania, in other words becoming obsessively responsive to every passing whim of the customer.

Marketers also need to avoid alienating customers with reactive approaches to environmental changes. The development of the company-customer relationship needs to be carefully managed, and unwanted advances, for example in the name of relationship marketing, should be avoided (Griffith, 1998). Judgment should also be used in assessing new marketing tools or techniques. The pros and cons should be evaluated before decisions are made.

In this chapter we have considered the nature of marketing and the concepts that underpin it. As we have seen, the activities of marketers often generate controversy—consider for example the debate about marketing alcohol and the influence that marketing activities have on teenagers and young people in particular.

THE MARKETING OF ALCOHOL TO TEENAGERS AND YOUNG PEOPLE

Three out of every 10 teenagers between the ages of 16 and 17 in Ireland has viewed an alcohol advertisement online, according to research carried out in 2010 by Behaviour & Attitudes, and commissioned by Action Alcohol Ireland, a charity that seeks to recognise and challenge the harm that alcohol does. The charity states that it is not anti-alcohol, but is anti the harm that alcohol can do.

When the same peer group was asked what its favourite television advertisements were, five of the top 10 advertisements noted were alcohol related. In 2010 a National Substance Misuse Strategy was being developed in Ireland and there was pressure on the government to end alcohol sponsorship in sport. This follows similar moves in France in recent years, and coincided with an ongoing debate in the UK about whether or not to curtail the activities of the drinks industry in sponsorship, advertising, and marketing.

Alcohol is one of the most heavily marketed products on our shelves. The alcohol market in Ireland was worth over €6 billion in 2010. Several research studies have established that alcohol advertising increases the likelihood that some young people will start drinking earlier, and those who are already drinking will drink more. The World Health Organization, in its strategy to reduce alcohol-related harm, cites alcohol marketing and pricing as key action areas for delivering change.

In 2009 more than €68 million was spent on advertising both alcoholic and non-alcoholic drinks products in Ireland using traditional advertising techniques. Diageo spent more than €18 million on advertising, while Heineken spent more than €11 million.

A 2010 report by the Working Group on Sports Sponsorship by the Alcohol Industry, convened by the Department of Health and Children, concluded that it 'had not been possible' to establish the full financial extent of the existing sponsorship of sports events by the alcohol industry, or the terms and lengths of existing contracts. The report went on to state that the financial contribution to sport in Ireland is 'very significant'.

However, any debate that focuses solely on traditional advertising models, such as television or print, is in danger of failing to tackle growing online marketing techniques. Dr Patrick Kenny, a lecturer in the School of Marketing in DIT, makes the point that younger people can now be accessed easily through their online activities. 'From a marketer's point of view, the online world is a dream, as you can get people to engage with your brand and start promoting it on Facebook or Twitter or whatever. If you go and ban TV advertising on its own, then I believe alcohol marketing budgets will be pushed into other areas, which are harder to regulate.'

Professor Gerard Hastings, Director of the Institute for Social Marketing in Scotland and a leading expert on alcohol marketing, is also of the belief that we must look at alcohol advertising. 'The attempt to get across moderation messages are being drowned out in a cacophony of messages in all sorts of media encouraging young people to consume alcohol in every possible way and time,' he says.

In recent years, particularly since 2000, more responsible television campaigns and warnings (such as the 'Don't see a great night wasted' promotion) have begun to appear. Surely this is evidence of the drinks industry taking its responsibilities on board and pursuing a more health-conscious agenda?

'The only way to sort the problem in Ireland and Britain is by reducing per-capita consumption,' says Professor Hastings, 'yet the industry doesn't buy into that analysis at all. We should recognise corporate social responsibility (CSR) programmes and advertisements for what they are. It is not Mother Teresa territory. They use these campaigns to improve and enhance corporate image with policymakers, so that they can be part of the solution. Diageo's *raison d'être* is to enhance shareholder value, let's not forget that.'

Restrictions aimed at reducing the exposure of children to alcohol advertising came into effect in 2008. The Codes on Alcohol Advertising, Placement and Sponsorship were agreed between the drinks industry and the Department of Health. Print and digital media, including social networking sites, came under the codes for the first time.

The code imposed a limit on alcohol advertising to 25 per cent of advertising space in any media at any time. Advertising drink on media where more than 25 per cent of the audience is under 18 is banned. There is also a ban on sponsorship by drink companies of sports events where participants are under 18. Placing ads on television between 6 a.m. and 10 a.m. is prohibited and the amount of advertising per viewing in cinemas has been reduced by 15 per cent.

At the time the restrictions were introduced the Drinks Industry Group of Ireland, a representative body for the marketers of alcohol, said that the measures would seriously restrict the amount of alcohol advertising and that they would be very challenging for the industry.

Two years later, a report in the *Irish Medical Journal* found that female students appeared to be binge-drinking at least as often as their male counterparts and would sometimes match them drink for drink. The study, by UCC's student health department, expressed concerns at the changing drinking behaviour of female students. It found that almost 45 per cent of students surveyed at UCC's health centre went binge-drinking once a week. A binge was defined as at least four pints or a bottle of wine, or its equivalent, in a single sitting.

More than eight students in 10 said they had binged in the previous year. Some 45.5 per cent of male students said they had binged more than once a week compared with 44.5 per cent of female students. The Clan life-style survey conducted in 2002–2003 found that the male–female binge-drinking ratio was 60–40.

'Females are drinking similar numbers of measures of drinks as males which is a particular concern given that the recommended maximum weekly alcohol intake for females is only two-thirds recommended for males [14 units versus 21 units a week],' the study said.

When females drank spirits, they had an average of five a session while males drank 4.7 measures. With beer and cider, males drank an average 4.5 pints compared with women's 3.7 pints.

Nearly one in four male drinkers said they had been in a fight as a result of their drinking and one in 10 students reported unintentional or unprotected sex as a result of alcohol. Men were more likely to have been abused or assaulted because of someone else's drinking, while women were more likely to have arguments about someone else's drinking.

The study recommended that alcohol and drug groups be set up in every third-level institution.

Speaking in 2010, Ireland's Chief Medical Officer, Dr Tony Holohan, summarised the medical and social evidence:

> Alcohol, even in small amounts, increases the risk of cancer of the mouth, oesophagus, breast, colon, liver and pancreas. On the other hand, alcohol in very low quantities spread over time may indeed have a protective effect against cancer and cardiovascular disease. However, higher levels consumed over shorter periods, not only have no protective effect against heart disease but in fact increase the risk. Alcohol, even at moderate levels, can lead to injury and death in the short term from accidental and non-accidental injuries. Alcohol can cause a wide range of family problems from marital breakdown to child abuse and domestic violence. Children of alcoholic parents can suffer the effects of alcohol throughout their lives. Alcohol leads to loss of work productivity and absenteeism and is associated with crime.

Dr Holohan pointed out that over 10 per cent of all general in-patient hospital costs, 14 per cent of psychiatric hospital costs, 7 per cent of GP costs, and up to 30 per cent of emergency department costs are a result of the effects of alcohol. For 2007 the total costs imposed by alcohol on the public health care system were €1.2 billion. Dr Holohan considered that Ireland is:

> … a country with a proven track record of an ability to change our ways for the improvement of our society. We have shown for example, in relation to cigarettes, that we put the health of our population first. We led the world in terms of regulatory and pricing measures to control consumption of tobacco. We have acted decisively and gained significant success in our fight against smoking which has reduced from 46% and 36% of men and women smoking in the 1970s to 31% and 27% of men and women respectively, currently smoking. If we were able to achieve success to the extent that has been achieved in road safety i.e. a reduction of harm of 30% we would save 30 lives per month, 600 overnight hospital admissions per day and a cost saving to the exchequer of €1 billion.

Sources: RTÉ News, 'Code on Alcohol Advertising Introduced', 1 July 2008; Dr Tony Holohan, opening speech at Alcohol Action Ireland Conference, 'Have We Bottled It? Alcohol Marketing and Young People', 15 September 2010; Brian O'Connell, 'Caught in a Web of Alcohol Ads', *Irish Times*, 14 September 2010; Alison Healy, 'Student Drinking Almost Equal by Gender', *Irish Times*, 29 September 2010.

DISCUSSION QUESTIONS

1. Lawther, Hastings and Lowry (1997) described the idea of 'de-marketing'. Do you think it is time to de-market alcohol in Ireland?
2. What need does alcohol satisfy? What need does over-consumption satisfy?
3. Using the concepts of marketing, elaborate on how they relate to alcohol.
4. Does the debate about the marketing of alcohol in Ireland represent a threat or an opportunity to the marketers of alcohol?

FURTHER READING

Carlson, J., *Moments of Truth*, Cambridge (MA): Ballinger 1987.
Kotler, Philip and Armstrong, G., *Principles of Marketing*, 13th edition, New Jersey: Pearson 2010.
Quinn, Feargal, *Crowning the Customer*, Dublin: O'Brien Press 1990.

DISCUSSION QUESTIONS

1. Explain why not all organisations are marketing-oriented. List examples of organisations you would consider to be very customer-oriented and some that are not.
2. Research by the Marketing Institute (page 28) suggested that more importance should be given to marketing. State why you think marketing will become more important.
3. Is there an inherent conflict between the concepts of marketing and ethics?

REFERENCES

Bagozzi, R., 'Marketing as exchange', *Journal of Marketing*, vol. 39, October 1975.
Bank, J., *The Essence of Quality Management*, Englewood Cliffs (NJ): Prentice-Hall 1992.
Butler, S., 'Ireland's Star Brands', *Strategies Europe*, February 2001.
Brown, S. 'Postmodern Marketing?', *European Journal of Marketing*, vol. 27, (1993), no. 4.
Carrigan, M. and Attalla, A., 'The myth of the ethical consumer—do ethics matter in purchase behaviour', *Journal of Consumer Marketing*, vol. 18 (2001), no.7.
Christopher, M., Payne, A., and Ballantyne, D., *Relationship Marketing: Bringing Quality, Customer Service and Marketing Together*, London: Butterworth-Heinemann 1992.
Condon, S., 'Marketing the key to growth', *Business and Finance*, November 1985.
Consultative Committee on Marketing, *Ireland and Marketing: Report of the Sectoral Development Committee*, Dublin: Stationery Office 1984.
Cook, T., 'What's wrong with Irish marketing practice?', *Irish Business*, October 1987.
Culliton, J., *The Culliton Report*, Dublin: Stationery Office 1992.
Cunningham, A., 'Where are our marketing samurai?' (presentation to Campus Ireland—Commerce and Industry), University College, Dublin, September 1987.
Davidow, W., and Uttal, B., *Total Customer Service: The Ultimate Weapon*, New York: Harper Perennial 1989.
Deming, W., *Out of the Crisis*, Cambridge: Cambridge University Press 1986.
Doyle, P., 'Marketing in the new millennium', *European Journal of Marketing*, vol. 29 (1995), no. 13.

Enterprise Strategy Group, 'Ahead of the curve: Ireland's place in the global economy', Dublin: Forfás, July 2004.

Federation of Irish Industry, *Annual Report*, 1968.

Firat, F. 'The consumer in Postmodernity', *Advances in Consumer Research*, vol. 18 (1991).

Fournier, S. 'Consumers and Their Brands: Developing Relationship Theory in Consumer Research', *Journal of Consumer Research*, 24 March 1998.

Griffith, V., 'Knowing when to be of service', *Financial Times*, 12 February 1998.

Grönroos, Christian, 'From marketing mix to relationship marketing: towards a paradigm shift in marketing', *Management Decision*, vol. 32 (1994).

Harrington, L., and Reed, G., 'E-commerce (finally) comes of age', *McKinsey Quarterly*, (1996), no. 2.

Ishikawa, K., *What is Total Quality Control?: The Japanese Way*, Englewood Cliffs (NJ): Prentice-Hall 1985.

Juran, J., *Leadership for Quality: An Executive Handbook*, New York: Free Press 1989.

Knutton, P., 'Customer strategy: start at the core, not at the edges', Works Management, July 1996.

Kotler, P., and Levy, S., 'Broadening the concept of marketing', *Journal of Marketing*, 10–15 January 1969.

Kotler, P. and Armstrong, G., *Principles of Marketing*, 13th edition, New Jersey: Pearson 2010.

Lawther, S., Hastings, G., and Lowry, R., 'De-marketing: putting Kotler and Levy's ideas into practice', *Journal of Marketing Management*, May 1997.

Levitt, T., 'Marketing myopia', *Harvard Business Review*, July–August 1960.

Levitt, T., 'Marketing myopia', *Harvard Business Review*, September 1975.

Low, W., and Davenport, E., 'Has the medium (roast) become the message? The ethics of marketing fair trade in the mainstream', *European Journal of Marketing*, vol. 22 (2005), no. 5.

Maslow, A., 'A theory of human motivation', *Psychological Review*, no. 50 (1943).

Quinn, Feargal, *Crowning the Customer*, Dublin: O'Brien Press 1990.

Quinn, Feargal, 'Becoming a customer-driven organisation: three key questions', *Managing Service Quality*, vol. 6 (1996), no. 6.

Sectoral Committee Report on Industrial Organisation, Dublin: Stationery Office 1965.

Telesis Consultancy Group, *A Review of Irish Industrial Policy* (ESRI report no. 64), Dublin: Economic and Social Research Institute 1982.

Tierney, E., 'Lessons from the scandals', *Management*, January 1992.

Ward, J., 'Marketing myopia in industrial development', *Irish Marketing Review*, vol. 2 (1987).

Zwass, V., 'Electronic commerce: structures and issues', *International Journal of Electronic Commerce*, 1996.

2

Marketing and Enterprise Development

Chapter 1 drew attention to the importance of understanding customers' needs. Understanding needs is a fundamental starting point for establishing a new business venture or developing an existing business. If a firm gets into difficulties, marketing will also play a role in the refocusing and turnaround efforts. Firms exist to serve needs, and an understanding of marketing is required if the firm is to understand these. The survival and development of a business will ultimately depend on its ability to serve market needs.

The formation and development of enterprises is important for Irish society, as it creates wealth and provides jobs. Historically, the establishment of new indigenous business ventures has not met the needs of society in job creation and economic development. As a result, state involvement and foreign direct investment have been significant. In the past two decades there has been some evidence of change. Greater encouragement has been given to indigenous enterprise in the form of support services available from both the public and the private sector. Marketing will be fundamental in any attempts to increase the level of entrepreneurial activity in Ireland. Marketing can help identify unserved needs in both the domestic and the international markets. It will play a role in researching those needs and developing, communicating, and delivering the product to these markets.

As the firm grows and develops, marketing will continue to be a vital feature. In subsequent chapters the principal elements of the firm's marketing management and practice are described and illustrated. Activities such as marketing research and the development of new products play an important role in continuing business success.

Marketing is also important if the business faces difficult circumstances, such as recession, declining sales, or performance difficulties. The firm may require a complete turnaround. In this chapter we explore the links between marketing and enterprise development and examine the role of marketing in achieving continued business success.

This chapter seeks to define the nature of entrepreneurship and intrapreneurship; to demonstrate the importance of entrepreneurship and intrapreneurship to Irish society; to evaluate the link between marketing and entrepreneurship and intrapreneurship; to describe the sources of new business ideas; to explain the role of marketing in enterprise development; and to analyse the role of marketing in corporate turnaround.

THE NATURE OF ENTREPRENEURSHIP AND INTRAPRENEURSHIP

Entrepreneurship is the fundamental principle underlying the establishment of most business and commercial activities. It is the process of organising, operating and assuming the risk of a business venture (Low and MacMillan, 1988). It typically characterises the start-up of small business operations. *Intrapreneurship* describes the initiation of ventures within a larger firm. The concepts and practice of marketing are inseparable from both entrepreneurship and intrapreneurship.

Both entrepreneurship and intrapreneurship are necessary for the creation, growth and development of business. In Ireland, economic commentators have considered that there is a weakness in entrepreneurship. This has largely been ascribed to cultural and historical factors, which it is felt discouraged or inhibited enterprise. Entrepreneurs apply marketing practice to research, develop and manage their enterprises. Marketing is a requirement for continuing success.

Intrapreneurs, while not assuming the risk of the business venture, will also apply marketing practices, such as research, product development, the generation of ideas, and innovative promotional and communication campaigns.

ENTREPRENEURSHIP AND IRISH SOCIETY

Successive economic commentaries on the Irish state since independence in 1922 have demonstrated the need for enterprise. Whether through direct state involvement or the encouragement of indigenous enterprise, the importance of the concept has long been recognised and has become a significant aspect of economic policy. In the 1980s the Telesis Report (1982) on industrial policy recommended that more support be given to indigenous enterprise. In the 1990s the Culliton Report (1992) also recommended that more support be given to indigenous entrepreneurs.

In November 2004, Forfás published a review of the sales, marketing and innovation capabilities of Irish exporting SMEs. The review highlighted a number of pertinent findings in relation to marketing and enterprise development in Ireland:

- SMEs find it difficult to source suitable qualified and experienced sales staff
- third-level marketing and sales courses are not sufficiently aligned to SME needs
- SME sales personnel receive insufficient sales and marketing training
- sales management, marketing planning, and new product development are key areas for improvement
- market research capabilities need to be strengthened
- scope exists for improved use of information technology
- corporate branding and promotion are lacking in many SMEs.

The Enterprise Strategy Group, which had also reported in 2004, felt that, overall, firms in Ireland needed to complement their existing production and operational strengths with new capabilities, specifically:

- developing expertise in international markets, to promote sales growth
- building technological and applied research and development capability, to support the development of high-value products and services.

This group made a number of recommendations on how they felt these things could be achieved.

Entrepreneurship is encouraged because of the role that entrepreneurs play in society. This role can be broadly summarised under three headings: innovation, job creation, and linkages.

Innovation

Entrepreneurs and intrapreneurs foster innovation. They may create products and processes that are new to the world, or make developments and improvements to existing ones. By using their ideas, skills and resources they are an engine for economic growth. Many products that we use every day as consumers or for our work—such as calculators, microwave ovens, and personal computers—were originally developed by entrepreneurial or intrapreneurial minds. Innovations and treatments in health care have contributed to longer life expectancy; again, many of these were the result of entrepreneurial and intrapreneurial activities. In 2010 the Innovation Ireland report produced 24 recommendations on ways that innovation could create over 100,000 jobs in Ireland.

INNOVATION IRELAND

The Innovation Ireland report published in March 2010 contained 24 key recommendations, and an additional 38 supporting proposals, to transform Ireland into an 'international innovation hub'.

It calls for innovation and entrepreneurship to be placed at the heart of enterprise policy and says that Irish culture needs to stop stigmatising business failure.

Among the main recommendations included in the report are: the implementation of a more efficient approach to identifying and accessing intellectual property arising from public research investment; investing 3 per cent of gross domestic product in research and development; the creation of a national network of angel funds to invest in early-stage companies; the attraction of new investment and the consolidation of existing foreign-direct investment; the introduction of additional measures to promote the study of maths and science; the creation of placement schemes in companies for both graduate and undergraduates; and the marketing of Ireland as a leading innovation location and destination of choice for European and other overseas investors. While no specific details of the costs involved for each recommendation were contained in the report, it did classify them as cost neutral, low cost or high cost.

Each recommendation was accompanied by one of four 'timeline' indications: 'immediate', which indicates that action should be taken within three months; 'short-term', which refers to an implementation period of less than a year; 'medium-term', which indicates a timeframe of one to two years; and 'long-term' which suggests a realisation period longer than two years.

The report states that regular reports on the progress of the implementation of recommendations should be prepared for consideration by the government and for publication.

One of the stated aims of the report is that, by 2020, Ireland will have a significant number of 'large, innovation-intensive companies, which are Irish headquartered and owned'. The taskforce also stressed the importance of fostering indigenous entrepreneurial enterprises, rather than focusing solely on multinationals, which already have a strong base here.

Sources: Suzanne Lynch and John Collins, 'Innovation Report highlights 24 points', *Irish Times*, 12 March 2010; www.innovationstaskforce.ie.

An example of one Irish company that had been putting some of the ideas of the taskforce into action is Treemetrics.

TREEMETRICS

Treemetrics is a software producer that enables tree producers and saw mills to measure the standing trees in a forest before calculating the timber yield per tree. Prior to the development of the firm's software, this had to be done manually or after the tree had been cut down, which was less accurate and often meant that trees were cut before they had reached optimum yield levels.

Treemetrics was formed in 2005 by two entrepreneurs, Enda Keane and Garret Mullooly, who developed the software which enabled the scanning of a tree in the forest and the production of a 3D image to calculate the timber yield. The software could therefore be used by both forest owners and saw mills. Both men had worked in the forestry sector and had spotted the opportunity for the new product development based on their work experience.

Some of the advantages of the software are that it reduces measurement costs by 75 per cent, can predetermine the product assortment in the forest (type of tree) and can maximise product recovery in the forest and the saw mill. This enables producers and processors to maximise their commercial and ecological returns.

The firm received support from Enterprise Ireland and has established a link with University College Cork to further its software research and development.

Source: www.treemetrics.com.

Job creation

In general, smaller business and commercial ventures tend to create more jobs than larger ones. There are more small business and commercial firms than larger ones. With regard to state support and grants it is estimated that jobs can be generated in small businesses at a much lower cost per job than in larger companies. Many smaller businesses operate in areas where large-scale job developments may be rare but where even a small number of jobs can prevent significant depopulation. Consider the example of Ireland's speciality food producers.

IRISH SPECIALITY FOODS

The estimated turnover of Irish speciality foods companies was estimated to be €475 million in 2005. The majority of producers (80 per cent) were based in Munster and Leinster. Many of these small enterprises are established in areas where there may not be significant job opportunities. Some are in rural areas where there may have been some depopulation.

Speciality foods are a niche in the food industry with products that appeal to discerning buyers. Examples include: James McGeough, a butcher from Oughterard, County Galway, who produces air-dried beef and lamb; Fíor Uisce premium spring water from Tourmakeady (one of only two Irish bottled waters that was licensed for sale in the United States); and Danucci artisan chocolates from County Louth. One of the biggest challenges for speciality food producers is gaining distribution. One Cork firm— the Alternative Pizza Company—secured distribution with Superquinn for a range of premium pizzas, including one with a Clonakilty black pudding topping. Other companies have managed to secure distribution with up-market food retailers, such as Selfridges and Fortnum and Mason in London, that concentrate on selling speciality foods.

Source: Aine Coffey, 'The cheese sandwich is dead; long live the brie on sourdough', *Sunday Tribune*, 14 May 2006.

Linkages

Many small business ventures establish linkages with larger firms, for example to supply raw materials, components or services that the larger undertaking may need, such as catering, transport, or security. Many channel members will be small businesses with linkages to larger manufacturers or service providers. These satellite businesses create jobs and contribute to the success of the larger firm; they are a source of information to larger businesses. They may have direct contact with customers, and any innovation they engage in will ultimately benefit the larger firm. The recycling firm Greyhound, which originally began life as a refuse collection service, has broadened its business so that it provides a more sophisticated and value-added recycling service for its mainly business customers.

GREYHOUND RECYCLING

Greyhound Recycling operates the largest recycling plant in Ireland. Opened in Clondalkin in 2005, the plant uses state-of-the-art technology to separate paper, metal and plastic waste into distinct groups. The segregated waste is then repackaged and sold on to be used again by manufacturers. Much of the recycled material is exported to Europe and China where it is used as raw material in the packaging and consumer goods industries.

Greyhound is a family-owned business run by three brothers, Brian, Michael, and Stephen Buckley. Originally, the company provided a service transporting waste to landfill sites. Increases in the volume of waste generated in Ireland and targets of reducing the amount of waste dumped in landfill sites provided Greyhound with an opportunity to develop its business activities. Waste, according to Greyhound, is a commodity that can command a price. Waste paper, for example, when properly segregated, can be sold as a perfect substitute for paper pulp used in the packaging and publishing industries. In addition, government plans require a reduction in landfill dumping of household waste of 50 per cent by 2013, and a reduction of 85 per cent in commercial waste dumping is also required.

In addition to waste separation the Clondalkin plant can convert waste cooking oil into bio-diesel, which is predicted to be a potential substitute for oil in coming years.

Greyhound provides its customers, mainly large commercial firms such as Diageo, with a waste audit, instructing them on how to separate their recyclable waste. They collect the material and the customer is paid for their waste.

The company has noticed changes in the public's attitudes towards waste and recycling. Campaigns such as Reduce, Re-use, Recycle, and the plastic bag tax, have contributed to this. There is also increased awareness of environmental issues generally.

Source: Conor Brophy, 'Racing ahead on recycling', *Sunday Tribune*, 27 February 2005.

INTRAPRENEURSHIP

Intrapreneurs are enterprising individuals who work in successful organisations. This implies that, just as with entrepreneurs, there are enterprising traits and characteristics that the organisation can develop. The organisation has a role in the development of intrapreneurs in the form of support and encouragement.

Intrapreneurs share the traits of entrepreneurs and may indeed go on to establish their own business and become entrepreneurs. Intrapreneurs are typically people with good commercial insights. They are capable of understanding the forces at work in the business environment and are able to adapt to them. Intrapreneurs will spot opportunities and will usually possess innovative and creative abilities. They will have a capacity for analysis, implementation and control and will be good problem-solvers. It is likely that they will be good communicators and will have the ability to work with others.

Intrapreneurs will usually possess skills that suit them to marketing, communication and creative roles in the business. It is important for the firm to recognise the talents and intrapreneurial potential of individuals, as these can lead to mutually beneficial and profitable activities.

Intrapreneurship will take place within the firm, but its results will ultimately benefit society to the extent that they lead to the development of new and better products, increased employment, and employee motivation and satisfaction. Intrapreneurship may also involve the creation of linkages. Fundamentally, intrapreneurship should benefit the firm in growth, profit, and employee commitment and motivation.

Stimulating intrapreneurship

One of the issues with which large companies have had to contend is the promotion of an enterprise culture. It can certainly be argued that an enterprise culture in a firm is necessary for the marketing policy to thrive also.

Entrepreneurs will have a personal interest in the success of the venture. This personal interest may be harder to generate in large companies. Internal marketing can certainly play a role in the creation and support of intrapreneurship. *Internal marketing* describes the application of the marketing policy within the firm. (This is discussed in more detail in chapter 3.) The desired result is that employees serve the customers' needs and provide high levels of customer satisfaction. Internal marketing will only be successful, however, to the extent that the firm values and encourages it.

Strategic orientation and organisational style will be significant determining factors in encouraging intrapreneurship (Pearson, 1989). *Strategy* describes what a firm does to achieve its objectives, while *organisational style* describes the way in which the firm operates. (These are considered in more detail in chapter 7.) Strategic orientation and organisational style have implications for organisational success. In addition, Drucker (1994) pointed out that success in the stimulation of enterprise within the firm must lead to strategies that work in the external market. This emphasises the importance of not losing sight of the customer in any entrepreneurial or intrapreneurial activities.

The conditions required for intrapreneurship to flourish in the firm have implications for procedures, structures, management development, performance appraisal, and job content (Jansen and van Wees, 1994). Burnside (1990) suggested that there were a number of stimulants that would improve the corporate climate for creativity and therefore of enterprise. There were also potential obstacles. The stimulants included the person's fellow-workers, the allocation of resources, and the nature of supervision. Creating supports for creativity, an environment where challenges were encouraged, and creative freedom were also significant stimulants. Obstacles to creativity included insufficient time, a desire to maintain the status quo, internal politics, and the ways in which creativity was evaluated.

Innovation—the process of identifying, creating and delivering new product or service values that did not exist before in the market—is another important factor in the stimulation of enterprise. Together with creativity, it will also be significant in the success of the firm's marketing efforts. Innovation is a prerequisite for enterprise creation and continued survival.

Innovation will be especially important for Ireland's manufacturing sector in a business environment in which labour costs are often cheaper in other countries. Innovation means that the firm can develop products that have a competitive advantage.

The *corporate culture* prevailing in the firm should therefore encourage creativity and innovation, in addition to an understanding of customers' needs. Corporate culture is the set of values that defines for members what an organisation stands for, how it operates, and what it considers important.

Corporate culture will therefore play an important role not only in encouraging enterprise but also in instilling a marketing orientation.

THE LINK BETWEEN MARKETING, ENTREPRENEURSHIP, AND INTRAPRENEURSHIP

The link between marketing and both entrepreneurship and intrapreneurship exists at two broad levels: the philosophical and the practical. Marketing as a philosophy, or way of thinking, implies putting the customer at the centre of the business. Ultimately both the entrepreneur and the intrapreneur have to acknowledge that there must be customers for their products or ideas. Putting themselves in the position of the ultimate customer is therefore a prerequisite for success.

One research study concluded that both marketing and entrepreneurship are opportunity-driven, value-creating processes that can be applied in a wide variety of situations (Morris and Lewis, 1995). These would include any exchange relationship. Marketers, entrepreneurs and intrapreneurs, regardless of the nature of their firm, will look for opportunities to serve customers' needs.

At the practical level, the research, product development techniques, strategy, planning, and management of the marketing mix will be used by both entrepreneurs and intrapreneurs. In the case of the entrepreneur the responsibility for marketing will rest completely with him or her as owner. In the case of the intrapreneur the responsibility for marketing will probably be corporate and will usually be taken over by the marketing department within the firm. Corporate intrapreneurship, however, is not the preserve of marketers or the marketing department; intrapreneurship should be encouraged among all employees.

There is evidence that, with regard to personality traits, marketing and entrepreneurship are linked. Entrepreneurship can also be linked to other management functions within the business (Foxall and Minkes, 1996). *Personality traits* are any relatively enduring ways in which one person differs from another (Guilford, 1959). Those associated with entrepreneurship include a desire for autonomy, social independence, a high tolerance of ambiguity, and a propensity for risk taking (West and Farr, 1990). Researchers would also agree that traits such as a need for control and independence, achievement, persistence, and a positive self-image are also significant. Generally, money is a means rather than an end.

It is possible to suggest that some of these traits may also be required to be a successful marketing practitioner. Research has established that marketing and entrepreneurship are correlated but that marketing can exist independently of the innovative, risk-taking climate of the entrepreneur (Miles and Arnold, 1991).

Innovation, new-product development, and enterprise

Innovation, according to Drucker (1994), is '... the specific tool of entrepreneurs, the means by which they exploit change as an opportunity for a different business or a different service. It is capable of being presented as a discipline, capable of being learned, and capable of being practised.'

Rosenfield and Servo (1990) considered that innovation consists of three essential elements:

$$innovation = conception + invention + exploitation$$

This implies that an idea must not only be conceived but must be translated into a product and successfully sold in the market. The starting-point is therefore the generation of ideas.

SOURCES OF IDEAS

Ideas for new enterprises or products, or for improvements to existing ones, can come from a number of sources. There is a strong relationship between the development process of a new product and the establishment of new enterprises. The new-product development process—whereby ideas are translated into successful products—is commonly used by both entrepreneurs and intrapreneurs. (This is considered in more detail in chapter 7.)

Typically, entrepreneurial ideas come from individual work experience, domestic experience, hobbies and leisure interests, competitors' offerings, market gap analysis, research and development activities, or import substitution. Intrapreneurial ideas may come from the same sources, though many companies devote considerable resources to research and development. Intrapreneurial sources may also include competitor analysis and market gap analysis.

Individual work experience

As in the case of Treemetrics, many ideas for new enterprises come from a person's work experience. In the work setting, opportunities may emerge for new products or services or for improvements to existing ones. In addition, the experience the person gains in the firm, in applied skills or management expertise, will be beneficial if they establish their own enterprise.

Domestic experience

The home may be a source of ideas. We use many products and services in our homes, and many ideas for new products have come from people's domestic experience, as the next panel demonstrates.

LIR CHOCOLATES

Lir Chocolates is one of a number of successful handmade chocolate companies. It was established by Mary White and Connie Doody. The idea came from experimenting with handmade chocolates at home; the positive reaction from family and friends encouraged them to consider setting up a small business.

Lir competes in the high-priced segment of the handmade chocolates market. Its main sales outlets are Brown Thomas, selected Tesco, Superquinn and Dunnes stores, and duty-free shops at Dublin Airport. Thirty-four per cent of output is exported.

Sources: Richard Brophy, 'Behind bars', *Checkout Ireland*, July 1997; www.lir.ie.

Hobbies and leisure interests

People's hobbies and leisure interests can yield ideas for new ventures, as happened with the Cavan and Leitrim Railway Company, which began operations in 1994, one of a number of railway restoration projects in different parts of the country.

THE CAVAN AND LEITRIM RAILWAY

The original Cavan and Leitrim Railway Company was established in 1887 to provide a narrow-gauge passenger and freight service on a line between Drumod, County Leitrim, and Belturbet, County Cavan, with a branch serving coal mines in Arigna. Eventually taken over by CIÉ, the lines were ultimately deemed to be uneconomic, and in 1959 they were closed.

In 1994 a group of railway enthusiasts decided to establish a museum and working railway at the Drumod end of the old line. The old company was re-incorporated as a limited liability company. The original station building was bought and restored, along with the engine shed, platforms and other buildings that had been abandoned in 1959. Track was relaid for about half a mile on the route of the former line, and the company began to offer trips using historic engines and carriages.

Finance for the venture was provided from the EU Interreg programme, the International Fund for Ireland, and private donations. The railway proved popular with tourists and school tours and was promoted as an interactive experience for visitors. This experience included a trip on a restored train and a guided tour of the company's workshops, where various items of rolling stock were in the process of being restored. Eventually the company hoped to fully restore the railway line to Mohill, approximately five miles away.

Source: *Cavan and Leitrim Railway Company Guidebook*, 1995.

Analysis of competitors

Observing competitors and analysing their product or service offerings can yield ideas for improvements or alternatives. Obviously, competitors' products cannot be directly copied, but they can provide ideas for variations. In many competitive markets firms will closely follow competitors' activities, and there may be scope for improving or building on what they have done.

Market gap analysis

Market gap analysis involves examining the market for unserved segments or niches. It is a common method used by marketers to find opportunities either for new or existing products. An increase in the number of large-scale events in Ireland was to prove the catalyst in the establishment of Ryan's Cleaning Event Specialists.

EVENT CLEANING

Ryan's Cleaning Event Specialists was founded by Pat Ryan, who spotted an opportunity to establish a business providing a clean-up service after big events such as concerts and race meetings. The firm's first big contract was cleaning up after a concert at Slane Castle. In 2006 Ryan's had contracts to clean up after the Oxegen festival at Punchestown, the Galway races, and the European Open and the Ryder Cup at the K Club. The Oxegen contract was worth about €400,000 to the company. Its biggest contract was the opening and closing ceremonies of the Special Olympics in 2003.

The business started as a one-man operation. 'I remember moving the whole family to Slane for a week to help with the clean-up of the concert there,' says Pat Ryan. The company started offering its service in the UK, where it had a contract to clean up after the V festival. It has invested about €3 million in specialist equipment.

About 90 per cent of turnover is generated from big events, but the company also cleans up after small private events, 'You'd be surprised at the number of people who are getting married in their back gardens these days,' says Ryan.

Source: Mark Paul, 'Event specialists clean up from a messy business', *Sunday Times*, 9 July 2006.

Even in markets that are dominated by large firms, opportunities may emerge for entrepreneurs to compete in niches.

NEW PRODUCTS CHALLENGE MARKET LEADERS IN THE BEER MARKET

While three large brewers—Guinness, Heineken, and Beamish and Crawford—dominate the Irish beer market, opportunities have also emerged for smaller brewers. In the late 1990s a number of micro-breweries were established; by 2000, they held 1 per cent of sales in the beer market but believed that this could increase to the 5–7 per cent that such craft beers enjoy in other European countries.

In Dublin, three micro-breweries—Porterhouse, Messrs Maguire and the Dublin Brewing Company—began producing stouts and ales; in Clare, the Biddy Early Brewery produces stout, ale, and lager; and in Carlow, the Carlow Brewing Company produces a range of lagers and ales.

The success of these products, albeit on a small scale, is attributed to discerning consumers who prefer to avoid mass-produced brands and seek out products with unique flavours. While the large producers use chemicals to preserve, colour, sweeten, and flavour their beers, many of the smaller producers use natural ingredients. Some ale producers, for example, add ingredients such as coriander, figs or elderberries to give their products unique flavour.

Source: Kieron Wood, 'New brews are good news if your tipple tastes tired', *Sunday Business Post*, 15 July 2001.

Research and development

Research and development may be a feature of both entrepreneurship and intrapreneurship. Companies may establish R&D departments or programmes to yield new ideas.

Import substitution

Imports may yield ideas for products that could be manufactured in Ireland.

THE LIFE-CYCLE FOR ENTREPRENEURIAL FIRMS

The generation of ideas is the first step in developing a successful enterprise. The examples given in previous sections illustrate where ideas could come from and how they could be translated into successful businesses. The new-product development process provides a framework for taking ideas, critically assessing them, and converting them into successful products.

The creation of a successful product is the first stage in the entrepreneurial life-cycle of the firm. Just as products have a life-cycle—they are born, grow, and ultimately mature— so too do entrepreneurial firms. According to Siropolis (1990), the entrepreneurial firm goes through three distinct stages: *acceptance*, *breakthrough*, and *maturity*.

The acceptance stage is characterised by the firm struggling to break even and having low cash flows. The challenge is gaining acceptance for the product on the market. The product or service may have to be adjusted to suit market demands, and the essential communication objective is the creation of awareness. Little money may be available for marketing activities and promotion, and communication may be largely personal.

Breakthrough comes with rapid sales growth. This requires effective management of cash flow and an emphasis on improved production performance to meet the increased demand. Quality and delivery also become important, and the business needs to ensure that standards are not compromised with a larger body of customers. At this stage more funds may be available for marketing activities, and research will be required on product and market prospects.

The firm reaches maturity when there is stable, balanced growth. Management skills will need to be developed or fine-tuned. At this stage the firm may consider expansion options: for example, the successful fast-food chain Abrakebabra decided at an early stage to expand through franchising. In so doing they created opportunities for others to set up new businesses.

ABRAKEBABRA

The name Abrakebabra—a combination of 'kebab' and 'abracadabra'—was chosen by two brothers, Graham and Wyndham Beere, for their kebab restaurant, which they opened in the Dublin suburb of Rathmines in 1982. The brothers had seen the success of kebab outlets in London and decided to try it out in Dublin.

The concept proved equally popular in Dublin, and within a few years the brothers had opened several more outlets. They believed there was more potential and decided to use franchising as a means of expanding throughout the country. The franchise to run an individual restaurant could be bought for €12,700. It was estimated that the cost of providing a fully fitted new outlet was €114,000; if an existing fast-food outlet was being renovated this was reduced to €50,800. By 1997 there were 50 Abrakebabra outlets, nine of which were owned by the Beere brothers.

Sources: *Sunday Business Post*, 6 December 1992, 16 May 1993, 9 March 1997; *Examiner*, 23 December 1996; *Sunday Tribune*, 2 November 1997.

ENTREPRENEURIAL ROLES

Entrepreneurs perform a number of roles in the management and development of their business. They will have been the innovators, responsible for the initial establishment of the enterprise. In start-up ventures they will also have complete responsibility for marketing. They may have done all the initial research and development, and they will be responsible for the communication and promotion of their enterprise. It is not unusual, therefore, for entrepreneurs to work long hours developing prototypes and establishing the business. As the firm grows, the roles will change. The number of employees will grow, and tasks will be delegated; management skills will need to be further developed.

HORSEWEAR

The idea for specialist horse clothing came to a riding instructor, Tom McGuinness, from a frustration with the inadequacy of horse blankets on the market in the early 1980s. He conducted a survey of 50 people in the industry on their needs and priorities; he then bought a sewing machine and worked for 12 weeks to develop a prototype. The blanket had an improved strapping system, so that it stayed on the horse properly, and was made of synthetic materials rather than the traditional woven jute.

Sales were very good, and production began in 1985. Ten years later the company was the largest manufacturer of horse blankets in Europe, employing 85 people in Dundalk and Cavan.

McGuinness attributes his success to good instincts about marketing and product development. As the business expanded, however, he realised he needed to develop his management skills, and he enrolled in two courses run by the Irish Management Institute: the effective marketing course and the business development course. These gave him the ability to analyse what was right in the business and to apply this so that it would keep on working.

The development of management and marketing skills was essential in the business, where 90 per cent of output was exported, mainly to the continent and the United States. The company's policy has been to develop well-researched products in a range of colours and finishes to suit customers' needs.

The company developed a brand, Rambo, which enjoys success in international markets.

In 2009 the company committed €500,000 to promote the equestrian sector in Ireland in the period 2009–2013.

Sources: *Sunday Business Post*, 29 May 1994, 31 March 1996; *Sunday Tribune*, 7 May 1995.

MARKETING WITHOUT MONEY

At the early stages in its life-cycle the entrepreneurial firm may have little money for marketing activities or for engaging marketing services. This is not necessarily a drawback, as there are many ways for the small business to market without significant amounts of money. Initial market research, whether primary or secondary, can be carried out by the entrepreneur: understanding the stages in the research process is the key.

Communication will be especially important. The entrepreneur should be able to explain clearly what the business is about, as there may be limited time to hold the attention of potential buyers or investors. Communication opportunities should be exploited. Local or national media may be interested in new business start-ups and may give coverage. Press statements can be prepared and sent to selected media, which may be interested in following up with a story.

Allied to the need for communication skills is the need for selling skills. The entrepreneur will have to convince buyers of the benefits of the product or service being offered and be able to negotiate the sale.

Many catalogues, guides or brochures will give free listings or charge small amounts for a listing or profile. Specific publications, such as *Your Business*, published by the Small Firms Association, regularly feature items on small business and development. Networking through business events, firms or social contacts is taken for granted in business and is a means of establishing contacts or following up leads. Advertising need not cost a lot: specific media, such as the Golden Pages, may be quite affordable.

The internet provides an opportunity for the entrepreneur to communicate with a selected group of customers. Its interactive nature means that it can also be used for taking orders or for providing additional information to potential customers. There are certainly implications for other companies identifying such consumers. One Australian study (Poon and Swatman, 1997) conducted among small businesses found that the perceived long-term benefits of the use of the internet, such as business development, far outweighed the perceived short-term benefits, such as cost savings and communications efficiency. The internet, therefore, has significant short-term and long-term benefits. The costs associated with website would obviously need to be assessed, and factors such as the cost of the site's design and continued site management will be important.

Concentrating on the smaller market means that the entrepreneur can be closer to customers and can build relationships with them. Close familiarisation with customers and their needs means that feedback and speed of reaction can be much faster than for larger firms. Smaller firms can therefore practise relationship marketing quite easily.

As the business expands and sales increase, more funds should become available for marketing, and the entrepreneur's responsibility for carrying out all the firm's marketing activities may then be reduced. It is also possible that, in addition to the availability of finance for enterprise development from state agencies, specific funds for marketing activities may also be available.

FINANCING FOR ENTERPRISE

One of the factors that many people have suggested contributed to the lower rate of new business start-ups in Ireland is the lack of funds. In particular, the lack of equity finance has been cited as a problem. In other words, businesses have been too small to finance growth from profits and not profitable enough to attract the attention of most venture capitalists.

The problem was recognised by the government as being especially significant for small firms. Approximately 800,000 people (54 per cent of the private sector workforce) are employed in businesses with fewer than 50 employees. In 2006 a venture capital package of more than €150 million was announced by the Department of Enterprise, Trade and Employment. In addition, knowledge acquisition grants of up to €20,000 as well as financial support for information and communications technology (ICT) audits were introduced. The venture capital package came about as a result of the Small Business Forum report (set up in 2005 to examine the environment for Irish small businesses and recommend measures to improve the sector's performance). The report identified access to finance as a major difficulty for the small business sector (see www.smallbusinessforum.ie).

SUPPORT FOR ENTERPRISE

Considerable support is provided for entrepreneurs starting new businesses and for existing enterprises, in an effort to stimulate and encourage indigenous enterprise, and some of this support is specifically aimed at marketing development or initiatives. Support can come from the state sector, such as third-level colleges, Enterprise Ireland and the county enterprise boards; from banks and financial institutions; and from voluntary bodies, such as the Small Firms Association, Plato, and First Step.

Most support agencies will assess closely the entrepreneur's marketing plans, proposals, or assumptions. These should provide an indication of the thoroughness of the marketing research that has been carried out and the assumptions made in planning the marketing strategy.

The following section describes some of the main state and private-sector bodies that are involved in the support of enterprise and have a role in the development of marketing in Irish business. (The role of Enterprise Ireland in international marketing is further discussed in chapter 12.)

County Enterprise Boards

Originally established in 1993 and given status under the Industrial Development Act of 1995, the 35 County Enterprise Boards (CEB) exist to support the micro-enterprise sector. A specific objective is to cultivate and expand an ethos of local entrepreneurship. Each CEB is a stand-alone limited company with funding provided from the Exchequer and European Regional Development Funds.

Each board has an evaluation committee which makes recommendations on the most appropriate form or level of support for the board to give to individual projects.

Enterprise Ireland

Enterprise Ireland is the state development agency focused on transforming Irish industry. Its core mission is 'to accelerate the development of world-class Irish companies to achieve strong positions in global markets resulting in increased national and regional prosperity'.

To do this, the organisation focuses on five main areas of activity: achieving export sales; investing in research and innovation; competing through productivity; starting up and scaling up; and driving regional enterprise.

Incubation

Enterprise Ireland has also been involved in the development of incubation units for new enterprises. The concept of incubation first emerged in the United States in the 1950s and 1960s. However, it was not until the mid-1980s that it began to be widely used as an economic development tool. Business incubation is a dynamic process of enterprise development that nurtures young firms, helping them to survive and grow during the start-up period when they are most vulnerable. The objective of incubation is to provide hands-on management assistance, access to finance and orchestrated exposure to critical business or technical support services. Combined together, these services create an environment conducive to new venture creation and survival (National Business Incubation Association, 2000).

Initially, incubators followed a strategy of focusing on the more tangible resource requirements of firms, directly related to their capital requirements. The main aim was to provide low-cost office or laboratory space, administrative services, access to library and computer services, skilled consultants and an inexpensive workforce in the form of graduate and undergraduate students (Smilor and Gill, 1986). It is now generally recognised, however, that the support required by entrepreneurs includes less tangible resources such as personal experiences in industry, and know-how. Incubators can also help to develop credibility for tenant firms and provide them with a network of contacts, which enables them to develop the relationship to grow.

The stronger and more diverse a web of relationships an entrepreneur has, the greater the chance they have of identifying market opportunities, solving problems quickly by targeting the right problem, and locating the appropriate individual to assist and help to implement the solution. In short, incubators shorten the learning curve for start-up firms and can prevent them from having to reinvent the wheel each time they undertake a specific activity. Finally, by locating many different start-ups and growing enterprises in one building, as the incubator does, there is the possibility for tenants to advise one another and, in some cases, share in the development of products or technologies (Bolton, 1997).

Enterprise Ireland and e-business

In the late 1990s, Enterprise Ireland began a number of initiatives to help illustrate the advantages of e-business. Guides are provided on e-business topics and the Enterprise Ireland website offers a discussion forum and events guide. In addition, an eBusiness Acceleration Fund was established.

An Bord Bia

An Bord Bia assists in the development and marketing of food and beverages. It can provide grants for marketing programmes and strategic marketing development. Other services include carrying out research and support for international trade shows. The board has a strong role in the development of export markets for food and beverages.

Business innovation centres

There are four business innovation centres: in Dublin, Cork, Limerick, and Galway. They are non-profit organisations and their main role is to be a facilitator, providing advice, finance and support to projects in the medium- to high-technology sector. The centres have a capital seed fund, which is provided by the state and the private sector. They can provide professional advisers on marketing, financial control, and strategy.

Plato

Plato is a small-business development network established by the Tallaght Partnership in 1993. It is primarily supported by the Local Urban and Rural Development Operational Programme, 1995–9. The network encourages co-operation between large companies and small- to medium-sized companies. It involves large companies releasing senior managers to work in smaller firms as part of an arrangement lasting for two years. A report carried out by Goodbody Economic Consultants in 1998 for Plato found that participating companies reported an increase in turnover of 22 per cent. Employment in the companies involved rose by 18 per cent. By 2010 Plato had 1,000 participating SMEs in seven regional networks around Ireland (www.plato.ie). Companies that join must have been in business for at least three years and must have a significant potential for growth.

Plato proved useful to Yvonne and Derek Kelly, the owners of Nourish Wholefoods.

NOURISH WHOLEFOODS

Originally established in 1985 as the General Health Food Store, Nourish is run by Yvonne and Derek Kelly. In 2005 it had a turnover of €3.2 million and employed 40 people. Nourish have five shops in Dublin, three in the city centre and one each in Santry and Rathfarnham.

Wholefoods are foods that have not had any of their natural features taken away or any artificial substances added. When the firm was first established wholefoods were not as mainstream as they are today. In the late 1980s, for example, the company started to sell organic vegetables but found that there was virtually no demand.

Gross margins in the business are around 40 per cent. Sixty per cent of sales are food products, with the remainder being supplements, natural remedies, cosmetics, and skin care products.

As the business expanded, Yvonne and Derek realised they needed to develop a more formal management structure and to improve their systems. Managers were recruited for each store and a full-time stock controller was hired to introduce a computerised stock management system. This revolutionised business efficiency, especially as each shop bought its own stock independently: this was because of the wide variations in what would sell in different locations.

The company became involved with Plato, the business development organisation, which it found to be a very rewarding experience. The business coaching module was particularly useful and Plato provided a support structure.

When they established the business neither Yvonne nor Derek had any formal business qualifications and they had limited experience of the retail trade. If doing it again, Derek says, 'I would draw up very detailed plans with a proper structure for the business from day one.'

Source: Olive Keogh, 'Wholefoods reap robust returns', *Sunday Times*, 12 June 2005.

First Step

First Step was an initiative of the entrepreneur Norma Smurfit. It is a private, non-profit organisation financed by private companies and involves the provision of repayable loans, advice and support to start-up businesses. First Step is staffed by managers who have been seconded from industry. They continue to be paid by sponsoring companies.

INTERACTION BETWEEN EDUCATION AND ENTERPRISE

Universities and third-level colleges are involved not only in the research and teaching of business and enterprise courses but also in liaison with entrepreneurs and businesses. This may involve research, consultancy, training, or short-term courses.

One study (Clark and Carson, 1986) looked at how academic staff assisted in the development of marketing expertise in smaller enterprises. It examined the principles of *action learning*—which means learning by doing—and how these were useful in the development of approaches. It is important that colleges link with industry to keep abreast of developments and to provide graduates who can meet the needs of employers.

Earlier we saw how Treemetrics had collaborated with UCC. In 2010 another collaborative development, this time in TCD led to the development of an aircraft anti-collision system.

AIRCRAFT ANTI-COLLISION SYSTEM DEVELOPED AT TCD

A new warning system to cut the number of collisions between aircraft on the ground at airports has been invented at Trinity College, Dublin The college was approached in 2006 to look into the issue by an Aer Lingus pilot, Captain William Butler, who expressed concern over the risks of aircraft collisions. Bigger aircraft and congestion at airports have led to a spike in collision rates.

According to the international Flight Safety Foundation, on-the-ground damage to aircraft can cost an estimated $10 billion worldwide. Wing-tip collisions alone can cost up to $5 billion a year. The college hopes that the new device, named WingWatch, will reduce these costs and is also looking into expanding it for use on other vehicles, such as heavy goods vehicles.

The system uses cameras positioned on the tail of the plane which give a 3D picture of the area around the aircraft.

'It's basically a parking sensor for an airplane,' said principal investigator Dr Gerard Lacey. 'The pilot would no longer have difficulty assessing the proximity of nearby objects. If an aircraft is dangerously close to another aircraft or object that could potentially cause damage the WingWatch system alerts the pilot by displaying, on screen, the proximity of objects and the level of risk they pose.'

This enables the pilot to take immediate corrective action, avoiding any possible damage to the aircraft. The research was carried out in conjunction with TCD's Aircraft Psychology Research Group which was looking at how pilots could be warned of the dangers, without being distracted.

The system is to be tested at Dublin Airport and it is then hoped that investment can be obtained to bring it to the market.

Source: Martha Kearns, 'Aircraft anti-collision system developed at TCD', *Irish Times*, 17 October 2010.

Typically the colleges act as incubator units for the enterprise; generally companies that will be assisted are those that can demonstrate a need for linkage with the colleges.

EU funds

The EU is a significant provider of funds for supporting the development of small business. There are four broad areas of relevance: human resources; research and technological development; European structural fund initiatives; and subsidised loans. Under the Leonardo programme, for example, the design and development of training materials and human resource programmes, as well as short intensive courses that rely on industry and universities, could be subsidised. The Fourth Framework programme covered research on 20 specific areas and was administered by Forbairt.

There were 13 separate structural fund initiatives. The most relevant in Ireland were the ADAPT programme, which aimed to make industry more competitive by facilitating adaptation to industrial change. The Interreg II programme was also significant: this related to cross-border co-operation and applied also in the north-east and south-east of the country.

Subsidised loans were administered by the European Investment Bank, with AIB and ICC co-ordinating the loan facilities in Ireland. Loans could be provided under the SME facility, which aimed to support the creation of employment in growing companies by subsidising capital investment in the industrial, agri-industrial, tourism, and service sectors.

OVERVIEW OF SUPPORT FOR ENTERPRISE

This overview of the support available for enterprise from both the state and the private sector gives some indication of the supportive environment for enterprise in Ireland. A common factor is the importance placed on marketing research, plans, and proposals. This applies equally to start-up ventures and developing enterprises. An understanding of the fundamental principles underlying marketing and the role it plays in the business is essential.

MARKETING AND CONTINUED BUSINESS SUCCESS

Marketing plays a crucial role at the start-up and initial development of a business. It is also required to ensure continued business success. This implies a need to constantly review and evaluate the firm's marketing strategies and activities.

Environmental changes may require marketing changes. (In chapter 5 the role of the marketing audit—which provides a structure for a comprehensive review of the firm's marketing—is demonstrated.) The following panel illustrates the changes made by the multinational firm Procter & Gamble. In this case the company reorganised itself in an attempt to become more responsive to market changes.

PROCTER & GAMBLE: RESPONDING MORE QUICKLY TO MARKET CHANGE

In 1998 Procter & Gamble, the world's largest home products company, announced the appointment of a new chairman and its decision to split itself into seven business units based on product lines. This would replace its existing structure of four geographical units and was a reaction to the financial upheaval that had taken place in Russia and Asia. The rationale for the change given by the company was the need to become more efficient and innovative and to get to the market faster with new products.

Procter & Gamble, whose brands include Ariel, Pampers, Tampax, Max Factor, and Fairy Liquid, had not been achieving its planned sales growth. It had planned to double global sales to $70,000 million by 2006, which required an annual sales growth of 7 per cent. Under the reorganisation, the new chairman planned to get more out of the firm's researchers, who include 1,250 scientists with a PhD. In spite of spending $1,500 million a year on research and development, most of the company's new products were improvements to existing lines, such as Crest toothpaste and Pantene hairspray. In some cases, such as the launch of the new product Febreze, which removed odours from fabrics, sales were originally confined to America, with the result that potential sales in other countries were lost.

The new global business units will divide the company into seven sections under the following titles: baby care, beauty care, fabric and home care, feminine protection, food and beverages, health care, and tissues and paper towels. The objective of the new plan will be to cut costs and make the company more responsive to the market. Though the company is being divided essentially along product lines, the global business units will be complemented by eight market development organisations that will work at regional and national levels to develop strategies for expanding business.

Source: G. Alexander, 'P&G gambles on shake-up to beat crisis', *Sunday Times*, 13 September 1998.

MARKETING AND TURNAROUND

The life-cycle for entrepreneurial firms illustrates the stages a business can go through as it seeks to become established. Once established, it will continue to face challenges. The changing needs of customer and environmental forces will have to be monitored constantly, and the firm may have to implement changes in response. The worst case is when the business gets into difficulties or collapses and the failure rate for new business ventures is quite high.

While many new and established businesses will get into difficulties and even disappear, there are also examples of firms that have been successfully turned around. Marketing can play an important role in achieving this.

FURTHER READING

Burns, P., and Dewhurst, J., (eds), *Small Business and Entrepreneurship* (second edition), London: Macmillan 1996.
Carson, D., Cromie, S., McGowan, P., and Hill, J., *Marketing and Entrepreneurship in SMEs*, Englewood Cliffs (NJ): Prentice-Hall 1995.
Cooney, T. (ed.), *Irish Cases in Entrepreneurship*, Dublin: Enterprise Ireland, Blackhall Publishing 2005.
Garavan, T., Ó Cinnéide, B., and Fleming, P., *Entrepreneurship and Business Start-ups in Ireland*, Dublin: Oak Tree Press 1997.
O'Gorman, C., and Cunningham, J., *Enterprise in Action: An Introduction to Enterprise in an Irish Context*, Dublin: Oak Tree Press 1997.

DISCUSSION QUESTIONS

1. Analyse the pros and cons of running your own business. Have you got what it takes to be an entrepreneur?
2. Where do you think business opportunities will exist in Ireland in the future? Give reasons for your answer.
3. 'No business or organisation can exist without marketing.' Comment on this statement.
4. Explain the link between marketing, entrepreneurship, and intrapreneurship. Can they be mutually exclusive? Give examples.
5. The state devotes considerable resources to the encouragement of enterprise. Are there any disadvantages to this? Should the state have a more laissez-faire approach?

REFERENCES

Bolton, W., *The University Handbook on Enterprise Development*, Columbus University 1997.
Burnside, R., 'Improving the corporate climate for creativity' in J. West and M. A. Farr (eds), *Innovation and Creativity at Work*, New York: John Wiley & Sons 1990.
Clark, W., and Carson, D., 'Marketing and the small business: a case history of education development', *Irish Marketing Review*, vol. 1 (1986).
Culliton, J., *The Culliton Report*, Dublin: Stationery Office 1992.

Drucker, P., *Innovation and Entrepreneurship* (third edition), London: Butterworth-Heinemann 1994.

Enterprise Strategy Group, 'Ahead of the curve: Ireland's place in the global economy', Dublin: Forfás, July 2004.

Forfás, *Innovate, Market, Sell: Review of the Sales, Marketing and Innovation Capabilities of Irish Exporting SMEs*, Dublin: Forfás, November 2004.

Foxall, G., and Minkes, A., 'Beyond marketing: the diffusion of entrepreneurship in the modern corporation', *Journal of Strategic Marketing*, June 1996.

Guilford, J., *Personality*, New York: McGraw-Hill 1959.

Jansen, P., and van Wees, L., 'Conditions for internal entrepreneurship', *Journal of Management Development*, vol. 13 (1994), no. 9.

Low, M., and MacMillan, I., 'Entrepreneurship: past research and future challenges', *Journal of Management*, June 1988.

Miles, A., and Arnold, D., 'Marketing orientation and entrepreneurial orientation', *Entrepreneurship Theory and Practice*, summer 1991.

Morris, M., and Lewis, P., 'The determinants of entrepreneurial activity: implications for marketers', *European Journal of Marketing*, vol. 29 (1995), no. 7.

National Business Incubation Association, 'Industry facts and figures', January 2000.

Pearson, G., 'Promoting entrepreneurship in large companies', *Long-Range Planning*, June 1989.

Poon, S., and Swatman, P., 'Small business use of the internet: findings from Australian case studies', *International Marketing Review*, vol. 14 (1997), no. 5.

Rosenfield, R., and Servo, J. C., 'Facilitating innovations in large organisations', in J. West and M. A. Farr (eds), *Innovation and Creativity at Work*, New York: John Wiley & Sons 1990.

Siropolis, N., *Small Business Management: A Guide to Entrepreneurship*, New York: Houghton-Mifflin 1990.

Smilor, R., and Gill, D., *The New Business Incubator Linking Talent, Technology, Capital and Know-how*, Lexington (MA): DC Heath and Company 1986.

Telesis Consulting Group, *Report on Irish Industrial Policy*, Dublin: Stationery Office 1982.

West, M. A., and Farr, J., *Innovation and Creativity at Work*, New York: John Wiley & Sons 1990.

SURVIVING AS A CRAFT ENTERPRISE, NICHOLAS MOSSE POTTERY

by Hilda Burton

With the changes in the economic climate in Ireland that have occurred over the past number of years come new challenges for craft enterprises who, now have to take stock to ensure their survival. Irish craft enterprises reported a 48 per cent downturn in sales in 2009. While competition from abroad is a key concern for the Irish craft sector its most significant challenge is the decline in consumer spending worldwide. Household consumption throughout Europe has contracted by 0.5 per cent with exports dropping 8.1 per cent and imports by 7.2 per cent. (Thomas, 2009) This has been labelled the worst global recession in six decades and, as a result, consumers have become more value conscious. However, research has shown that there is a place in the market for both low-cost imports and high-value, home-produced craft products. The hardest hit sectors have been products related to housing and discretionary items.

Innovation and creativity is the way forward in all industries and the craft sector has clearly embraced this idea. In a recent survey of craft workers in Ireland 55 per cent reported deriving revenue from new products in the past three years while 31 per cent stated that all of their revenue came from new products (CCOI, 2010). The craft sector contributes greatly to employment currently employing an estimated 5,771 people, many in rural areas, and exporting €124.5 million of craft products worldwide. It is also an important contributor to tourism and the building of the brand of Ireland internationally (ibid.).

Nicholas Mosse Pottery was established in 1975 in an old flour mill in Bennettsbridge, County Kilkenny. In the early days of production, with only a few staff, about 200 items were produced a week. Over the years the business has evolved into the largest craft business in Ireland and today employs 80 people and produces over 6,000 items of pottery per week. Increasing labour costs, strict EU regulations regarding health and safety and employment law have impacted on the company in the past decade and, in response, the company has switched from employing all locals to recruiting from Eastern Europe. Relocating production abroad has been considered by Mosse but, as yet, production remains in Kilkenny. Mosse feels such a move in the future would not adversely affect the Irishness of the brand as consumers are quite used to firms relocating. He also recognises that strong brand recognition both at home and abroad is not enough to insulate the firm against foreign competition and the decline in consumer spending. Traditional purchasing patterns have changed and both the retail and product brands are key influencers on today's consumer. In particular retailers are seen as central to reaching the younger consumer.

In recent years Nicholas Mosse has gone from strength to strength adding to its products and services year on year. The mill in Bennetsbridge has been turned into a mini paradise for tourists and craft enthusiasts. The ground floor of the mill houses a working pottery and country shop where customers can see the product being thrown and decorated and then examine the finished product for themselves. Linen and glass products, bearing the

Nicholas Mosse brand name and patterns are also available along with many other decorative home and garden accessories from outside suppliers. The second floor of the mill, houses the Riverside café where customers can dine surrounded again by a range of Nicholas Mosse giftware. There is a further giftware section on the third floor, stocking larger items of furniture and textiles and the most recent addition to the mill is a self-decorating studio to draw in school tours and increase appreciation of hand-made pottery amongst consumers generally.

Building a ceramics enterprise in Ireland

Central to the development any craft enterprise in Ireland is the Craft Council of Ireland (CCOI). Established in 1971 it is the national design and economic development organisation for the country's craft industry and has on its register approximately 2,000 workers. It is responsible for generating growth, developing competitiveness, and stimulating quality design and innovation within the sector. Some of its initiatives in recent years have been: 'Buy Irish Craft', a national campaign to promote Irish craft; the creation of a craft area at Bloom, Ireland's premier consumer show celebrating garden life; the development of exhibition and touring programmes; and an ongoing review of craft education and training in Ireland.

The largest group of its craft workers are 272 ceramicists. The CCOI potentially add to this number of ceramicists by running a pottery skills course taking on 12 new potters every two years. While there is a positive side to skills development within the sector as many of these new potters to the market are successfully attracting younger customers with their designs, there are those who feel that there is already a surplus of potters and any newcomers to the market actually cannibalise the existing market rather than grow it. Research by Indecon International Economic consultants has suggested that there is potential to increase employment in the craft sector by approximately 30 per cent over the coming years.

Ceramics Ireland, set up in 1977 as a voluntary, non-profit organisation to support potters in Ireland, also plays a significant role within the sector. Entirely reliant on fees from its members and some grant assistance, it hosts workshops, three exhibitions annually and publishes the magazine *Ceramics Ireland* twice yearly. Its main objective is to promote Irish ceramicists collectively and raise their profile internationally as providers of a collectable art form. Many of Nicholas Mosse's competitors are member of Ceramics Ireland but as yet Nicholas Mosse is not involved with the organisation.

Ceramics customers

Ceramics styles vary widely within and across European countries (Massot, 2005). Ceramic ware is very often bought as a gift or for decorative purposes but is also bought for its functionality. As a product group it includes items like table-top pottery and kitchen items for which functionality is key. These items are no longer kept for good use only, as would have been the case in the past, but are rather used day to day and are expected to be oven and dishwasher proof. Lamps, candle holders, desk sets, ornaments, animal figurines, and vases also fall into the product category and are used throughout the house for both their functional and decorative value. Outside the home ceramic flower pots and statuettes are often used to decorate gardens, terraces, and sunroofs.

Nicholas Mosse attributes approximately 10 per cent of its company sales to the UK where they have 30 stockists and 6 per cent to the rest of Europe, where they have approximately three stockists in each European country. European consumers when buying ceramics or giftware are looking for one-of-a-kind items which personalise their homes. Older European couples, aged 45–65, are less sensitive to fashion and more concerned with value for money and functionality and spend the most on their interior. Environmental awareness also influences consumers when they are purchasing giftware with producers who take account of the environment generally gaining more appreciation from European customers (CBI, 2004). Craft purchasers in Ireland typically spend €248 annually on Irish craft and view craft mainly as a gift item (CCOI, 2010).

Thirty per cent of Nicholas Mosse customers are tourists, many of them becoming familiar with the products while visiting Kilkenny but purchasing from a stockist when they return home. For tourists products with stories or local folklore attached to them have enjoyed success. This is particularly true of the Celtic market in America which represents the company's largest foreign market. Approximately 24 per cent of the company's sales can be attributed to its 200 stockists in North America. According to the United State's *Census 2000* report 10.8 per cent of the US population claims Irish ancestry (www.Euro Americans.net). Typically these customers are 50 plus with a natural and emotional link to Ireland and Irish products. They like products that are almost old fashioned and are not particularly concerned whether or not they are made in Ireland but rather that they have a story connecting them to Ireland (Lynch, 2005). Americans are also avid collectors of craft and have as a nation an appreciation of owning decorative items indicating good appreciation of applied art.

In 2005 Nicholas Mosse started to see changes to their core customer profile, which was traditionally 95 per cent female and 30–60 years of age, when customers as young as 15 started to show an interest in the brand. While these younger customers may have been starting a collection they had nowhere near the disposable income of those 40–60-year-old AB's who were often buying for a second home.

A major difficulty identified for the sector in 2006 was that the Irish consumer did not appreciate what handmade quality was and older Irish Consumers found the 'handmade' label more desirable than younger consumers. To combat this lack of awareness 'Craft in the Classroom' was initiated nationally between 2007–2009 at primary level and has involved 2,000 students and 77 craft makers. Also many new craft awards have been developed to raise the profile of craft. When consumers are informed of the craftsmanship and story behind the creation of a piece of craft 'handmade' becomes a more valuable label (CCOI, 2006). This is significant as, on average, over half of craft companies in Ireland report selling 90–100 per cent of their products to the domestic market (Technology Ireland, 2002). For Nicholas Mosse this figure is around 70 per cent.

Irish consumers have reported being influenced by a broad variety of internal and external factors when buying craft products. The three key influencing factors are life stage, affluence, and purchase occasions. Purchase occasions can be further split into buying for others, buying for self, home focus, and non-home focus. Gift needs can be broken down into big occasions, such as weddings, anniversaries, or a new house, and smaller occasions, such as birthdays, thank-you gifts, and Christmas presents. There are a number of challenges facing craftspeople of Ireland regarding perceptions of craft among Irish consumers. There are clear perceptual differences depending on life stage, with the affluent over 35s being most disposed to buying and appreciating craft. The older, less affluent groups see craft as a tourist product. Generally gifts aimed at tourists are viewed negatively and the association of 'craft' with 'tourist gift' has made the term a liability when marketing to the home buyer. The younger age group of 25–35 while reacting positively to products when exposed to them, seeing them as contemporary and relevant to their life-styles, are unlikely to find these products in the shops that they frequent. Younger consumers are not inclined to travel to a craft studio or small rural outlets and 40 per cent of craft purchasers in Ireland find it hard to locate stockists of Irish crafts when searching for products (CCOI, 2003).

Some other smaller customer niches for craft and ceramics in Ireland are: the corporate sector, either buying gifts for their staff/business associates or tableware for upmarket restaurants; the collectables market; and interior designers and architects. The collectables market consists of specialist buyers who are willing to pay high prices for one-off pieces. These buyers can be museums, galleries, and corporate or private collectors. It is a very underdeveloped niche for a number of reasons. Firstly a there is no gallery system in place in Ireland with only three relatively large galleries operating which limits accessibility to the market. Secondly Irish collectors are few in number, very discrete and difficult to identify (Flegg, 2005).

Regarding the latter niche there is potential for ceramic products in all rooms of the house and into the garden not just in the traditional form of tableware, lighting, and decorative pieces but also in surfaces, such as tiling, and bigger household appliances, such as sinks and baths (Mabelson, 2005).

Competitors

The company's location in Kilkenny, the creative heart of Ireland, has clearly contributed to its success. Since the mid-1960s when the first Kilkenny Design Centre was established, crafts people have been locating there. Within this setting Nicholas Mosse find themselves surrounded by 70 other craft businesses and are one of 26 professional craft studios that can be visited on the Kilkenny Craft Trail. Collectively these studios market themselves under the 'Made in Kilkenny' banner (Parsons, 2009). The key players in the ceramics market in Ireland are Nicholas Mosse and Louis Mulchay, both of whom have been in operation over 35 years. Nicholas Mosse is the largest potter in the south of Ireland in terms of production volume, selling its products through one self-owned retail outlet at the Mill in Kilkenny, a company website and a chain of some 500 retail stores at home and abroad. Louis Mulcahy sells through his own studio pottery on the Dingle peninsula, his wife's textile shop in Dingle town and another self-owned retail outlet on Dawson Street in Dublin. They have actively been selling their products through the web for many years and are artists of some acclaim.

Stephen Pearce Pottery was a major player in the market until 2008 when it went into receivership. In operation since 1960 it was an east Cork institution drawing many people to the area and providing valuable, skilled employment. Despite its obvious appeal it was thought that because of the intricate processes that each piece of pottery must go through, profits could never be huge. Its 12,000-square-foot retail emporium was bought by the top Irish craft retailers the Kilkenny Group, and its 5,000-square-foot manufacturing base was subsequently bought out by Youghal's Jack O'Patsy Pottery which had been closed for six years previous to this acquisition. Jack O'Patsy also own Badger Hill a Wexford brand of pottery. Pat Collins the founder of Jack O'Patsy's aims to grow the domestic business gradually while also keeping a keen eye on the American market developing a mail order and catalogue business there. The purchase of Pearce's production facilities means a further ability to develop a technique called reduction gas-fired pottery which offers great potential to create stunning and vibrant colours. Collins aims to keep the brand unique by continually adding innovative designs reflecting Irish historical and mythological themes, along with local and national landscapes and seascapes.

In Northern Ireland potteries such as Ballydoughan and Belleek are successfully developing contemporary tableware and giftware brands. There are also numerous medium-sized players in the sector that employ up to 10 people, such as Stoneware Jackson, Michael Kennedy, Judy Greene, Rossmore Country Pottery, and countless other small-scale operations countrywide. Like their larger counterparts they too, in a bid to gain more control and higher income from their sales, are choosing to sell direct more and more and open their own galleries and shops where possible and in many cases provide short courses in ceramics giving consumers a chance to experience this craft.

In the early 1980s and 1990s retail sales of craft were dominated by indigenous retailers carrying a substantial amount of mainstream Irish craft as part of their sales offering. Since the late 1990s there has been an explosion of retail options in the form of national and international chains, high street stores, internet shopping, and mail order companies all vying to attract consumer spending. Retail giants, such as IKEA, House of Frazer and John Lewis, are all upping their game with own-label and foreign-produced products in the gift and tableware sectors. Within this new retail mix Irish craft is a smaller, even diminishing, part of the offering. As the Irish population ages the older affluent groups of consumers who are more disposed to shop in craft, gift or specialist outlets will become less active purchasers while younger consumers, who frequent the high street and larger international shopping centres, will become a more influential consumer group for craft. They however have very different shopping needs (CCOI, 2006). Clearly channel management and selection will be important in facilitating growth since most craft producers rely heavily on their studio as a point of sale for their products while only 11 per cent of craft purchasers buy through studios.

Nicholas Mosse marketing mix

'Broadly speaking every pottery does the same thing, use clay, energy and water to make beautiful fragile objects that require very careful and copious packaging' (Cullen, 2005). Nicholas Mosse Pottery is instantly recognisable and as functional as it is appealing. Each piece goes through a six-week production process, during which it is checked for quality three times. The final quality check occurs after firing and faulty items are used for landfill or driveways. Out of every 100 pieces 45 per cent pass the quality-control procedures but still have to make it through the transport stage. Transport is critical due to the products fragility and the company use plastic returnable boxes, which the company deliver and collect from customers themselves. Nicholas Mosse Pottery use an integrated accounts and stock system that provides full visibility and recording of information necessary to manage order processing, manufacturing, quality control, and dispatch. These tasks were up to recently performed on spreadsheets and were very time consuming. In the future it is intended to streamline business processes further and automate other manual processes to achieve more efficiencies.

Nick Mosse has always been mindful of the environment and buys up clay from an old coal pit in England, which has enabled the company to produce its own clay without impacting on its local environment for 40 years. The kilns used in the production process are fired by hydropower from the nearby River Nore and ongoing research is being conducted by the firm into a heat exchange system for the kiln flues which would power a water-heating system for the mill complex.

The company's core product category is tableware and, at any one time, around 20 patterns and 42 shapes are available to the customer along with special ranges, such as the Christmas, and floral and fruit ranges, each of which has four patterns that can be mixed and matched. This helps collectors substantially when patterns are discontinued. Approximately 20 per cent of patterns are changed yearly, but customers will always be facilitated if they are looking for a specific piece. The same patterns are used on lighting pieces, flower pots, linens, and candles. A change in style for the company occurred in 2003 and while they held on to their more traditional round-shaped pottery, which is designed and coloured around country-living concept, a more modern and contemporary-styled product was introduced with a view to establishing the company in the European marketplace.

Nicholas Mosse products are aimed at the higher end of the market. Almost every product is available in a number of sizes and prices vary accordingly. For example a mug could range from €14.95 to €16.95, a jug from €17.50 to €56.25, a bowl from €11.50 to €68.75, a plate from €24.50 to €133.99, and a lamp from €34.00 to €191.00. Lamps, serving dishes, and artistic centrepieces generate the higher value sales for the company. Nick Mosse does not believe in discounting his products and will consider dropping a stockist if they do not follow his pricing recommendations. The company keep their prices in Bennettsbridge and their mail order catalogue the same, however consumers can source selected items on eBay. Nicholas Mosse does not want to be competing with their stockists and for this reason has not pushed a mail order business which accounts for approximately 4 per cent of company sales. While looking after their stockists very well, Mosse is not foolish and will not give more then 15 per cent of his company's business to any one retailer.

Nicholas Mosse invests 5–7 per cent of sales annually into advertising, trade fairs, and promotions. Showcase, Ireland's annual craft fair, is used as the primary networking and relationship exercise of the year where they can generate up to 60 per cent of their annual sales orders. The company also exhibits at Birmingham Spring Fair, New York Craft Fair twice yearly, and in Enterprise Ireland's permanent showrooms in Atlanta year round. The company sells its products through a network of 500 speciality stores throughout Ireland, the UK, Europe, and America. These stores operate on a small scale, selling one-of-a-kind, limited-edition craft products and focusing on building relationships with customers. They look to suppliers for in-depth product information and service. Nick Mosse has started doing demonstrations of his throwing and decorating processes in some larger stores and feels that this may be the only way to educate consumers as to the nature of 'handmade' ceramics.

Two thousand and eleven has been designated 'Year of Craft' in Ireland when Ireland will be hosting the Annual General Assembly of the World Craft Council. This coincides with the 40th anniversary of the establishment of CCOI and increasing efforts to strengthen crafts as a profession and a product choice. Innovation in design and production of Irish craft products will be high on the agenda and will continue to play an important role for growth and competitiveness of the sector into the future. Competition from imported goods is not going away and consumer caution will continue to be a cause for concern and so product marketing and the branding of Irish craft will be critical.

FURTHER READING

Flegg, E.,'Philadelphia-A follow up', *Stopress*, Jan/Feb 2005, p. 12.

Thompson, J., 'The rise and fall of Waterford Wedgewood', *Irish Independent*, 6th January 2009.

Torres, A., 'Marketing networks as a form of strategic alliance among craft enterprises', *Journal of Nonprofit and Voluntary Sector Marketing*, vol. 7 (August 2002), no. 3, pp. 229–43.

Torres, A., European Case Clearing House Case Study Winner, SME/Venture Creation Category, 'Judy Greene Pottery: Marketing Irish Handcrafted Pottery'.

Useful Websites

www.cso.ie/statistics
www.ccoi.ie
www.ceramicsireland.com
www.irishpotters.comn
www.nicholasmosse.com
www.belleek.ie
www.ballydouganpottery.co.uk

DISCUSSION QUESTIONS

1. Indicate how a knowledge of marketing can be used by firms like Nicholas Mosse as they face a difficult consumer environment.
2. How should Nicholas Mosse take advantage of the 'Year of Craft'? Try to think of some specific things it should do.

REFERENCES

CBI (Centre for the Promotion of Imports from Developing Countries), *EU Market Survey—Gifts and Decorative articles*, Rotterdam 2004.

CCOI (Crafts Council of Ireland), *The Irish Craft Industry a Summary*, Kilkenny 2003.

CCOI (Crafts Council of Ireland), *Annual report,* Kilkenny 2006.

CCOI (Crafts Council of Ireland), Strategic Plan 2010–2012, 2010.

Cullen, D., 'Crafts and the Environment', *Stopress,* January 2005, pp. 6–7.

Flegg, E., 'An insight into the collectors market', *Stopress,* March/April 2005, pp. 4–5.

Lynch, H. (development officer, CCOI), Personal communication, 20 September 2005.

Mabelson, G. (pottery trainer CCOI), Personal communication, July 2005.

Massot, R. (Craft industry consultant), Personal communication, September 2005.

Parsons, M., 'The art of Irish crafts', *Irish Times,* 12 December 2009.

Technology Ireland, 2002 *Crafts.* Accessed at: www.arcturus.businessandfinance.ie/cgi-bin/frags/advanced-news.

Thomas, E.R, 'European Spending, Exports decline most in 14 years', 3 June 2009. Accessed at: http://www.bloomberg.com/apps/news?pid=newsarchive&sid=aQeIuRCoYMZw.

Fig 2.1: Nicholas Mosse Pottery

PART 2

The Market

3

The Forces in the Irish Marketing Environment

The *environment* refers to the forces external to the firm that affect its ability to develop and maintain successful transactions. The environment is composed of a number of elements that, individually or jointly, can determine success or failure for the business.

Environmental forces can represent threats to the firm, but they can also present opportunities. Environmental forces can change, and therefore marketers need to be flexible and able to adapt to these changes. The environment requires constant monitoring. Some changes may be well heralded; others may take the firm by surprise. This chapter explores the main elements in the environment and examines some of the environmental influences that marketers need to take into account.

Kourteli (2000) argued that organisations must develop the appropriate sensitivity towards the changes and differentiations in their environment.

The level of complexity of the environment imposes on the organisation a specific environmental monitoring process. This in turn requires an internal communication system so that decision makers are aware of and respond to environmental influences. Kourteli argued that this internal communication system is in effect the structure of the organisation itself.

The idea that environmental monitoring is analogous to the structure of the organisation illustrates very powerfully the defining role of environmental analysis for any organisation. The results of this monitoring can, for example, provide new business opportunities. It would also suggest that in fast-changing environments the organisation's structure must be designed for quick decision making and rapid response.

The environment can be divided into two main areas: the *micro-environment* and the *macro-environment*. The micro-environment consists of forces that are closest to the firm, including the elements or functions within the firm itself, competitors, and customers. The macro-environment consists of broader social forces, such as demographics; these are further removed from the firm but are no less significant. In this chapter, these forces are examined mainly in the context of the Irish marketing environment.

THE MICRO-ENVIRONMENT

The micro-environment refers to a collection of forces that include the company itself, its suppliers, intermediaries, competitors, customers, and publics.

The company

Most companies and organisations are composed of individuals or groups of people working together to achieve a common purpose. This common purpose can be defined as serving the needs of the customer. The firm engages in a value-adding process: it takes inputs such as raw materials and, using its skills and resources, transforms them into products or services. If customers place enough value on the result of this process, they may buy the product or service. The firm must therefore be concerned about getting the value-adding process right. This will be based on understanding needs. If, for example, a coffee-producer obtains coffee beans from coffee plantations, processes them into instant coffee granules, gives them a brand name, and distributes them on the market, they have added value for the consumer. This value could be expressed in the form of such factors as convenience, taste, quality, and price.

All organisations add value. When a theatre stages a play, for example, it is adding value in the form of enjoyment, creativity, or artistic merit.

In general, firms tend to be divided according to functional speciality and responsibility. Therefore there will usually be functional departments, such as marketing, finance, production or operations, and personnel or human resources. Each of these functions is involved in adding value.

The extent to which these functions are oriented towards serving customers' needs and are integrated is important. It is easy for functional specialists to concentrate on or become completely absorbed with their own specialism. Marketers, for example, will usually want to spend money to attract more customers; the finance department, however, may want to cut costs, leading to tension between the two. Functions will usually compete with each other for a greater share of internal resources. All of this may distract attention from the customer and an understanding of the customer's needs. Firms are myopic if they concentrate on internal rivalry at the expense of customers' needs. Serving the needs of customers should be an integrating force for all functions. The need for integration of functions emphasises the role of internal marketing.

Internal marketing

Internal marketing involves the application of the marketing policy within the firm. Expressed in simple terms, if the staff won't buy the product, then why should the customer (Barnes, 1989)? The objective of internal marketing is for all the firm's employees to be committed to the goal of ensuring the best possible treatment of customers. It complements the company's external marketing efforts, plays a role in customer satisfaction, and is directed at producing and maintaining a motivated and satisfied group of employees who will support the company's external marketing objectives.

Internal marketing is important because of the role it can play in focusing or refocusing the company's personnel on the importance of the customer. Firms can lose sight of the customer. Internal politics and the culture of the firm may mean that individual functions or departments spend more time competing for resources than attempting to achieve integration. Integration implies that all elements in the firm are working together with a common purpose. The customers' needs should be the means of achieving this integration.

Internal marketing therefore encompasses issues such as communication, discussion, corporate culture, quality standards, and change.

Suppliers

Most firms rely on suppliers to provide them with goods and services. Raw materials, equipment, and transport are just some of the areas in which firms may rely on suppliers. Firms will also buy from marketing-related suppliers, such as advertising agencies, market research companies, and public relations consultants. Financial service suppliers, such as banks and insurance companies, are also important.

Business-to-business marketing covers the marketing activities of firms that supply other firms with goods and services that are incorporated into the value-adding process. It is important that the marketer is aware of the changes that may be taking place in the supplier environment. Factors such as scarcity of raw material or changes in technology may be experienced by suppliers first, but they have a knock-on effect on the firm and may cause increases in costs or require changes in the firm's value-adding process.

Intermediaries

Intermediaries include wholesalers, distributors, agents, and retailers. These are all elements of the *marketing channel*. (This is discussed in more detail in chapter 10.) A significant issue will be the development of relationships with intermediaries; *relationship marketing theory* (discussed in chapter 1) provides some insights on how to do this.

Relationship marketing with suppliers and intermediaries

Relationship marketing is important in managing the interaction between the firm and its suppliers and intermediaries. Relationship marketing simply involves the firm applying the marketing policy to those firms or individuals with which it deals. It involves treating them all as customers. It can therefore be applied to the supplier–marketer exchange and the marketer–intermediary exchange, and of course it is the basis of the marketer–customer exchange.

In relation to the supplier–marketer and the marketer–intermediary exchanges, relationship marketing is based on the well-established business principle that co-operation between businesses should be mutually beneficial. Suppliers and intermediaries have an interest in ensuring that the firm prospers; similarly, the firm has an interest in ensuring that its suppliers and channel members prosper.

One study has examined how aquaculture went from being a cottage industry—fragmented, undercapitalised, with uneven product quality, and at the mercy of larger, foreign-owned distributors—to become the Irish Seafood Producers' Group, a successful, internationally competitive firm (Garvey and Torres, 1993). Significantly, relationship marketing approaches played an important part in this process. The company undertook a value chain analysis of its industry (see fig. 3.1). The value chain demonstrates how value is added in successive stages, from the obtaining of raw material to ultimate consumption by the consumer. This value chain analysis demonstrated a need for the producers' group to build co-operative relationships with producers, distributors, and retailers. The key to capturing value was considered to be getting to know the customer's customer (i.e. the retailer or caterer) and the customer's customer's customer (i.e. the consumer). One of the results of this approach was the ability of the group to negotiate promotions directly with large supermarket chains, which led to lower margins for the distributor but guaranteed higher volumes, which more than compensated for this.

Figure 3.1: The aquabusiness chain

Commercialise
Produce ➤ Package ➤ Supply, Sell, Promote ➤ Distribute ➤ Retail ➤ Consume

If the firm and the members of the value chain have a strong relationship, this should help to ensure that needs are satisfied.

Customers

Central to any marketing is the customer. Customers can be classified as being *consumers*, *business-to-business*, or *international*. In this book, particular attention is paid to understanding consumers' behaviour (chapter 6), international marketing (chapter 12), and business-to-business markets (chapter 13). The role of marketing involves not just creating customers but also developing a relationship with those customers. Though marketers want to develop relationships with their suppliers and intermediaries, the fundamental relationship is between the marketer and the customer. The marketer needs to consider what the relationship means to the customer.

Barnes (1995) suggested viewing firm–customer relationships along a spectrum of intensity, from mere transactions to genuine relationships. Genuine relationships are characterised by the consumer experiencing a stronger sense of closeness to the marketer, which should contribute to a stronger desire to return to do business than if no relationship existed. The marketer therefore needs to understand customers' needs fully. Barnes suggested that this understanding could be facilitated with information on how pertinent dimensions or characteristics of the relationship are to the consumer, how the consumer views his or her interaction with the company, and how the consumer engages in that interaction.

Relationship marketing is therefore much more than retaining customers, developing customer databases, or locking customers into relationships that are difficult to get out of: it involves putting into practice the core principles of marketing, which require a more holistic view of the customer.

Customer care will be important in the maintenance of relationships. One model of customer care suggests that both quantitative and qualitative issues are involved (Carson and Gilmore, 1989). Quantitative issues include factors such as speed of delivery, while qualitative issues include factors such as courtesy. While rules and procedures are common for the former, in the qualitative or psychological areas it is the perceptions, attitudes and behaviour of customer-contact personnel that are important. These are areas where marketing managers can have an impact or can implement improvements.

Competitors

Competition describes the rivalry that exists between firms in the market. Most markets are characterised by competition; and even where traditionally very little competition existed, rivalries are increasing. Greater integration in the European Union, for example, has meant more competition in many markets. The changing nature of competition can also present opportunities; such was the case when Tayto (Northern Ireland) purchased the Golden Wonder brand in the United Kingdom.

TAYTO (NORTHERN IRELAND)

In February 2006, Tayto (Northern Ireland) acquired the Golden Wonder brand for £15 million. Tayto (Northern Ireland) is based in Tandragee, County Armagh, and owed its origins to a deal between Thomas Hutchinson and Joe Murphy (who established the Tayto brand in the Republic) in 1956. Hutchinson bought the rights to the Tayto brand in Northern Ireland for £250. There was an agreement that neither party would sell in the other's territory. In 2006 the company had a 44 per cent share of the Northern Ireland crisp market.

The Hutchinson family still runs the business. Thomas's three sons and one daughter comprise the board of directors. The company produces 6 million packets of a 100-strong range per week and supply most of the big British supermarket chains such as Tesco and Sainsbury's as well as the German company Aldi.

The acquisition of Golden Wonder provided the company with the opportunity to expand. Golden Wonder had been the market leader in the UK crisp market but had come under pressure from the PepsiCo-owned Walkers brand. In 2004, it recorded losses of £10.8 million.

Hutchinson had tried to acquire the Tayto brand in the Republic in 1999, but had been beaten to it by Cantrell and Cochrane.

Tayto continued its strategy of expansion by acquisition and in 2007 acquired Sirhowy Valley Foods, the makers of the Real Crisps brand, while in 2008 it acquired Red Mill Snack Foods, the third largest crisp manufacturer in the UK. In 2009 another English crisp manufacturer Jonathan Crisp was added and, by that stage, company turnover was £150 million.

An interesting and popular feature of the brand's marketing is its Tayto Castle Tour; visitors can visit the firm's manufacturing facility in Tandragee where they are taken on a tour and shown the manufacturing process. Like the Tayto brand in the Republic, the company also has a Mr Tayto, who meets and greets visitors to the factory; he is described by the company as the brand mascot.

Sources: Mark Paul, 'Deal is in the bag for Ulster's potato man', *Sunday Times*, 5 March 2006. *Irish Times*, 21 January 2009; www.tayto.com.

Defining or identifying who competitors are may not always be easy. Some may be direct competitors, and these can usually be easily identified and will typically be the focus of most brand competition.

Indirect competitors for a product or service may be quite diverse. In the case of lager, for example, the consumer may decide to go to the cinema rather than to the pub; in that case the cinema would be an indirect competitor. Obviously there can be many possible indirect competitors for most products and services, and the marketer may not be able to precisely determine them all. The important point is, who or what does the consumer perceive to be a competitor, and in what circumstances? Research into consumers' perceptions of competitors is therefore vital.

Competition can exist at different levels. Consider the example of the person who is hungry and decides to buy a snack (see fig. 3.2). *Generic competitors* are the broad range of products from which the consumer may choose. If the consumer decides to buy a bar of chocolate, they then move on to what *product form* they will buy. If the decision here is a toffee-centre product, they will have a number of *brand competitors* from which to choose.

Figure 3.2: Levels of competition

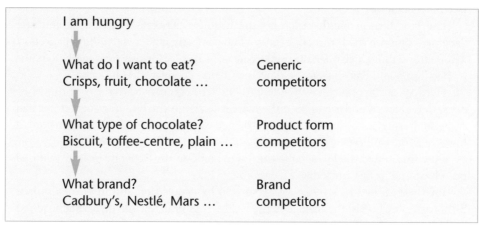

Marketers, therefore, should not concentrate their attention only on brand competitors. It would be myopic for companies like Cadbury, Nestlé or Mars, for example, not to consider Tayto or Perri to be competitors.

Publics

In addition to the various forces described in the previous section, the firm will also interact at a microlevel with various publics. These may be other organisations, such as providers of financial services, government departments, or the media, or they may be the general public. All these publics may influence the company very directly: for example, if the company is planning to float on the stock exchange, the views or opinions of leading stockbrokers or financial analysts may influence potential investors. News media coverage of the company or its products may influence perceptions or opinion.

THE MACRO-ENVIRONMENT

The *macro-environment* refers to a broad range of social forces, external to the business, that influence its activities. The following section describes some of the main forces in the macro-environment and their implications for marketers.

Demographics

Since the Great Famine of the 1840s, the population of Ireland has exhibited a fairly steady decline. The rate of decline varied as economic and social conditions varied, but the underlying trend from 1900 to the 1970s was downwards, as table 3.1 shows. By 1971 the decline had ceased, and by the 1981 census the total exceeded what it had been at the turn of the century.

The results of the census conducted in April 2006 revealed that the Irish population had increased by 8.1 per cent since the previous census in 2002. The total population was 4,234,925. As table 3.1 indicates, Ireland's population has increased steadily since the middle of the 20th century.

Table 3.1: Population (26 counties)

1901	3.221 million
1911	3.139 million
1926	2.971 million
1936	2.968 million
1946	2.955 million
1951	2.960 million
1961	2.818 million
1971	2.978 million
1981	3.443 million
1991	3.525 million
1996	3.626 million
2002	3.917 million
2006	4.235 million

Source: Central Statistics Office.

In September 2010 the CSO estimated that the Irish population was 4,470,700; it also reported an increase in emigration. The main features of the estimates for 2010 were:

- of the 65,300 people who emigrated in the year to April 2010, Irish nationals were the largest group, accounting for 42 per cent
- the number of immigrants from the EU12 states continued to decline
- the estimated number of persons aged 65 years and over exceeded 500,000 for the first time
- the overall population increase of 0.3 per cent (compared to 2009) was unevenly distributed, with the mid-east showing the strongest growth at 1.6 per cent and Dublin showing the largest decrease of 0.3 per cent.

Improved economic conditions in the 1990s contributed to the overall increase in population, and this has continued during the past decade. The natural rate of increase (i.e. births minus deaths) has increased, but the most significant contributor to population growth has been immigration. The 2006 census estimated that there were 400,000 non-nationals living in the Republic that year, compared with 220,000 in 2002 (table 3.2). Ireland's demography was described by Fitzgerald (2003) as one of the most unstable in the world, the country having changed from one of the highest population densities in Europe in the 1840s to one of the lowest today (about two-fifths of the European average). The distinctive features of Ireland's demography had been established in the early 19th century and included:

- late age of marriage
- high fertility within marriage
- a low level of births outside marriage
- an overall low rate of fertility across the population as a whole
- high levels of emigration.

While there have been changes, as cited by Fitzgerald, and in some cases reversals in these trends, emigration was to last (with the exception of a period in the late 1960s/mid-1970s) until the early 1990s. According to Akenson (1991), from the 19th century, the Irish became the most internationally dispersed of the European national cultures.

Table 3.2: Nationalities living in Ireland

Country	Number
Irish	**3,706,683**
United Kingdom	112,548
Rest of EU	163,227
Rest of Europe	24,425
Africa	35,326
Asia	46,952
America	21,124
Other nationalities	16,131
Not stated	45,597

Source: Central Statistics Office.

Birth rates in Ireland decreased slightly in 2009 as table 3.3 indicates, death rates increased slightly, but the underlying trends in the past decade have been an increasing birth rate and a reduced death rate.

Table 3.3: Birth and death rates 1990 and 2000–2009 (Per 1,000 of the population)

Year	Birth rate	Death rate
1990	15.1	9.0
2000	14.5	8.3
2001	15.0	7.9
2002	15.4	7.6
2003	15.5	7.2
2004	15.3	7.0
2005	14.8	6.6
2006	15.2	6.5
2007	16.3	6.5
2008	17.0	6.4
2009	16.7	6.5

Source: Central Statistics Office.

Life expectancy in Ireland is 76.8 years for men and 81.6 years for women.

Ireland's population, unlike many other European Union countries, is expected to grow steadily over the next 50 years (see table 3.4).

Table 3.4: European population projections 2008–2060

Population at 1 January	2008	2035	2060
EU27	495,394	520,654	505,719
Belgium	10,656	11,906	12,295
Bulgaria	7,642	6,535	5,485
Czech Republic	10,346	10,288	9,514
Denmark	5,476	5,858	5,920
Germany	82,179	79,150	70,759
Estonia	1,339	1,243	1,132
Ireland	4,415	6,057	6,752
Greece	11,217	11,575	11,118
Spain	45,283	53,027	51,913
France	61,876	69,021	71,800
Italy	59,529	61,995	59,390
Cyprus	795	1,121	1,320
Latvia	2,269	1,970	1,682
Lithuania	3,365	2,998	2,548
Luxembourg	482	633	732
Hungary	10,045	9,501	8,717
Malta	410	429	405
Netherlands	16,404	17,271	16,596

continued overleaf

Austria	8,334	9,075	9,037
Poland	38,116	36,141	31,139
Portugal	10,617	11,395	11,265
Romania	21,423	19,619	16,921
Slovenia	2,023	1,992	1,779
Slovakia	5,399	5,231	4,547
Finland	5,300	5,557	5,402
Sweden	9,183	10,382	10,875
United Kingdom	61,270	70,685	76,677
Norway	4,737	5,634	6,037
Switzerland	7,591	8,798	9,193

Source: Eurostat.

Courtney (1995) described Ireland as experiencing a second demographic transition, in other words contemporary demographic patterns in Ireland were becoming increasingly similar to those of Western Europe and countries like Australia. The principal trends in this transition refer to marriage (declining rates, later age, increased co-habitation, increased rates of separation and divorce, increasing rates of remarriage, and more homosexual unions), fertility (smaller family size, later motherhood, more voluntary childlessness, more single-parent families, and more births outside marriage), and ageing (people living longer, better health, more 'old elderly', later retirement rates for some, and longer periods of retirement).

While Ireland is converging with these trends, there are also some differences most notably in relation to ageing. While many European countries are faced with the challenge of an ageing and increasingly dependent population in the coming decades, the opposite is true in the case of Ireland where a proportionately larger number of the population (38 per cent) are aged under 25. The age profile of migrants, with significant numbers in the under 25 age group, has helped to boost this proportion.

Overall, the changing Irish population profile presents both opportunities and challenges for marketers, not least the multicultural nature of the market.

Research on migrants

The addition of 10 new member states to the EU in 2004 resulted in substantial immigration from these countries. In 2002 and 2003 there were fewer than 10,000 arrivals from these accession states; in 2004 this had increased to 59,000 and by 2006 it had reached 139,000, or 61 per cent of all arrivals.

In 2006 94,000 arrivals were from Poland, representing 67 per cent of arrivals from the accession states. The other significant sources were Latvia and Lithuania who between them accounted for 18 per cent.

The majority of immigrant workers can be found in lower paid and lower skilled occupations in the services, catering, and agriculture/fishery sectors. Minimal numbers are found in the higher skilled/professional categories.

The inflow of immigrants has led to debates about refugee and labour rights, racism, integration, and inter-culturalism. Immigration is a complex phenomenon, the push factors that send people from Central and Eastern Europe and the developing world to Ireland include poverty and unemployment. Structural conditions, for example the ability to work legally, and technical infrastructure, for example the internet, have also helped. In addition to labour market issues, how people who come from different cultures consume in Ireland presents interesting research possibilities.

Some recent research has focused on the importance of networks and clusters. Corrigan (2006) for example, highlights the importance of how emigrants and potential emigrants draw on social networks as a form of capital; this analysis was based on Irish-born entrepreneurs in the United States. A study on Vietnamese immigrants (Maguire, 2004) revealed that first generation migrants do not speak English and therefore have little interaction with Irish people.

The inflow of migrants into Ireland has led to the development of a body of research on the topic. Castles and Millar (1998) pointed out that the experiences of immigrants are significantly shaped by the policies and practices of the state. As immigration is a relatively new phenomenon in Ireland, it may not be surprising that state policy is evolving. In practice, the state has encouraged immigration, principally to fill shortages in labour supply. As a result, much of the research conducted so far has focused on the labour market characteristics of immigrants, for example Barrett and Trace (1998) examined the educational profile of arrivals, their research indicated that in the 25–29-age category, almost 70 per cent of immigrants had some form of third-level qualification, compared with just 32 per cent of the native population in that age category. Subsequent research (Barrett, Bergin and Duffy, 2006) supported this finding and also showed that immigrants were not, on average, working in occupations that fully reflected their educational attainment, when compared with the host population. A follow-on study (Barrett and Duffy, 2008) sought evidence about whether or not the length of time that immigrants had been in Ireland was associated with improved occupational attainment. Their study found no evidence that this was the case.

Russell, Quinn, King-O'Riain and McGinnity (2008), in a study of experiences of discrimination, found that while 12 per cent of Irish adults felt that they had been discriminated against in the labour market, the figure for non-nationals was 24 per cent. This finding was supported in O'Connell and McGinnity's (2008) research which concluded that in addition to experience of discrimination, migrants to Ireland fared less well than Irish nationals in the Irish labour market, in terms of unemployment levels and in access to privileged occupations in the occupational structure. They also found that English-language skills were a determining factor in the quality of the migrants' experience. Dundon, González-Pérez and McDonagh (2008) in a study on immigrant workers and industrial relations concluded that some immigrant workers in Ireland 'have experienced a system of near-serfdom that perpetuates social, economic and cultural exclusion on a large scale'.

CONSUMER ACCULTURATION

According to Sam (2006), acculturation covers all the changes that arise following 'contact' between individuals and groups of different cultural backgrounds. The International Organisation for Migration defines acculturation as 'the progressive adoption of elements of a foreign culture (ideas, words, values, norms, behaviour, institutions) by persons, groups or classes of a given culture'. The definition put forward by Redfield, Linton and Herskovits

(1936), is considered by Sam to be the 'classical definition', they had described acculturation as 'those phenomena which result when groups of individuals having different cultures come into continuous first hand contact, with subsequent changes in the original culture patterns of either or both groups'.

Peñaloza (1989) was the first to define consumer acculturation which describes an eclectic process of learning and selectively displaying culturally defined consumption skills, knowledge, and behaviour. Peñaloza (1994) developed a model, based on a qualitative research study among Mexican migrants to a number of south-western US states (fig. 3.3) to clarify how people's consumer behaviour changes in a new cultural setting.

Figure 3.3: Peñaloza's model of consumer acculturation

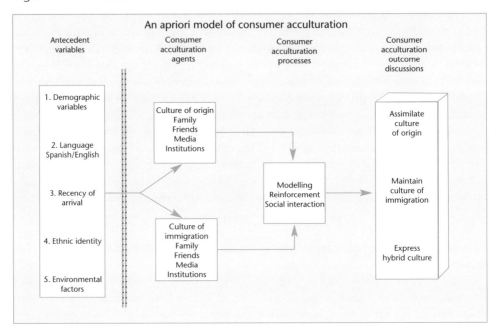

Consumers with disabilities

While they are not necessarily an age-dependent category, marketers should also be aware of the needs of disabled consumers. Disability affects people of all ages, but it does not necessarily affect their ability to buy. People with disability and their carers are an important pressure group, and they are also an important market, not just for specialist products (Reed, 1997). Advertising or communication activities aimed at this market should not emphasise disability, and they certainly should not be patronising.

Implications for marketers

In general, the changing population profile presents both opportunities and challenges. A declining birth rate had meant a reduced market for products related to babies and children, but on the other hand the increased life expectancy means that consumers will remain in the market for longer, and the demand for products and services for the elderly will increase.

Some have referred to this market as the 'golden years' or 'senior' market. One researcher noted that there was a danger of marketers stereotyping the senior market as lacking in spending power and innovation and being perceived as being difficult to segment (Turley, 1994). It was argued that there was an opportunity for marketers to direct their efforts at a segment that is active, engaged, and discerning.

A study in Britain suggested that the senior market could be segmented into four broad categories—'healthy indulgers', 'healthy hermits', 'ailing outgoers', and 'frail recluses'—and that marketing activities could be selected accordingly (Moschis and Mathur, 1997). Some manufacturers have undertaken research to assess the needs of older consumers, as the following panel demonstrates. There is certainly no doubt that the senior market is one that will present increased opportunities for marketers.

MARKETERS: IGNORE THE AGED AT YOUR PERIL

'Senior citizens' are a growing market force throughout Europe, and manufacturers of domestic appliances ignore this market at their peril. Not only is the proportion of people over 55 increasing in all European markets but this older generation of consumers needs labour-saving devices.

A survey by Electrolux showed that people over 55 have substantial purchasing power and increasingly discerning tastes. It showed that only two in five showed brand loyalty when replacing white goods; so manufacturers must understand how these more mature consumers think.

Their cognitive age—how old they feel—is often 10 or 15 years younger than their actual age. They think young and want to hold on to a life-style they enjoyed when they were younger. Older consumers tend to know what they want, but they are usually quite willing to experiment with new designs if there is a perceived benefit from the technology.

However, advancing years bring unavoidable changes, and manufacturers of consumer durables must make allowances for this:

- People grow shorter in stature after the age of 40, and women at a faster rate than men. Arthritis can limit mobility too; so a cooker with high-level controls or back-breakingly low shelves, for instance, is impractical.
- Eyesight deteriorates, so control panels should be clear and uncluttered. Labels should be in large type on non-reflective surfaces.
- Dexterity and the power to grip are diminished; so push-buttons and touch-pads should not be too small or too cramped.
- Clear and relevant instruction leaflets with household appliances are vital, with large type printed in black on a white background.

Youth culture has dominated marketing and advertising for at least four decades, and, relative to the rest of Europe, Ireland still has a young population; but demographic surveys carried out by Eurostat show that there were well over 100 million Europeans in the over-55 category at the turn of the century. In Germany, for instance, they will make up nearly a third of the population, and in Britain and Spain, a quarter.

Source: M. Markey, 'Marketers, ignore the aged at your peril', *Sunday Business Post*, 6 October 1996.

At the other end of the spectrum, any increase in the birth rate will increase the market for associated products and services. In between the children's and older market are the teenage market, the singles market, the 'family formation' market, and a number of other age-related markets, all of which are catered for by an ever-expanding range of products and services. In youth marketing, the 1990s witnessed 'generation X'—younger consumers who were more marketing-aware than previous generations and who appreciated direct and honest advertising (Dwek, 1997).

The youth market is one in which marketers have shown a particular interest, despite estimates that it will decline in size in the coming years.

THE IRISH YOUTH MARKET

Decode is a consortium of five organisations (98FM, the *Star*, TV3, Irish International OMD advertising, Clear Channel) who co-operate to research the life-styles of 18–24-year-olds in Ireland. The research is carried out for them by Amárach.

As fig. 3.4 shows, the number of Irish 18–24-year-olds is expected to decline from 475,000 in 2001 to 375,000 in 2011.

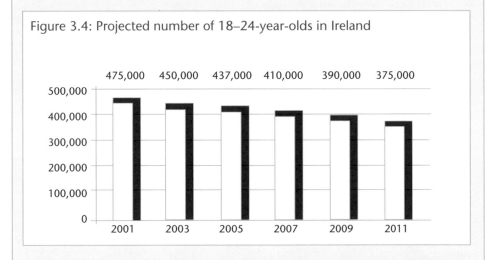

Figure 3.4: Projected number of 18–24-year-olds in Ireland

In spite of the decline in numbers it is felt that the value of the market will remain high. Employment levels are high, even among full-time students. Sixty-six per cent of all 18–24-year-olds are in some form of paid employment. Four in ten are still in full-time education.

Alcohol accounted for the bulk of discretionary spend, with food, transport and mobile phone calls also significant expenditure items. Out-of-home activities are concentrated on going to the pub, clubbing, going to the cinema, eating out, shopping, and participating in sporting activities.

Almost nine in every ten 18–24-year-olds had a mobile phone; the average number of text messages sent was 37 per week. Sixty-five per cent of 18–24-year-olds used the internet (these were more likely to be 18–19-year-old, ABC1, third-level students).

The research sought information on future expectations. As table 3.5 shows, there was an emphasis on material gain.

Table 3.5: Future expectations

How likely are you to do/have done the following in the next five years?

	Likely	Unlikely	Already have
Own a car	53%	20%	25%
Own a credit card	49%	34%	16%
Lived and worked abroad	41%	52%	4%
Own a home	29%	65%	5%
Skydived/bungee-jumped	27%	68%	2%
Married	21%	76%	2%
Had children	19%	75%	3%
Started a business	12%	83%	3%
Joined a political party	7%	91%	1%

Which of the following issues would you say are of most concern to you?

Having enough money to do the things I want	84%
Employment prospects	54%
Having enough time to do the things I want	48%
Health	47%
Violence/personal safety	33%
Environment/where I live	27%
House prices/rental costs	27%
Drug and alcohol abuse	26%
Traffic situation	20%
Political/business corruption	14%
Others/don't know	2%

Another age-dependent category, the 45–55 age group, was described as the 'baby-boomers'. These tend to be rational buyers who base their brand loyalty on product and manufacturer integrity and prefer brands offering stability and longevity (Bond, 1997). To the extent that marketers segment or sub-segment their markets demographically, these individual age-dependent groups will be important.

The economic environment

Economic factors affect our purchasing power and spending patterns; and inflation, interest rates and tax will all have a bearing on the market. Inflation—which represents increases in the cost of living resulting from a sustained increase in the general price level—will have a direct effect on the consumer's purchasing power. If the rate of inflation is high and if incomes are not increasing, people may cut back on consumption, switch their purchases from expensive to cheaper items, or completely avoid certain purchases, such as luxury goods. In periods of low inflation the consumer's spending power is in effect increased. The consumer price index (CPI) gives an indication of the rate of inflation: this is calculated by taking the prices of a range of consumer products and services and measuring any price changes over time.

Interest rates, which represent the price of money, will also affect purchasing. When interest rates are high, consumers will be encouraged to save rather than to borrow; when they are low, the opposite is usually the case.

Rates of personal tax have a direct bearing on employees' take-home pay. High tax rates reduce disposable income and will therefore have an influence on the consumer's purchasing decisions.

Economic conditions at any given time will have a bearing on consumer and business confidence. If confidence levels are low, investment may be reduced and purchases postponed or re-evaluated. Between 1995 and 2006, Ireland experienced significant increases in economic growth (table 3.5), growth declined in 2007, but has dropped dramatically in the years since then.

Table 3.6: Volume changes in GNP and GDP 2000–2009

2000	10.0	9.7
2001	3.7	3.7
2002	3.0	6.5
2003	5.8	4.4
2004	4.3	4.6
2005	6.0	6.0
2006	6.5	5.3
2007	4.5	5.6
2008	−3.5	−3.5
2009 (estimate)	−10.7	−7.6

Source: Central Statistics Office/Department of Finance.

Reasons for the decline in economic growth include:

• reliance on construction sector for growth and tax revenue (creation of a 'property bubble')
• poor regulation and control of financial services sector
• over-extended banks (significant bad debts tied to the property sector) leading to a banking crisis
• global economic downturn
• lack of competitiveness.

Two reports on the banking crisis in 2008 (the outcome of which was a government guarantee on Irish banks and financial institutions) were critical of government fiscal policy, the system of regulation and the lending policies of the banks (Honohan, 2008; Regling and Watson, 2008). Estimates of the cost of the bank guarantee scheme vary, but will likely involve tens of billions of euro.

While the benefits of economic expansion were apparent, Fanning (2001) argued that Ireland's economic growth and development had led to:

• increased anxiety among consumers about the pace of life and choice of life-style
• fears about losing traditional aspects of Irish identity
• a sense of aimlessness brought about by the decline in authority of religious institutions.

He predicted that people would look for greater convenience and that there would be increased levels of participation in sport, adult education, the arts, and hobbies.

RETAIL SALES

The retail sales index (fig. 3.5) indicates increases in the value and volume of sales in Ireland until 2007. There were further declines in value and volume in 2008, while in 2009 value dropped to 134 and volume to 118.

Figure 3.5: Retail sales index

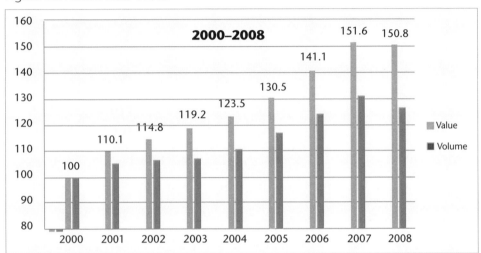

Source: Central Statistics Office.

Economic conditions affect consumer confidence. Levels of consumer confidence in Ireland reached an all time low in 2008 (fig. 3.6). The consumer price index (CPI) which represents the change in the average level of prices paid by consumers for goods and services, had increased by 4.1 per cent in 2008, but dropped by 4.5 per cent in 2009. The CPI tended to increase in Ireland as rates of economic growth increased, until 2008 it was consistently higher than the EU average.

Figure 3.6: Consumer confidence

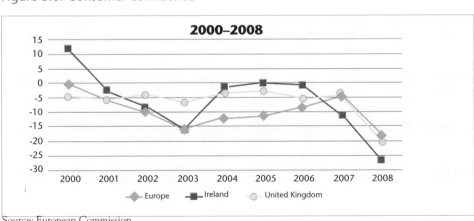

Source: European Commission.

Since the mid-1990s interest rates have remained low. This encouraged a significant increase in consumer borrowing. For example, outstanding levels of debt on credit cards has almost doubled since 2004 (fig. 3.7).

Figure 3.7: Outstanding levels of debt on personal credit cards

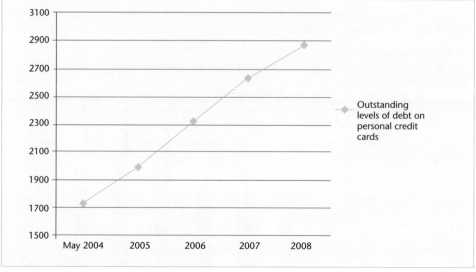

Source: Central Bank annual statistical bulletin.

Consumers also appear to have responded to the economic uncertainty by increased saving (fig. 3.8).

Figure 3.8: Personal savings as a percentage of disposable income

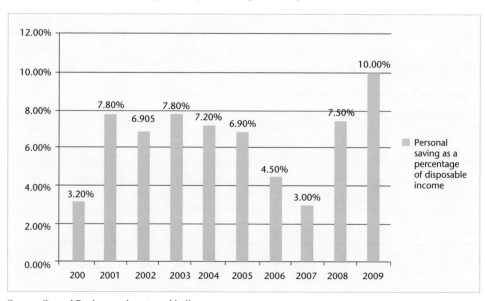

Source: Central Bank annual statistical bulletin.

Employment

The number of people employed in Ireland peaked in 2007 and has been in decline since, dropping to below the 2005 level in 2010, as table 3.7 indicates.

In August 2010 the unemployment rate had increased to 13.8 per cent of the labour force. The ESRI have predicted that this could be as high as 15 per cent by the end of 2010.

Table 3.7: Employment and unemployment

	2005	2006	2007	2008	2009	2010
Total in employment (million)	1,944.6	2,034.9	2,113.9	2,112.8	1,938.5	1,859.5
Rate of unemployment (%)	4.4	4.4	4.6	6.4	11.8	13.8*

*August 2010

Implications for marketers

Increased income levels led to growth in demand for many products and services. Household budget surveys conducted by the CSO in recent years have indicated that there has also been a shift in patterns of consumer spending:

- real expenditure on food, drink and tobacco declined
- consumers spend more on alcoholic drink than on food
- almost 6 per cent of consumer spending is spent abroad
- spending on recreation, entertainment and education is flat
- expenditure on housing now accounts for one-fifth of total consumer spending
- consumers spend almost 9 per cent of their cash on services.

The increased participation of women in the workforce has led to increased demand for childcare services.

The technological environment

New technology creates opportunities, but it can also create a need for change. Technology can be a source of competitive advantage for firms that can use it to introduce or develop superior products or processes. It can also render existing products and processes obsolete and leave the unprepared firm behind.

Society is now experiencing a faster pace of technological change than ever before. In telecommunications, for example, there has been a rapid change from mechanical systems to computerised and cellular technology. This change, coupled with deregulation in telecommunications, has resulted in more choice for the consumer and more competition in the sector. Improvements in health technology have helped increase the average life-span, with surgical procedures such as transplants and heart bypasses becoming routine.

Technology has also had a very direct effect on marketers. In the retail sector, barcode scanning has improved stock management techniques and can provide up-to-date information for marketers on stock levels or reorder quantities. Satellite television has increased the potential for global advertising campaigns, and the internet has just begun to have an impact on communication and the transfer of information. Digital television is also likely to become a significant development. Technological change can present challenges to firms in many ways.

ELECTRONIC COMMERCE

A number of definitions have been proposed for this increasingly important concept. Zwass (1996) described it as sharing business information, maintaining business relationships, and conducting business transactions by means of telecommunications networks. It was also defined by Andersen Consulting (1998), in a major research exercise on the use and perception of electronic commerce throughout Europe, as an interchange of goods and services or property of any kind through an electronic medium.

Electronic commerce has grown in importance because of developments in electronic technology in areas such as telecommunications, networking, and data interchange. The technology has led to such developments as an increase in telephone transactions through call centres, the internet as a medium, and electronic data interchange (EDI), which has enabled firms to centralise purchasing and administrative functions.

There have been increased levels of internet access in EU states; by 2009 Ireland had a household access level just above the EU27 average, as table 3.8 indicates.

Table 3.8: Internet access by households, 2006–2009 (%)

	2006	2007	2008	2009
EU27	49	54	60	65
Austria	52	60	69	70
Belgium	54	60	64	67
Bulgaria	17	19	25	30
Cyprus	37	39	43	53
Czech Republic	29	35	46	54
Denmark	79	78	82	83
Estonia	46	53	58	63
Finland	65	69	72	78
France	41	49	62	63
Germany	67	71	75	79
Greece	23	25	31	38
Hungary	32	38	48	55
Ireland	*50*	*57*	*63*	*67*
Italy	40	43	47	53
Latvia	42	51	53	58
Lithuania	35	44	51	60
Luxembourg	70	75	80	87
Malta	53	54	59	64

Netherlands	80	83	86	90
Poland	36	41	48	59
Portugal	35	40	46	48
Romania	14	22	30	38
Spain	39	45	51	54
Slovenia	54	58	59	64
Slovakia	27	46	58	62
Sweden	77	79	84	86
United Kingdom	63	67	71	77
Other Countries				
Croatia	–	41	45	50
FYR Macedonia	14	–	29	42
Turkey	–	20	–	–
Iceland	83	84	88	90
Norway	69	78	84	86
Republic of Serbia	–	26	–	37

Source: Eurostat.

In 2009 most homes in Ireland that had an internet connection used broadband. Broadband describes a transmission medium capable of supporting a wide range of frequencies, typically from audio up to video frequencies. It can carry multiple signals by dividing the total capacity of the medium into multiple, independent bandwidth channels, where each channel operates only on a specific range of frequencies. This is done at high speed. There are however differences in access levels to broadband in Ireland, with many rural households having no access.

Implications for marketers

Technology is a source of competitive advantage for a firm. It leads to the development of new products and services and new processes; it is also an aid to marketers in their practice. Information technology, for example, has had a significant impact in areas such as marketing research, sales reporting, and budgeting and decision support systems.

The impact of new technology, especially in the area of electronic commerce, is likely to be a significant element in the environment of many firms. It is probable that the introduction of a single EU currency, the increasing penetration of cellular phones, digital television, increased internet usage, and an increased use of EDI will hasten the process. The ability to link phones to computers, televisions to computers, and computers to computers means that the ability of the marketer to interact with the customer will improve. This has obvious implications in areas such as marketing communication, customer service, product order and delivery, and payment.

The political and regulatory environment

Political stability is important for business. Instability causes uncertainty, which affects investment levels and trade. Ireland has a stable political environment and one that is generally supportive of investment and job creation.

The aspects of the political environment of most relevance to business are the laws enacted by the Oireachtas and the various government agencies involved in the support and development of business and enterprise. The Companies Acts (1963 and 1986), the Sale of Goods and Supply of Services Act (1980) and the Consumer Information Act (1978) are all examples of legislation that has a direct influence on business and marketing practice. Increasingly, directives from the European Commission are having an influence on competition and on corporate governance and activities. The Competition Act (1991), for example, required firms to ensure that their business and marketing strategies were in compliance with the law (Meade, 1993). The act was based on the competition rules of the European Community contained in the Treaty of Rome (1957) and led to the introduction of comprehensive competition rules, established a competition authority, prohibited restrictive arrangements, and regulated the dominant positions that some firms enjoyed.

It is likely that changes at EU level will have most impact here, where a number of priorities have been established (table 3.9). Other examples of EU-inspired changes include regulation of advertising to children and a directive affecting airlines.

Table 3.9: Ten major priorities for the future development of consumer policy in the EU

1. Major improvement in the education and information of consumers.
2. Completion, review, and updating of the legislative framework to protect consumer interests in the internal market.
3. Review of consumer aspects of financial services.
4. Review of the protection of consumer interests in the supply of essential public utility services.
5. Helping consumers to benefit from the information society.
6. Improving consumer confidence in food stuffs.
7. Practical encouragement of sustainable consumption.
8. Strengthening and increasing consumer representation.
9. Helping the development of consumer policies in Central and Eastern Europe.
10. Review of consumer policy in developing countries.

Source: The EU Commission.

In 2009 the Broadcasting Authority of Ireland published a review of regulations relating to advertising to children, arising out of this, the authority will review the rules relating to diet and nutrition, especially products that contain high levels of fat, sugar, or salt.

In March 2005 the EU airline directive came into force. This requires airlines to pay defined levels of compensation to passengers for delays, cancellations or 'bumping'.

Statutory bodies, for example the ESB and CIÉ, are directly involved in providing goods and services. Other agencies provide services and support to business: for example, Enterprise Ireland has a central role in the development of indigenous enterprise and foreign markets. All statutory bodies and other government agencies report to the relevant government minister and department.

Given the role that forces in the political environment can have, business interests will often seek to lobby or influence political decision-makers. Representative bodies, trade unions, and individual organisations use lobbying to present their point of view, seek to have changes made, or emphasise particular issues. This lobbying may be conducted at local, national, or EU level. In other cases, lobby groups may have an impact on particular businesses.

EFFECTIVE LOBBYING PREVENTS INTRODUCTION OF CHEWING GUM TAX

In 2004, the Irish government proposed a 10 per cent tax on chewing gum, with the revenue raised being used to clean up discarded gum from streets and pavements.

The chewing gum manufacturers lobbied the government and proposed instead to spend €6 million on an anti-litter awareness campaign as well as €1 million on research into making gum less difficult to clean off surfaces.

Environmental groups such as An Taisce were critical of the government's decision, while the largest brand in the market, Wrigley, stated that the approach it suggested was more sustainable than a tax.

Dublin City Council estimates that it costs €250,000 per year to clean chewing gum off Dublin's streets and footpaths.

Source: Peter Stiff, 'Gum tax prevented as industry steps in', *Confectionary News*, January 2006.

Implications for marketers

The political environment can be a source of rules and regulations that can have an impact on the marketer or on the way in which business is done. A central issue is adapting the business to change. But changes in laws or regulation can present opportunities: for example, the Galway company Thermo King reacted to a change in European regulation by developing a new product (Watson, 1993). In 1989 the EC Transport Commission introduced legislation deregulating the length of trailers and regulated instead the total length of the trailer and tractor unit. The result was that no front-mounted refrigeration unit existed that could fit inside the dimensions prescribed in the new regulations. Thermo King developed a new refrigeration unit and in doing so was able to compress the design and development time usually required for developing such a product from between three and five years to 18 months. This quick response showed how it was possible for a company to react quickly to an environmental threat.

Changes in regulations may pose threats to businesses. In 2006, for example, Greencore announced the closure of its sugar processing operations in Ireland. Sugar beet had been a crop that was supported by EU subsidies and trade quotas; however, agricultural reforms meant that these were to be phased out in favour of creating a free market with more access for producers from developing countries.

The socio-cultural environment

The socio-cultural environment involves forces that affect our values, beliefs, perceptions, and behaviour. Culture is a broad phenomenon and comprises a number of different elements, including material culture, social institutions, human culture, aesthetics, and language.

Cultural change can be reflected in consumption. Increased prosperity and affluence have resulted in significant growth in many consumer markets. The consumption of products such as wine has increased. The number of wine drinkers in Ireland increased from 728,000 in 1990 to 1,441,000 in 2003 (*Checkout*, May 2005). Ireland's changing population profile means that the country is now a more culturally diverse market.

Keohane and Kuhling (2004) examined the microprocesses of everyday Irish life to extrapolate broader discussions on the nature of change in Irish society. They use the term 'collision culture' as a metaphor for contemporary Irish society, where rapid social change leads to clashes between different ways of living, for example different life-styles, values, and opinions.

Friel, Walsh and McCarthy (2004), for example pointed out that in Ireland 'across all income groupings, large amounts are spent on sweets, soft drinks, biscuits, crisps, sauces and creams, cakes and buns and tea'. Although Inglis (2002) suggested that Irish people were becoming more rational, circumspect, and educated about the pleasures of food and drink.

In 2010, the Oireachtas passed the Civil Partnership and Certain Rights and Obligation of Co-habitants Act, an outcome of which is legal recognition for same-sex partnerships. Some marketers were quick to highlight the change in the law (see fig. 9.7, page 242).

Material culture refers to a country's economic and technological profile and gives an indication of economic strength and technical advancement. Ireland is categorised as a developed country by the OECD.

Social institutions are the educational and political systems that exist, both of which play a role in the encouragement, fostering, and support of enterprise. In Ireland, levels of educational attainment are high in comparison with those in other EU countries.

Religion can be an important cultural determinant and influence. In Ireland the importance of religious institutions in determining culture was found to be above the European average in the 1980s (Turley, 1986); by the 1990s there was some evidence of change. According to research carried out by Millward Brown IMS, weekly attendance at church/Mass fell to 48 per cent in 2002. Of this 48 per cent, attendance is more prevalent among the elderly and rural population and is lowest among the younger population living in urban areas.

Human culture refers to the values, beliefs, and attitudes held by the population and is strongly influenced by factors such as family socialisation, religion, social class, and peers. The *aesthetic* aspects of culture are demonstrated in art, music, and folklore and from the marketing viewpoint will often be used in national advertising and promotional campaigns. *Language* can also be significant, as seen in the launch of Teilifís na Gaeilge (now TG4) in 1997.

In the area of social changes, the 1990s saw alterations in the law allowing for the wider sale of contraceptives, the decriminalisation of homosexuality, and the introduction of divorce. Social changes like these may present opportunities for marketers: for example, sales of contraceptives increased throughout the 1990s, particularly through vending machines, which were introduced in 1993.

As the following panel indicates, changing tastes have presented opportunities for many marketers.

ETHNIC FOODS

The appeal of ethnic foods has grown, with Irish consumers more willing than ever to experiment with Thai, Indian, Japanese, and Mexican foods. In addition, with an estimated 400,000 foreign nationals living in Ireland, the foods of Eastern Europe, Africa, Asia, and India are becoming more common. There has been an increase in Russian and Polish delicatessens, Asian and halal food shops, as well as authentic Chinese restaurants catering for Eastern rather than Western palates. Mexican food gained popularity due to its appeal in the snacking category, with convenience the main consumer motivation to purchase.

There was an overall perception that ethnic foods are higher in calories than traditional fare; this is to some extent true given the emphasis on frying and creamy sauces. As a result there is a perception that these foods should be an occasional indulgence. The exception was Italian food, with consumers likely to prepare Italian meals on a weekly basis. Roma was the market leader in the pasta market with a 47 per cent share, while Dolmio had a 62 per cent share across the pasta and pasta sauce market combined. The market for rice was valued at €17.9 million in 2006 and had grown by 3.6 per cent in sales and 2.2 per cent in volume. Convenience was important to consumers, with both boil-in-the-bag and microwaveable products proving popular.

In the cooking sauce market, Italian sauces held 57.2 per cent of the market with Chinese and other Asian sauces having 42.8 per cent. This market was also growing, by about 2 per cent.

Source: *Checkout*, March 2006.

The changing population profile means that Ireland is now a more culturally diverse market (see panel on page 96).

DIVERSITY IN IRELAND

Official CSO figures showed that, in 2006, 9 per cent of the workforce and 10 per cent of the population were born outside Ireland. Between 1991 and 2003, for example, the Muslim population quadrupled to 19,000, due mainly to inward migration. The Traveller Community is one of the largest minority groups, estimated at 27,000.

The increased numbers of immigrants coming to Ireland led to the establishment of several new media. In Dublin a multi-ethnic radio station called Sunrise FM began broadcasting in March 2006. Programmes in Polish, Russian, Chinese, Lithuanian, Latvian, and Estonian, and in African, Indian, and Pakistani languages, were broadcast at weekends. Other radio stations broadcast weekly shows to immigrant groups. Anna Livia FM's most popular show, *Marhaba*, covers topics from the Eastern Mediterranean and the Lebanon in Arabic, Greek, and Spanish. City Channel targets the Polish community with a programme called *Oto Polska Extra*, which combines local news about Poles living in Ireland with a current affairs programme from Poland.

Metro Éireann is Ireland's longest-established multicultural publication and has a circulation of 8,000 copies per week. It was launched in 2000 and targets the wider immigrant community. *Metro Éireann* has attracted several advertisers including AIB, Bus Éireann, Dublin Bus, Eircom and O_2. In addition, universities, colleges and various government departments use it as an advertising medium. One company that was quick to target the immigrant community from the start was Western Union, which advertised in the first issue of *Metro Éireann*.

Other publications include *Xclusive*, a glossy equivalent of *Hello* magazine for the African community, and *Gazeta*, a weekly Russian-language newspaper that has attracted advertisers such as Western Union, Aer Lingus and Bank of Ireland, the latter taking out advertisements in Russian. The Chinese community is catered for with a publication called *Tiao Wang* and its advertisers have included Bord na gCon, extolling the virtues of greyhound racing in Chinese.

The *Evening Herald* was the only national title to cater for immigrants with its *Polski Herald*, an eight-page supplement published on Fridays. The only regional newspaper to target the immigrant community was the *Limerick Leader*, which devoted a page to news in Chinese, Polish, and Russian, and reports in English from South Africa.

Sources: Hugh Oram, 'Dividends from diversity', *Marketing*, vol. 17, April 2006, no. 4; Padraic Guilfoyle, 'Ireland is a changed place', *Marketing*, vol. 17, April 2006, no. 4, .

While prosperity has brought many benefits, it also poses many challenges to Irish consumers. As the following example illustrates, fast-food restaurants experienced growth in sales in recent years. As if to underline the buoyancy of this market, the National Health and Lifestyle survey, published in 2003, showed that six out of 10 adult men are overweight and 12 per cent are clinically obese. Nearly a third of Irish children are overweight and 10 per cent are obese (*Sunday Times*, 22 February 2004).

Consumption of alcohol was also increasing.

Marketers are interested in consumers' perception of their overall well-being. This also gives some indication of consumer confidence and therefore spending patterns. One such study is carried out by Amárach (see panel on page 97).

The fact that cultures vary from country to country has implications for international marketers. The same product or promotional campaign may not be suitable for all markets. Bord Fáilte, for example, varies the themes of its advertising and promotional campaigns in different markets. In markets like Italy it emphasises culture, nature, and scenery, while in the United States ancestry, music, and history are the main themes.

IRISH QUALITY OF LIFE

Amárach Consulting carried out two studies on Irish quality of life, in 2001 and in 2004. The research was carried out for Diageo and in 2004 was conducted in the Republic and in Northern Ireland (1,000 adults aged 15–74 in the Republic and 400 adults aged 16–74 in Northern Ireland). In addition, the survey included 200 non-nationals living in the Republic.

The study sought to measure four aspects of satisfaction:

* emotional goodness
* family goodness
* physical goodness
* financial goodness.

In addition, an overall satisfaction score was calculated based on these.

The study showed that there was an increase in overall satisfaction level with the quality of life between 2001 and 2003 in the Republic (from 72.3 per cent satisfaction to 74.9 per cent).

The study showed that, for the most part, people in the Republic were increasingly satisfied with their financial circumstances; the majority of people were also more satisfied with their family relations.

In spite of increased economic prosperity, the research showed that the proportion of people who stated that they were very satisfied with the life they led remained fairly static. In comparison with the results obtained in similar studies in the 1980s, the percentage had actually declined.

The research also showed that the proportion of people suffering from stress had increased, half the population reporting that they suffered from stress sometimes or often. Almost half of all workers stated that they would like to retire before the age of 55.

In Northern Ireland there were marked differences between people's opinions on their personal quality of life when compared with the Republic. Fewer than half (47 per cent) of those in Northern Ireland believed that their personal quality of life had improved in the previous three years, compared with 60 per cent in the Republic. Northerners were more satisfied with their family relations, however, with 69 per cent very satisfied, compared with 52 per cent in the Republic. Nearly one in 10 employees in Northern Ireland was worried about being made redundant within the next 12 months compared with one in 20 in the Republic.

In relation to non-nationals, 52 per cent considered that the quality of life in the Republic to be better than in their home country. In general, non-national levels of satisfaction with life were on a par with the rest of the population. The main difference was financial happiness; this was 64.2 per cent for non-nationals compared with 68.6 per cent for the indigenous population.

Source: www.amarach.com/diageo_qualityoflife.

Socio-cultural factors influence many product purchases. In Ireland, 80 per cent of homes are owner-occupied; this compares with an EU average of 56 per cent (*Irish Times*, 4 March 1998). This tendency can probably be explained by a combination of historical and cultural factors, which manifest themselves in the desire for ownership and security. Increased property prices in Dublin and the greater Dublin area in the middle and late 1990s, however, meant that many people could no longer afford to buy in those areas, and the market for property became buoyant in surrounding towns and counties and many people began to commute longer distances to work.

Implications for marketers

Cultural change provides opportunities for marketers. It can also be a threat for the marketer who cannot react or adapt. While the rate of cultural change can be quite slow—concepts such as tastes and values rarely change overnight—it is an important phenomenon. Cultural change may present opportunities for the development of new products or services.

A growth area in the publishing market in the 1990s was men's magazines, featuring articles on style, life-style, health, and fashion. The market was largely catered for by imported magazines, such as GQ. Cultural change may also mean that marketers have to re-evaluate the ways in which they segment the market and the development of positioning strategy.

The natural environment

In recent years there has been an increased awareness of the natural environment and its protection. The devastation of the rainforests of the Amazon, the effects of the Chernobyl nuclear leak in 1986, the effects of acid rain and the threat posed to rare or endangered flora and fauna have all received coverage. For some it was a call to action, as pressure groups were established and consumers began to seek out environmentally unharmful products.

Environmental protection took on added importance, and in the European Union many initiatives and directives were introduced. In some cases, such as the use of chlorofluorocarbon (CFC), which contributed to the depletion of the ozone layer, manufacturers began to produce aerosol products without this gas.

In addition to product development and support for environmental issues, firms often devote considerable resources to attempts to improve their environmental image. The Shell petroleum company, for example, planned to spend $200 million in 1998 on an international campaign aimed at improving its image in the aftermath of allegations about its environmental and human rights record. The company had been criticised by the environmental group Greenpeace over its plans for the disposal of the *Brent Spar* oil platform in the North Sea and for its failure to defend a writer and environmental campaigner who was put to death by the Nigerian government (*Marketing*, March 1998).

Many marketers were quick to jump on the environmental bandwagon in the 1990s. One study on cosmetic products, for example, found that of all competitors, the Body Shop came closest to openly explaining issues to consumers. While most competitors printed environmental information on their packaging, some of them made largely meaningless claims (Prothero, Peattie, and McDonagh, 1997). Consumers may be influenced by environmental information: for many it will be a factor used in evaluating a product.

With regard to consumer behaviour patterns, many people now recycle household waste that previously they would have dumped. Several advertising campaigns have been conducted encouraging people to reduce, reuse and recycle (fig. 3.9).

In 2006, the government announced that grants would be made available to home owners who wanted to install solar heating panels, wood pellet burning stoves and geo-thermal heating systems in their homes.

In January 1998 the European Union announced limits on the number of landfill dumping sites that will be allowed in Ireland. It is probable, therefore, that recycling will take on added significance in the future.

Figure 3.10: 'Race Against Waste'

Agency: Lyle Bailie International.

One issue that has dominated discussion of the natural environment at an international level is the greenhouse effect. This refers to the emission of gases that results from burning fossil fuels. These gases cause significant warming of the earth and lead to changes in the natural environment such as violent storms, expanding deserts, melting ice caps, and rising sea levels. The main greenhouse gases include carbon dioxide, methane, nitrous oxide, ozone, chlorofluorocarbons, and perfluorinated carbons. Carbon dioxide is believed to be responsible for 70 per cent of global warming. As table 3.10 indicates, the United States is the world's biggest generator of greenhouse gases.

Table 3.10 Percentage of greenhouse gas emissions by country

United States	19.1%
China	9.9%
Japan	5.1%
Brazil	4.3%
Germany	3.8%
India	3.7%
United Kingdom	2.4%
Indonesia	1.9%
Italy	1.7%

Source: United Nations.

In 1997, representatives from 180 countries met in Kyoto, Japan, to negotiate limits on greenhouse gas emissions among the developed nations of the world. The result was the Kyoto Protocol, which required 38 developed countries to limit their greenhouse gas emissions between 2008 and 2012 to levels that are 5.2 per cent below the 1990 levels. Progress in ratifying the protocol has been varied. The United States, for example, which signed the protocol, did not submit it to its senate and congress for ratification. It argues that there is a need for developing countries to give specific undertakings to reduce greenhouse gases. It is also argued that the protocol will impose costs on developed economies that will make their products more expensive, while similar costs will not be imposed on developing countries' products.

Implications for marketers

Businesses exist within the natural environment and should therefore be sensitive to the preservation and protection of that environment. In many cases, regulations and controls must be complied with. There are, however, potentially more advantages for a marketer who takes the initiative rather than simply reacting to circumstances. Many marketers, such as the Body Shop chain for example, have demonstrated that consumers are environmentally aware and will respond favourably to genuine environmentally unharmful products.

McDonagh and Prothero (1993) suggest that the basic requirement for marketers in relation to environmental marketing is a communication regime of integrity and clear-sightedness, both within companies and between companies and their relevant publics. They proposed a diagnostic tool that would enable the marketing manager to assess whether or not the company had a structure on which it could develop an environmental orientation. This involves an assessment of external communication on environmental issues, establishing who was responsible for environmental issues within the company, internal communication about the environment, and whether or not the firm had a written environmental policy.

CONSUMERISM

Consumerism is a force in the macro-environment designed to aid and protect the consumer by exerting moral, economic, political, and legal pressures on business.

It may appear strange that consumers should need to be protected if the fundamental principle guiding the business is serving their needs. Consumerism as a force grew because of many cases of fraud, deceit, or misleading claims about products and services. Consumerism it is not a new phenomenon. From earliest times it was recognised that businesses or trades were in a stronger position relative to the customer. The customer needed to be protected from poor quality or fake products. The mediaeval guilds, for example, were established not just to regulate and control trades and professions but also to provide the customer with reassurance that when they bought from a member of the guild they were buying a genuine product. Goldsmiths and silversmiths, for example, had their products assayed and hallmarked.

Contemporary consumerism had its beginnings in the 1960s and was particularly strong in the United States. One of the leading proponents there was Ralph Nader, who came to national attention when he led a campaign to draw attention to design defects in a particular brand of car. The campaign gathered momentum because the manufacturer did nothing to rectify the defects, in spite of several accidents. This case, along with many others, demonstrated the need for consumer protection, and ultimately a Consumer Bill of Rights was introduced in 1969.

In Ireland the consumer movement has also grown. In 1966 the Consumers' Association of Ireland was founded to 'protect and promote the interests of the consumers of goods and services, and to enhance the quality of life for consumers'. The association is an independent, non-profit-making body and seeks to influence and lobby decision-makers on behalf of the consumer.

With greater European integration, consumer protection has become more standardised throughout EU member states. A Department of Consumer Protection (DG XXIV) has been established by the European Union, with the power to propose new legislation, scrutinise draft directives, and financially support consumers' associations taking test cases in the courts. An ombudsman can receive and investigate complaints from a citizen of any EU country (Lansman, 1995).

The goals of consumerism

Consumerism and consumers' associations have a number of goals, which include:

- helping buyers cope with complexity
- protection from fraud
- representing consumers' interests
- protecting consumers' rights
- protecting the less well off.

The Consumers' Association of Ireland has been involved in identifying issues of concern to consumers, such as product safety. It has also sought to have consumer representation on state bodies. The association publishes a magazine, *Consumer Choice*, which reports on issues of interest to consumers and also publishes reports on product tests. These tests are based on market research, laboratory tests, or surveys of users, and they are independently and scientifically conducted (see panel on page 102).

PRODUCT TESTING BY THE CONSUMERS' ASSOCIATION

Comparative testing of products by independent organisations gives consumers unbiased information about the performance and characteristics of goods on the market. The Consumers' Association of Ireland is the only organisation in Ireland to carry out independent testing of goods and services. There are similar organisations in other European countries and in the United States, New Zealand, Australia, and other countries, each of which carries out similar tests and surveys.

A comparative test subjects different products designed for the same purpose to the same analyses and tests. The tests are conducted by expert testers in independent laboratories that specialise in the type of testing required. All products tested are bought anonymously in retail outlets, without manufacturers or suppliers being informed.

The test methods are scientific, repeatable, and transparent, with a relevant choice of criteria reflecting consumer usage. User trials are carried out by a selection of consumers, including those who are left-handed, those who are smaller or taller than average, and those with limiting disabilities. Men and women volunteers are used.

In some cases the association adapts tests reports from *Which?*, the magazine of the Consumers' Association in Britain; however, it reports only on products that are available in Ireland. International comparative tests are also conducted through International Research and Testing Ltd, a consortium of consumer firms from around the world.

Product tests aim to be representative and usually include the most widely available models. There are limits to the number of brands that can be tested, so the association will carry out research to establish which brands are most popular or widely available or have a particular feature worth investigating.

Source: *Consumer Choice*, May 1997.

The 1969 Consumer Bill of Rights in the United States established that consumers had the right to safety, the right to be informed, the right to choose, and the right to be heard. There is no similar statute in Ireland; consumers are, however, protected by the provisions of various pieces of legislation. The main purpose of the Consumer Information Act (1978), for example, is to prevent false or misleading indications about goods, services or prices being given in the course of a business, trade, or profession. The scope of this particular act is quite wide, covering descriptions of products and services, price indications, and advertising claims. The act also established the Office of the Director of Consumer Affairs, who can receive and investigate complaints and has significant legal powers.

The Sale of Goods and Supply of Services Act (1980) amended and updated the law governing the relationship between consumers and suppliers of goods and services, while the Liability for Defective Products Act (1991) came about as the result of a directive of the EU. Under this act the producers of a product are liable in tort for any damage caused wholly or partly by a defect in their product. Other acts and regulations also apply.

These acts do not confer rights on the consumer but are part of the criminal law. In relation to advertising, consumers can make complaints to the Advertising Standards Authority if they feel an advertisement has been misleading or is in breach of the code of standards. (A detailed discussion of the various acts, regulations and standards that have implications for marketing practice is beyond the scope of this book. The reader should refer to the recommended reading at the end of the chapter.)

Reasons for the growth of consumerism

The consumer movement has grown in line with the growth in the availability of products on the market. As economies have grown, so too has the number of products and services. Many of these are technically advanced and complex, and consumers may not have the ability to understand or differentiate between them. Consumers may also have become sceptical about claims made in advertising or claims made by different competitors.

Increasingly, consumers are concerned about quality and safety controls, especially in cases where poor quality or safety have been demonstrated. The 1990s witnessed a greater interest among consumers in food additives and food safety and in environmental and health issues.

An examination of what consumers complain about also gives an indication of why the consumer movement has become a strong force. Complaints may include deceptive advertising, deceptive packaging, the exploitation of children, slow or inadequate servicing, misleading guarantees or warranties, poor product quality, and badly trained sales staff, or the attitude of customer service staff. These complaints have one thing in common: a lack of understanding of the customer's needs.

Enlightened firms tend to view complaints as an opportunity to learn and to react quickly to solve problems. It is important for firms to have an effective complaints-handling procedure. Consumers are not unreasonable, and while mistakes should not happen, customer dissatisfaction may be considerably reduced by the way in which the firm deals with their complaint. Poor complaint handling serves to increase consumers' dissatisfaction and scepticism. It also leads to lost customers.

Implications for marketers

The consumer movement represents a threat to those firms that do not listen to their customers, that do not try to satisfy their needs, that provide misleading or scant information, or that have poor quality control—in other words, firms that are not marketing-oriented. If firms were truly marketing-oriented there would be no need for a consumer movement.

The objectives of marketers and the consumer movement are in fact the same. The consumer movement can be a source of information and ideas for marketers. It demonstrates what may be of concern to them; it may also alert the business to changes in the market. In 1998, for example, the SuperValu supermarket chain began buying beef from suppliers who used 'Enfer' testing (*Checkout*, January–February 1998). This test claims to establish whether the beef is free from BSE. Consumers had become increasingly concerned about this disease after a number of people developed a human variant form of the disease from eating beef.

Marketers need to be familiar with the factors in the regulatory environment. In relation to product liability, for example, it is also advisable to investigate the desirability of taking out product liability insurance. While there may be rigorous quality control practices, it is possible for defective products to make it onto the market.

THE YEARS AHEAD

The analysis of the forces in the micro and macro environment described in this chapter has given some indication of how environmental influences have affected firms in the past. Some ideas of probable future environmental trends have also been given.

In 2010 some of the significant issues that were affecting the Irish business environment were:

1. **The banking sector bailout**
   By November 2010, the state's financial position became so uncertain that the Irish government applied to the EU and the International Monetary Fund for a financial-aid package to be used to restructure the Irish banks and reduce the state deficit. The EU and the IMF subsequently agreed a €67.5 billion package, which required the government to enage in significant expenditure reductions over the period 2011–2014.
2. **Significant government cutbacks in spending**
   The government is the largest purchaser of goods and services, reductions in spending had an impact on many businesses.
3. **Inability of businesses to borrow**
   As banks tried to restore market confidence, many businesses reported difficulties in securing loans or credit, with many banks being reported as unwilling to lend.
4. **Exchange rate fluctuations**
   As the world experienced a recession, the dollar and sterling exchange rates against the euro weakened, making Irish goods more expensive to buy in these markets.
5. **Eurozone improving slightly but consumer demand still weak**
   There was some evidence of economic recovery in many EU economies, but consumers remained cautious and were therefore more likely to save money rather than spend.
6. **Domestic price/cost competitiveness**
   Ireland is an expensive country to produce goods and services with high energy costs in particular.
7. **Consumer debt**
   The high levels of individual consumer debt in Ireland mean that for many consumers, their priority will be debt reduction. This may mean reduced consumer spending on goods and services.

The Economist Intelligence Unit (EIU) predicted in 2010 that it would be 2012–2015 before modest levels of economic growth would return. A return to the heady growth rates before the recessionary crisis, which were only possible because of excessive credit growth, was not in prospect. The EIU felt that the US will need several years during which private consumption would grow by less than overall demand, while the public sector will also have to retrench in the medium term. In Western Europe, fiscal tightening will weigh on growth in many countries. In addition, as wage subsidies have encouraged labour hoarding to contain unemployment, a return to healthy job growth will take a long time, as companies have ample room to increase production without hiring new workers. Given more favourable demographics and stronger balance sheets, it expected that emerging markets would continue to outperform. Asia will be the fastest growing region, led by China and India. China will face some policy challenges, as the labour force is set to stop expanding from 2011, which will push up the price of labour. This will encourage more balanced growth in China, with consumption accounting for a greater share of demand. A rebalancing of China's economy away from fixed investment and exports will help to alleviate imbalances in the global economy, but this will be a drawn-out process, and while imbalances persist, they will carry the risk of trade and currency wars.

Concerns about fiscal sustainability in the developed world will remain a potential source of market turbulence and instability. The EIU expect that Greece will ultimately have to restructure its public debt, probably in 2012. This could lead to fresh fears about contagion within the eurozone and thus new turbulence. Other countries with high public debt burdens and poor fiscal dynamics, including the UK, Japan and even the US, could come under scrutiny by the markets. Some predictions made by the EIU were:

- A forecast of US GDP growth of 1.5 per cent in 2011. The US labour and housing markets would be 'frail' and it suggested that domestic demand in the US will remain weak in the short term, and any further fiscal stimulus is likely to be too small to have a significant impact on growth.
- It expected interest rates in the developed world to remain close to zero until the second half of 2012.
- In Japan, the government intervened in the foreign-exchange market in September 2010 in an attempt to prevent the yen appreciating in value, but the EIU did not expect these measures to stem the yen's strength. Other countries, such as Brazil and South Korea, have been taking steps to halt the appreciation of their currencies. This raises the risk of currency wars as economies try to maintain competitiveness in a world characterised by deficient aggregate demand.
- The euro had strengthened against the US dollar, but it maintained a forecast for a weaker euro against the US dollar in the medium term, as concerns about debt default and the viability of the eurozone resurfaced.
- In the eurozone, concerns centred on Ireland. The cost to the government of bailing out Anglo Irish Bank, its most distressed bank, had risen to €30 billion. Consequently, Ireland's budget deficit will exceed 30 per cent of GDP in 2010.

As we have seen, economic trends affect people's consumer behaviour, the EIU forecast in 2010 suggested that the period 2010–2015 may see declining consumer demand and therefore difficulties for many marketers.

FURTHER READING

Bird, T., *Consumer Law in Ireland*, Dublin: Round Hall Sweet and Maxwell 1999.

Brooks, I. and Weatherston, J., *The Business Environment: Challenges and Changes*, Prentice Hall Europe 2000.

Clancy, P., Drudy, S., Lynch, K. and O'Dowd, L., *Irish Society: Sociological Perspectives*, Dublin: Institute of Public Administration 1995.

Coulter, C. and Coleman, S. (eds), , *The end of Irish history? Critical reflections on the Celtic Tiger*, Manchester: Manchester University Press, 2003.

Doolan, B., *Principles of Irish Law* (third edition), Dublin: Gill & Macmillan 1991.

Foley, E., *The Irish Market: A Profile*, Dublin: Marketing Institute 1996.

Lambkin, M., *The Irish Consumer Market*, Dublin: Marketing Society 1993.

Murphy, E., *Legal Framework for Irish ACCA Students*, Dublin: Gill & Macmillan 1997.

O'Hagan, J. W. and Newman, C., *The Economy of Ireland* (9th edition), Dublin: Gill & Macmillan 2005.

Share, P., Tovey, H. and Corcoran, M., *A Sociology of Ireland* (third edition), Gill & Macmillan, Dublin 2007.

Whelan, C. (ed.), *Values and Social Change in Ireland*, Dublin: Gill & Macmillan 1994.

Central Statistics Office (www.cso.ie).

DISCUSSION QUESTIONS

1. Describe the micro and macro forces likely to impinge on each of the following:
   (*a*) HB ice cream
   (*b*) DVD players
   (*c*) The GAA
   (*d*) A third-level college
   (*e*) Batchelors canned vegetables.
2. Explain why marketers must monitor environmental change constantly.
3. Explain the term 'internal marketing'. Why is it important in all firms?
4. Outline the possible relationship dimensions for each of the following:
   (*a*) A national daily newspaper and reader
   (*b*) Ryanair and customer
   (*c*) The National Gallery and visitor
   (*d*) College restaurant and student.
5. Outline, using examples, how you feel each of the elements in the environment will change in the next five years.

REFERENCES

Akenson, D., *Small Differences: Irish Catholics and Irish Protestants, 1815–1922*, Dublin: McGill-Queen's University Press/Gill & Macmillan 1991.

Anderson Consulting, *One Choice: E-commerce and Ireland's Future*, Dublin: Anderson Consulting 1998.

Barnes, J., 'Internal marketing: if the staff won't buy it why should the customer?', *Irish Marketing Review*, vol. 4 (1989), no. 2.

Barnes, J., 'Establishing relationships: getting closer to the customer may be more difficult than you think', *Irish Marketing Review*, vol. 8 (1995).

Barrett, A., and Duffy, D., 'Are Ireland's immigrants integrating into its labour market', *International Migration Review*, vol. 42 (2008), no. 3.

Barrett, A., and Trace, F., 'Who is coming back? The educational profile of returning migrants in the 1990s', *Irish Banking Review*, Summer (1998), 38–52.

Bond, C., 'Frightened and fifty: marketing to baby boomers', *Marketing*, 22 May 1997.

Carson, D., and Gilmore, A., 'Customer care: the neglected domain', *Irish Marketing Review*, vol. 4 (1989), no. 3.

Castles, S., and Millar, M., *The Age of Migration: International Population Movements in the Modern World*, Basingstoke: Palgrave 1998.

Courtney, D., 'Demographic structure and change in the Republic of Ireland and Northern Ireland' in P. Clancy et al. (eds), *Irish Society: Sociological Perspectives*, Dublin: Institute of Public Administration/Sociological Association of Ireland 1995.

Corrigan, Á., 'Irish immigrant entrepreneurs in the United States: Ethnic strategies and transnational identities'. Unpublished PhD thesis, Department of Sociology, NUI, Maynooth 2006.

Dundon, T., González-Pérez, M.A., and McDonough, T., 'Bitten by the Celtic Tiger: Immigrant workers and industrial relations in the new 'glocalised' Ireland', *Economic and Industrial Democracy*, vol. 28 (2008), no. 4, 501–22.

Dwek, R., 'Cool Customers', *Marketing Business*, February 1997.

Fanning, J., 'Celtic tiger, hidden dragons', *Irish Marketing Review*, vol. 14 (2001), no. 2.

Fitzgerald, G., *Reflections on the Irish State*, Dublin: Irish Academic Press 2003.

Friel, S., Walsh, O., and McCarthy, D., *The financial cost of healthy eating in Ireland*, Working Paper 04/01, Dublin: Combat Poverty Agency 2004.

Garvey, S. and Torres, A., 'Winning success in aquaculture marketing', *Irish Marketing Review*, vol. 6 (1993).

Honohan, P., *The Irish Banking Crisis: Regulatory and Financial Stability Policy 2003–2008*, Dublin: Central Bank of Ireland 2008.

Inglis, T., 'Pleasure Pursuits', in M. Corcoran and M. Peillon (eds), *Ireland Unbound: A Turn of the Century Chronicle*, Dublin: Institute of Public Administration 2002.

Keohane, K. and Kuhling, C., *Collision Culture: Transformations in everyday life in Ireland*, Dublin: Liffey Press 2004.

Kourteli, L., 'Scanning the business environment: some conceptual issues', *Benchmarking: An International Journal*, vol. 7 (2000), no. 5.

Lansman, N., 'Consumer protection and the single market', *Company Secretary's Review*, 27 December 1995.

McDonagh, P. and Prothero, A., 'Environmental marketing: some practical guidelines for marketers', *Irish Marketing Review*, vol. 6 (1993).

Maguire, M., *Differently Irish: A Cultural history exploring twenty-five years of Vietnamese Irish Identity*, Dublin: Woodfield 2004.

Meade, J., 'The Competition Act: the implications for business', *Irish Marketing Review*, vol. 6 (1993).

Moschis, G., Lee, E., and Mathur, A., 'Targeting the mature market: opportunities and challenges', *Journal of Consumer Marketing*, vol. 14, (1997), no. 4.

O'Connell, P. J. and McGinnity, F., *Immigrants at Work: Ethnicity and Nationality in the Irish Labour Market*, Dublin: The Equality Authority/ESRI 2008.

Peñaloza, Lisa N., 'Altravesando Fronteras/Border crossing: A critical ethnographic exploration of the consumer acculturation of Mexican Immigrants', *Journal of Consumer Research*, 12 (2) (1994), 32–50.

Peñaloza, Lisa N., 'Immigrant consumer acculturation', *Advances in Consumer Research*, vol.16 (1989), 110–118.

Prothero, A., Peattie, K., and McDonagh, P., 'Communicating greener strategies: a study of on-pack communication', *Business Strategy and the Environment*, May 1997.

Redfield, R., Linton, R., and Herskovits, M.J., 'Memorandum for the study of acculturation', *American Anthropologist*, 38, (1936), 149–52.

Reed, D., 'Disabled people: consumers able to buy', *Precision Marketing*, 12 May 1997.

Regling K. and Watson, M., 'A Preliminary Report on the Sources of Ireland's Banking Crisis', Dublin: Government Publications, 2008.

Russell, H., Quinn, E., King-O'Riain, R. and McGinnity, F., *The Experience of Discrimination in Ireland: Analysis of the QNHS Equality Module*, ESRI Research Series, number 3, Dublin: ESRI and The Equality Authority 2008.

Sam, D. L. 'Acculturation: conceptual background and core components' in D. L. Sam and J. W. Berry (eds), *The Cambridge Handbook of Acculturation Psychology*, Cambridge: Cambridge University Press, 2006.

Turley, D., 'Some perspectives on the Irish consumer', *Irish Marketing Review*, vol. 1 (1986).
Turley, D., 'The senior market: opportunity or oxymoron?', *Irish Marketing Review*, vol. 7 (1994).
Watson, M., 'Quick response as a competitive tool: Thermo King Europe's SMX', *Irish Marketing Review*, vol. 6 (1993).
Zwass, V., 'Electronic commerce: structures and issues', *International Journal of Electronic Commerce* (1996).

4

Marketing Research

Marketers require information in order to make decisions about markets, customers, competitors, and the marketing mix. The changing marketing environment requires new information and requires existing information to be brought up to date.

Information can be gathered from a variety of sources. In particular, marketers need to be familiar with the theory and practice of market research. Research is vital to marketers, as it can provide them with information on the consumer's needs and wants. Market research plays an important role in developing effective marketing strategies and in understanding what is happening in the company's marketing environment. This chapter examines the sources of information available to marketers and the market research process, including the factors that must be taken into account in designing a research exercise.

THE NATURE OF RESEARCH

Research is the systematic collection and analysis of data that is relevant to the particular product or service. It is carried out in the context of political, economic and social influences, and it can apply to any aspect of the marketing process that requires investigation. Typically, research is conducted on markets, sales, products, advertising, promotion, distribution, and pricing. Within each of these, specialist research techniques and studies have developed.

The main purpose of research is to facilitate decision-making and to reduce risk. Managers need information to help them make decisions, and the more information they have and the more accurate and reliable that information is, the lower the risk will be in making those decisions. A manager considering the introduction of a new product to the market, for instance, will require information about the market, potential buyers, distribution channels and competitors to help them make that decision. Research will be used to determine whether a potential market exists, to profile potential buyers, and to help in the design of the marketing mix.

The importance of listening to the customer

If the customer is at the centre of the business, it is important that the marketer listens to the customer. This is particularly so where the marketer does not come into regular face-to-face contact with the customer. Marketing research methods facilitate listening to the customer and finding out why the customer buys from the certain firm and identifying customers' attitudes, perceptions, opinions, and expectations of their future needs. Customer research also provides first-hand information on how they perceive competitors. Customers may be quick to point out where improvements can be made.

INFORMATION TYPES

Information is the basis of all research. The research process involves the gathering, analysis, interpretation and presentation of information. Usually the information that marketers collect is broadly classified under three headings: *internal information*, *secondary information*, and *primary information*.

Internal information

Internal information is information that is available through the firm's own records and information system. Company accounts will provide information on sales and profits, which can be further analysed, for example by product category, retail outlet, or market area. Accounts information will also yield cost and revenue budgets, which can be used in making decisions on such issues as the development of new products, communication campaigns, and marketing plans. Sales representatives' reports will give information on the sales of products within the geographical areas or retail outlets for which they are responsible.

With the advent of new scanning technology and electronic data interchange, many marketers can get rapid information from retail outlets on the sales of particular products or product lines. As products are scanned at the checkout, an information database can be updated not only according to units sold but also to record stock levels.

All departments in the firm are providers of information: it is not purely a function of the marketing department. All companies and organisations have information available to them from internal sources, and marketers should be familiar with these sources and ensure that internal information is being regularly and reliably reported.

Secondary information

Secondary information is any published information that is available to the marketer, for example the census of population, industry reports, or published market research reports. It is information that already exists and has been compiled for a particular purpose. Typically, secondary information is useful for environmental monitoring, and it can be obtained from a variety of sources. The following panel lists some of the most commonly used secondary sources.

SOME SECONDARY MARKET RESEARCH SOURCES

- Government publications
- Economic and Social Research Institute
- Central Statistics Office:
    Census of population
    Irish Statistical Bulletin (quarterly)

- Trade Statistics of Ireland
    Labour Force Survey
    Census of Industrial Production
    National Income and Expenditure
    Census of Services
    Business of Advertising Agencies
    Statistics of port traffic
- Tourism and Travel (quarterly)
- Statistical Report of the Revenue Commissioners
- Eurostat—basic statistics of the European Union
- Representative associations—*IPA Yearbook and Diary* gives a detailed listing
- State bodies—e.g. Enterprise Ireland, Bord Fáilte, An Bord Bia
- Libraries—university libraries, business information libraries, IMI library
- Third-level colleges—published research findings
- Marketing research companies—e.g. JNLR and JNMR, Henley Centre of Ireland

Primary information

Primary information is information that has to be generated at first hand, because no published sources are available or accessible, or because such information does not meet the information needs of the marketer. For instance, a company may wish to ascertain the attitudes or opinions of its own customers, and this information will not be available from secondary sources.

Quantitative or qualitative research?

There are two broad research approaches that can be considered when contemplating how to solve a research problem. Quantitative approaches concentrate on generating quantifiable statistics, such as percentages, means, and modes. A sample is usually taken from a defined population and specific questions are asked. A marketer of coffee, for example, could take a sample of shoppers in a supermarket and ask them questions, such as how often they buy coffee, which brand they prefer, and how many cups of coffee are consumed per day in their household. This would yield quantitative data and would enable the researcher to quantify average household consumption or brand preference statistics.

Qualitative approaches do not involve statistical sampling and typically focus on studying research participants in their natural setting, for example the home or the workplace. The researcher attempts to make sense and communicate phenomena in terms of the meaning that participants bring to them. In the case of coffee, the researcher who wants to gain qualitative insights might decide to go to a café and observe how people consume coffee, the researcher might engage with people and ask them what coffee means to them and try to get them to elaborate on this meaning.

The broad differences between quantitative and qualitative research are given in the panel below.

Quantitative research	Qualitative research
• Strong positivist influence (e.g. measuring scientifically)	• Contemporary methods are more social constructivist (e.g. constructing a social picture)
• Detached methods used (e.g. surveys)	• Intimate methods used (e.g. one-to-one personal interview)
• Emphasis on quantifying phenomena	• Emphasis on the qualities of phenomena
• Isolating cause and effect	• Studying phenomena in context
• Searches for common denominators	• Searches for variation
• Generalises based on large samples	• Individualises by describing in detail individual cases

It is not the case that one approach is better than the other—indeed the researcher can use both approaches in the same study—the important point is that the researcher chooses an approach that is best for the research problem that needs to be addressed. In the following sections, we will elaborate and give examples of the different ways in which these two methods can be used.

Figure 4.1: Stages in the market research process

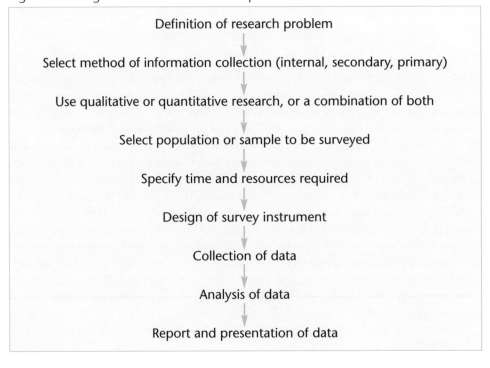

Definition of research problem

↓

Select method of information collection (internal, secondary, primary)

↓

Use qualitative or quantitative research, or a combination of both

↓

Select population or sample to be surveyed

↓

Specify time and resources required

↓

Design of survey instrument

↓

Collection of data

↓

Analysis of data

↓

Report and presentation of data

THE MARKET RESEARCH PROCESS

The *market research process* is the systematic way in which information is procured and provided in a usable form to the decision-maker. The process involves a series of stages. Fig. 4.1 on page 112 outlines the stages commonly used in gathering market information from primary sources.

Definition of research problem

This stage may prove the most difficult, as the marketer has to specify in advance what the research problem is. Sometimes it can be difficult to get agreement from the company or organisation on what the objectives of the research should be. It is vital, however, that the person carrying out the research has a clear and unambiguous brief.

The problem should not be defined too broadly or too narrowly. Too broad a definition can lead to unnecessary information being gathered, while too narrow a definition can result in important information being overlooked. A precise statement of the research problem is required, and this can then be translated into specific research objectives. Consider the example below, where researchers had to design a research study on people's opinions about public parks.

RESEARCH ON PARKS IN SOUTH COUNTY DUBLIN

In 2004, students from IT Tallaght carried out a survey for the Parks Department of South Dublin County Council.

The Parks Department wanted to carry out a research project to establish levels of public use and satisfaction with the parks under their management. As part of the process they wished to construct a profile of users and non-users of public parks and determine their expectations, attitudes, and opinions.

Research objectives:

1. Profile the characteristics of users and non-users of parks in the South Dublin County Council area.
2. Establish the main purposes of use among users.
3. Identify the reasons for non-use among non-users.
4. Establish levels of public awareness for park location and amenities.
5. Measure respondents' attitudes and perceptions to the parks as a public amenity.
6. Determine overall levels of public satisfaction.
7. Seek ideas and suggestions from respondents on the future development of parks.
8. Compare results with findings obtained in a similar survey in 1999.

In many cases it may be difficult for the marketer to be specific, and some research will be *exploratory* in nature. This describes the assessment of general information to find relevant points to concentrate on: for example, a marketer wishing to expand into overseas markets may scan a number of markets before deciding which one to select. Other research projects will be *descriptive*, such as those dealing with the size of the market, the market share of the main competitors, or the attitudes and opinions of customers. *Causal* research describes research into cause-and-effect relationships: for instance, a company might be interested in finding out the effects, if any, an increase in price will have on sales of a product.

Method of information collection: internal, secondary, primary

The researcher needs to specify what methods of information collection will be used. In many cases companies will have information available to them internally from their own reporting system, and this may be enough to provide the marketer with the information needed. It is important that firms have an organised information reporting system, otherwise decision-makers may waste time and money because their system is not being properly used, or they may not realise the usefulness of internal information, because it is not being communicated or compiled in a meaningful way.

Secondary research is used frequently by decision-makers. It will usually be required in advance of meetings about the product or industry so that participants are informed about general background issues, or it may be required to build up specific knowledge of the industry or sector in which the business operates. Marketing practitioners need to keep themselves informed on developments in their business environment, and secondary research can be particularly useful in this regard.

In relation to the research problem itself, sometimes it can be wholly or partially solved using secondary sources of information. The difficulty for Irish marketers is that, in general, very little published research is available on specific markets or product categories: most research commissioned by marketers through market research companies is proprietary and is not generally published.

Primary research will be generated at first hand using one or a combination of research techniques. Primary research can be time-consuming and expensive, and the researcher therefore should be sure, before embarking on such a project, that all possible secondary sources have been examined. Primary research can involve a number of alternatives, as shown in the following panel.

METHODS OF PRIMARY RESEARCH

Observation: for example, observing the number of people selecting a particular product in a supermarket during a particular period.

Experiments: selecting subjects, giving them different treatments, controlling related factors, and measuring the results. A company wishing to test a new product before launch may experiment by using a test market or area. The product can be promoted in this area and stocked in a selected number of shops, and consumers' response can be measured. The test market should be representative of the total market, and this will give an indication of the probable success of the product.

Surveys: questioning people directly about their behaviour, attitudes, or opinions. The survey will usually involve the use of a questionnaire, which is a structured research instrument.

Qualitative and quantitative research

Qualitative research

Qualitative research involves attempting to gain insights into respondents' perceptions, attitudes, and motives. It is based on an understanding of psychology, and therefore the researcher should ideally have a background in psychology before attempting qualitative research. The main methods used by researchers are *depth interviews, focus groups*, and *projective techniques*.

In recent years there has been an increase in the use of qualitative research. One study reviewed some of the creative techniques used in qualitative research (O'Leary, 1993); it found that analysis was primarily based on psychological and sociological dimensions.

Depth interviews are usually conducted individually and are therefore ideal for dealing with sensitive subjects. The form of the interview is typically unstructured, so that the respondent is encouraged to open up to the researcher rather than simply answer a list of questions. The interviewer needs to be skilled at dealing with people, so that the respondent feels at ease and is willing to answer the questions. Depth interviews are time-consuming and can also be expensive if several are needed.

Focus groups usually consist of eight to 10 people, together with a moderator, who meet for a group discussion about a particular subject. Respondents are encouraged to discuss their attitudes, reactions, motives, life-styles, or feelings about the subject. They are recruited from specific groups: for example, a hotel interested in developing a new short holiday break for people over 55 might conduct a focus group comprising men and women over 55. The new product could be explained to them and their opinions and ideas sought. The moderator will usually have a psychology background, as skill is required to analyse responses. The moderator will also have to ensure that the discussion does not become sidetracked and that no one person attempts to dominate the discussion.

Projective techniques will sometimes be used in both qualitative and quantitative research. Essentially these are attempts to understand the individual's underlying motives and feelings. Two of the main techniques used are *word association* and *sentence completion*; the panel on page 116 gives some examples of each.

Quantitative research

Quantitative research involves the analysis and manipulation of facts and figures—the collection of sufficient data to enable statistical analysis. Data for analysis may be available from secondary sources or it may have to be generated by primary means.

The techniques for the design, administration and analysis of questionnaires are particularly important in quantitative research, as in many research projects the questionnaire will usually be the means of obtaining the data for analysis. Questionnaires are structured research instruments and are used to measure behaviour, demographic characteristics, knowledge levels, attitudes, and opinions.

PROJECTIVE TECHNIQUES

Word association involves asking interviewees to respond immediately to a word with the first word that comes to mind; respondents are therefore communicating their feelings indirectly. Asking the respondent for an immediate response is important, as it means they don't spend time searching for the answer they feel they should give. It is also usual to present a list of words, only some of which are actually of interest to the researcher; this disguises the purpose of the research when the researcher does not want the respondent to bias answers to later questions based on their earlier responses.

For example, a chocolate producer interested in the perception of its brand might want to research spontaneous response to a number of brands.

Stimulus word	*Response*
Yorkie	....
Flake	....
Fry's Chocolate Cream	....
Lion Bar	....
Snickers	....

Sentence completion requires the respondent to be a little bit more descriptive and forthcoming; for example:

People who eat Flake are ....

....

....

Sampling

The *sample* refers to those respondents selected for survey. They must be representative of the whole population of interest, and this implies a need to consider what will be a statistically valid sample. The researcher has therefore to decide who is to be surveyed, how many should be surveyed, and how respondents should be chosen.

It is rare that a census of the population of interest will be undertaken, unless it is physically and financially possible to do so. A census implies that the researcher will survey every member of a population, and there are cases where it may be possible to do so: for example, if Boeing were carrying out research on the needs of airlines in Ireland it would be quite feasible for them to survey all Irish airlines, as the total population is quite small. But in general, researchers will select a representative sample from the population of interest.

There are a number of different approaches to sampling.

Probability samples: Each element of a population from which the sample is drawn has a known chance (non-zero) of being selected. This is the only truly objective method of sampling. Its main drawback is that a *sampling frame* (a list of the population under survey) is necessary, and this is not always possible. An example of where it is possible would be

Eircom conducting research among subscribers listed in a particular area's telephone directory.

Non-probability samples: This is a type of stratified sampling in which the selection of sampling units is within specified strata and is done non-randomly, usually controlled by quotas. A quota should be representative of the total population. For example, if 55 per cent of a population is female and 45 per cent is male, a quota sample of 100 people should comprise 55 females and 45 males.

Computing the size of the sample: Sample size depends on the basic characteristics of the population, the type of information required, and the costs entailed. In general the rule is: the larger the sample size, the greater the reliability. When sample size is being computed the *non-response factor* should be borne in mind: in other words, there may be members of a particular population who will not consent to be surveyed. If the researcher carrying out a survey for Boeing, for example, approached all Irish airlines but only one agreed to participate, the response error would be quite high and would have to be reported in the research findings.

With *random sampling* the size of the sample can be computed mathematically in order to achieve a stated degree of precision. Random samples can be drawn where a complete list of the relevant population is available and each therefore has a calculable chance of being selected for survey. This involves the evaluation of a *confidence coefficient*, which indicates the specified degree of certainty with which a particular sample estimate can be accepted as a true estimator of the population being surveyed: for example, a level of confidence of 95 per cent would result in a 5 per cent level of significance. (For a detailed discussion of sampling the reader should consult the texts given in the further reading list at the end of the chapter.)

Time and resources required

The time taken to complete the research, and the resources required, must be included in any research plan. Decision-makers will usually not have unlimited time or resources to complete the research; the time and resources available will, for instance, determine the extent of sampling that might be possible. In addition to the general costs of carrying out the research, such as the fees of a market research company, the marketer may also consider incentives to encourage a higher response rate, such as free products for participants or participation in a prize draw. Incentives should not, however, be such that they would bias the research findings.

Design of survey instrument

In most cases the survey instrument will be a questionnaire, the nature and design of which will vary according to the research being undertaken.

Questionnaires are structured survey instruments used by researchers to interact with interviewees. They are widely used by researchers conducting quantitative research. They can be of varying lengths and forms, but they should be kept short, simple, and easy to understand.

A number of questions should be borne in mind when a questionnaire is being designed, including:

- Exactly what information is required, and from whom?
- Will respondents be able to understand the questions, and will they be able to answer them?
- Are the words used in the questions clear and unambiguous?
- Are the words used likely to result in biased answers?
- Are the questions arranged in the correct sequence?
- Is the layout of the questionnaire clear and free from confusion?

The design of the survey instrument is a separate stage in the process, but it is important to note that it follows on from the research objectives. Researchers should ensure that the objectives have been clearly established before beginning the design of a questionnaire. The survey instrument will also determine the subsequent stages in the research process. Problems with the questionnaire will inevitably lead to difficulties in data collection and analysis. Poorly designed and structured questionnaires will probably yield low response rates or vague and unreliable data.

Questionnaires should always be tested among some representative respondents before the survey is undertaken. This should ensure that any potential difficulties are identified and can be dealt with before the survey takes place.

When the questionnaire is being designed, the method of analysis that will be used should also be borne in mind. If a statistical computer program is being used it must be possible for the researcher to code the answers into a form that is compatible with the program.

Question sequence

The following are some guidelines relating to the sequence of the questions:

1. Open the questionnaire with a few factual, easily answered questions.
2. Lead in to a small number of factual multiple-choice questions.
3. Follow with questions designed to gauge whether the interviewee has thought about or knows about the topic under review.
4. Move to a series of structured and semi-structured questions designed to cover very specific issues.
5. Introduce a selection of open-ended or wide-open questions so that the respondent can fully express himself or herself.
6. Close with 'filter' questions—those designed to place the respondent according to the sampling frame.

It is not unusual for the 'say/do' phenomenon to appear in market research. Respondents may give the answer they think they ought to give but will in fact engage in quite different behaviour. In new-product research, for example, the respondent may say that they will buy the product but will not. While it is very difficult—in most cases impossible—to monitor this, a well-designed questionnaire will have questions that verify the answers given by the respondent. In the case of new-product research, for example, the marketer could seek information on other new products the respondent has bought in order to determine their interest in new products in general.

Classification questions

Questionnaires will usually seek background information on respondents, such as their age, marital status, and social class. Usually, factors such as age will be presented on a scale, unless it is important to know the exact age.

Social class in Ireland is measured according to the respondent's occupation or the occupation of the head of household. This yields a number of groupings, commonly referred to as the ABC1 scale. The Central Statistics Office also produces socio-economic groupings, but the ABC1 scale is the most widely used in marketing. Researchers use a fairly comprehensive list of occupations for classifying people.

Rating scales

Questionnaires will often require respondents to *rate* something. There are three types of rating scale. The *Likert scale* and the *semantic differential* are the most commonly used; the *Stapel scale* is probably used less frequently. The Likert scale asks the respondent to indicate agreement or disagreement with something.

THE LIKERT SCALE

Brand A provides customers with high standards of service.

Strongly agree	Agree	Neither agree nor disagree	Disagree	Strongly disagree
☐	☐	☐	☐	☐

The *semantic differential* presents bipolar adjectives on a scale, and respondents are asked to indicate on the scale the point that reflects their view.

THE SEMANTIC DIFFERENTIAL

Rise and Shine orange juice is:

good value for money	☐ ☐ ☐ ☐ ☐ ☐ ☐	poor value for money
conveniently packaged	☐ ☐ ☐ ☐ ☐ ☐ ☐	inconveniently packaged

The *Stapel scale* consists of a single adjective in the middle of an even-numbered range of values.

THE STAPEL SCALE

Please indicate how accurately you think each of the following words describes our service:

+5	+4	+3	+2	+1		−1	−2	−3	−4	−5
+5	+4	+3	+2	+1	Fast	−1	−2	−3	−4	−5
+5	+4	+3	+2	+1	Slow	−1	−2	−3	−4	−5
+5	+4	+3	+2	+1	Reliable	−1	−2	−3	−4	−5
+5	+4	+3	+2	+1	Unreliable	−1	−2	−3	−4	−5

Referring back to the example of the research objectives on page 113, the following is the questionnaire that was used for the subsequent survey.

We are students at the Institute of Technology, Tallaght, and as part of our course work we are conducting research on park usage. Would you be interested in participating in this survey, which involves answering a short questionnaire? This will take about 5–10 minutes.

All information received will be treated in the strictest confidence.

Date: _____   Weather Conditions: _____

Time: _____

Location: _____

Have you participated in a survey about parks within the past week?
Yes   ❏   1   (If 'Yes' Terminate Interview)
No   ❏   2

Section 1: Personal Details (Please tick only one box per question.)

Q. 1) Gender: Male   ❏   1 Female   ❏   2

Q. 2) Which of the following age categories do you belong to?
        0–17 yrs   ❏   1   35–50   ❏   4
        18–24   ❏   2   51–64   ❏   5
        25–34   ❏   3   65+   ❏   6

Q. 3) Do you have any children under 16 years of age?
        Yes   ❏   1   No   ❏   2
        If yes, please indicate how many _____

Q. 4) Whereabouts do you live? _____
        (*e.g. Oldbawn, Tallaght*)

Section 2: Public Awareness

Q. 5) Which public body is responsible for managing and maintaining parks in this area?
        Answer _____

        Don't Know   ❏

Q. 6) What is your overall opinion of parks in this area?
        Very good ❏ 1   Good ❏ 2   Fair ❏ 3   Poor ❏ 4   Very poor ❏ 5

Q. 7) Do you think that more information about parks in this area should be made
available?
Yes   ❏   1   No   ❏   2

Q. 8) Do you currently use any public parks, for any reason?
Yes   ❏   1   No   ❏   2 (If No, skip Section 3)

Section 3: User Information

Q. 9) Today, are you using the park for:
| | | | |
Shortcut   ❏ 1   Recreation   ❏ 5
Walking   ❏ 2   Exercise   ❏ 6
Event/Festival   ❏ 3   Organised Sports   ❏ 4

Other _____

Q. 10) a) How often do you use the park?
Every day   ❏ 1   Once per week   ❏ 4
Only at weekends   ❏ 2   Once per month   ❏ 5
2–3 times per week   ❏ 3   Once/twice per year ❏ 6

b) How much time do you usually spend in the park?
Less than 30 minutes   ❏ 1   1–2 hours   ❏ 3
30 minutes–1 hour   ❏ 2   More than 2 hours   ❏ 4

Q. 11) a) When did you last use the park? _____

b) Did you enjoy your last visit to the park?
Yes   ❏ 1   No   ❏ 2   Indifferent   ❏ 3

Q. 12) Approximately how far do you live from the park you are visiting today?
<1km ❏   1–3 km ❏   3–5 km ❏   5–10 km ❏   10km+ ❏

Q. 13 a) How did you travel to the park today?
Car ❏ 1   Bus ❏ 2   Cycle ❏ 3   Walk ❏ 4   Other _____
(In the case of bicycles or motorised vehicles, please answer Part B)

b) Please rate the parking facilities at this park:
Very good ❏ 1   Good ❏ 2   Fair ❏ 3   Poor ❏ 4   Very poor ❏ 5

Q. 14) Do you know the opening hours of the park?
Yes   ❏   1   No   ❏   2

Q. 15) At what time do you most often use the park?
Early morning   ❏ 1   Late afternoon   ❏ 4
Late morning   ❏ 2   Evening   ❏ 5
Early afternoon   ❏ 3

Q. 16) Have you ever attended any family days organised in your local park?
    Yes   ❑   1   No   ❑   2 (If No, skip Q.17)

Q. 17) How did you find out about such an event?
    Radio   ❑ 1   Television   ❑ 5
    Local newspaper   ❑ 2   Word of mouth   ❑ 6
    National newspaper ❑ 3   Signage   ❑ 7
    Mailshot/flyer   ❑ 4   Other _____

Q. 18) Were you aware that the council organises such events during the summer?
    Yes   ❑   1   No   ❑   2

Q. 19) Would you allow your younger children to visit the park without supervision?
    Yes   ❑   1   No   ❑   2   N/A   ❑

Q. 20) Did you have any difficulty in finding this park today?
    Yes   ❑   1   No   ❑   2

Q. 21) Please respond to the following statements regarding the park you are in today
    by indicating your level of agreement.

	Strongly Agree	Agree	Neutral	Disagree	Strongly Disagree
a) I always look forward to visiting this park	❑	❑	❑	❑	❑
b) I feel safe while in this park	❑	❑	❑	❑	❑
c) The park is always well kept	❑	❑	❑	❑	❑
d) There is plenty for all ages to do in this park	❑	❑	❑	❑	❑
e) It can be difficult to find my way around the park	❑	❑	❑	❑	❑
f) The park's opening hours suit me	❑	❑	❑	❑	❑
g) There are too many sports pitches in this park	❑	❑	❑	❑	❑
h) There should be some sheltered areas in the park	❑	❑	❑	❑	❑
i) There are not enough litter bins in the park	❑	❑	❑	❑	❑
j) The park is only for young people	❑	❑	❑	❑	❑
k) There aren't enough flowers in the park	❑	❑	❑	❑	❑
l) There are too many trees in the park	❑	❑	❑	❑	❑
m) The park serves no purpose	❑	❑	❑	❑	❑
n) The park is an important part of the community	❑	❑	❑	❑	❑
o) The staff are very friendly	❑	❑	❑	❑	❑
p) There should be more park rangers	❑	❑	❑	❑	❑
q) The park is accessible for prams/wheelchairs	❑	❑	❑	❑	❑
r) The park caters for people with learning disability	❑	❑	❑	❑	❑

Q. 22) Would you recommend this park to others?
    Yes   ❑   1   No   ❑   2

Q. 23 a) Have you experienced a problem(s) with any aspect of this park?
Yes ❏ 1   No ❏ 2 (If No, skip parts b & c)

b) Did you report the problem to staff?
Yes ❏ 1   No ❏ 2 (If No, skip part c)

c) Was the problem resolved to your satisfaction?
Yes ❏ 1   No ❏ 2

Q. 24) The council has a policy of letting areas grow naturally at certain sites in order to return the area to a more natural habitat, such as long grass and wild flower meadows. What do you think about this policy?

Very favourable   Favourable   Indifferent   Unfavourable   Very unfavourable
❏ 1   ❏ 2   ❏ 3   ❏ 4   ❏ 5

Q. 25 a) Do you own a dog?
Yes ❏ 1 No   ❏ 2 (If No go to part b)
If yes, do you walk your dog in the park?
Yes ❏ 1 No   ❏ 2
If yes, at what time?
Morning ❏ 1 Afternoon ❏ 2 Evening ❏ 3

b) Please indicate the strength of your agreement with the following statements.
I feel dogs are properly controlled in this park.
Strongly Agree Agree Neutral Disagree Strongly Disagree
❏   ❏   ❏   ❏   ❏
I think all dogs should be muzzled in the park.
Strongly Agree   Agree Neutral Disagree Strongly Disagree
❏   ❏   ❏   ❏   ❏
I think dogs should be allowed run free in the park.
Strongly Agree   Agree Neutral Disagree Strongly Disagree
❏   ❏   ❏   ❏   ❏
Should a time be provided to allow dogs run free in the park?
Yes ❏ 1 No   ❏ 2

Q. 26) Do you know any of the rules that govern the use of the park?
Interviewer: Record any responses
Litter ❏   Cycling ❏   Alcohol ❏   Dogs ❏

Other _____

Q. 27) Currently the bye-laws prohibit cycling in parks.
Do you agree that cycling should not be allowed?
Yes ❏ 1   No ❏ 2

Should the council provide dedicated cycle-paths in parks?
Yes   ❏   1   No   ❏   2

Q. 28) Please indicate your level of satisfaction with the following features in this park.
(If the facilities are not available in this park, tick N/A.)

	N/A	Very Satisfied	Satisfied	Indifferent	Dissatisfied	Very Dissatisfied
a) Picnic site	❏	❏	❏	❏	❏	❏
b) Community centre	❏	❏	❏	❏	❏	❏
c) Floral display	❏	❏	❏	❏	❏	❏
d) Wildlife interests	❏	❏	❏	❏	❏	❏
e) Trees/wood	❏	❏	❏	❏	❏	❏
f) Children's playground	❏	❏	❏	❏	❏	❏
g) Historical interests	❏	❏	❏	❏	❏	❏
h) Fishing	❏	❏	❏	❏	❏	❏
i) Rivers/lakes	❏	❏	❏	❏	❏	❏
j) Tennis courts	❏	❏	❏	❏	❏	❏
k) Seating/benches	❏	❏	❏	❏	❏	❏
l) Signage	❏	❏	❏	❏	❏	❏

Q. 29) In the past five years . . .
I feel that facilities in this park have improved.

Strongly Agree	Agree	Neutral	Disagree	Strongly Disagree
❏	❏	❏	❏	❏

I feel that the general appearance of this park has improved.

Strongly Agree	Agree	Neutral	Disagree	Strongly Disagree
❏	❏	❏	❏	❏

I feel that the overall management of this park has improved.

Strongly Agree	Agree	Neutral	Disagree	Strongly Disagree
❏	❏	❏	❏	❏

Q. 30 How does this park compare with any other park you are familiar with?
Better   ❏   The same   ❏   Worse   ❏
Why? _____

Q. 31) Does the Parks Department do anything other than manage parks?
Yes   ❏   1   No   ❏   2   Don't know   ❏

Q. 32) Overall, what is the single most important issue about this park that concerns
you?

Note Response: _____

Section 4: Non-User Information

Q. 33 a) Do you know where your local park is located?

Yes   ❑   1

If yes, what is its name? _____

No   ❑   2 (If No, skip part b)

b) Please indicate the distance from your home to the nearest park:

<1km ❑ 1 1–3km ❑ 2   3–5km ❑ 3   5–10km ❑ 4   10km+ ❑ 5

Q. 34) Please indicate the reasons for which you choose not to use the parks.

	Very Influential	Influential	Not Influential
a) Security	❑	❑	❑
b) Weather	❑	❑	❑
c) Distance	❑	❑	❑
d) Inconvenience	❑	❑	❑
e) Atmosphere	❑	❑	❑
f) Maintenance	❑	❑	❑
g) Facilities	❑	❑	❑
h) Other	❑	❑	❑

Q. 35 a) Are you aware of the facilities available at the parks in the South Dublin County Council area?

Yes   ❑   1   No   ❑   2

b) Do the facilities at these parks meet your needs?

Yes   ❑   1   No   ❑   2

Q. 36) Parks play an important role in the community.

Strongly Agree	Agree	Neutral	Disagree	Strongly Disagree
❑	❑	❑	❑	❑

Q. 37) It doesn't matter if any landscaped area were rezoned for development.

Strongly Agree	Agree	Neutral	Disagree	Strongly Disagree
❑	❑	❑	❑	❑

Additional Comments:

_____

_____

_____

_____

Thank you for your time and co-operation.

Contact methods

If a structured questionnaire is being used, the main contact methods are personal interviews, telephone interviews, and postal interviews.

Personal interviews include interviewers stopping people on the street, giving out questionnaires on a train, and calling at people's homes. They are time-consuming and more expensive than the other two contact methods but are more flexible.

Telephone interviews have the advantage of being more cost-effective and less time-consuming, but they need to be highly structured, and the interviewer may not be able to verify the accuracy of data, for example the respondent's age.

Postal interviews are very cost-effective and can be highly structured but do not allow for respondents' questions and can have low response rates. If a more unstructured research approach is being adopted, depth interviews or focus groups will be more appropriate. Here the questionnaire will be a series of general questions or discussion points designed to prompt the interviewer or moderator.

A particular survey form that has grown in importance is 'mystery shopping'. This involves trained assessors visiting retail outlets, presenting themselves as customers, and talking to sales staff. The purpose is to assess whether or not sales staff can explain the benefits of products and can answer questions; it therefore provides an assessment of the firm's sales and customer care training schemes.

Assessors usually complete a detailed questionnaire, which may cover such factors as initial greeting, general customer service, sales ability, and product knowledge. (See the extracts from a questionnaire used by UCI Cinemas in fig. 4.2.) The assessor or mystery shopper has to answer each of these questions with respect to the experience they had when they visited one of UCI's cinemas. In addition to the questions listed in fig. 4.2 the mystery UCI shopper also had to assess making a telephone booking, the external lobby, toilets, main foyer, and the quality of the food and beverages.

Figure 4.2: UCI mystery visitor scheme

		Points	Points
Site Location:			
Date of Visit:			
Show Time:			
Film Seen:			
Weather:			
External Impressions			
		Points	*Points*
	Yes or No	*Possible*	*Scored*
Car park neat, tidy and litter or weed free		3	
All lights on		1	
All signage clean and well illuminated		1	
Film display fully illuminated		1	
Film titles and certificates clearly on display		1	
All windows clean and free of smudges		1	
All film posters neatly presented		1	

Box office
Number of customers in the queue:
Number of kiosks open:
Number of staff members in the kiosks:
Time taken to receive tickets:
Name of person serving:

	Yes or No	Points Possible	Points Scored
Clear where tickets booked by phone could be collected		1	
All staff not smoking, chewing or eating		2	
Clear display of films, show times, certificates and prices		1	
Inside of the kiosk clean and tidy		1	
Tickets came directly from dispenser		3	
All staff neatly dressed in uniform and wearing name badge		4	
Greeted with eye contact or smile and all staff polite and courteous		6	
The box office appeared secure		2	

Concession stand

	Yes or No	Points Possible	Points Scored
All staff neat, tidy and in full uniform		4	
All food displays adequately stocked		2	
Straw and napkin dispensers adequately stocked		2	
Counter neat, tidy and free of spillages		2	
Staff member attempted to trade up order		10	
Correct change tendered		2	
Greeted with eye contact or smile and all staff polite and courteous		6	
All displays fully illuminated		1	
All staff observing the no smoking or drinking or eating rule		2	

Auditorium

	Yes or No	Points Possible	Points Scored
Queue well controlled or informed of show time		3	
Ticket checked or stub put into box		2	
If seat booked, shown or clearly directed to seat		1	
Seat clean and free of rips		3	
All floor areas clear of food or litter, etc.		3	
Exit signs illuminated		2	
Temperature comfortable		4	
Screen slides in focus or well presented		2	
Film picture and sound quality good		5	

Show started on time	3
Audience quiet and controlled by staff	5
All staff neatly dressed in uniform and wearing name badge	4
Greeted with eye contact or smile and all staff polite and courteous	6
Asked for ticket stub on return to cinema	5

Source: UCI.

The assessor can also present problems to members of the staff to see how they are dealt with, or complain about something and measure the reaction. Employees usually know that mystery shoppers are calling, but not when. Schemes will usually be spread over time, so that the performance of individual branches can be tracked. Usually, firms with several outlets or branches use the scores received by each outlet to make comparisons. An important aspect of this research is that employees should receive feedback, and the results can be used in training schemes. They can also be used to benchmark performance against that of competitors.

Collection of data

The method used will depend on the type of research being conducted. If a quantitative survey of consumers is being undertaken, this usually involves administering a questionnaire. The questionnaire is therefore the data collection instrument. If qualitative research is being undertaken the data will usually be collected through depth interviews or focus groups. The period for the collection of data may need to be specified. This ensures that the research is not limited to particular days.

Analysis of data

If the information generated has been mostly qualitative in nature, the analysis will concentrate on the principal opinions, attitudes, or perceptions. This requires an objective analysis of respondents' opinions and viewpoints. Quantitative information will usually be subjected to various degrees of statistical analysis. As statistical analysis can be a laborious process, it will usually be done by computer, using a specialised statistical and research program. The analysis process involves the editing, coding, and tabulation of data. Degrees of statistical analysis will depend on the complexity of the information collected. A number of statistical programs are available that can be used for the analysis of quantitative information, including SPSS, SAS, Systat, Minitab, and Microstat. These programs permit the tabulation and analysis of large quantities of information.

The statistical measures used will depend on the objectives of the research. At a basic level this will usually involve descriptions of averages, percentages, distributions, and measures of dispersion. Cross-tabulations that show the number of cases that have particular combinations of responses with two or more questions are useful for providing a more detailed analysis of information obtained.

Cross-tabulations usually involve taking variables relating to the respondents, such as sex, age, or class, and cross-tabulating them with other variables, such as brands bought, quantity of the product bought, or opinions expressed. It is also usual to examine data for correlations, but care must be exercised, as a correlation indicates a degree of movement between two or more variables: it does not necessarily imply a causal relationship. For example, a research study on the consumption of household products might show that in particular households there was a correlation between the consumption of candles and the consumption of milk, but obviously there is no causal relationship between the two.

Report and presentation of data

The general guidelines for report-writing should be followed, in that the style should relate to the person who will receive it, clear language should be used, and diagrams and tables should be used for presenting quantitative information. The following panel gives a suggested framework for a research report.

SUGGESTED FORMAT FOR A RESEARCH REPORT

- Title page
- Table of contents
- List of appendixes
- Introduction
- Main conclusions
- Details of survey methods
- Survey findings
- Conclusions
- Recommendations
- List of tables
- List of diagrams
- References
- Appendixes

Things that can go wrong

Researchers are concerned to ensure that any research carried out is reliable and accurate; otherwise it is impossible to base decisions on research findings. There are a number of possible errors that researchers must be careful to avoid.

Sampling errors can occur where the sample taken is not representative of the population of interest. Care needs to be exercised in sample design.

Non-response error can occur when the researcher does not receive a response from the target sample. Possible reasons could be where the research topic is sensitive or embarrassing or where respondents are approached at an awkward or inconvenient time.

Data collection errors occur when respondents do not understand the questions asked. Researchers have to ensure that the wording used does not confuse the respondent.

Analysis errors happen when the researcher wrongly interprets research findings. Researchers need to view research findings objectively and should ensure that data has been accurately tabulated and analysed.

Report errors can occur if the researcher comes to the wrong conclusion or if the research findings are poorly communicated.

Needless to say, these sources of error should be avoided, and can be avoided with careful planning of the research project.

RESEARCH ETHICS

Ethics refers to moral rules, standards, codes or principles that provide guidelines for right and truthful behaviour in specific situations. Research practitioners are governed by codes of conduct and ethics that are designed to protect people from exploitation and ensure that research is conducted in an ethical manner. Researchers have responsibilities to their clients, to respondents, to the public, and to themselves. Researchers should honestly do what they purport to do: they should not manipulate research techniques to produce desired findings, and they should not undertake research assignments that are ethically unacceptable.

CODE OF PROFESSIONAL ETHICS AND PRACTICES

1. To maintain high standards of competence and integrity in survey design.
2. To maintain high levels of business and professional conduct.
3. To observe reasonable care and to be objective and accurate in the use of data.
4. To protect the anonymity of respondents.
5. To thoroughly instruct and supervise those responsible for carrying out the research.
6. To observe the rights of ownership of any materials received.
7. To make available to clients such details on the research methods and techniques used as may be reasonably required for proper interpretation of data.
8. To promote trust of the public for marketing and survey research activities.
9. To encourage observance of ethical practice among the research profession.

Source: Abstracted from text supplied by the Marketing Research Association, Inc., Chicago.

Warren (1998) argued that the marketing research industry was making considerable, increasingly unwelcome, and perhaps unreasonable demands on respondents. He maintained that the industry needed to change its procedures and suggested that researchers should consider reducing the length of questionnaires, setting quotas in simpler ways, making better use of interviewers, and educating the general public on the methods and benefits of research.

The code of research ethics developed by the Market Research Association in the United States is summarised in the above panel.

In general it can be taken that respondents have the right to choose whether or not to participate in the research, the right to have confidentiality protected, and the right to be informed about the nature of the research. A company cannot misrepresent a sales pitch as a research exercise; and research can be conducted on minors only with the consent of a parent or guardian.

The net result of unethical research practices would include the unwillingness of companies, organisations, or the public to take part in research surveys, the distortion of policy-makers' and decision-makers' perceptions of issues, and a reduction in the public's ability to distinguish between valid and invalid research findings. Observance of the codes of ethical research practice ensures that respondents, clients and researchers are not compromised.

The following panel reproduces a leaflet given to participants in surveys by Lansdowne Market Research to explain the reasons why respondents were selected and the responsibilities the research company has to them.

STATEMENT TO RESPONDENTS

LANSDOWNE MARKET RESEARCH
12 Lower Hatch Street
Dublin 2

Thank you for helping with our survey by giving this interview.

Since its foundation in 1979, Lansdowne Market Research has grown to become Ireland's leading consumer research company.

In the course of a year, many thousands of people are interviewed by Lansdowne Market Research. However, those who help us do not always know why we ask so many questions or the uses to which we put the information. Here is a short explanation of what it is all about.

Q. Why were you chosen for interview?

A. On most surveys we have to interview a cross-section of the public, people from all walks of life and of all ages. The answers given by all the different types of people are analysed together to give an accurate picture of the country as a whole.

Q. Will someone try to sell me something?

A. No. You will not be approached by anyone selling anything as a result of this interview, and you will not be contacted again, unless:
   (a)   the interview is one of a series in which you agree to take part
   (b)   you stated your willingness for reinterview
   (c)   as part of our Quality Control Procedure.

Q. Who commissioned this survey?

A. As stated earlier, market research is controlled by a strict code of standards. The person being interviewed does not know the name of the client, nor does the client know the names of the people who have been interviewed. This way we can guarantee that the information given to us is not biased by any preconceived ideas.

Q. How can I be sure that someone is a genuine market research interviewer?

A. (a)   Ask to see an identity card. All our interviewers carry an identity card with their photo attached.

(b)   Ring one of our telephone numbers and ask to speak to the field controller or manager.

Q. Why do you want my name, address, and telephone number?

A. It is possible that you might receive a letter or phone call from one of our supervisors. This letter or call will be to thank you once again for taking part in the survey and to find out if you were happy with the way the interview was carried out. You may also be asked a few questions about the survey itself to ensure that the answers you gave were recorded correctly. This forms part of our Quality Control Procedure, and your co-operation is greatly appreciated.

Q. How am I protected?

A. Market research is controlled by a strict code of standards, which guarantees anonymity both to the person who is interviewed and to the client for whom the research is being conducted. The interview you give is strictly confidential.

Unless your explicit permission has been obtained, the name and address of you or your family will not be disclosed to anyone.

Finally, we would like to thank you once again for agreeing to take part in this survey. We hope this leaflet will have helped to explain the background to market research. If you have any further questions, concerns or comments, please contact us at [telephone numbers].

MARKETING RESEARCH APPLICATIONS

Marketing research has several applications. It is used to measure and investigate aspects of consumers' behaviour, advertising and promotion effectiveness, new product or service ideas, package design, and price-sensitivity. Advertisers, for example, pay particular attention to the annual JNRR, JNLR, and JNMR. FMCG (fast moving consumer goods) companies tend to buy continuous tracking research on their brands; this provides continuous information on the sales performance and market share of brands in the product category. Some researchers specialise in particular applications, and a significant body of knowledge has been built up in each. In general, regardless of the particular application, the research process includes the factors described in this chapter.

Consider the research conducted on the Lynx and Harvey's Bristol Cream brands.

LYNX: CONTINUOUS PRODUCT RESEARCH

The Lynx brand of deodorant, as the product is known in Britain, Ireland, Australia and New Zealand—or Axe in all other markets—is the world's most successful deodorant for young men. In Britain, for example, one in every two men has a can in his bathroom. Unilever produces it.

In addition to spending heavily on advertising, the company has also invested in product research. This research focuses on product development and subsequent testing among consumers.

Deodorant does not stop perspiration, but it minimises under-arm odour by killing the bacteria that feed on the sweat, usually with ethanol. The bacteria can grow back quickly. New deodorant technology works by denying the bacteria the iron they need for growth. Unilever added a chemical called DTPA that binds the iron floating around in the sweat, making it unavailable to the bacteria. It has also added an anti-oxidant called BHT that releases iron from the proteins in the sweat, allowing the DTPA to bind it before the bacteria can get hold of it. In tests among 4,000 consumers in Europe and Latin America, 95 per cent of respondents thought the new product worked better than the old.

At Unilever's research centre in Britain, 12 expert human odour assessors are used to test the product on volunteers, simply using their sense of smell. In the case of antiperspirants that work by blocking the sweat glands, the research involves volunteers sitting in a sauna-like hot room. Each volunteer has a sample applied under one arm and a control under the other, together with pads to collect the sweat.

Unilever considers this research to be essential as it gives the company technological lead time. It has also invested in new packaging and borrowed from technology developed in the soft drinks industry to produce a shaped and moulded pressurised can that can be used without removing the cap.

Source: Richard Tomkins, 'Deodorants push ahead by a nose', *Financial Times*, 12 April 2002.

In the case of Harvey's Bristol Cream, the research involved blind taste testing.

HARVEY'S BRISTOL CREAM

Sometimes it's illuminating to demonstrate the kind of emotional baggage that products collect over the years. Ahead of a series of discussion groups, consumers were given samples, unbranded bottles of 'a new alcoholic drink' from a 'reputable manufacturer'. They were asked to keep diaries of how they used the drink, and what they thought of it.

Reactions were enthusiastic—it could be drunk neat or with mixers, with ice or at room temperature. When chilled and 'long', it was seen as outgoing, attractive, stylish, relaxing, and fun. Smooth, full-bodied, rich and herby were some of the words used to describe the taste.

In fact, the drink was Harvey's Bristol Cream, in an anonymous bottle. The brand was in desperate need of relaunch in the face of declining sales. Total sherry consumption in Britain had more or less halved to 2.5 million cases in the 12 years to 1994.

The research demonstrated that the product could have appeal to a wider market but it would have to be repositioned. The company decided that there was need for a packaging change. A design company came up with a cobalt-blue bottle with a black label. New research was commissioned, the results of which showed that consumers preferred the change.

The new bottle was launched in the autumn of 1994; in the first quarter of 1995, deliveries to the trade were up 46 per cent on the same period in 1994.

Source: *Marketing*, 19 October 1995.

FURTHER READING

Domegan, C. and Fleming, D., *Marketing Research in Ireland* (third edition), Dublin: Gill & Macmillan 2007.

Malhotra, N., *Marketing Research: An Applied Orientation* (fifth edition), Englewood Cliffs (NJ): Prentice-Hall 2007.

Morris, Clare, *Quantitative Approaches in Business Studies* (third edition), London: Pitman 1993.

Reilly, J., *Using Statistics*, Dublin: Gill & Macmillan 2006.

DISCUSSION QUESTIONS

1. Describe the steps in the research process you would adopt for each of the following projects:

    (*a*) A manufacturer wishes to research the market for a new fat-free, ready-to-serve trifle.

    (*b*) A tour operator feels that the 18–30-year-old market is potentially lucrative and wishes to establish the type of holiday package (or packages) that would be most attractive.

    (*c*) A theatre group wants to discover how often people visit the theatre and the types of performances they prefer.

    In your answers you should clearly indicate how you would go about carrying out the research, specify your population of interest, and state what information you would require from them and how you would go about collecting it.

2. You have to chair a discussion in a focus group on people's attitudes to recycling domestic waste, such as glass and plastic. Prepare an outline of how you would select people for the group and the discussion points you feel should be covered.

3. A distributor of eggs wishes to find out about household use and consumption patterns in their area. Design a questionnaire that would elicit information on the size and composition of the household, how often eggs are bought, where they are bought, consumption rates, how eggs are cooked or prepared, and general classification of respondents' age and social class.

4. Comment on the issues that can affect the validity of marketing research.
5. Explain the importance of ethics in marketing research. Give some examples of unethical activities.

REFERENCES

O'Leary, P., 'Qualitative research: where it's at, where it's going', *Irish Marketing Review*, vol. 6 (1993).

Warren, M., 'Killing the golden goose: survey research and the public', *Irish Marketing Review*, vol. 11 (1998), no. 2.

5

Market Segmentation, Targeting, and Positioning

This chapter discusses the segmentation, targeting, and positioning decisions that must be considered by marketers. Each is a step in the process of understanding the needs of the customer and attempting to match those needs with a marketing mix that the company can deliver capably. The process is part of the marketer's strategy: it enables the marketer to select the most profitable and viable customers to serve, to reach them with an offering that has a competitive advantage, and to communicate a position that is clearly perceived.

Research studies are often conducted to profile or construct segments. Segments may emerge from changing beliefs or values and as the following example indicates, it is not just product markets that can be segmented.

FOUR TYPES OF CATHOLICS IN IRELAND

A research study carried out by academics at UCD, found that there was little evidence of religious adventurism among Irish people. While the number of people who belong to minority religions, such as Buddhism or Hinduism, has increased, more than half of the adherents of minority religions are non-Irish nationals.

In relation to Catholicism, one of the researchers Professor Tom Inglis, considered that the lack of religious adventurism was 'related to the monopoly position that the Catholic church developed in the religious field from the 19th century. During this long reign, the church effectively managed to eliminate any form of opposition, or thinking outside the Catholic box'.

Qualitative research revealed that there were new types of Catholic, emerging in Ireland and that Catholics could be broadly grouped as:
1. Orthodox Catholics who remain loyal to the institutional Church.
2. Cultural Catholics who identify more with Catholic heritage and being Catholic.
3. Creative Catholics who not only choose between different Catholic beliefs, teachings and practices but mix these with non-Catholic beliefs and practices.
4. Individualist Catholics who identify themselves as Catholic, but do not believe in some of the Church's fundamental teachings.

Source: Patsy McGarry, 'Irish do not 'shop around' for religion, conference told', *Irish Times*, 31 October 2009.

MARKET SEGMENTATION

Market segmentation literally means the division of the market. It is based on the fact that most markets consist of buyers who have different needs and who cannot all be served with the same product offering. From a business point of view it is also based on the idea that by identifying buyers whose needs the firm can serve and by aiming a product at them, the marketer can be more effective and profitable. Segmentation is the first stage in the sequential process illustrated in fig. 5.1.

Figure 5.1: The segmentation, targeting, and positioning process

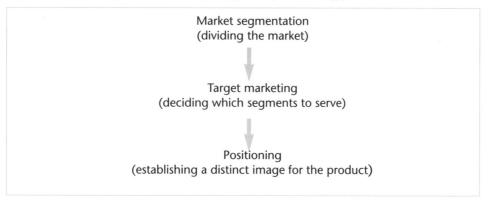

There are very few examples of products that are marketed in the same way to everyone. Marketers tend to divide up markets in an attempt to find the segment or segments they can best serve. Sometimes, when products are new to the market, they may be limited in their options or segments.

Market growth, however, may be dependent on producing variants and finding new segments. Few marketers attempt to be all things to all people, and many marketers engage in *product-differentiated marketing*, whereby two or more products with different features, benefits, options, or sizes are offered.

Environmental changes can mean that markets become more segmented. For example, in addition to normal milk, consumers' health and dietary needs are catered for with low-fat milk, calcium- and vitamin-enriched milk, and skimmed milk.

Markets in general are becoming more segmented. If there is only a small number of buyers it may be possible to customise the product for each buyer. For example, business-to-business marketers typically sell products to a small number of large customers, and their competitive advantage may be their ability to offer a customised product. For most other marketers, segmentation is a requirement, and, in general, buyers will be grouped into broad categories with similar needs. There is no single basis on which to do this, and the marketer should consider all the alternative ways of dividing up the market.

Bases for segmentation

A number of different bases are used for market segmentation, and most marketers will use a combination of them, as no single base may be completely descriptive of the segments that exist. The most commonly used segmentation variables include *geographical area*, *demographics*, *behaviour*, and *psychographics*.

Geographical segmentation involves dividing the market by geographical area. This can be done by region, city, postal district, county, or any number of sub-divisions. Census data can be used to establish population numbers in particular areas. Population statistics provided by the Central Statistics Office, for example, divide the Irish population by province, county, age, sex, and other descriptors. These can be used by marketers to assess the size and profile of the market for their products.

In the Irish market, many products and services are available nationally. There are, however, many regional and local brands and in some cases national marketers with regional brands. In the bread and confectionery market, for example, a small number of large bakeries control the market, but there is also a larger number of smaller bakeries that serve local markets.

Guinness has one significant regional brand, Macardle's ale. This has a strong market presence in the north-east, the product having been brewed in Dundalk since the last century. Similarly, Beamish and Crawford's Beamish brand has a strong presence in Munster.

Geographical segmentation is also useful for international marketers. While the Irish market is quite small and homogeneous, the international markets that many companies compete in are much larger and more diverse, and this diversity can be more manifest in different geographical areas.

Consider the geographic profile of Ireland's tourism source markets in table 5.6. This geographic breakdown enables Ireland's tourism marketers to target their marketing communications in particular countries. In addition, information is collected on other descriptors of the overseas visitor, such as age, socio-economic background, and interests. This can be used to design particular campaigns aimed at target segments, as fig. 5.2, which was used in the USA, illustrates.

Table 5.1: Where visitors to the island of Ireland came from, 2005–2009 (in 000s)

	2005	2006	2007	2008	2009	2009/2008 % difference
Great Britain	4,810	4,970	4,920	4,650	3,955	−15
Mainland Europe	1,991	2,350	2,706	2,669	2,404	−10
Germany	417	432	464	470	422	−10
France	320	370	407	423	399	−6
Italy	196	253	271	234	276	+18
Spain	178	219	267	262	264	+1
Nordic countries	166	190	259	228	175	−23
The Netherlands	169	167	169	162	143	−12
North America	993	1,065	1,097	992	937	−6
United States	890	965	995	885	842	−5
Canada	102	100	103	108	95	−12
Other areas	319	340	346	377	339	−13
Australia and New Zealand	154	153	167	176	153	–13
TOTAL	8,114	8,725	9,070	8,688	7,636	−12%

Source: Tourism Ireland.

Figure 5.2: Tourism Ireland advertising

Source: Tourism Ireland.

In addition to where visitors have come from, tourism research also seeks to clarify the reasons why people visit Ireland.

MOTIVATION FOR VISITING IRELAND

Research by Tourism Ireland reveals that while visitors to Ireland have a variety of motives for visiting, there are six broad motives that bring visitors here. These have been used to classify visitors into distinct groups:

1. Sightseers and culture seekers—these are visitors who like exploring the country's sights and finding out about its culture
2. Social adventurers—these are visitors who like meeting the locals and other new people during their visit
3. Outdoor actives—these are visitors who want to spend time on outdoor pursuits and being physically active
4. Luxury lovers—these are visitors who like luxurious accommodation and are willing to spend more on luxuries when on holiday
5. Affinity groups—these are visitors who like an organised element to the holiday and being with friends or a group of like-minded people
6. Family and loved ones—these are visitors who like spending time with family and loved ones on holiday.

Tourism Ireland has identified the first group as being the most important, estimating that it is the main motivation for about 60 per cent of visitors to Ireland. Its research reveals that people who have this motivation to visit:

*   are slightly older (42 per cent are aged at least 45)
*   have higher disposable income
*   travel with others, usually as part of a couple or with other family members
*   travel by air (82 per cent)
*   are more likely to be first-time visitors to Ireland
*   have problems with the high cost of living in Ireland (especially food and accommodation), weather, roads, and sign-posting.

Ninety-four per cent of sightseers and culture seekers leave Ireland happy, stating that they would unreservedly recommend Ireland as a holiday destination.

Source: Tourism Ireland

Demographic segmentation involves dividing the market according to demographic factors, namely age, sex, and income. In 2010 a research study commissioned by the Arts Council and the Temple Bar Cultural Trust profiled attendance at a variety of arts events and activities. One aspect of the demographic profile was the age of regular attendees.

Table 5.2: Percentage of regular attendees by age group

	15–24	25–34	35–44	45–54	55–64	65+
Theatre	14	18	18	17	15	17
Classical music	14	14	12	17	17	26
Contemporary dance	28	26	15	13	9	8
Folk concerts	10	20	12	22	21	14
Jazz	18	30	13	18	13	8
Opera	10	14	10	11	19	36
Art galleries	14	21	16	13	17	21
Ballet	13	21	16	13	17	21
Plays	14	19	16	19	16	16

Source: TGI Report, 'Arts Attendance in Ireland', June 2010.

Income is another possible demographic segmentation base. In general, income per capita will give an indication of the spending power of consumers in particular markets. This may be particularly relevant when examining international markets, as a low income per capita will indicate a poorer economy. Demographic segmentation may not be as useful to industrial marketers as they are to product or services marketers. Business-to-business marketers tend to sell to businesses or organisations rather than to individual consumers.

Behavioural segmentation is based on buyers' behaviour patterns. These can include the occasion when the buyer uses the product: for example, the business traveller may use a particular scheduled airline for normal business travel but when going on holiday may use a charter airline. Timing of use is also a basis on which the marketer can expand the use of the product. For instance, most consumers of Kellogg's Corn Fakes ate the product at breakfast, but the company mounted an advertising campaign to encourage consumers to use the product at other times of the day as a snack. Kellogg's hoped that this would open up a new segment for them. An Post produces St Patrick's Day cards every year to increase use of the postal service and in doing so has further segmented the greeting card market.

The *benefit* being sought by the consumer is another behavioural segmentation possibility. Consider the Swiss watch manufacturer Swatch, which has developed a range of watches suitable for casual, formal, sports, or fashion wear.

The *rate* of use is another segmentation base. Some consumers consume more of the product than others: for example, a beer company might segment the market into heavy, medium and light users. The economist Pareto discovered a universal law that held that 80 per cent of anything can be attributed to 20 per cent of its causes. If this law were applied to usage rates of a product, the marketer might find that 20 per cent of buyers account for 80 per cent of sales. Heavy users of a product will therefore be a small but highly significant segment in the form of sales and profits. Most airlines place a considerable emphasis on business travellers, who, compared with air travellers in general, buy a disproportionate number of first-class and business-class seats (Clemens, 1997).

Psychographics is essentially a technique for measuring people's life-style. (This is discussed in more detail in chapter 6.) As a segmentation variable it can be used to segment a market according to social class, life-style, personality, loyalty, or attitudes.

For marketing purposes, social class in Ireland is regarded as being derived from people's income. Table 5.3 gives the main grades used by marketers. These are sometimes used as a classification variable; however, they should be combined with other classification variables, as on their own they are of limited value.

Table 5.3: ABC1 social classification in Ireland

	Proportion of heads of household
AB (professional/managerial)	8.2%
C1 (white collar)	30.7%
C2 (skilled working class)	24.7%
DE (unskilled working class)	26.0%
Farmers	10.4%

Source: Lansdowne Market Research.

Life-style is probably a more meaningful basis for segmentation, as it builds up a broader profile of the buyer. It describes people's interests, activities, and opinions, and can be measured. Bord Bia research in 2009 indicated that Irish people were going out for meals less often.

SHARP RISE IN COOKING AT HOME

Research by Bord Bia in 2009 indicated a sharp increase in the number of people cooking at home, rather than going out for a meal, 63 per cent of people indicated that they cooked a meal at least a few times a week, compared with the 56 per cent who did so in 2005.

There was also an increase in the number of people who had taken cookery courses. One in five people interviewed in the Republic, Northern Ireland, and Britain, claimed to be entertaining more at home. Bord Bia considered that the changing trends were as a result of the recession.

The research also found that people were committed to buying local foods, with 71 per cent stating that they looked for a quality label when shopping, compared to 49 per cent in the UK. Country-of-origin labelling was significant for 71 per cent of people, compared to 50 per cent in 2001.

Bord Bia highlighted the research findings at its annual Food and Drinks Industry awards, where Kerry Foods received an outstanding achievement award for its Cheestrings product. Other winners were Oak Park Foods in Tipperary who produced an innovative bacon rib product and C&C for its development of the Bulmer's Pear Cider product. HighField nurseries won an award for its Living Flavour fresh herbs range, a product range that had been successfully repositioned to meet changing consumer demands.

Source: Seán Mac Connell, 'Sharp rise in cooking at home – Bord Bia', *Irish Times*, 6 November 2009.

Life-style profiling can be used to segment a market and is used by many advertising agencies in developing campaigns suitable for particular segments. People's interest in various products is influenced by their life-style, and many of the products they consume are an expression of life-style.

Personality can also be used for segmentation purposes. Marketers attempt to endow their products with a personality so that the consumer can relate to them. Car manufacturers, for example, use advertising to give different brands a personality; common traits used include 'secure', 'dependable', 'strong', 'sporty', and 'sophisticated'. Selected personalities will be suitable for the segments selected by the marketer: so marketers of children's products may use cartoon characters in their advertising to appeal to children.

Attitudes can also be used as a segmentation variable. A political party might segment its target voters according to their attitudes towards a particular candidate or particular political issue. Attitudes have a direct influence on people's behaviour, and knowing buyers' attitudes may help the marketer identify segments most likely to buy a particular product or service or to vote in a particular way.

The segmentation process

Applying the possible bases for market segmentation to the market gives the marketer a greater understanding of the needs and behavioural profile of buyers. The segmentation process describes how the organisation goes about segmenting its market. The stages in the process are illustrated in fig. 5.3.

Figure 5.3: The segmentation process

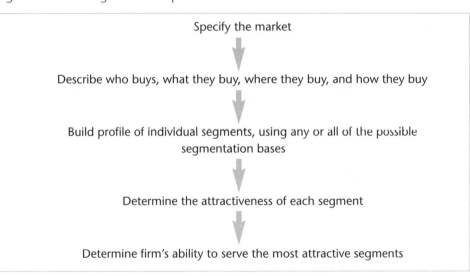

The process presents a sequential series of steps, the result of which should be a greater understanding of the profile of the segments in the market and the firm's ability to serve those segments profitably.

The process begins with the marketer specifying the market of interest and then attempting to outline specific aspects of buyers' behaviour, such as when, where, and how they buy. Any one, or all, of the possible bases for segmentation could be used to give a greater insight into the needs of particular segments. Primary or secondary research, or both, may be conducted to profile the behaviour and classification of individual segments.

To determine the attractiveness of segments and the firm's ability to serve them, the marketer should consider the following points.

- *It should be possible to measure or quantify the segment.* This implies a need for quantitative information on such aspects as the number of potential buyers in a particular segment, the quantity of the product they consume, or how often they consume. Quantifying the size and consumption profile of the segment enables marketers to determine whether they can meet demand levels or indeed whether the segment is large enough to be worth while.
- *Segments should be accessible to the marketer.* Accessibility can refer to geographical location, the ability of the marketer to gain access to the distribution channels used by the segment, and the ability of the marketer to communicate with the segment. If buyers are dispersed across a wide geographical area, if it is difficult to convince the distribution channel to stock the product, or if communication is expensive or difficult, the segment becomes less attractive to the marketer.
- *Segments should yield a profit to the marketer.* Quantification of the size of the segment will help the marketer to determine probable sales and profit levels. Small segments already well served by existing suppliers may not prove profitable. The profitability of individual segments will be determined by the cost of producing, delivering, and communicating the product to the segment. It will also be influenced by the actions of competitors.
- *The business should be able to attract, serve, and hold on to the segment.* This aspect, referred to as actionability, requires the firm to assess its ability to deliver value to the segment on a continuous basis. There will be a strong link between the firm's general marketing strategy and segment actionability. The firm must identify segments within which it has a competitive advantage.

There are a number of benefits to a firm that uses the segmentation process, not least a greater understanding of its ability to match the needs of the market with its own capabilities. Not every firm can serve all possible segments, and the most attractive segments may not be the best for the firm if competitive or market conditions are unfavourable or if the firm does not have the marketing capabilities to deliver the desired benefit to the buyer.

TARGET MARKETING

Target marketing follows on from the initial segmentation decision. Once the firm has segmented its market, it must decide which segment (or segments) it wishes to serve. *Targeting* means selecting particular customers or customer groups at which to aim the firm's marketing mix. It may involve the development of different marketing mixes for different segments. A targeted segment will be one in which the firm can have a competitive advantage. There must be a demand for the firm's product, and it must be possible for the firm to compete effectively with its offering.

Successful targeting helps the marketer fine tune and develop the product, as the Innocent brand discovered.

INNOCENT

Established in 1998 by three English entrepreneurs, the smoothie company Innocent had sales of €39.4 million in 2005. The company sells 90 per cent of its products in the UK and Ireland. The company's increased sales mirrored increased consumer interest in healthier food and drink products. The smoothies are made mainly with fruit and do not contain any additives or preservatives. The company creates its own recipes. It describes its target consumer as 'slightly more female, slightly more affluent, slightly younger'. The products sell at prices that push them to the high end of the fruit juice market. In addition to its healthy image, Innocent gives 10 per cent of its profits to charity. It concentrates on assisting projects in developing countries that enable sustainable farming.

In Ireland the brand has also become involved with charitable organisations. In 2010, for example, it invited consumers to knit small woolly hats for Innocent smoothie bottles, for each hat Innocent received, it donated €0.25 to Age Action Ireland.

Source: *Irish Times*, 26 August 2005; www.innocentdrinks.ie.

Many marketers have developed highly targeted marketing campaigns in response to the ever-increasing segmentation and sub-segmentation of markets. In broad terms, there are three approaches to target marketing: *undifferentiated marketing*, *differentiated marketing*, and *concentrated marketing*.

Undifferentiated marketing is essentially the mass marketing of the product. It is a suitable targeting approach where the needs of buyers are more or less the same and the market is not segmented. An example would be a campaign to encourage the population in general not to litter the countryside or to emphasise road safety to road users. In both cases the campaign would be aimed at a broad national audience.

With regard to consumer products and services and industrial products, few firms engage in undifferentiated marketing. This is mainly because these markets tend to be highly segmented, with different groups of buyers who have different needs.

Differentiated marketing is a characteristic of many firms and involves the development of a separate marketing mix for each segment the firm serves. A manufacturer such as Cadbury seeks to serve a number of different segments in the chocolate and confectionery market:

countline bars are aimed at the snack market, while boxed assortments are aimed at the gift or special occasion market, and drinking chocolate is aimed at the beverage market. Each segment, which has a different need profile, is catered for with a distinct product offering. Segments may differ in age or background characteristics, or there may be many similarities; however, the need in each case will be different. Thus the person looking for a gift is very different from the person seeking to replenish their supply of drinking chocolate; the same firm, however, can direct a particular product at each of these buyers.

Differentiated marketing is a feature of product, service, and industrial firms. In the detergent market, for example, Lever Brothers market the brand leader in the category, Persil. They also market the Surf brand, which is cheaper than Persil and aimed at the value-for-money segment (*Checkout Ireland*, April 1997).

Concentrated marketing means that even though there are a number of segments in the market, the marketer decides to concentrate on a particular one. Though there are several segments in the car market, for example, companies like Porsche and Ferrari tend to concentrate on high-value, prestige sports cars. There can be dangers inherent in relying on a concentrated approach: for example, in recessionary times the sales of high-value prestige products tend to decline.

Sometimes marketers may decide to enlarge their market coverage by identifying new niches. A concentrated approach can work very well for start-up ventures or newer companies that may not have the resources to serve a variety of segments and that can build up a loyal customer base by concentrating on a particular segment, whose needs they can serve. It may also be applicable to specialist industrial marketers that concentrate on serving a specific segment with their product, for example a manufacturer of packaging machinery for the dairy industry.

In many markets, consumer demand in different specialist segments requires the marketer to be able to keep up with the latest requirements. Consider the example of Dualit, which found that a retro product style helped it broaden its segments from the catering to the consumer market.

RETRO STYLE

The Dualit toaster was first produced in Britain in 1945. Initially a small electric toaster was produced for the domestic market, but the company switched to producing catering models when the market became intensely competitive. The company's toasters were the first to have in-built timers. They were also designed to be durable. Each product is made from start to finish by one worker who stamps a unique number on the base. If the product goes wrong it can be returned to that worker. The product is expensive; a basic model can cost £220.

By 2005, half the company's £10 million annual sales were to the catering trade. The successful return to the consumer market was attributed to a relaunch of the toaster in the 1980s. It is thought that the retro styling appealed to consumers, especially in the 1990s, when a retro-industrial style was popular in kitchen designs.

Source: Oliver Duff, 'Competitors turn up heat on Dualit, toast of the town', *Sunday Tribune*, 29 May 2005.

PRODUCT POSITIONING

Product positioning is the third stage in the process. It involves establishing a unique position for the product in the mind of the consumer. Product positioning is strongly related to perception and image. Marketers hope that the buyer will perceive their product to be unique and that they will have a distinctive image of the product and its benefits. The difficulty for buyers is that they are constantly being bombarded with advertising and promotions, all of which are attempts to position products distinctively. Marketers trying to find a distinct position must therefore compete for attention with all other competitors.

The product's positioning will be based on the value the marketing mix can deliver to the consumer. This value may be expressed in a number of ways, including product benefits, features, style, value for money, uniqueness, and sophistication. A number of broad positioning approaches are used by marketers; but whichever is used, the marketing mix must live up to the consumer's expectations: the position adopted must be realistic. Positioning decisions will be made in the context of general marketing and product strategies. Companies desire a distinct position not just for their products but for the company as well.

Positioning will be linked to ultimate product success in the marketplace. Failure to update or revitalise the positioning of a product can shorten its potential life in the market.

Positioning strategies

There are a number of product positioning strategies, and which one the marketer selects will depend on the nature of the buyer's needs. Positioning may be based on the features of the product, the benefits of the product, the occasion on which the product is used, the type of user, or the competitive conditions in the market.

Product features will be emphasised by some marketers to differentiate their products. Consider the example of the Eircom Break Free advertisement (fig. 5.4). Eircom credited

Figure 5.4: Product features—Eircom 'Break Free'

this campaign with persuading almost 200,000 Irish households to upgrade their home phones and purchase a new cordless model (IAPI Advertising Effectiveness Awards 2004).

Benefit positioning involves the marketer concentrating on the perceived benefits of the product. Benefits emphasised typically include value for money, quality, uniqueness, time and labour savings, and lifetime guarantees.

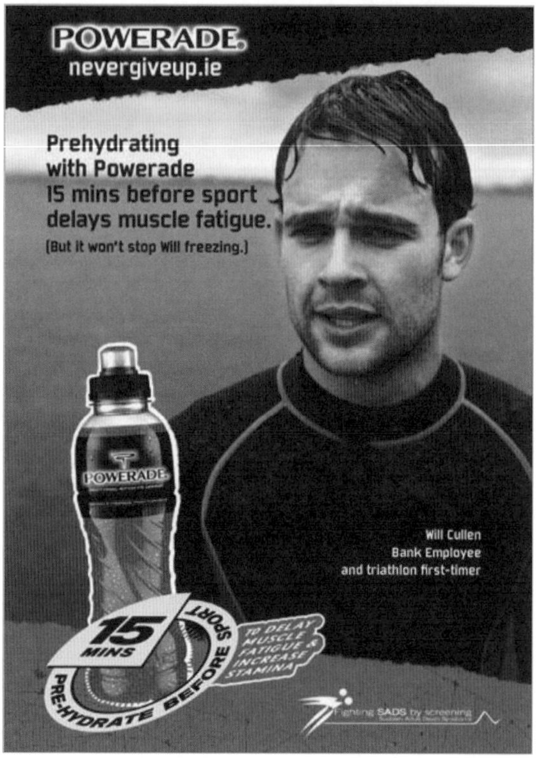

Consider the example of the advertisement developed by McCann Erickson for the Coca-Cola-owned Powerade brand. This sought to explain the benefits of pre-hydration, in other words hydrating before undertaking sport. Coca-Cola was facing stiff competition from rival brand Lucozade Sport and sought to differentiate itself from Lucozade by educating consumers on the importance of hydrating before exercise, not just during and after. The campaign involved the recruitment of a volunteer whose progress in training for the Irish National Triathlon Championships in 2007, was followed in the brand advertising. The campaign received a silver award in the IAPI Advertising Effectiveness Awards in 2008 (www.iapi.ie).

Figure 5.5: Product benefits – Powerade

Positioning on the basis of *usage occasion* is another possibility. Examples of usage occasion would include a fast-food restaurant emphasising the speed and convenience of its service for people in a hurry; and an insurance company that promises to deal with a particular emergency when the occasion arises. In 2007, for example, Fáilte Ireland ran a successful campaign encouraging Irish people to consider taking more holidays in Ireland (see fig. 5.6). The advertising campaign, which received an effectiveness award, was developed by the agency DDFH&B. Research conducted during and after the advertising was transmitted, revealed that there were high levels of awareness for the advertisements, people's perceptions of Ireland as a place for a holiday break improved and there was an increase in the number of people visiting the Discover Ireland website (www.iapi.ie).

The *type of user* can also be used as a positioning strategy. Heavy users can be encouraged to continue using the product, while medium and light users can be encouraged to increase their use. Guinness, for instance, was traditionally positioned as a male product; in the 1980s and 1990s, however, it aimed at the female market, who were either light or non-users. Kellogg's aim brands such as Special K at female users, while Frosties and Coco Pops are aimed at children (fig. 5.7).

Figure 5.6: Usage occasion—home holidays

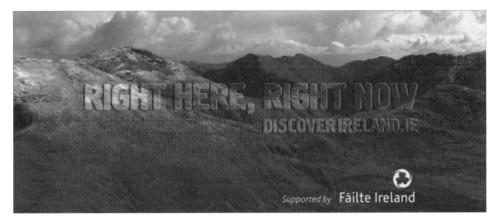

Figure 5.7: Type of user—Kellogg's cereals

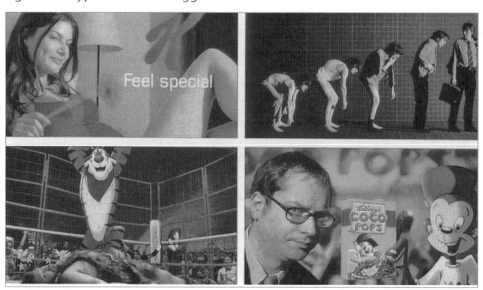

Competitive positioning is an extremely important aspect of a firm's marketing strategy. The competitive nature of most markets requires that firms differentiate their product offerings. Positioning can be used to demonstrate the advantages of one particular product over another, to reinforce what one competitor can do, or to motivate or reassure buyers.

Competitive positioning is in many ways the cutting edge of marketing practice. Firms may do battle with each other through their positioning: they may imitate each other, anticipate what their competitors are going to do, adapt their position as competitive conditions dictate, or use positioning in an effort to defend their market share. In general, firms use advertising as their main positioning tool.

Positioning needs to be flexible to changes not only in the competitive environment but also in the general business environment. Buyers' needs change and segment profiles change, so marketers may have to adapt or update their positioning accordingly.

In some cases, competitors position themselves directly against other competitors, usually in relation to differences in price or quality. As a positioning strategy this will only work if there is a difference and if the difference is perceived by the buyer. In the early 1980s, for example, British Airways sought to differentiate itself with the statement 'We'll take more care of you.' One of its rivals, British Caledonian, responded with 'We'll take less fare off you.' On the other hand, many marketers will not use positioning to take on competitors directly: instead they will concentrate on establishing a position that emphasises the value of their own product or service.

Positioning tends to evolve as markets and brands evolve. It is therefore a dynamic process. Firms need to be careful not to let their position become stereotyped or outdated. Johnson and Johnson, for instance, have successfully managed to position its baby care products, such as shampoo and soap, at adults; while the Lucozade brand, which traditionally was positioned as a product for people recovering from illness, has been repositioned as an energy-giving drink for active people. In both cases the firms were reacting to changes in the market and were seeking more profitable market segments to serve.

Positioning and product image are closely connected. On occasion, marketers may attempt to change the positioning if they feel the image needs to be changed, as Showerings, the cider producers, did in the mid-1990s.

A NEW IMAGE FOR CIDER

In 1990 Showerings decided they needed to change the image of cider. The popular image was of a product associated with underage drinking and not a drink to be seen with socially; some supermarkets were refusing to stock it. The company, which had an 85 per cent share of the cider market, became the principal force behind the establishment of the Cider Industry Council. The council began to lobby politicians and the media with information and videos on the product and the significance of the market. It also became involved in sponsoring efforts to combat underage drinking.

Research showed that cider was not in fact the favourite drink of underage drinkers, who were just as likely to consume other alcoholic drinks. The teenage 'cider party' image was strong, however, and Showerings decided that it needed to specifically promote its Bulmers brand. An advertising and promotional budget of €2.54 million a year was established, most of which was spent on television advertising, supported by cinema, poster, and radio campaigns. The advertising reflected the quality of the product and was aimed at the 18–34-year-old market. Long-neck bottles were launched in the pub trade to compete with higher-priced bottled lagers. The cider range was expanded in 1994 with the launch of the Coopers brand, which, unlike other ciders, has a head when poured, giving it a lager-like appearance.

The efforts of the Cider Industry Council and Showerings have seen the image of cider transformed. By 1995 the cider market was growing by 20 per cent per year, and Showerings' turnover had doubled to €89 million a year, 95 per cent of which was in the cider area.

Showerings continued to advertise the Bulmers brand in a series of advertisements that reinforced its brand values: craft, heritage, tradition, naturalness, and dedication. Market share continued to increase, from 6 per cent of the beer/cider market in 1997 to 10 per cent in 2000.

In 2004 the company decided to enter the cider market in Britain. It could not use the Bulmers brand name there because it was owned by Scottish and Newcastle breweries, so the Magners brand was introduced. The launch of this brand was successful and in 2006 it sold 30 million litres (in a total market of 470 million). One market analyst from Credit Suisse considered that serving the product on ice, coupled with the fact that the product had lower alcohol content, a higher price and a premium image, was the reason for its success.

In 2009, a new product, Bulmer's Pear was added to the range and this was followed in 2010 by Bulmer's Berry.

Sources: *Irish Times*, 30 June 1995; *Sunday Business Post*, 10 September 1995; IAPI Advertising Effectiveness Awards Case Study 2000; Alex Barker, 'Rediscovered taste for cider cheers brewers', *Financial Times*, 2 September 2006; www.bulmers.ie.

Positioning is strongly linked to product and corporate image.

In some cases marketers have to consider repositioning their products or brands. This usually happens as the result of declining sales, declining relevance of the product to buyers, or a need to update the product's image. The identification of new needs or new segments may also mean that the product or service has to be changed or reformulated and subsequently repositioned. It is important to note that if the product does not meet buyers' needs, a repositioning on its own will not work: the product's features or physical characteristics may need to be changed in a particular way.

Positioning maps

Positioning maps are a useful tool for marketers, especially in relation to competitive positioning decisions. Positioning maps are based on people's perception of particular products or services. They are useful when the marketer is examining the positions that competing products occupy in the consumer's mind and when attempting to find new positions that are unserved or poorly served by existing competitors.

Positioning maps can be constructed using information gathered from market research. Consider the example in the panel below, which demonstrates how the research in positioning might be carried out and how a positioning map is constructed.

The positioning map is a useful analytical tool for marketers. Any number of variables can be used for the axes on the map, and positions can be mapped on the basis of research into buyers' perceptions. The map can also be used to identify unserved positions in the market that may become new segments.

POSITIONING RESEARCH AND THE POSITIONING MAP

The marketer of a brand of orange juice (brand A) wishes to research how its brand is perceived relative to competitors. There are six brands in the market: A, B, C, D, E, and F. The marketer carries out market research to determine how consumers perceive the different brands according to factors such as taste, value for money, nutrition, and package convenience. Respondents are asked a series of questions to establish their perceptions.

In relation to the following brands of orange juice, please indicate on the scale your ratings in relation to the statements presented.

Brand A
The carton is easy to open and reseal.

Strongly agree   ☐   ☐   ☐   ☐   ☐   Strongly disagree

This brand is good value for money.

Strongly agree   ☐   ☐   ☐   ☐   ☐   Strongly disagree

This would be repeated for all other brands. The results would then be tabulated and the researcher would be in a position to develop a positioning map. Suppose a hundred consumers of orange juice were surveyed and the researcher decided to map all six brands according to these consumers' perceptions of ease of use of the carton and value for money. The results might look something like the positioning map below. One axis represents the scale value for money, while the other represents the ease of use of the carton. The position of each brand is mapped according to respondents' ratings. The map also indicates where the marketer of brand A might consider repositioning the brand; the A2 position could be reached if the carton were redesigned to improve ease of use and if buyers perceived this to be so. The A2 position would give brand A a positioning advantage over brand B, which is perceived to be better with regard to both value and ease of use. The marketer for brand A could thus investigate the cost of a package redesign to improve market position.

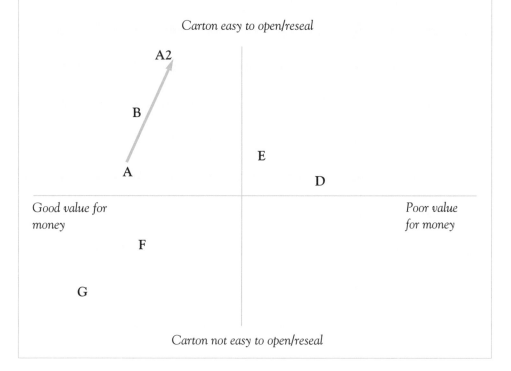

Carton easy to open/reseal

A2

B

E

A   D

Good value for money   *Poor value for money*

F

G

Carton not easy to open/reseal

FURTHER READING

McDonald, M., and Dunbar, I., *Market Segmentation*, London: Macmillan 1995.
Trout, J., and Rivkin, S., *Differentiate or Die*, New York: Wiley 2000.

DISCUSSION QUESTIONS

1. Outline the possible bases that a manager could use to segment the market for each of the following:
    (*a*) breakfast cereal
    (*b*) mobile phones
    (*c*) mechanical diggers

(*d*) garden sheds.
2. Explain the terms 'undifferentiated marketing', 'differentiated marketing' and 'concentrated marketing'. Give an example of a product or service that follows each approach.
3. Describe how the following marketers position their products:
    (*a*) Toyota
    (*b*) Tayto crisps
    (*c*) Permanent TSB
    (*d*) O_2.
4. Outline the variables you would use to construct positioning maps for each of the following:
    (*a*) brands of pasta sauce
    (*b*) brands of instant coffee
    (*c*) brands of canned fruit
    (*a*) brands of luggage.
5. List some products and services that you believe should consider repositioning. In each case, state what you feel the desired position should be.

REFERENCE

Clemens, J., 'Business flyers make profits soar', *Marketing Week*, 7 August 1997.

6

Understanding Consumer Behaviour

Marketing requires an understanding of the needs and wants of buyers. To achieve this, marketers must attempt to gain insights into buyers' behaviour. Understanding the reasons why people behave as they do in relation to the marketer's offering, or how they might behave in the future, helps the marketer make decisions.

Behaviour is not always predictable, and gaining an appreciation and understanding of buyers' behaviour can be interesting, complex, and puzzling. It can never be taken for granted that buyers will behave in a particular way, as behaviour is determined by both personal and social factors.

Behaviour always has a reason, even though it may appear illogical or irrational. The key to understanding behaviour is avoiding judgment on what may appear irrational and identifying the factors that determine behaviour in the market. Marketing strategies will be developed on the basis of behavioural determinants. In recent years, much has been written about the ways in which consumer behaviour is affected by recession, as the following example shows.

CHANGES IN CONSUMER BEHAVIOUR DURING RECESSION

The international consulting firm, Mc Kinsey, carried out research on changes in consumer behaviour in the United States during the recessionary period that began in 2008. Naturally, many consumers had become more price sensitive and had reduced consumption. The research also found that because many consumers had started to buy cheaper brands, they were learning to live with less expensive products. Of those consumers who had switched to buying cheaper products, the majority found that they performed better than expected and the premium brands were, therefore, perceived not to be worth the money. The researchers cautioned marketers not to assume a rapid rebound in consumer behaviour as had happened following previous recessions. McKinsey felt that the changed perception of cheaper brands in categories such as bottled water, beer, processed meats, sliced cheese, cold and allergy medicines, and facial moisturisers, could mean that consumers would see no reason to return to buying premium brands. Many consumers found that they no longer needed the benefits of the more expensive brands, their willingness to pay more, was therefore reduced. This research also echoed an earlier McKinsey study on consumer electronics in the United

States which found that 60 per cent of consumers were more interested in a core set of basic product features at a reasonable price, rather than the latest and greatest technology at a more expensive price. Some marketers had begun to take action, Procter & Gamble for instance, introduced Tide Basic in the US, after sales of Tide declined. Tide Basic was a cheaper version of the leading detergent brand.

Sources: Betsy Bohlen, Steve Carlotti, and Liz Mihas, 'How the recession has changed US consumer behaviour', McKinsey Quarterly.com, December 2009; Andre Dua, Lisa Hersch, and Manu Sivanandam, 'Consumer electronics get back to basics', McKinsey Quarterly.com, October 2009; 'Tide turns 'basic' for P&G in slump', *Wall Street Journal*, 6 August 2009.

There may be many underlying reasons for consumer behaviour patterns. Kellogg's, for example, have 60 per cent of the Irish breakfast cereal market, with annual sales of €100 million. The Irish eat more breakfast cereal per capita than any other country in the world (*Sunday Times*, 26 February 2006). There are probably several reasons for this, including the brand's history in the market, consumer tastes, convenience, and brand advertising. In this chapter we will examine the behavioural variables that might help explain why some brands and products enjoy such success.

THE NATURE OF CONSUMER BEHAVIOUR

The study of consumer behaviour gives the marketer an insight into how buyers establish a need for the product, how they identify and evaluate options, and the factors that influence their decision-making and ultimate choice. Consumer behaviour has been defined by Solomon, Bamossy, Askegaard, and Hogg (2010):

> The study of the processes involved when individuals or groups select, purchase, use or dispose of products, services, ideas or experiences to satisfy needs and desires.

Much of the theory that underlies buyer behaviour derives from the disciplines of psychology and sociology. Psychology is the study of human and animal behaviour, while sociology is the study of the collective behaviour of people in groups. In addition to these two disciplines, economics, geography, and history have also contributed to the understanding of why we behave as we do.

In 2010 for example, research indicated that Irish shoppers were buying more organic food products (see panel on page 157).

Consumer behaviour is a process of which the physical purchase of the product is only one stage. Many underlying influences, both internal and external, influence the consumer's decision. Market research can be used to assist the marketer in the process of understanding consumers' behaviour: research techniques can be used to assess and measure aspects of buyers' behaviour such as motivation, perception, and attitude. Consider the example in fig. 6.1, which could be used to measure respondents' attitudes to flying with an airline. The results of research exercises such as this give the marketer an overview of how buyers evaluate the product; they also help explain why buyers engage in different behaviour patterns.

MORE BUYING ORGANIC FOOD

Research conducted by Bord Bia in 2010, indicated that organic food is being purchased by a growing number of Irish shoppers every year. The research showed that 33 per cent of Irish grocery shoppers purchased an organic product in the week prior to the survey. This was a 2 per cent increase on figures for 2008 when this figure had been 31 per cent.

The research found 30 per cent of these consumers are purchasing more organic food than in the previous year. Sixty-two per cent were buying the same amount of organic food.

Fruit and vegetables accounted for the most popular purchased categories, but there had been a growth in the popularity of both dairy and meat, with 73 per cent and 69 per cent of organic buyers respectively purchasing in the past year.

Twenty per cent of non-organic buyers said they were 'likely or very likely' to buy organic products in the future.

Source: Seán MacConnell, 'More buying organic food', *Irish Times*, 14 September 2010.

Figure 6.1: Evaluative scale for measuring attitudes towards an airline

Compared with other airlines, flying with airline A is:

Good value	[1]	[2]	[3]	[4]	[5]	Poor value
Convenient	[1]	[2]	[3]	[4]	[5]	Inconvenient
Stressful	[1]	[2]	[3]	[4]	[5]	Relaxing
Pleasant	[1]	[2]	[3]	[4]	[5]	Unpleasant

CONSUMER SOVEREIGNTY

One of the fundamentals of marketing is that the consumer is sovereign. This implies that the consumer will ultimately make up his or her own mind about the purchase of a product. As we have seen in chapter 1, this decision will be needs-based. The marketer can attempt to influence the consumer's decision-making process with a product offering, but ultimately the decision is made by the consumer. This is an important principle: buyers are not unthinking beings that can be easily led or can be dictated to by marketers.

The consumer will not act in a way contradictory to his or her own goals or motives, though motivation and behaviour can undoubtedly be influenced by the activities of marketers. The consumer will consider the alternatives presented by the marketer but will ultimately make up his or her own mind about whether or not to buy.

In making up their own minds, consumers can exhibit varying degrees of involvement.

Involvement

Involvement refers to the perceived importance of an object or event to the person. In general, people will become more involved in decision-making regarding products that have high personal relevance and involve high risk, for example cars, computers, or clothes. Other product decisions will have low levels of involvement, for example products such as light bulbs, matches, or toilet rolls. Where consumers are making a high-involvement decision they will generally look for more options, carry out more evaluation, and look for advice.

For low-involvement decisions, consumers are less likely to engage in extensive search and evaluation. In many instances they will buy products essentially on grounds of convenience. A consumer may prefer a particular brand of milk, for example, if given a choice; but if they visit their local shop to buy milk and find that it does not stock the preferred brand, they are unlikely to leave to search for the preferred brand elsewhere.

In industrial buying situations it can be argued that employees are in fact being paid to make involved decisions, for example an analysis of different tenders from possible suppliers. In this situation the employee uses professional skills to make a decision that may involve high or low levels of involvement, depending on the product in question.

The level of consumer involvement is determined by a combination of personal and situational factors. It will depend on the importance of the decision to the consumer and the context in which the decision is being made.

Consumer involvement is particularly important in understanding the power of branding. Consumers may use the brand as a strategy for risk avoidance. They may become brand-loyal as a means of reducing tension and avoiding having to make involved decisions. Marketers may use their brand advertising to inform the consumer how their brand can take the risk out of potentially involved decisions. One brand that has been particularly successful and that positions itself as the best product in an appearance-conscious market is Gillette. As the following panel demonstrates, Gillette paid particular attention to researching buyers' behaviour, creating a powerful brand, and the development of new products.

GILLETTE: A CUT ABOVE THE REST

For the international toiletries giant Gillette, the success of the Sensor razor posed a problem. The razor might indeed be 'the best a man can get'—as people were constantly reminded in television advertising—but wasn't the hapless shaver entitled to equally mould-breaking toiletries to add style to his bathroom shelf? What could be done to make it more exciting?

Gillette dominates the wet shave market, with an estimated share of 60 per cent of worldwide sales. Gillette earned this dominant position through large investments in research and development and through careful consumer research. Every day about 10,000 men carefully record the results of their shaves for Gillette. Five hundred of these men shave in special cubicles under carefully controlled and monitored conditions, including observation through one-way glass and video cameras. Shavers record the precise number of nicks and cuts. In certain cases researchers even collect sheared whiskers to weigh and measure. As a result, Gillette scientists know that an average man's beard grows 0.4 mm a day. During an average lifetime a man will spend 3,350 hours scraping 27½ feet of whiskers from his face. Gillette even uses electron microscopes to study blade surfaces and miniature cameras to analyse the actual shaving process.

Gillette maintains that it has never been concerned with the low end of the market: status-seeking men, it believes, will always buy a 'classy' product. Most men, it considers, see shaving as a serious business and their appearance as a matter of importance. It also believes that men will pay more for a superior shaving product.

Since the safety razor was patented by Gillette in 1904, the company has always been innovative in product development. The safety razor changed shaving from being a tedious, difficult, time-consuming and often bloody task that was endured at most twice a week. Only the rich could afford to have a barber shave them daily. The safety razor gained wide acceptance during the First World War, when a free razor was given to every American soldier. In this manner millions of men just entering shaving age were introduced to the daily self-shaving habit.

Gillette was the first to develop the double-blade razor in 1971, the first with swivel-head razors in 1977 (the Contour), and in 1985 the first with the Contour Plus, which incorporated a lubricating strip for a smoother shave. The Sensor, launched in the late 1980s, was a development of the Contour and was designed with a more advanced lubricating strip and swivel head. The Sensor and a subsequent development, the Sensor Excel, were very successful, and Gillette increased its share to 71 per cent of the North American and European markets. The company's sales grew from $3,000 million in 1986 to $66,100 million in 1997.

Gillette was not the first to introduce disposable razors: this was done by Bic in Europe in 1975. Gillette introduced the first disposable in the United States the following year.

The morning shaving ritual continues to occupy a special place in most men's lives: it affirms their masculinity, and the first shave remains a rite of passage into manhood. A survey by New York psychologists reported that though men complain about the bother of shaving, 97 per cent of the sample would not want a cream that would permanently rid them of facial hair.

Though shaving may require less skill and danger than it once did, many men still want the razors they use to reflect their beliefs that shaving remains a serious business. A typical man regards his razor as an important personal tool, a kind of extension of self, like an expensive pen or set of golf clubs.

In 1991 Gillette launched a new range of shaving foams, gels, aftershave moisturiser, deodorants, and anti-perspirants, known as the Gillette Series. Gillette had already been a producer of shaving foams, but the new range was designed to be a complete revamp of pre-shaving and post-shaving products, as well as an entry for Gillette to the lucrative men's toiletries market. The award-winning containers made sparkling use of bare metal in their silver-and-blue colour scheme to suggest steel and water. Fresh thinking was given to the plastic actuator and cap to give a different look from the general run of aerosols. Futuristic graphics were used, and the products were advertised using strong life-style imagery as 'the best a man can get'. Almost all the products in the range have achieved number 1 or number 2 market share in their various categories.

In 1998, after spending $1,000 million in research and development, Gillette launched the Mach 3, a razor with three blades, each of which is 10 per cent thinner than previous blades and is made from a combination of steel and diamond-like carbon. The company planned to spend $300 million marketing the new product. The selling price was 35 per cent more than the existing Sensor Excel, and it was expected that the Mach 3 would ultimately eat into the sales of the Sensor Excel.

In 2006 Gillette launched the Fusion, which offered five blades compared to the three on the Mach 3, and also had a trimmer blade on the back. By this year, blades and razors accounted for more than two-thirds of Gillette's annual profits.

In the summer of 2010, Gillette introduced the Fusion ProGlide which it claimed gave the smoothest shave to date. The product had thinner blades than the Fusion and was launched in the North American market.

Gillette launch a new razor every seven or eight years, usually followed by increases in the price of its older razors to persuade men to switch to the new model. This strategy made the Mach 3, which was introduced in 1998, the best selling men's razor product of all time.

Sources: R. Cobb, 'Gillette: a cut above the rest', *Marketing*, 30 September 1993; T. McEnaney, 'Spending $1 billion to be a cut above the rest', *Sunday Tribune*, 19 April 1998; 'Gillette sharpens up', *Sunday Business Post*, 17 May 1998; Sarah Ellison and Charles Forelle, 'Gillette's smooth bet: men will pay more for five blade razor', *Wall Street Journal*, 15 September 2005.

The level of involvement will play a role in determining the amount of time and effort the consumer devotes to the buying process. This process can be explained and illustrated using a model of consumer behaviour.

A MODEL OF CONSUMER BEHAVIOUR

A basic model of buyer behaviour was developed by Howard and Sheth (1969) and is illustrated in fig. 6.2. This is a stimulus-response model: it proposes that the buyer is stimulated by marketing and other environmental factors and makes a response. The 'black box' describes all the psychological and decision factors specific to the buyer. These are a combination of personal traits and characteristics and the way in which the buyer makes decisions.

Figure 6.2: 'Black box' model of buyer behaviour

Marketing and other stimuli	Buyer's black box		Buyer's response
	Buyer's traits	Buyer's decision process	Product choice
Marketing mix			Brand choice
Economic			Outlet choice
Political			Purchase timing
Cultural			Purchase amount
Technological			

This basic model of buyer behaviour is a useful introduction to the process of understanding how we make decisions, the influences that may come into play, and the possible responses the buyer may make. The model shows that buyers do not make their decisions in a vacuum: most people will be influenced by a variety of sources. Even when consumers have made up their mind about what to buy, factors can intervene to change that decision. They may have seen the advertisements for a particular brand, may have processed the information received, and may have a positive intention to buy, but they may not end up buying the product. Other factors can intervene so that intention does not translate into purchase. For example, when the consumer reaches the supermarket they discover that a competing brand is on special promotion, and they opt for it instead.

The model, therefore, will not be a perfect description of behaviour, but it does give marketers a basic structure for understanding how buyers make their decisions and the factors that influence them. The consumer's decision process will be based on problem solving; usually our purchases occur as a result of a problem. There are three main perspectives on how consumers make decisions. Problems may be solved rationally (where we calmly and carefully weigh up the pros and cons before making our decision). In other cases we make decisions as a result of behavioural influence, for example learned responses to environmental cues as in making an impulse decision. The experiential perspective suggests that we won't make a rational decision but will respond in a more emotional way.

Marketing and other stimuli

The primary stimulant to buyers will be the firm's marketing mix—the bundle of benefits and added values that the marketer hopes will stimulate the buyer into action. (The components of the marketing mix—product, price, promotion, and place—are dealt with in chapters 7–10.) Suffice it to say that the marketing mix should be capable of meeting the buyer's needs if it is to have a chance of consideration.

In chapter 3 the factors in the marketer's environment were discussed. These environmental forces affect the firm's ability to meet the customer's needs. Changes and developments in the economic, demographic, technological, political, legal, or natural environments can influence buyers' decision-making.

Environmental factors that influence consumers' behaviour

As the 'black box' model illustrates, a number of factors influence and can stimulate the consumer.

Cultural factors

Human behaviour is learned. We learn our basic sets of values, perceptions, beliefs, and attitudes from our family, but also from the culture of our country. *Culture* describes the way of life or personality of a society. It exists to serve the needs of society and has an influence on consumers' behaviour within that society.

Culture has an influence on defining values. In one research study dealing with values, Ireland emerged as exceptional and idiosyncratic (Turley, 1995).

There are a number of different aspects to culture. These include:

- material culture: economics, technology
- social institutions: religion, education, politics
- human culture: values, beliefs, attitudes
- aesthetics: music, folklore, tradition.

Cultural analysis is relevant for marketers, not just in their home market but also in international markets, where different influences may affect how the product is marketed. Culture is dynamic in nature, though change tends to be a slow process and is heavily influenced by other cultures, by travel, and by the media.

In Ireland, as in other industrialised countries, cultural changes have taken place, and these can be reflected in our buying behaviour. Increased income levels have led to growth in the demand for many products and services. Consumers appeared to place more value on convenience, and this led to increase in consumption of products such as ready-to-serve meals and home delivery services.

The Henley Centre of Ireland produced some research findings in 1992 that indicated that the Irish adult population could be divided into five distinct groups, based on identity (Henley Centre, 1992). The research is specific to Ireland, and the identities are linked to cultural factors.

IRISH IDENTITIES IN THE 1990s

Young Irelanders (26 per cent)
Generally young people who are optimistic about the future in Ireland and believe that products made in Ireland are usually better than those from other countries. They have above average ability in the Irish language, which they believe will become more significant in the future.

Envious neighbours (26 per cent)
Also mainly young people. They believe that life in other European countries is more stylish and glamorous than in Ireland, and only a minority see themselves as having a future in Ireland. They do not think that Irish will become more important in the future.

Anglo-Hibernians (21 per cent)
The most affluent group, strongly based in Leinster, with a higher proportion of males than females. They are very confident about their future, are not envious of other European countries, and also think that Irish will increase in importance in the years ahead.

Future pessimists (18 per cent)
These see themselves as having no future in Ireland, and do not believe that Irish will become more important in the future.

Old romantics (9 per cent)
These show many of the characteristics of the 'Young Irelander' group but are older and more certain of the superiority of Irish goods. They are convinced of the increasing importance of Irish, but virtually none are capable of speaking or reading it.

Source: Henley Centre of Ireland, 1992.

The Henley Centre research presents some interesting points for marketers. For example, the groups could potentially be used as a basis for segmentation. The perception of Irish-made products undoubtedly influences their purchasing, and their views on Irish could possibly be of significance with regard to communication strategies or the media they may consume, for example TG4.

Social factors

Social factors are any influences that groups of which one is a member, or that one comes in contact with, have on the consumer's behaviour. People interact with other people in domestic, work, and social settings, and these interactions have an influence on our behaviour. A group that serves as a point of comparison for the individual and influences buyers' behaviour is known as a *reference group*.

There are both primary and secondary reference groups. *Primary reference groups* have most influence and include the person's family, friends, neighbours, and fellow-workers or fellow-students. *Secondary reference groups* usually have less influence and typically include churches, professional associations, and trade unions. It is also possible to have *aspirational reference groups*, which are groups of which the person is not actually a member but would like to be, for example a professional institute. The individual may engage in behaviour in an effort to join, for example by pursuing a course of study.

Opinion-leaders are referents who are the first to buy new products or to accept new ideas and whose opinion is sought by others. They play an important role in the adoption process for new products because of the influence they can have over other consumers, who, because of perceived risk, may be *opinion-seekers*.

The family is one of the most important reference groups, because it is within the family that people become socialised. The family, as a group, is also a significant purchasing unit, with many products being specifically marketed to families: consider 'family pack' products in the supermarket, or family holidays. The term *family* can also be interpreted quite widely.

Whatever its composition, the different members of the family can have varying amounts of influence on purchasing decisions. Some decisions will be husband-dominant, some will be wife-dominant, and some will be joint. One research study (Mohan, 1995) examined husbands' and wives' perceptions of their roles in the purchase of six chosen consumer products or services. It found that some decisions were more husband-dominant (lawnmower, car, and television), while the wife's influence was stronger for sitting-room suite and washing machine. There was a high level of joint decision-making for mortgage choice.

Where there are children in the family they will also influence family decisions. Many advertisements for food products, entertainment, toys, and holidays are specifically aimed at children, who can be quite a sceptical audience. A research study in 1988 drew some conclusions on how sceptical children are of the claims advanced in television commercials. It argued that successful campaigns are contingent on advertisers understanding the stages in the child's cognitive growth (Turley and Gallagher, 1988).

In the 1960s Walls, which marketed ice cream in Britain, segmented the children's market into three groups: 'adventurers', 'hungry Horaces', and 'little madams' ('Washes Whiter', Channel 4, 1991). They had found that the product type bought by the child was influenced by personality. 'Adventurers' liked shaped ice cream products, such as space rockets or characters, while 'hungry Horaces' were price-sensitive and wanted as much ice cream as possible for their money. 'Little madams' were girls who could relate to slightly more sophisticated products. Walls developed and aimed particular products at each of these segments.

In addition to family groups, one research study conducted in the United Kingdom revealed that there were significant numbers of single people and that they could be segmented by age.

SINGLETONS

Research in the UK in 2006 indicated that about 38 per cent of all 16–64-year-olds are single. This figure was predicted to grow to 45 per cent by 2010. The research was conducted by the British media agency Carat. The definition of a singleton was someone who was single, divorced, widowed, or separated, and did not plan to have a baby, marry or live with their partner in the next 12 months. Singletons tended to be more whimsical spenders than those in committed relationships. Products can be tailored to single people as part of an overall marketing strategy, for example Tesco's meals for one or Goodfellas' solo pizza portions. Carat identified four distinct segments of single consumers:

- social butterflies—aged 16–24, live at home with their parents
- achiever beavers—aged 25–34, more likely to be female, making the most of their youth and choosing success at work ahead of marriage
- pippa pans—women between 35 and 44 who are concerned about getting old
- silvertons—aged 45–64, tend to be happy with their single status.

The researchers felt that, overall, marketers were failing to cater adequately for single people and were therefore missing out on a lucrative group of people who, because of their relative lack of responsibilities, tend to spend more money on themselves.

Source: Ciar Byrne, 'Opportunity knocks in thriving singleton niches', *Sunday Tribune*, 29 January 2006.

The buyer's decision-making process

The central component of the model of buyer behaviour is the black box. Understanding the components of the black box involves examining the buyer's decision-making process and the personal and psychological forces that have an impact.

In trying to understand the buyer's decision-making process, it is useful to examine the 'hierarchy of effects' model, which proposes that people go through a number of sequential stages in making decisions (Dewey, 1910). The sequence can vary, depending on the level of involvement. Fig. 6.3 illustrates the hierarchy of effects decision-making model.

Problem recognition

Problem recognition can be stimulated in many ways. The consumer may feel hungry and want something to eat; they go to the fridge and find it is empty, and then decide to visit a local delicatessen. Problem recognition can also be stimulated by advertising and promotions, by social trends, or by sight, smell, or other stimuli.

Problem recognition will occur when the consumer notices that the present state of affairs is not the ideal or desired state. Because of this they will be motivated to do something about it. Depending on the importance of the problem to the person, a certain level of involvement will also be activated.

Figure 6.3: Hierarchy of effects decision-making model

Search for information

The amount of searching the consumer engages in will depend on the degree of risk involved. For routine purchases of staple products, this process will be limited and will depend more on factors such as availability. For purchases of consumer durables or high-involvement products in general, the search process may be quite extensive.

Evaluation of alternatives

The consumer will evaluate alternatives using three main criteria:

(*a*) the specifications the consumer sets
(*b*) the standards the consumer sets
(*c*) the expectations the consumer has.

These criteria will be heavily influenced by social factors and by advertising. Evaluative criteria will be based on beliefs. The consumer's beliefs will shape their attitude to the product, which can be positive or negative. Attitudes play an important part in the determination of purchasing intention; positive attitudes towards a particular product make it more likely that the consumer will buy it.

Choice

The consumer chooses not only what product to buy but also where to buy it. Choice involves evaluating alternative actions or behaviour and forming a behavioural intention or plan to engage in the selected behaviour. The consumer may use a number of choice criteria, for example price, features, quality, or guarantees.

Outcome

The outcome of the consumer's decision will either be satisfaction, which may lead to repeat purchases and positive word-of-mouth communication, or dissatisfaction, which will usually not result in repeat purchases and may lead to negative word-of-mouth communication. Marketers need to be just as concerned about the evaluation the consumer makes after the purchase as they are about the evaluation made when alternatives were being considered before purchase.

High involvement v. low involvement

Generally, for high-involvement decisions the consumer will follow the five stages described in fig. 6.3 above. The model can, however, be modified for low-involvement decisions, as fig. 6.4 demonstrates.

Figure 6.4: Hierarchy of effects for low-involvement decisions

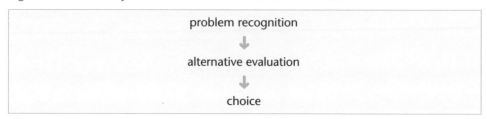

In the case of low-involvement decisions, problem recognition is typically non-complex. If, for example, the consumer runs out of milk, alternative evaluation may involve quite a limited search, and choice may depend more on factors such as availability or convenience than on more complex factors, such as choice of retail outlet.

Personal factors and psychological factors

The second component of the black box is the characteristics of the individual. These can be broadly described as personal and psychological.

Personal factors

Age: Consumers' tastes and behaviour will vary with age. For example, breakfast cereals aimed at children, such as Kellogg's Frosties or CocoPops, are sweet-tasting and use cartoon characters to communicate the benefits of the product. Cereals aimed at adults, such as Kellogg's All Bran, stress the importance of dietary fibre.

Occupation: In Ireland the ABC1 socio-economic classification, which is used predominantly by marketers, is based on the occupation of the head of the household (see page 142). There are two other scales derived by the Central Statistics Office from the census of population, but these are rarely used. Market segmentation may be based on occupation, and products may be developed for specific occupations. For example, advertising campaigns for cellular phones stress the benefits to people whose jobs may require them to travel or to work at different sites. Many computer programs have been developed with specific occupations in mind, for example accountants. Care has to be exercised in using social classification as a means of segmentation. The marketer should not stereotype buyers on grounds of social class. Also, many products are consumed by all classes.

Life-style: This refers to the person's pattern of living in the world, expressed in their activities, interests, and opinions. It is influenced by culture, values, demographics, social class, reference groups, and family, as well as by individual psychological characteristics.

The concept is widely used by marketers in segmentation and positioning decisions.

Life-styles are identified using the AIO (activities, interests, opinions) framework. Typical components used in AIO analysis are given in table 6.2. These can be used as the basis for measuring life-style, and researchers can build a profile of buyers on the basis of their activities, interests, and opinions. This can be used by marketers when making positioning decisions.

Life-style is particularly used in marketing communications, in the belief that people will identify with obvious life-style settings used in advertising, for instance. In theory, if a person identifies with the life-style portrayed in the advertising, it increases the probability that they will buy the product.

Table 6.1: Typical AIO life-style components

Activities	Interests	Opinions
work	family	themselves
hobbies	fashion	social issues
entertainment	food	education
sports	home	future
holidays	community	politics
shopping	achievement	culture

Life-style trends are increasingly a source insight into changes taking place in the marketplace. One research study considered the life-style trends that were relevant to the marketing of food and drink products.

THE BORD BIA CONSUMER LIFE-STYLE TRENDS PROGRAMME

Bord Bia, the Irish Food Board, has been researching consumer life-style trends to provide a framework for the marketers of food and drink products to improve understanding and make sense of how consumers' needs and wants are changing. The research has been developed in partnership with the Henley Centre, a research and consultancy firm. The research has focused on global trends, important for Irish marketers as they attempt to market their products in international markets. Both quantitative and qualitative research is conducted, for example the Henley Centre has a Global Streetscapes Network which involves interviews with independent, discerning, and culturally connected individuals in 40 cities around the world. Additional qualitative research has been carried out in the UK and Ireland to validate the global trends.

The research has concluded that there were six broad trends that were affecting consumers' attitudes, needs, wants, and behaviours. They suggest that marketers have responded to these trends with new products, advertising themes, and the development of positioning strategies. Researching the six trends involved Henley exploring people's agreement with the following six statements.

Trend 1: Life on-the-go—'I need to be able to cope with the demands of my busy day'

This trend is driven by changing work patterns, increased urbanisation and mobility and the rise of new communication technologies. As a result consumers are searching for simple solutions, greater convenience, energy control, time out, and short-cut language. The Flahavan's brand (see chapter 1) is a good example of a brand that has capitalised on this trend, while various energy drink brands can also be included.

Trend 2: Living life to the full—'I want experiences that help me get the most out of life'

Forces which affect this trend include increased consumer affluence, greater knowledge of the world's opportunities, demographic changes (for example, increased life expectancy), and changing work patterns. Increased travel and consumption of products such as wine might be considered as examples of this trend.

Trend 3: Making a difference—'I want to feel good about the choices I make and do my bit when I can'

Issues such as rising globalisation, growing awareness of environmental and social issues, declining trust in governments and big business, and rising consumer affluence have shaped this trend. Examples such as the success of Fairtrade and increased consumption of free range and organic foods illustrate this trend.

Trend 4: Quest for health and wellness—'I want to manage or improve my health and wellness'

Previous generations relied on governments to provide healthcare and regulatory bodies to inform them about issues such as food safety. The research indicated that many question whether these institutions can be trusted. Additionally, media focus on health and well-being; scientific advances, ageing populations, and increased availability of information are the driving forces for this trend. Foods with enhanced properties such as added vitamins or minerals, alternative medicines and increased numbers of people engaging in yoga are examples of this trend in action.

Trend 5: Smart shoppers—'I like to make smart choices when I buy things and want to feel I'm getting a good deal'

Consumers are becoming more price sensitive and are conscious of getting value for money. Growing market competition and greater access to information has given people increased power to compare prices, shop around, and demand more for their money. The basics of life are getting cheaper and luxury items are becoming more accessible. The internet is making it easier for consumers to shop around, so comparison websites such as tripadvisor.com are increasingly being used. It is also likely that this trend has benefitted retailers such as Lidl and Aldi.

Trend 6: The real thing—'I am looking for the real thing; I care where it came from and how it is made'

This trend focuses on issues such as provenance, fair trade, and ethical production. Comfort and reassurance can come from products that have integrity, history, and an honest approach to life. Stories about the product or brand, resonate with consumers who are looking for something 'real' among a mass of faceless global brands. In 2009, for example, Guinness sought to establish 29 September as 'Arthur's Day', to celebrate the brand's founder Arthur Guinness.

Source: www.bordbia.ie.

Personality: This refers to a person's distinguishing psychological characteristics, which lead to relatively consistent and enduring responses to his or her environment. Every person has a unique personality, which manifests itself in traits such as dominance, self-confidence, innovativeness, or autonomy.

Marketers attempt to endow products with personalities in the belief that people will identify with particular personality traits. Personality is particularly associated with brands. The following panel, for example, lists some of the brand personalities that one commentator suggests are a feature of some leading British brands, many of which are available in Ireland. Some of these 'personalities' have been built up over several decades as part of concerted positioning campaigns. The personality derives from how the brand is communicated and perceived. It also demonstrates the difficulty that marketers can have if the personality of the brand does not change as times change: for example, according to are commentator, Barclay's Bank still had a 1970s personality.

BRAND PERSONALITIES

Barclay's Bank	1970s-style high-street banking
Cadbury	Small purple pleasures; world of chocolate
Coca-Cola	America for everyone
Levi's	Classic style, authenticity
Mars	Countlines
Marks and Spencer	Editorial ability, innovative luxury
Nescafé	Suburban niceness, familiar product brand
Nike	Just do it (youth and attitude)
Persil	Caring household cleaning
Sainsbury's	Middle-class quartermaster
Sony	Innovative design in gizmos
Virgin	David v. Goliath

Source: Peter Wallis (SRU Management Consultancy), 'Elastic brands', *Sunday Times*, 3 November 1996.

One research study in the United States suggested that there were five brand personality dimensions: sincerity, excitement, competence, sophistication, and ruggedness (Aaker,

1997). The research had been conducted among a representative sample of the American population based on these five demographic characteristics. It is certainly possible to relate various well-known brands to these dimensions.

Psychological factors

Motivation exists when a need is sufficiently pressing to direct a person to seek satisfaction of that need. It is a force that impels us into action. People feel tension if a need exists; to reduce this tension we will take action. Our behaviour will be goal-oriented: we are motivated to achieve particular goals.

Marketers are interested in motivation because consumers' needs and goals will be determinants of the products and brands they consider to be relevant to them as a means of achieving their goals. Some of these goals are generic (for example, if a person is hungry they will be motivated to do something about it), while some goals will be brand-specific or product-specific (so the person who is hungry might decide to buy a specific product, such as a packet of Tayto crisps).

There are several theories of motivation, but this chapter will limit its discussion to one, Maslow's hierarchy of needs. Maslow (1943) proposed that people were driven by needs that can be arranged in a hierarchy (fig. 6.5). The needs ascend; as needs at the bottom of the hierarchy are satisfied, the person moves on to the next level. As soon as the needs on one level have been satisfied, the needs on the next level will come into play. This is relevant to marketers, as various products and services can be seen as possible satisfiers of particular types of needs. An insurance company sells products on the basis of safety needs, while the motives for buying an expensive car may have more to do with prestige and esteem than with transport. Maslow's hierarchy is particularly useful when considering positioning and communication strategies.

Figure 6.5: Maslow's hierarchy of needs

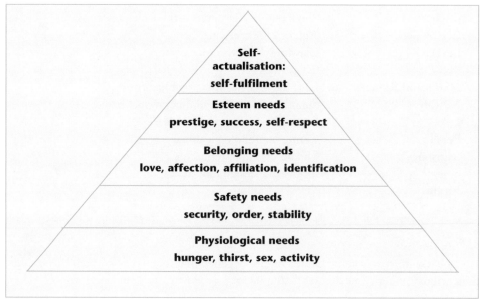

Consumers' motives will be a strong influence on the products or type of products they buy. In the boxed chocolate assortment market, for example, different sets of motives can apply to different brands.

MILK TRAY: SATISFYING A NEED SINCE THE 1930S

Cadbury, the manufacturer of two leading assortments, Milk Tray and Roses, considers that different motives come into play for each of the brands.

A person who buys a box of Milk Tray as a gift has a different set of motives from someone who buys Roses. According to the brand manager, 'Roses are a gesture. There are no symbolic purchasing reasons attached to buying a box of Roses. With Milk Tray, though, you are talking about a different set of standards. It could be love. It could be sincerity. It could be emotive reasons.'

The brand was launched in Ireland in the 1930s, and over time the appearance has changed. In 1997, for example, the company devised a new, curved shape for the box. This was the third change to the box during the 1990s, though the distinctive purple-and-gold colouring has always been retained. New chocolates have been added and the selection changed to suit changing tastes.

Cadbury typically spends €635,000 a year on marketing the brand. Its original television advertising campaign was inspired by the James Bond era, 'where the guy would go to any length to get the lady a box of Milk Tray'. In the 1960s and 1970s this appeal was appropriate because there was a clear role distinction between men and women. The role of women has changed since then: women have become more powerful, and the advertising has changed to reflect this. The catch-line 'and all because the lady loves Milk Tray' has, however, been retained. Not surprisingly, women eat more Milk Tray than men. In the broader chocolate market, sales are split equally by sex: in the formal chocolate gift market, women account for 65 per cent of purchases.

Source: A. O'Toole, 'Most chocaholics are women', *Sunday Business Post*, 21 December 1997.

PERCEPTION

A motivated person is ready to act; how they do so is influenced by their perception of the situation. *Perception* is the process by which a person selects, organises, and interprets stimuli to create a meaningful picture of the world. Perception is therefore important in the product evaluation process with regard to the buyer's perception both of the marketing mix and its ability to satisfy needs.

Perception is a physiological process, because it involves the use of sensory receptors such as the eyes and ears, which send impulses to the brain through the central nervous system.

The lowest level at which a person can perceive a stimulus is called the *absolute threshold*. The minimum difference that can be perceived between two stimuli is called the *just noticeable difference*. These are important concepts with regard to communication and product or pricing changes. An advertisement has to reach the absolute threshold to register in the person's mind. A chocolate manufacturer faced with rising cocoa costs might decide to reduce the amount of cocoa in each bar rather than increase the price of the product. If the consumer noticed the change this would be above the just noticeable difference; if not, it would be below. Similarly, if the price of a product was changed and was above the just noticeable difference, the consumer might decide to reconsider their choice.

People generally select stimuli according to interest, expectations, and motives. They are therefore selective in what they perceive. With regard to advertising, we will be more likely to perceive advertisements for products that we are interested in. Selective perception can manifest itself in a number of ways.

Selective exposure: People will only notice certain stimuli. For example, if we are hungry we are more likely to notice the smell coming from a coffee shop, or advertisements for food products. This caused one company in Britain to investigate using 'sensory' advertising.

Selective distortion: People can distort the stimuli to suit themselves, so as to support rather than challenge their preconceptions. Advertising campaigns may demonstrate the dangers of smoking to people's health, but people may distort the message by convincing themselves that it will never happen to them.

Selective retention: People retain only a certain amount of information, usually what is of most interest. Marketers cannot expect the individual to remember everything, so in many advertising campaigns the same short message is repeated many times.

Perception and company or product image are strongly related. In general, marketers attempt to create and maintain a positive image for their company and products through their communication activities. Retailers pay particular attention to shop design and image, whether in supermarkets, where the first sensory experience is the smell from the in-store bakery or the display of fresh fruit and vegetables, or a fashion retailer, where garments are displayed using creative and innovative window dressing.

ASSAULTS ON THE SENSES AT BUS STOPS

In 1996 the advertising agency Young and Rubicam in Britain devised a promotional campaign for the Batik range of soft drinks marketed by Del Monte. Ten bus shelters were selected for the promotion and were specially adapted so that a citrus fragrance was released automatically by means of an infrared device when someone came within range. The advertising panels on the shelter featured the Batik range.

Del Monte hoped the fragrance would add an extra dimension to their advertising and act as a stimulus to perception. As people waiting at a bus stop were unlikely to associate a citrus fragrance with the experience, the chances were they would notice.

Source: *Irish Times*, 31 August 1996

LEARNING

Learning involves changes in people's behaviour arising from experience. It is of interest to marketers because consumers learn about concepts, products, and brands. There are two broad schools of thought about learning: the behavioural theories and the cognitive theories.

Behavioural theories view learning as observable responses to stimuli. The two main theorists were Pavlov (1927) and Skinner (1938). Pavlov showed in his experiments with animals that *conditioned learning* occurs when a stimulus that is paired with another stimulus that elicits a known response serves to produce the same response when used alone. By combining the sound of a bell with giving a dog food, he showed that eventually the dog will associate the sound of the bell with the food and will salivate merely on hearing the bell. This is known as *classical conditioning*. Its relevance for marketers derives from association and repetition. For example, many advertisers have used pieces of classical music or invented jingles in their advertising. If this is repeated often enough, the person may come to associate the music with the product.

Instrumental conditioning was demonstrated by Skinner, again using animals. Here learning occurs by a process of trial and error, in which rewards result in repeat behaviour. Every time the animal engaged in the desired behaviour it was rewarded. Laboratory animals therefore associated particular behaviour with rewards and would repeat the behaviour to obtain the reward.

With regard to human behaviour, instrumental conditioning theory suggests that the buyer will associate particular behaviour with a reward and may engage in purchasing behaviour to obtain that reward. Consider the example of supermarkets rewarding loyalty, as described below. Members of these 'loyalty clubs' learned that engaging in purchasing behaviour with participating firms was instrumental in their receiving rewards.

The examples in the panel below are indicative of the increased prevalence of loyalty schemes in the 1990s. Airlines and petrol retailers had in many cases led the way with such schemes. From a psychological viewpoint, three main effects determine whether a loyalty scheme will alter consumers' behaviour. Loyalty can be measured directly, whether to the brand or indirectly to the scheme itself. The value the consumer places on the reward will also be a determinant, as will the timing or the time allowed for the scheme (Dowling and Uncles, 1997). Generally, marketers consider that loyalty schemes encourage loyal customers to pass on recommendations to others and to offer advice and feedback to the marketer on the scheme. Loyalty schemes are usually designed to ensure that they maximise the buyers' motivation to make further purchases.

REWARDING LOYALTY

Superclub was the first supermarket loyalty scheme, launched in 1993 by the Superquinn chain. It also involved a number of partner firms, ranging from Texaco service stations to UCI cinemas. These pay a fee for the service and buy points that they distribute to their own customers. Consumers could join the club and were given a membership card with a bar-coded membership number. Every pound spent with any participating company earned points, which could be redeemed for a range of gifts, including electrical goods, household items, and flights to a number of destinations. The scheme was run by a company called Superclub Target Marketing.

By 1998 Superclub had over 350,000 members, and Superquinn had franchised the system to a chain of Brazilian shops. They had also carried out consultancy work for companies in Scandinavia and Portugal. The company had calculated that average expenditure per customer had increased since the scheme was launched. Many participating firms give bonus points from time to time on selected items and services, so the careful shopper has the chance to considerably increase the total number of points.

Other supermarkets watched with interest, but it was 1997 before Dunnes Stores and Quinnsworth (Tesco Ireland) launched their Value Card and Tesco Clubcard, respectively. Dunnes Value Card concept was different from Superclub, in that points were converted into cash vouchers that could be used to pay for purchases. The Tesco Clubcard also involved the consumer receiving vouchers, redeemable when making purchases in the shop.

In 1998 the Spar chain launched a scheme involving itself and the phone card company Switchcom. They produced branded pre-paid phone cards that could be used from any phone, including mobiles. Consumers could collect points and redeem them for phone cards.

The appeal of these cards was in the fact that points could be accumulated quite quickly. Many consumers were members of more than one scheme. For retailers it provided a database of club members and enabled them to monitor customer loyalty. If items with bonus points could be shown to sell faster than items without, manufacturers could be encouraged to give price reductions or incentives.

The general reaction of customers to loyalty cards has been positive. Lansdowne Market Research carried out some research on consumers' attitudes to loyalty schemes in 1997, and the results were published in the trade magazine *Checkout* in September 1997. A number of questions were asked, including questions about what shoppers thought of loyalty schemes and why they participated.

Are loyalty schemes a good or a bad idea?

Very good	26%
Good	45%
Neither good nor bad	17%
Bad	9%
Very bad	3%

Reasons for participation:

To receive goods on offer	38%
I'm shopping, so I might as well	36%
To save money or receive discounts	22%
Other reasons	4%

Shoppers were also asked if they would switch shops as a result of loyalty schemes. The majority would not, as the following figures indicate. This suggests that loyalty cards have an important role in reinforcing loyal behaviour.

Likelihood of switching shops because of loyalty schemes

Very likely	9%
Likely	17%
Neither likely nor unlikely	17%
Unlikely	22%
Very unlikely	35%

Sources: *Sunday Tribune*, 3 November 1996; *Irish Times*, 27 June 1997; 'New loyalists in the Republic', *Checkout Ireland*, September 1997; Christine Doherty, 'Changing face of loyalty schemes', *Sunday Business Post*, 17 May 1998.

Cognitive learning theory

Cognitive learning theory holds that the kind of learning most characteristic of humans is problem-solving. The individual processes information, stores it, retains it, and retrieves it. Memory is therefore important in the process. For memory to function, the information must be rehearsed, encoded, stored, and retrieved.

People are most likely to memorise advertisements that they find interesting or of relevance to them and that are repeated often enough. The individual may see and hear many advertisements, but only some will be committed to memory. These will have been rehearsed and encoded. When the need arises, they can be retrieved from memory.

While cognitive learning theory is probably the most relevant theory with regard to understanding human learning, classical and instrumental learning are also relevant with regard to learning associated with advertising and promotion. The repeated use of the same message or of free gifts with the product that reinforce the consumer's decision are examples of this. In the area of branding, brand extensions demonstrate that consumers can generalise. Pavlov showed in his experiments that dogs would react in the same way to the sound of jingling keys as to the sound of the bell. This is known as *stimulus generalisation*. Marketers such as Cadbury have used this concept in extending their brand from chocolate bars to cakes, biscuits, desserts, and cream liqueurs. All these products are branded with the Cadbury name, and the familiar purple colour appears on many of them. Cadbury hope that the consumer will generalise and consider any Cadbury product to be a good choice.

ATTITUDES

Attitudes are learned predispositions to respond in a consistently favourable or unfavourable way with respect to product, brand, person, idea, or organisation.

Attitudes consist of three components:

- **cognitive**—the consumer's beliefs about the object
- **affective**—the consumer's emotions or feeling about the product
- **conative**—the likelihood that the consumer will act in a particular manner.

These three components are related. If the consumer believes that the product is good they will have a positive feeling about the product and will be more likely to buy it. Attitudes are therefore important determinants of behaviour. Attitudes can be measured using *attitude scales* (see fig. 6.6), which are quite common in research questionnaires. The results from questions like those in the following questionnaire can be numerically tabulated, giving a quantifiable indication of attitude.

Marketers may attempt to change or influence attitudes by trying to influence one or other of the attitude components. It can be difficult to get people to change their beliefs about something; the marketer may therefore have to encourage a re-evaluation or attempt to change the image of the attitude object. Advertising campaigns to encourage consumers to switch from spreads to butter or to revert to using sugar are examples of this.

Figure 6.6: Attitude scales

Semantic differential scale—measures attitudes by getting the respondent to rate the attitude object using bipolar adjectives; for example:

We would like you to tell us what you think about our shop. Please tick the point in the scale that reflects your feelings.

Modern	☐ ☐ ☐ ☐ ☐	Old-fashioned
Low prices	☐ ☐ ☐ ☐ ☐	High prices
Good service	☐ ☐ ☐ ☐ ☐	Poor service
Convenient	☐ ☐ ☐ ☐ ☐	Inconvenient

Likert scale—consists of a number of evaluative statements, which the respondent is asked to agree or disagree with; for example:

	Strongly agree	Agree	Neutral	Disagree	Strongly disagree
This shop offers a wide product range	☐	☐	☐	☐	☐
This shop has an easy-to-follow layout	☐	☐	☐	☐	☐

INFLUENCERS ON THE BUYING DECISION

The consumer will usually go through a decision-making process that may or may not involve outside influencers. As stated in the definition of buyer behaviour, the physical purchase is only one part of the process. There are a number of roles in the decision process, and these can be performed by different people. The essential roles are:

1. **initiator**—the person who first suggests the idea to buy;
2. **influencer**—whose views carry weight in the final decision;
3. **decider**—who ultimately decides what to buy, in what quantity, and where to buy;
4. **buyer**—who actually makes the purchase;
5. **user**—who actually uses the product.

These roles can be particularly pronounced in family buying and in industrial buying situations. In most families, different family members may take on different roles, which may vary depending on the product. For example, children may be an influence on the holiday the family takes but may not be an influence on the power tools the family buys. In the industrial buying situation it may be a particular person's job to perform one of the roles: for example, the buyer might be the purchasing manager. Understanding that there are different buyer roles is important, as the marketer may want to select particular role members. Most in-store promotions, for instance, are aimed at the buyer, as they are being asked to make a decision about the promoted item there and then.

Buyer's response

The third element of the black box model is the buyer's response. Marketers typically measure response in sales of the product; however, the timing of the response, the retail outlet chosen and the amount bought are other possible responses. The consumer may see an advertisement for a new model of car and may be quite impressed. They may commit the advertisement to memory and retrieve it when they are actually changing their car or buying their first car at some later time. Responses, therefore, are not always immediate. Buyers also make decisions about the outlets they will use. Outlets that are perceived to be inconvenient or offering poor choice may not be considered. Buyers may go to outlets that they feel are consistent with their life-style.

The timing of the buyer's response is also important. Many airlines and travel companies attempt to fill spare capacity in the winter months by offering special deals; but consumers who cannot take holidays at that time of year may not be able to respond. The amount that buyers buy is also a response variable; this is especially a factor in sales promotions, where banded offers, special price offers and promotional packs may encourage the buyer to buy more.

It is important to note that it is possible for marketers to have an influence at the response stage. Advertising and promotion can be used to attract undecided buyers or consumers who are willing to switch brands.

REPEAT PURCHASE AND BRAND LOYALTY

A desirable behavioural response is repeat purchase and brand loyalty. Consumers tend to buy products and brands continuously that they like and that meet their needs.

Loyalty cannot be taken for granted. Changing needs, competitive product offerings and sales promotions aim to tempt buyers away. Loyalty schemes, such as those described above, are an attempt to secure consumer loyalty. Loyalty, however, is much more than simple repeat purchase: there can be different dimensions to loyalty. One study examined the nature of loyalty and suggested a matrix with four dimensions, as fig. 6.7 illustrates. This demonstrates the importance of the relationship between customer attitude and loyal behaviour.

Figure 6.7: Dimensions of customer loyalty

		Repeat patronage	
		High	Low
Relative attitude	High	**Loyalty**	**Latent loyalty**
	Low	**Sporadic**	**No loyalty**

Source: A. Dick and K. Basu, 'Customer loyalty: towards an integrated conceptual framework', *Journal of the Academy of Marketing Science*, vol. 22 (1994), no. 2.

Marketers, therefore, need to follow changing trends and where necessary adapt products or develop new offerings to keep pace with changing market conditions. Advertising can be used to encourage the customer to be loyal, not only by reminding the customer that the product is still there but also by helping to reinforce the buyer's decision.

Holding on to loyal customers is a core principle of marketing. It generally costs a lot more to create new customers than to hold on to existing ones. Customers can of course switch to other products or service providers; marketers, however, can influence these defection rates in an attempt to keep them low. Banks, for example, will aim their advertising at students, many of whom open an account for the first time when they go to university.

One study measured defection rates from financial service institutions among students (Colgate, Stewart, and Kinsella, 1996), which found that the defection rate was 18 per cent. Banks have certainly realised the importance of holding on to student customers. They have also provided inducements to students to stay, such as minimised bank charges, good customer service, access to overdrafts, and accessibility.

Airlines have 'frequent flier' schemes to reward loyal users, while Superclub members can receive rewards by remaining loyal to a range of firms. In competitive markets, brand loyalty will come under pressure, and understanding the nature of buyer behaviour with regard to the influences and the personal and psychological forces that are at work can help the marketer in the process of maintaining brand loyalty.

FURTHER READING

Arnould, E., Price, L., and Zinkhan, G., *Consumers* (second edition), New York: McGraw-Hill 2004.
Solomon, M., Bamossy, G., Askegaard, S., and Hogg, M. K., *Consumer Behaviour: A European Perspective* (fourth edition), Harlow, England: FT Prentice Hall 2010.

DISCUSSION QUESTIONS

1. Using the black box model presented in this chapter, comment on the behavioural factors that would be of interest to the marketers of the following products:
   (*a*) Bord na Móna peat briquettes
   (*b*) Kerrygold butter
   (*c*) Knorr packaged soup
   (*d*) Dulux paint.
2. Outline, using examples, how marketers attempt to influence consumer behaviour at different stages in the decision-making process.
3. Can markets be segmented using buyer behaviour as a base? Please give some examples to support your answer.
4. Using the advertisements illustrated in this chapter, identify which needs from Maslow's hierarchy are being addressed.
5. Outline the benefits of customer loyalty schemes to marketers. Do you think loyalty schemes will become more important in the future?
6. Do you think the Irish identities highlighted by the Henley Centre's research have changed in the 2000s?

REFERENCES

Aaker, J., 'Dimensions of brand personality', *Journal of Marketing Research*, August 1997.

Colgate, M., Stewart, K., and Kinsella, R., 'Customer defection: a study of the student market in Ireland', *International Journal of Bank Marketing*, March 1996.

Dewey, J., *How We Think*, New York: Heath 1910.

Dowling, G., and Uncles, Mark, 'Do customer loyalty programs really work?', *Sloan Management Review*, summer 1997.

Henley Centre of Ireland, *Planning for Social Change*, Dublin: Henley Centre of Ireland 1992.

Howard, J., and Sheth, J., *The Theory of Buyer Behaviour*, New York: Wiley 1969.

Maslow, A., 'A theory of human motivation', *Psychological Review*, vol. 50 (1943).

Mohan, Mark, 'The influence of marital roles in consumer decision-making', *Irish Marketing Review,* vol. 8 (1995).

Pavlov, I., *Conditioned Reflexes*, London: Oxford University Press 1927.

Schiffman, L., and Kanuk, L., *Consumer Behaviour* (fifth edition), Englewood Cliffs (NJ): Prentice-Hall 1994.

Skinner, B., *The Behaviour of Organisms*, New York: Appleton-Century-Crofts 1938.

Solomon, M., Bamossy, G., Askegaard, S. and Hogg, M. K., *Consumer Behaviour: A European Perspective* (fourth edition),Harlow, England: FT Prentice Hall 2010.

Turley, D., 'The Irish consumer through Irish eyes: European values survey, 1990', *Irish Marketing Review,* vol. 8 (1995).

Turley, D., and Gallagher, H., 'Children and television advertising: a cognitive development perspective', *Irish Marketing Review*, vol. 3 (1988).

LOVE IRISH FOOD INITIATIVE

Love Irish Food is a promotional initiative created by a number of Irish food and drink manufacturers to encourage the consumption of their brands. The initiative came about in late 2009 when, in an increasingly competitive grocery market, many Irish brands were experiencing difficulties, especially competing with international or global brands. In a period of economic recession, consumers had become much more price sensitive, as a result discount retailers such as Aldi and Lidl had increased their share of the grocery market and supermarket chains such as Tesco and Dunnes Stores had begun to source more products outside Ireland in an attempt to reduce costs.

Love Irish Food was established as a non-profit entity with the purpose of promoting Irish food and drink brands to consumers. Initially there were 29 members but this rapidly expanded (see fig. 6.8 which is an example of one of the print advertisements used to promote the brand members). There were two criteria for joining Love Irish Foods, the product had to be manufactured in Ireland and ingredients had to be sourced in Ireland where possible.

The objectives of the campaign were to encourage consumers to think about the positive consequences (for example, employment) of purchasing Irish food and drink brands. A logo was developed which members used on their packaging and the philosophy of the campaign was communicated in advertising and public relations initiatives. A 30-second television commercial was produced and screened on national channels over a 10-week period to create awareness and explain the concept behind the logo. In addition a press campaign was developed with the theme 'One more makes all the difference' (see fig 6.9).

Figure 6.8: Example of Love Irish Foods membership press advertisement

Figure 6.9: 'One more makes all the difference' press advertisement

A website www.loveirishfood.ie was created to inform, educate, and engage consumers. Visitors to the site could download discount coupons, enter competitions, and find out more about the Irish food and drink brands participating in the campaign.

To assess the initial effectiveness of the various promotional activities, research was conducted among a sample of 400 shoppers from different parts of the country. Twenty-six per cent of those questioned claimed they could recall the campaign, but when probed (by showing them examples) this increased to 58 per cent. Ninety-six per cent of people had seen the logo and 47 per cent could recall seeing the television advertising. When asked what they thought the campaign was about, people answered with statements such as: 'Buy Irish', 'Buy home produced food', 'Buy local', 'Guarantee of Irish origin', 'Not imported', 'Support Irish jobs', 'Keep Irish people in work', 'Support the economy', 'Quality product', and 'Better quality product'.

The research indicated that consumers had got the message, with most indicating that it had made them more receptive to purchasing Irish food and drink brands.

Sources: Dervila Mc Garry, Programme Co-ordinator, Love Irish Food, Presentation, ITT Dublin, November 2009, www.loveirishfood.ie.

DISCUSSION QUESTIONS

1. Explain why you feel the Love Irish Food Initiative was successful.
2. How will this success be maintained?

ROMA PASTA AND THE ORGANIC MARKET

The Roma brand was market leader in the Irish pasta market, with a 47 per cent share in 2006. The Roma range also included pasta sauces and canned tomatoes.

In response to changing consumer tastes, the marketing manager of Roma wishes to assess the position of the Roma brand in the organic food market. The company has a number of organic products including pastas and pasta sauce and would like to determine consumer familiarity with and reaction to these. The company would like to assess its overall position in the organic market compared with other brands.

The competing brands on the market that offer organic variants are Dolmio, Ragu, Bunalun and Agnessi.

The marketing manager has outlined the following research objectives.

Research objectives

1. To assess consumer attitudes and perceptions to organic food products in general.
2. To profile consumers who buy organic food products.
3. To determine consumers' price sensitivity to organic products.
4. To determine consumer perceptions of the Roma brand and its position in the organic market.
5. To evaluate existing Roma packaging and assess whether it conveys an organic image, what expectations consumers have of organic packaging and, if necessary, how the packaging could be changed.

Design a questionnaire that will achieve these objectives. Your questionnaire should provide clear instructions to both the interviewer and the respondent.

PART 3

The Marketing Mix

7

The Product

Marketers tend to use the term *product* in a very broad sense. Kotler and Armstrong (1994) defined a product as anything that can be offered to a market for attention, acquisition, use or consumption that might satisfy a want or need. It includes physical objects, services, people, places, organisations, and ideas. This chapter examines the nature of the product and the marketing decisions required in the creation and development of product strategy.

Firms devote considerable skills and resources to the management and development of their products. Products should meet the needs of the market. The creation and development of products to meet these needs, and sustaining products or brands that have developed strong relationships in the market, will be vital. Branding, for example, is one dimension of the product that requires careful management and that can yield significant benefits, as the following panel illustrates.

TOP GLOBAL BRANDS

Once a year Interbrand, a global brand and marketing consultancy firm, publishes its estimates of the top 100 global brands. It bases its calculation on a number of factors, including its '10 Principles of Strong Brands':

1. **Commitment**—the extent to which the brand receives organisational support in terms of time, influence, and investment.
2. **Protection**—the organisation seeks to secure the brand across a number of dimensions from legal protection and proprietary ingredients to design, scale, and geographic spread.
3. **Clarity**—the brand's values, position, and proposition must be clearly articulated and shared across the organisation.
4. **Responsiveness**—the brand must adapt to market changes, challenges, and opportunities.
5. **Authenticity**—the brand has a defined heritage and a well-grounded value set, as well as an ability to deliver on customer expectations.
6. **Relevance**—the brand fits with customer needs, desires, and decision criteria across all appropriate demographics and geographies.
7. **Understanding**—customers must not only recognise the brand but have an in-depth understanding of its distinctive qualities and characteristics, as well as those of the brand owner.

8. **Consistency**—the brand is experienced without fail 'across all touch points and formats' (for example advertising, websites, in-store displays).
9. **Presence**—the degree to which the brand feels omnipresent and how positively consumers, customers, and opinion formers discuss it in both traditional and social media.
10. **Differentiation**—the degree to which the customer perceives the brand to have a positioning that is distinct from the competition.

Criteria for inclusion

The brand must be truly global and have successfully transcended geographic and cultural differences. In measurable terms, at least 30 per cent of revenue must come from outside the home country, and no more that 50 per cent of revenue must come from one continent. The brand must have a presence on at least three continents and have broad geographic coverage in growing and emerging markets. There must be substantial, publically available data on the brand's financial performance; economic profit must be positive and show a return above the operating and financing costs. The brand must also have a public profile and awareness beyond its own marketplace.

To calculate the brand values, Interbrand has developed a formula based on the brand's financial performance, its role and its strength. The financial performance involves calculating the economic profit (a measure that Interbrand derived by taking the net operating profit after tax and subtracting a capital charge which is based on a weighted industry average). The role of the brand involves measuring the proportion of the decision to purchase that is attributable to the brand. This is a notional concept and is based on an estimate of the portion of demand that exceeds what demand would be if the product was unbranded. Brand strength is calculated using the 10 principles of brand strength.

Interbrand's research estimates the values of the top 100 global brands. In 2010, the top 20 brands are given in Table 7.1.

Table 7.1

Brand	$ million
Coca-Cola	70,452
IBM	64,727
Microsoft	60,895
Google	43,557
General Electric	42,808
McDonald's	33,578
Intel	32,015
Nokia	29,495
Disney	28, 731
Hewlett Packard	26,867
Toyota	26,192

Mercedes-Benz	25,179
Gillette	23,298
Cisco	23,219
BMW	22,322
Louis Vuitton	21,860
Apple	21,143
Marlboro	19,961
Samsung	19,491
Honda	18,506

Source: www.interbrand.com

This account shows that the dimensions of the product are wide and make a significant contribution to the general success of the company. In this chapter these dimensions are considered in more detail.

PRODUCT LEVELS

Products can be considered as having different *levels* or *dimensions*. The *core level* is what the consumer is really buying: for example, the National Lottery considers that when consumers buy a lotto ticket they are buying a dream. The core dimensions of the product should meet the core needs of the buyer.

The next product level is the tangible aspects of the product, including the product's features, quality level, styling, design, branding, and packaging. Tangible aspects can be readily perceived by the consumer and will often be used by marketers in positioning the product.

PERSIL: CONTINUOUS PRODUCT DEVELOPMENT

Persil aloe vera, a product development of the leading detergent brand, was launched in Britain in April 2002 and in Ireland in June of that year. The product was the result of a research initiative by Unilever who wanted to develop a milder version of the brand. Researchers at Unilever had discovered that one in four people in Britain believe that they have sensitive skin and are concerned that detergent could aggravate the situation. The people surveyed said that they would even compromise the cleaning power of a detergent if it were milder on their skin. Moreover, consumers seem to have faith in the aloe vera plant, the sap of which has long been recognised for its moisturising and soothing properties.

Detergent has gone from powders to liquids to tablets and then to dissolvable liquid detergent pouches. Manufacturers have been keen on continuous product development, not least because the detergent market in the United States and Europe has shown little growth.

The launch of Persil with aloe vera followed almost five years of research—7,000 people participated in market and clinical research. Market research was conducted among consumers who were asked to rate different natural ingredients, including camomile, tea leaves, and vitamin E, for their perceived gentleness on skin. The results of this research showed that aloe vera was the only one in whose properties consumers believed. Clinical research was carried out to measure the level of skin itchiness and redness that could be caused by different surfactants that are commonly used in detergents.

In 2003 Persil liquids were replaced with Persil liquigels, which the company claimed worked through the fibres of clothes to give a deeper clean. In that year Persil Perfomance tablets were also introduced; these had an effervescent fizzing action in the wash.

In 2007 Unilever launched Persil small & mighty, a double-concentrated liquid detergent that contains a pre-treating agent so that only a small amount of product is needed for the wash.

Continuous product development has helped this brand maintain market share leadership both in Ireland, where it outsells its nearest rival by a ratio of 2:1, and the UK, where it holds 21 per cent of the detergent market. It is likely that future product development will focus more on detergents that can be used at low temperatures, even in cold water, thus reducing energy costs.

Sources: Alessandra Galloni, 'Unilever reaches out for sensitive customers', *Wall Street Journal Europe*, 26–28 April 2002; www.unilever.ie.

The *augmented product level* is the guarantee or warranty that may come with the product, delivery, credit, installation, customer service, and after-sales service. The augmented aspects of products will differ: electrical retailers will usually provide many aspects of augmented service, a TSN (tobacconist, stationer, and newsagent) may not. The augmented level of the product should not necessarily be viewed as an extra. Customers may expect high levels of service and will expect difficulties or product failures to be sorted out.

The *potential product* refers to the level the product may reach or be developed towards. Arguably, all products can be developed by means of new benefits or added values. The potential product level describes how products might compete in the future, as the example of Persil detergent has shown.

THE PRODUCT MIX

The product mix is the set of all products the marketer makes available to the seller. For an individual company this is a complete description of its range: for example, for a company such as Guinness it would include its stouts, ales, and lagers. These can be further subdivided. For example, in the ale category there are three brands: Smithwick's, Kilkenny, and Macardle's. Each of these brands is retailed in draught, bottled, and canned form. Smithwick's and Kilkenny are national brands, while the Macardle's brand is strong in the north-east.

The product mix can therefore be considered as having width, length, and depth. The width refers to the number of different product lines offered. The length refers to the number of items in the product mix. The depth describes the number of variations of each product that is offered. Ale represents one product line for Guinness; length is determined by the number of ales (three), and depth by the number of variations of each, for example different bottle or can sizes.

In general, firms will seek to achieve consistency among the products in the mix. Obviously for Guinness there is consistency in the production, packaging, and distribution of stouts, ales, and lagers. Similar plant and machinery may be used for all three. There is also consistency in distribution, in that all the products in the mix are sold in pubs and off-licences, and they can be transported and delivered to outlets in the same delivery. Strategically, Guinness maintains three brands of ale to maximise its presence in the channels of distribution. The Macardle's brand is maintained because of its historically strong position in the north-east region.

Branding can also be used to achieve marketing consistency among products. For example, the Golden Vale brand appears on a range of dairy and meat products, and the Tayto brand appears on a range of crisps and extruded snacks.

PRODUCT CLASSIFICATION

Products can be classified in a number of ways. *Non-durable goods* are products that are consumed in one or a few uses. These include most foods and drinks. *Durable goods* are designed to last longer and include such products as household electrical items, cooking utensils, personal computers, and sports wear.

Convenience goods are goods that are bought frequently and with a minimum of effort. In recent years the convenience market has grown in importance. It includes products such as soft drinks and snacks, chilled ready meals, and fast-food restaurants. All are designed to minimise the consumer's efforts in preparation and search. Consumer staples such as milk, bread, and newspapers are largely classified as convenience goods, as are most impulse purchases.

Shopping goods are goods that the consumer spends some time considering before purchasing. These typically represent high-involvement purchases for the consumer, who may go to considerable lengths to analyse and evaluate the different products on offer. *Speciality goods* usually have a high involvement also; these are goods with unique characteristics for which the consumer will make a special purchasing effort, for example an expensive brand of clothing or products related to a specialist hobby.

The classification of the product will be a determinant of distribution policy. Convenience and impulse products tend to be widely available and distributed in a variety of retail outlets and by other means, including vending machines. Shopping and speciality goods are more selectively distributed; for some speciality goods only a small number of outlets in the country may stock the product.

PRODUCT MANAGEMENT

In small, single-product firms there may be few variations in the width, depth, or length of the product mix. In larger, multi-product companies there may be more variation. An examination of the top 100 grocery brands in Ireland, for example, reveals that within many product categories, and among categories, many brands are owned by a single parent firm. Multinationals such as Procter & Gamble, which owns seven of the top brands, and Van den Bergh Foods, which owns 10, have a presence in several product categories.

Product management also applies in services and in business-to-business markets. Again, an individual manager could be assigned to specific products or services. In the 1960s the concept of product management was first introduced by Procter & Gamble. Product managers were given responsibility for a brand or a number of brands, the idea being that they would become, in effect, small-scale marketing managers. Product managers concentrate their efforts on the products or brands assigned to them, and they are responsible for the research, promotion and advertising of the brands, reporting to a marketing manager or marketing director.

According to Lysanski (1985), the product manager performs a 'boundary role' in the

Figure 7.1: The product manager's boundary role

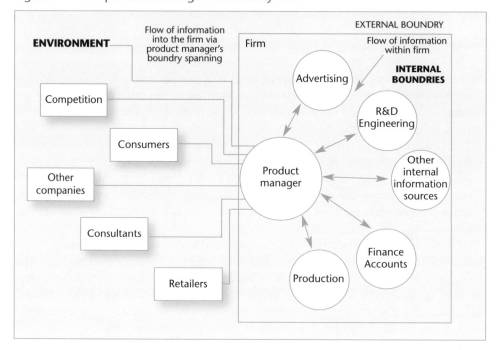

firm. This is illustrated in fig. 7.1.

The concept of product management gained popularity, especially in large multi-product companies. In many cases, within brands there could be quite extensive variations in packet sizes or varieties. Similarly, product managers were often given responsibility for *product lines*. These are groups of products that are closely related because they function in a similar manner, are sold to the same groups of customers, are marketed through the same outlets, or fall within given price ranges. In the case of Procter & Gamble, three of the top brands are detergents: Ariel, Bold, and Daz. These constitute a product line. Another one of its brands is Fairy Liquid; this would belong to a separate product line.

BRANDING

Brands have been used for many years to distinguish products. In the past hundred years or so there has been a significant growth in branding activities. This growth can be ascribed to the industrial revolution and the development of marketing practice. More products and services are produced, more means of communication and promotion are available, and there is greater competition for the consumer's attention.

Holt (2003) argued that every society needs myths—simple stories that help people deal with tensions in their lives. He considered that today's most potent brands succeed by providing these myths. Icons are encapsulated myths and they are powerful because they deliver myths to us in a tangible form, thereby making them more accessible. If a brand becomes an icon, such as Nike, Harley-Davidson, or Volkswagen, it wins competitive battles, not just by delivering on quality or innovation but by forging a deep connection with the culture.

A brand is a name, sign, symbol, or design—or a combination of these—intended to identify the goods or services of one seller and to distinguish them from those of competitors. A brand has been defined by de Chernatony and McDonald (1993) as an identifiable product, service, person, or place augmented in such a way that the buyer or user perceives relevant unique added values that match their needs most closely. Furthermore, its success results from being able to sustain these added values in the face of competition.

Branding helps to differentiate products and is a powerful competitive tool. Inanimate objects can be given an identity and image to enable them to compete in the market, and the brand owner can create a valuable company asset. Branding has been described as the DNA of the business (Macrae, Parkinson, and Sheerman, 1995). DNA contains the unique inherited codes that determine the shape, form and function of an organism; branding may be viewed analogously as a business process that determines the particular combination of product quality, innovation, technology, trade partnerships, logistics, and other factors crucial to a firm's sustainable competitive advantage.

Brand names give the owner proprietorial rights, which can be legally protected. Many brands have been on the market for generations, such as Guinness; some brands have disappeared, such as Phoenix ale and Halpin's tea, which were significant brands in the 1950s and 1960s. Other brands have been revived, as the following panel shows.

REVIVING 18TH-CENTURY WHISKEY BRANDS

In 1987 Cooley Distillery was founded by two businessmen, John Teeling and Dónal Kinsella. The company acquired the assets of John Locke and Company, which in 1757 had received the world's first licence to operate a distillery, at Kilbeggan, County Westmeath. The production of whiskey had ceased at Locke's in the 1950s. Cooley Distillery renovated and reopened the plant and set about reviving the brand.

In 1994 the company relaunched Locke's Irish Whiskey, a quality blended whiskey containing 40 per cent malt. Another Locke's brand, Kilbeggan Irish Whiskey, a standard blend, originally introduced in the late 19th century, was also relaunched. A third brand, Tyrconnell, was relaunched to compete in the single-malt segment of the market. This brand had been introduced by Watt's Distillery in Derry in 1762. The

Connemara brand was the only peated single malt Irish whiskey on the market.

Brands were esssential for Cooley if it was to compete in the brand-conscious national and international whiskey market. The brands it revived had considerable heritage and historical associations.

Sources: *Sunday Tribune*, 25 May 1997; *Irish Times*, 11 June 1997; *Sunday Business Post*, 16 June 1997; Cooley Distillery Annual Report, 2000.

The benefits of brands to the buyer

Brands can communicate the product's benefits and tell the buyer something about the product. Brands such as the Wash 'n' Go range of hair care products or Shake 'n' Vac carpet freshener suggest something of the products' benefits and how they can be used. Branding is an aid to recognition. The colours, shapes, and names used make it easier for the consumer to identify products in the shop. The brand can also be used to draw attention to new and beneficial products or services. The chocolate and confectionery manufacturer Cadbury tends to use purple in the packaging of its range of products. The Cadbury name appears in its distinctive lettering, and the result is packaging that is instantly recognisable.

Psychologically, brands may satisfy identification and security needs. Consumers may feel comfortable or reassured when a brand provides them with the value they want. The purchaser of designer-label clothing or of a particular brand of car may be looking to the brand to provide them with the added benefit of being socially acceptable or well recognised.

Brand loyalty may be rewarded not just with continued satisfaction but also with gifts or added benefits, such as the rewards frequent travellers can obtain from some airlines or that the regular shopper can obtain from the multiple supermarkets as part of their loyalty schemes.

The benefits of brands to the company

Brands can represent significant assets to the business. In 1996 the multinational FMCG company Unilever paid €92.85 million for a 75 per cent stake in Lyon's tea. This represented several times the asset value of the company. Unilever wanted to add the brand leader in the Irish tea market to its range.

Brand equity is the power and value the brand holds in the market. Some of this power is financial, in the form of market share or profitability; the rest is more psychological, in the form of recognition and attractiveness to buyers. Generally, brands with high equity have high levels of brand loyalty and name-awareness. There are usually strong brand associations and other assets, such as patents or strong trade relationships.

Brand names and trade marks can be registered and legally protected. A trade mark is a word or device used to distinguish the goods of one enterprise from those of another and can include labels, individual brand names, signatures, and shapes. It therefore has two functions: an identification for the owner and a quality guarantee for the customer. Trade marks are a means of legally protecting the goodwill of the business.

Trade marks can be registered in any country. This is important, as in some countries an unregistered trade mark confers no rights on the owner.

Marketers have frequently gone to court in an attempt to protect their brands, as the following case demonstrates. Following the successful introduction of own-label products, many supermarkets began to produce imitations of branded products. A number of legal cases have been taken, which emphasise the need for manufacturers to register not just the brand name but also the packaging and labelling styles as trade marks. In one case in Britain, taken by United Biscuits against Asda supermarkets, the supermarket chain was found guilty of passing off, because of the great similarities between its own label, Puffin biscuits, and United Biscuits' well-known Penguin brand (Benson, 1997).

Brands aid the sale of the product. The image, personality, and identity given to the brand become associated with the product. The brand can be used as the centrepiece in advertising and promotional campaigns and is part of the total communication package. Loyal and profitable users can be attracted with focused brand positioning, and many marketers will use brands as a base for segmentation.

Brands help the marketer deliver meaning to the buyer and the market. The brand name itself may convey attributes of the product: for example, Duracell suggests something about the long life of the product, and Tayto is a play on the word 'potato'.

Functional and emotional benefits can be linked to the brand through advertising and promotion. Panafluke emphasises the functional nature of liver-fluke eradication, while CK One, the fragrance for men and women from Calvin Klein, has a more emotive proposition.

Marketers may attempt to link the brand with certain consumer or social values. Low Low, the sunflower spread from the Kerry Group, is linked with diet and health, while the charitable organisation Alone emphasises the importance of visiting or keeping in touch with the elderly.

Successful brands can be further extended by increasing sales and market share. Lucozade was launched as a drink for convalescents in 1927. In the 1980s, with sport and life-style becoming ever more significant, Smith-Kline Beecham developed Lucozade Sport. Mars has extended its business into ice cream; and the Virgin brand covers air and rail travel, music, financial services, and computers.

Brand personality

Advertisers have considerable scope for giving brands a personality, which does not have to involve humans. Brands can be endowed with personality traits so that people can better relate to them. The Andrex brand of toilet roll and Dulux paint have consistently used dogs in their advertising. Cartoon or animated characters can also be developed, as the food company Batchelor did with the characters Beany and Barney, used for many years to promote the company's range of canned products. An Bord Gáis has used animated teddy bears in its advertising and promotion.

Brand personality reflects the nature of the product and the target market. Banks and financial institutions tend to emphasise traits such as security, service, dependability, and friendliness. Drink brands may emphasise sociability, trendiness, and attractiveness, while many chocolate brands have been given strong sex-role traits, as with Cadbury's Flake and Nestlé's Yorkie, which have been endowed with female and male personalities, respectively.

Brand valuation

Brand valuation can be difficult; generally, it is only when brands or companies are sold that brand values are realised in cash. In 2005, for example, Procter & Gamble paid $57 billion for Gillette (*Wall Street Journal*, 21 June 2005). The *Business Week*/Interbrand value for Gillette in 2005 was $17.5 billion. In 2006, Largo foods paid €62.3 million for the Tayto brand (*Irish Times*, 6 July 2006).

In other cases, declining or low sales brands that may appear to have little value can often be successfully turned around. One American company, Prestige Brand Holdings, spotted a business opportunity when companies like Procter & Gamble and GlaxoSmithKline sold off brands such as Compound W, Chloraseptic and Cutex nail polish remover. Prestige Brand Holdings stepped in and acquired them and was able to turn many of its acquisitions (often referred to as orphan brands) around by investing more money in marketing them (*Wall Street Journal*, 29 June 2005).

TOP IRISH BRANDS

Every year the research company AC Nielsen carries out research to calculate the top 100 grocery brands in Ireland. The results are published in the grocery trade magazine *Checkout*. For the purposes of its survey it defines a grocery brand as every product falling under a brand banner within a specific product class. A product class is defined as the specific generic to which a collection of brands, sharing common perceived characteristics, belong, for example, all Jacob's biscuits belong to the biscuits product class, whereas Knorr soup and Knorr sauces are separate product classes. In 2010 the research indicated that Coca-Cola was the top grocery brand in terms of sales, the other top 10 brands were:

1. Coca-Cola
2. Avonmore Milk
3. Brennan's Bread
4. Lucozade
5. Tayto
6. Cadbury's Dairy Milk
7. 7-Up
8. Danone
9. Jacob's
10. Denny Sliced Meats

The Nielsen research revealed that about 20 per cent of groceries purchased were own-label and it forecast that, by 2012, this would increase to 28 per cent. Most of the country's big grocery retailers had been increasing the number of own-label products on their shelves, for example, in 2010 Superquinn launched an 'Essentials' range of grocery products aimed at the price-conscious consumer. At the same time, there had also been opportunities for brands, especially among retailers that traditionally concentrated on own-label. Marks and Spencer began stocking 50 Irish brands such as

Tayto and Lyons tea in its food outlets and the discounters Lidl and Aldi increased the number of Irish brands stocked on their shelves, adding brands such as Cully and Sully, Denny, and Cooleeny cheese in 2010.

Source: www.checkout.ie; John Ruddy, 'Own-label brands a major challenge for shelf stalwarts', *Sunday Business Post*, 12 September 2010.

Brand extensions

A brand extension is any attempt to extend a successful brand name to cover new or related products or services. In psychology this is known as the 'halo' effect, which has been defined as a judgment or perception made on the basis of one characteristic (MacDonagh and Weldridge, 1994). In other words, consumers may make a judgment on a new product or a modified product on the basis of the brand name they are already familiar with. If they have a positive disposition towards the brand, this may transfer to other brand offerings.

The concept has been used by marketers to extend their brand coverage and to build market share. The Avonmore brand, for example, has been extended from its original base, which was whole milk, into low-fat and calcium-enriched milk. Cheese and dairy spreads were added, and in the early 1990s a range of fresh soup, Avonmore Country Ladle, was launched. The range was further extended in the 1990s with dessert products, and in 1997 a range of fresh cooking sauces, Avonmore Art of Sauce, was introduced.

Brand extensions may prolong the life of the brand and reduce the risks involved in the launch of new products, but it is not always a successful strategy. Avonmore Afters, a dessert product launched by Avonmore in the late 1980s, did not succeed in capturing a satisfactory market share for the company and was withdrawn in the mid-1990s.

Many global marketers, such as Hoover and Black & Decker, have used brand extension strategies in international markets, and their names appear on a wide variety of related electrical products. Another brand that has been successfully extended is Lucozade.

LUCOZADE

The Lucozade brand was first launched in the United Kingdom in 1927 and in Ireland in the 1930s when it was taken over by Beechams. Today, Lucozade is Ireland's eighth largest grocery brand and one of the fastest-growing soft-drink brands.

Lucozade actually started life as Glucozade, a brand originally formulated by a Newcastle pharmacist; it was renamed Lucozade two years later. Introduced to the market as a food energy source for those unable to eat solids, it was based on a glucose formulation that was quickly absorbed and easily digested.

By 1954, Beechams had extended distribution of Lucozade from chemists to pubs and then to grocery outlets. In 1956, a production facility was opened in Dublin. By the 1970s, sales of Lucozade had slowed. Up to this point, Lucozade had been targeted mainly at housewives with children. The brand was seen as reliable but a slightly old-fashioned product. In 1979, it was repositioned as a pick-me-up for healthy people who felt ups and downs. This meant that Lucozade was being aimed at a new target audience, namely, young adults. The product was extended to new pack formats including a 250ml bottle with dimples as well as a new 1-litre bottle. A new advertising slogan was developed—'Lucozade replaces lost energy'—and this, with a new advertising campaign, was launched using the well-known sports personality Daley Thompson. Sales of the product grew by 300 per cent over a six-year period, while Daley Thompson was replaced with another athlete, Linford Christie.

In 1990, Lucozade Sport was launched. This was an isotonic product formulated to give essential fluid back to the body after glucose had been lost during sport. Another sports star, the soccer player John Barnes, was used in advertising campaigns. Lucozade Sport proved to be a successful product, but it had a negative effect on the sales of Lucozade. In 1995, Lucozade was re-launched as Lucozade Energy. A new Linford Christie bottle was created; this was easy to hold and carry but its shape had no dimples. The company had worried about changing the shape of the bottle but the new look proved successful. In 1999, Linford Christie was replaced by the cyber-character, Lara Croft; at this point, sales reached a record high.

Lucozade Sport and Lucozade Energy have both become successful brands. The former has successfully used sponsorship of sporting events as a means of communication, while the latter has consistently emphasised its role as an energy boost.

Source: Rosemary Lyster, 'Lucozade from sick bed to sports field' *Marketing News*, November/December 2000.

Brand extensions can sometimes be quite improbable. A fashion success in the 1990s was the Caterpillar range of footwear, clothing, and fashion accessories, an extension of a brand of earth-moving and construction equipment.

Marketing mature brands

One of the challenges that brands face as they get older is the need to position themselves as being relevant to the contemporary consumer; otherwise they can face decline. There are several examples of what are sometimes referred to as heritage brands, in other words brands that successfully repositioned.

Sometimes manufacturers can revive brand fortunes by appealing to consumers' interest in retro styles.

Brand repositioning

Consumer needs, market conditions or the activities of competitors may require the updating or repositioning of the brand. Repositioning can make the life of the brand potentially infinite.

Irish Distillers have several whiskey brands in their range, each of which has an individual image and identity. In the mid-1980s they concentrated considerable marketing effort on Power's Gold Label, which proved to be the most difficult and elusive to position. Power's was the best selling Irish whiskey, yet its product image was the most diffuse. The majority of the brand's drinkers were over 50, and it was largely consumed outside Dublin. The company's research confirmed that the brand was generally perceived as long-established and traditional, with a distinctive flavour. The company developed a communication theme and an advertising campaign that integrated the brand's existing qualities of tradition and 'earthiness' into a product image that sought to woo a target audience of men and women from their mid-20s upwards (Cummins, 1986).

Keeping up with trends or changing social conditions may be necessary for the survival of a brand. Marketers will therefore update advertising, logos, packaging design, and promotional activities.

Occasionally marketers will change brand names. Mars changed the name of one of its British and Irish countline bars, Marathon, to Snickers, which was the brand name used on the product in the United States. In 1998 another of the company's leading brands, Opal Fruits, was changed to Starburst (*Sunday Business Post*, 12 April 1998). Extreme care is needed in considering such a change if consumers are not be confused. Mars chose to change the names because it wanted a single brand name to be used in all markets. It did not make the change for Opal Fruits overnight. The packaging was first changed to incorporate 'Opal Fruits—internationally known as Starburst.' This was followed some months later by 'Starburst—formerly known as Opal Fruits.' The company estimated that it would take customers six months to get used to the change. In 2000, Lever Brothers changed the name of one of its cleaning products, Jif, to Cif. Once again, having a single brand name for all markets was the motivation for the change. The Jif name had been used in Britain, Ireland, and the Netherlands, while the Cif name was used in all other markets.

Daly and Moloney (2005) examined the corporate rebranding process. They viewed the process as a continuum that ranged from revitalising a current brand to a full name change involving alterations in brand values promises. Four approaches to rebranding were suggested:

1. *Interim/Dual*—some form of interim arrangement is used before the new name replaces the old name: for example, Eircell-Vodafone was used for a six-month period following the acquisition of Eircell by Vodafone. After this period the Eircell name was dropped.
2. *Prefix*—two or more brands merge but none of the existing brands will be used as the new brand. For example, First Trust was created in Northern Ireland when AIB and TSB merged their businesses in that market.
3. *Substitution*—a new name is substituted for an old name, for example the Northern Bank became National Irish Bank.
4. *Brand amalgamation*—two strong brands merge; for example Jurys-Doyle Hotels.

Rebranding requires careful planning. When Vodafone changed its corporate brand a marketing programme included internal marketing to employees prior to the introduction of the interim/dual name. The launch of the new name then followed; the culmination of a process that lasted 11 months.

The own-label challenge

Retailers' own-label brands have steadily increased their share in many markets. In 1994 it was estimated that they accounted for 15 per cent of the total Irish grocery market (Pratt, 1994). By 2010 the figure was 20 per cent, with the research firm Nielsen predicting that this would increase to 28 per cent in 2012 (*Sunday Business Post*, 12 September 2010). In

Germany the equivalent figure is 31 per cent and in Switzerland just over 50 per cent of the grocery market is own-label.

The challenge from these brands has been felt by both national and international manufacturers. Retailers have used own-label brands to create and enhance their image and to give them more power in distribution channels.

The challenge in the Irish market began principally with staple products, such as bread and milk, but has gradually been extended. In the grocery sector all the major multiples and retail groups have developed ranges of own-label products. The fundamental reasons why retailers have developed own-label brands are:

- to give them more control in the distribution channel
- to improve the margin they can earn from products
- to maximise control on the use of shelf space
- to enhance their reputation for quality and value.

Retailers argue that they bring quality own-label products to the consumer at reduced prices. But the own-label challenge has not been without criticism. Many manufacturers argue that the quality of products can suffer in the search for lower costs, and that many of the retailer's own brands are in effect 'copycat' products. It is also argued that smaller manufacturers that devote a large proportion of their production to own-label products become tied into a highly controlled relationship.

In the 1990s there was considerable debate about the future of brands. Discounting and the proliferation of supermarket own-brand products convinced some that branding was in peril. Some argued that the 'crisis' in branding had occurred because of the accelerating power of retailers and the sophistication of retailer brands. It was also argued that increased awareness among consumers impaired the power of the traditional mass media, and this was exacerbated by the weakness of marketing departments in major companies (Fanning, 2006).

The debate on brands demonstrates the importance of market research and of senior managers taking responsibility for their brands. The growth in distributors' own brands led to intense competition with and between manufacturers' brands. It was argued that imitation and passing off by copycat retailer products would lead manufacturers to accelerate their innovation and R&D (Romeo, 1995). In most cases, retailers introduced own-label products in well-proven product categories. By being more innovative in their product offerings, manufacturers could successfully differentiate themselves from the retailers' brands.

Increased price competition among retailers is likely to be good for manufacturers' brands, as is the development of new modes of shopping, such as home shopping by means of multimedia technology.

According to Fanning (2006), as the public becomes more adept at decoding and deconstructing the most sophisticated brand communications messages, businesses will be forced to adopt more imaginative solutions to attract and retain their attention. He suggested six possible directions for branding in the 21st century.

Cultural branding refers to brands that resolve cultural contradictions in the society in which they operate because they address the collective anxieties and desires of a nation. In the past, for example, emigration was a significant issue for Irish people. Some advertisers used the theme of emigration, an example being a 1980s ESB advertisement that showed a son returning to see his parents, whose preparations for the visit were helped with various electrical products.

Fusion branding suggests that in the future successful brands will be based on service excellence, rather than technical innovation. Products such as ready meals and Tesco's 'every little helps' slogan were considered examples.

Quaker branding: consumers seek out brands that espouse the values to which they themselves aspire. Many household brands that were established in the 19th century were founded by individuals inspired by the ethically based Quaker ideal of alleviating poverty in their local area: Hershey (chocolate) in the United States; Cadbury and Rowntree in Britain; and Jacob's and Bewley's in Ireland. In more recent times, brands such as the Body Shop and Ben and Jerry's have been associated with a reputation for good corporate citizenship, ecological awareness, being good places to work and playing an active role in the communities in which they operate.

Positional brands are brands that avoid the risks of decreased value as more people can afford them. In other words, if the brand is perceived to be too common it may lose its appeal. Thus car manufacturers have introduced limited editions, confectionery companies have done the same and the fashion brand Puma introduced a limited range of shoes of which only 888 pairs were made.

Trickster branding suggests that consumers sometimes find products or brands that tell tall tales (such as the Carbolic Smoke Ball in the 19th century) entertaining and subversive. Consumers don't believe what the brand is saying, but they don't care and they enjoy the entertainment.

Puritan branding are brands that seek to make their point discretely, with signals that only people in the know can pick up. Fanning considered that the steady growth of farmers' markets in Ireland, catering for consumers who wanted quality and simplicity, was an example of this.

The brand name

In many cases, companies have put considerable effort into the creation of brand names. Names have been created by word association, word play, and the development of new words. Attempts will be made to come up with words that describe the product or service. Some companies simply use their own trade name or company name.

The process of successfully selecting brand names can be based on seven essential steps, as fig. 7.2 illustrates. This demonstrates the seven-step selection process that was used in selecting the Finches brand name for a range of soft drinks. The expert use of market research in choosing a final brand name is of critical importance.

Another study suggests that there are five different types of brand name: *generic*, *descriptive*, *suggestive*, *arbitrary*, and *coined* (Kohli and Thakor, 1997). Generic names include most company trade names, for example Avonmore and Cadbury. Descriptive names describe the product, for example Night Saver or Powerscreen. Suggestive would include Premium Choice and First Trust; while arbitrary names would include such names as Kodak. Coined names usually represent a play on words, for example Weetabix, Tayto, or Waifos.

Figure 7.2: Selecting a brand name

1.	Defining the product and the market
2.	Selecting branding objectives
3.	Selecting a branding strategy
4.	Choosing a type of commercial name
5.	Name generation
6.	Assessing and selecting brand names
7.	The brand name in action

Source: D. McLoughlin and F. Feely, 'Successful brand name selection: Finches soft drinks', *Irish Marketing Review*, vol. 9 (1996).

PACKAGING

Packaging adds value to products. It is a means of differentiation and can be a source of competitive advantage. Many products are instantly recognisable because of the shape or design of the packaging, some of which are patented and legally protected, such as the traditional Coca-Cola bottle and the Perrier bottle.

Packaging and product are in many cases synonymous, as for example the packaging used for the correction fluid Tippex; in other cases there may be no packaging, as for example with shovels in a hardware shop.

Innovative or novel packaging can gain attention, as with the Pringle brand of potato crisps, packed in a cylindrical container. This differentiates it significantly from most of its competitors. For most products, packaging is an inherent part of the product, serving a number of functions.

Protection

The packaging may protect the product during storage and handling. In addition, it may protect the product from contamination and maintain the contents in a fit state for consumption or use, as with food, drink, pharmaceuticals, cosmetics, and petroleum products. The biscuit manufacturer Jacob introduced resealable tubs for its range of mallow biscuits, Kimberley, Mikado, and Coconut Creams, in 1997. These were designed to keep the product fresher for longer and were reusable (*Checkout Ireland*, November 1997).

Convenience

Packaging is convenient for the consumer if it facilitates use or storage. Ready-to-serve food products, microwaveable containers and built-in measures make products more convenient to use.

Convenience is also important for channel members involved in distribution, transport, and storage. How the package is to be transported and how much handling or stacking is required may influence the materials used and the design of the packaging. Many packaging innovations have come about in an attempt to make products more convenient and attractive to consumers.

SHERIDAN'S: CREATING A CONVENIENT POUR

In October 1992 Gilbey, the manufacturer of Bailey's Irish Cream, launched the Sheridan's liqueur brand, a unique product development combining two separate liquids: a coffee-chocolate liqueur and a vanilla cream liqueur. When poured, the vanilla cream settles on the top, giving the product a Guinness-like appearance.

Sheridan's was the result of a £1 million research and development programme. The product would not have been possible without the design of the distinctive package, a bottle divided in two to contain the separate liquids. At first a screw-on top was provided for each part of the bottle, and the consumer poured first from one part, then the other. This proved inconvenient for consumers, and research showed that they wanted a quicker, easier way to pour the product. Gilbey began a research programme, the result of which was a new, integrated pouring mechanism, which they described as their 'perfect-pour cap'. This gave the consumer a perfectly layered serving of one-third vanilla cream and two-thirds coffee chocolate in one pour.

The innovation increased the appeal of the brand by making the product easier to serve. In 1995 it became the best-selling liqueur in Ireland after Bailey's Irish Cream.

Sources: *Irish Independent*, 2 December 1993; *Sunday Business Post*, 5 March 1995.

Economy

Packaging makes products economical to buy and use. Generally, the larger the package the lower the cost of the individual serving or measure will be. In the case of many household products, such as detergent or breakfast cereal, a variety of packet sizes is available. For other products, such as raw materials or components, packet sizes also vary. It is more economical for manufacturers to buy in bulk, and therefore packaging will be designed to suit their requirements.

Promotion

Packaging plays an important part in communicating and promoting the product. The colours used and the shape, design, illustrations, labels, and information on the packet may attract attention and be used by the consumer to make comparisons. On-pack promotions, such as competitions, discount coupons, and special offers, play an important part in sales promotion.

Information

Packaging not only identifies and promotes the product but also provides information, some of which may be legally required, such as ingredients on food products or health warnings on tobacco products. Other labelling requirements include the country of origin and country of manufacture.

Increasingly, EU packaging regulations are having an influence. The packaging directive issued in 1996, for example, aimed at a 25 per cent reduction in packaging waste by 2001. More emphasis is being placed on the recycling of packaging materials, with a common symbol to show that the packet is recyclable.

Instructions on how to use or assemble the product may be given on the packaging. Many products have a barcode printed on the packet, which enables the product to be scanned, facilitating pricing and stock control. Manufacturers who have received quality approval by associations or government bodies may also indicate this on their packaging: in Ireland the Q mark of the Irish Quality Association or the ISO 9000 designation appear on many packets, as does the Guaranteed Irish symbol. Guaranteed Irish is a limited company that has as its objective increasing the awareness of, and demand for, Irish products and services. Manufacturers and service providers can become registered users of the Guaranteed Irish mark, provided their products and services originate in Ireland and they comply with the company's regulations. The mark can be used on packaging and also in advertising and point-of-sale and promotional materials.

Other marks or symbols that can appear on packaging include the royal warrants that some manufacturers are granted for supplying members of European royal families. This applies to a large number of British products, ranging from Barbour outdoor clothing to Gordon's gin. Other European examples include the Danish beer Carlsberg. In Britain, royal warrants are granted to companies that have regularly supplied goods or services for a minimum of five years to any of the three senior members of the royal family. They are normally granted for 10 years, and there are rules to ensure that high standards are maintained. A number of Irish companies hold warrants, including Ulster Weavers, which produces linen tea-towels, calendar towels, table napkins, and other kitchen co-ordinates (Gunin, 1998). In some cases, such as the Smirnoff vodka brand, the coat of arms of the Russian imperial family is still used on the label, indicating something of the brand's heritage. To some extent these marks were an early form of quality approval, with royal warrants in England dating from the time of King Henry VIII (www.royal.gov.uk/faq/warrant.htm.).

Packaging design

Given the functions the packaging has to perform, packaging design needs to be carefully planned. Typically, marketers use the services of design consultants to create or modify packaging. Designers consider the nature and positioning of the product and the needs of the marketer. Materials, colours, illustrations, typefaces, and shapes will all be co-ordinated to get the message across. Sometimes packaging redesign is necessary as part of a product revamp. Allied Domecq, the owner of the Harvey's Bristol Cream brand of sherry, redesigned its bottle in cobalt blue as part of its repositioning of sherry from a sweet drink consumed only at Christmas to something dry and exclusive (*Marketing*, 28 November 1998).

PACKAGING DESIGN

Bailey's Irish Cream: The bottle shape was originally designed to reflect an old Irish whiskey crock. The Bailey's symbol was inspired by the age of master-craftsmen, and the rural scene depicted on the label was commissioned to convey the Irishness of the drink.

Smirnoff Mule: The product is a cocktail of vodka, ginger beer, and lime, invented in 1940s Hollywood, where it was served in copper mugs. Copper was chosen as the colour for the bottle when it was launched in 1996.

Premier Milk: Premier was the first dairy to produce milk in cardboard cartons, in 1962; previously, milk was supplied only in glass bottles. In 1993 Premier introduced the snap-pack resealable carton, designed to be easier for the consumer to use.

Chocolate Kimberley: Black packaging was used for this extension of the Kimberley brand. Few competing products used black, especially for countline products. Part of Irish Biscuits' strategy was to establish the single-serve product in the countline market.

Source: *Checkout Ireland*, August 1997

THE PRODUCT LIFE-CYCLE

The sales potential and profitability of a product change over time. Product life-cycle theory is an attempt to recognise distinct stages in the sales and profit history of the product. It is based on a biological analogy, whereby products are introduced, grow, mature, and ultimately decline. Unlike many biological examples, however, many products may have potentially infinite lives if they are changed and adapted. Many brands have been around for hundreds of years and continue to prosper.

Life-cycle theory has four basic assertions: products have a limited life, product sales pass through distinct stages over time, profits rise and fall at different stages, and products require different management strategies at each stage in the cycle.

There are four distinct stages in the life-cycle: introduction, growth, maturity, and decline, as illustrated in fig. 7.3.

Figure 7.3: The product life-cycle

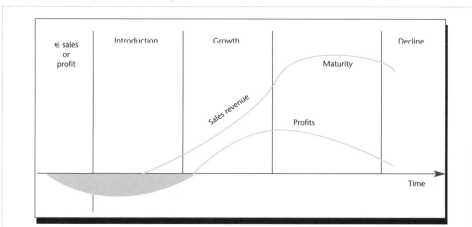

Introduction

At the introductory stage, the principal marketing consideration is creating awareness among channel members and potential consumers. New products usually have to be marketed to channel members first, so that they can place orders and have the product in stock when consumer advertising or communication begins. The creation of consumer awareness should be followed by encouragement to try the product. Marketers may therefore have to consider using sampling, couponing, or other forms of promotion to facilitate trial.

Growth

The growth phase is characterised by an acceptance of the product in the market and a consequent growth in sales. The business must therefore have the production, marketing and management ability to meet the increased demand. This can pose particular problems where the product has gained a rapid acceptance in the market: if the marketer cannot supply the demand, there is a shortage and prices go up. If demand continues to increase, competitors will be attracted to the market. If, however, demand is somewhat transient, or it is just a fad, the delay in supply may result in lost sales.

Competitors generally closely monitor the introduction and early growth stages of new products, and this may determine whether they enter the market or how quickly they will follow. They will have had the advantage of observing how the product has performed at the early stages and can learn from any mistakes made. The marketer must therefore be ready to make changes to fend off attack by competitors. Factors such as design, which would have been vital in the initial development of the product, will also be important throughout the product life-cycle.

The successful mineral water brand Ballygowan, launched in the mid-1980s, was followed by several other Irish spring water brands. This showed the need for the company to reconsider the package design, as consumers were finding it difficult to differentiate between the many imitation products. Ballygowan moved to a complete redesign to deal with this and also to produce a design that would be suitable in overseas markets, where it hoped to achieve sales growth. In overseas markets the packaging needed to be a little more sophisticated. A design company's services were engaged, and a new range of bottles was designed (Mortell, 1993).

Maturity

The maturity phase is characterised by a slowing down in sales as the product reaches market saturation. Maturity is a critical point for many products and brands; without development or extension the product may go into decline. The principal issue for the marketer is extending maturity and determining how the product or brand can best be developed. The product may not have to be changed: additional sales may be achieved in new segments or markets, for example overseas markets. In many cases, however, mature products will need to have marketing resources devoted to them. Possibilities include repositioning, adding extensions, and new variations.

Decline

The decline phase is apparent when sales and profits begin to fall. The difficulty for the marketer is in determining whether the decline is terminal or whether the product can be saved. If the marketer does not react, the decline may occur more quickly. It is necessary to determine whether marketing resources should be devoted to a declining product or brand. In many cases products or brands do indeed disappear from the market, though they may reappear again, as happened with the Cooley Distillery whiskey brands. In the clothing market, fashions or styles can also be resurrected and reintroduced.

For other products, decline ultimately means the end. This demonstrates the importance of the marketer reacting in time by changing, innovating, or developing alternatives to the declining product.

Determinants of the product life-cycle

The product life-cycle is measured over time. For some products and brands the life-cycle can be measured in weeks or months, for others it is years. It is important that marketers do not consider it to be a self-fulfilling prophecy: in other words, a product or brand may not necessarily have to decline or disappear.

Several factors can explain the shape and length of the product's life-cycle: the product's characteristics, the marketing strategies employed, external environmental factors, and market-related factors (Meenaghan and O'Sullivan, 1986). The shape is determined not only by analysing these factors but also by the interaction between them. The product's life-cycle, therefore, is not necessarily time dependent. The management will have a critical strategic role in effecting changes over the life-cycle of the product.

Diffusion of innovations

Diffusion refers to how products spread in the market. It has been defined as the process whereby an innovation is communicated through certain channels over time among members of a social system (Rogers, 1983). Marketers have been interested in the topic because of the regular launch of new products and a desire to ensure that they are effective.

Marketers want to guide and control the diffusion process by adjusting the marketing mix to elicit the desired response from the market. The diffusion process is related to the product life-cycle but different in that it refers to the proportion of potential adopters within a social system, whereas the product life-cycle is based on absolute sales over time.

Innovators: Innovators represent the first $2\frac{1}{2}$ per cent of adopters. They are venturesome, willing to take risks, and quite outward-looking. They are communicative and are involved in many networks of people. Given that they are the first buyers of new products that may be expensive, they will usually have above-average income. They tend to be well educated, open-minded, and cosmopolitan. The first people to adopt mobile cellular phones, for example, displayed these characteristics (Rogan, 1988).

Early adopters: Representing the next $13\frac{1}{2}$ per cent of adopters, this group enjoys the prestige and respect that early purchasing brings. They tend to be opinion-leaders, who influence others. Like the innovators, they have higher-than-average incomes. One study on the adoption of direct banking services, for example, found that the early adopters exerted a higher degree of opinion-leadership and had a more favourable attitude to change (Lockett and Littler, 1997). It also found that they were more involved in related product categories, for example in buying products over the phone.

Early majority: The early majority represent a significant 34 per cent of potential adopters. They tend to have status within their social class. They are communicative and attentive to sources of information. They tend to be deliberate and to interact frequently with their peers.

Late majority: Also accounting for 34 per cent of adopters, the late majority differ from the early majority in being less cosmopolitan and less well off. They tend also to be older. They will be sceptical about new products, cautious, and subject to economic necessity.

Laggards: Laggards represent the last group of adopters. They are price-conscious, and suspicious of novelty and change. They tend to be conservative in behaviour and have lower levels of income. They tend to be traditional and to have a local view of the world.

CATEGORIES OF ADOPTERS

Rogers, in his research on the adoption of new products, concluded that the adoption process could be illustrated as a normal distribution and that, depending on the time of adoption, there were five broad categories of adopters, as illustrated in fig. 7.4.

Figure 7.4: Categories of adopters

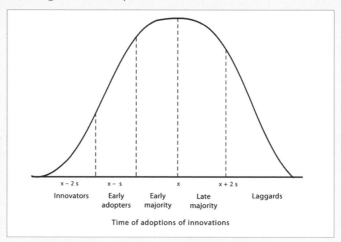

Source: Rogers, *Diffusion of Innovations*, 1983.

These categories of adopter can be used by marketers as a means of segmenting the market for new products. It is important at the outset to select the innovators and early adopters. Communications may need to be tailored to them: for example, advertising may depict people with similar traits or life-styles. As the product diffuses, communication may be adapted to cater for broader buyer characteristics. Caution is required, however. There is a danger inherent in early communication. If the product is portrayed in too narrow a way, this may inhibit subsequent adopters.

The rate of adoption of innovations can be explained by a number of factors, and the characteristics of the product itself will have a bearing. Five characteristics in particular are important (Rogers, 1983). The *relative advantage* of using the product is the degree to which the innovation is perceived as better than the product or idea it supersedes. The *compatibility* of the innovation with the consumer's existing values, past experiences, and needs will be important. The degree of *complexity* refers to the degree to which the innovation is perceived as being difficult to understand; and the degree of *trialability* refers to how easy it is for the consumer to try out the innovation. *Observability* refers to the extent to which the product stimulates word-of-mouth comment or conversation.

Product diffusion will also be influenced by other factors, including competition, pricing and economic conditions. Over time, the relative diffusion patterns of products in the market place can be determined, as the household budget survey indicates (table 7.2).

Table 7.2: Household appliances and facilities

Percentage of households with:	1994–1995	1999–2000	2004–2005
Household Appliances	(%)	(%)	(%)
Tumble dryer	26.3	42.0	61.7
Washing machine	85.6	93.4	95.3
Dishwasher	18.7	32.0	50.1
Microwave oven	46.6	71.5	86.0
Communal TV reception	40.3	51.2	44.3
Home computer	16.0	29.3	56.2
Household Facilities			
Telephone (landline)	75.9	89.2	85.9
Mobile phone	*	44.3	84.3
Internet access, *of which*:	*	14.2	42.2
ISDN	*	*	3.0
Broadband	*	*	7.6
Phone link	*	*	31.6
Burglar alarm	11.7	23.9	32.6
Two or more cars	14.0	24.2	32.8

* Not included in reference year

Source: Central Statistics Office, Household Budget Survey.

The adoption and diffusion of industrial products

With regard to the adoption and diffusion of new industrial products, it has been suggested that the process is influenced by behavioural variables generically categorised as organisational traits, environmental aspects, and individual factors (Kennedy, 1983). Organisational traits include such factors as the structure, size, and climate prevailing in the firm. The environmental aspects include both the micro- and macro-forces that impinge on the firm. The individual factors refer to the individual's characteristics and traits that they will bring with them into the firm.

The *new-product development process* describes how firms or individuals find new ideas for products or services and convert them into commercial successes. It is based essentially on the principle that consumers or firms want new goods and services and that the development of these helps a business to achieve growth and profitability. The new-product development process precedes the introduction phase of the product life-cycle. It is also required to extend the life of the product or to replace it with something else.

What is a new product?

The term *new* in a business or marketing context is rather broad. A new product or service is one that is essentially different from those already marketed by the firm. Products can be technically new, such as a personal CD player, or they may be a new consumer concept, for example designer sunglasses. A packaging change, such as an aerosol deodorant, may also constitute newness. New products can be classified in two ways: from the consumer's viewpoint and from the firm's viewpoint.

Classification of new products from the consumer's viewpoint

In determining newness from the consumer's viewpoint, the central issue is the effect of the product on the consumer—in other words, the disruptive influence the use of the product has on established consumption patterns. *Continuous innovations* are continuing changes that may take place: for example, every few years car manufacturers may update their models by adding new features. In some instances the manufacturer may also change the brand name, as when Ford revealed its replacement for the Escort, the Focus, in 1998.

Consider how continuous innovation contributed to the growth of the ice cream market in Ireland. In the clothing industry, changes in fashion or style would usually be considered continuous.

Dynamically continuous innovations include products such as electric knives and cellular phones. The innovative aspect of these products is the way in which they are used. Products such as the Sony Walkman, introduced in 1979, could be included in this category. Other dynamically continuous innovations include the first disposable cameras, introduced by Fuji in 1985, and the first disposable contact lenses, which appeared on the market in 1987.

Discontinuous innovations are essentially products that are new to the world, such as personal computers and electronic calculators. In this case the product is radically different from anything that went before. Many products and services we take for granted were originally discontinuous innovations. The first television was demonstrated by John Logie Baird in 1926, and penicillin was discovered by Alexander Fleming in 1928.

CONTINUOUS INNOVATION IN ICE CREAM

The Irish have the third-highest level of consumption of ice cream in Europe (after Sweden and Denmark). In 2006, the Irish ice cream market was valued at €143 million per annum. There were two distinct market segments: out-of-home (impulse single-serve products), which accounted for €75 million; and take-home (e.g. tubs, bricks), which was worth €69 million. The main competitors were HB (which belonged to Unilever), Mars, and Nestlé.

Continuous product innovation has helped the market grow. In the 1930s, new packaging machines enabled manufacturers wrap ice cream in flat cardboard rectangles called bricks. This, along with the availability of deep freezes, revolutionised distribution. The bricks allowed the retailer slice the product into flat portions and serve them between two wafers—known as 'two penny wafers'. Ireland is the only country where bricks are still available. Subsequent innovations have been in product form and texture.

Ice cream is predominantly an impulse purchase: it is estimated that up to 70 per cent is bought on impulse. As a result, manufacturers are keen to promote and distribute their products widely and, as HB demonstrated, to protect their distribution channels.

In the 1990s a conscious effort was made to sell to the adult market, and in 1991 HB launched the Magnum brand, a higher-priced, high-quality product that proved extremely successful. The product and its subsequent variations were essentially combinations of ice cream and chocolate on a stick. The American company Häagen-Dazs entered the Irish market in 1992, supplying its product directly in refrigerated containers. This was similar to Magnum and was also aimed at the adult market, with an advertising campaign that sought to establish a connection between ice cream and sensuality. Both Magnum and Häagen-Dazs extended their ranges with different chocolate coverings and, in the case of Häagen-Dazs, with a Bailey's and a Malibu-flavoured product.

The confectionery manufacturers Mars and Nestlé had entered the market in 1990 and 1995 respectively. Both companies introduced ice cream versions of familiar confectionery brands, such as Mars and Aero. The innovation here was in the production process, with both companies investing in new plant to manufacture ice cream variants of their products.

While the market has been dominated by big global brands, a number of Irish brands have also been established, including Murphy's ice cream which was established by Brothers Sean and Ciaran Murphy in Dingle, County Kerry, in 2000. Sold initially in its own shop in Dingle, by 2010 there were additional shops in Killarney and Dublin. A product range in 500ml tubs was also stocked by an increasing number of retailers.

Sources: *Irish Independent*, 7 August 1995; *Examiner*, 1 May 1997; *Sunday Business Post*, 4 May 1997; *Checkout*, June 2006; www.murphyicecream.ie.

Classification of new products from the firm's viewpoint

The firm can assess newness in technological or market terms. This yields a number of possibilities, as fig. 7.5 demonstrates. It is apparent, therefore, that product life-cycles can be extended in technological and market terms. This helps explain why so many products have lasted for so long; it also indicates to the marketer that the marketing or the technological dimensions of the product can usually be developed.

The development, successful launch and subsequent improvement of a new product is well illustrated by the case of Fairy Liquid. Over time, the product was reformulated and improved, and new segments were added.

Figure 7.5: Dimensions of technological and market newness

Increasing technological newness ⟶

	Reformulation: Change in product formula or physical product to optimise costs and quality	**Replacement:** Replace existing product with new one based on improved technology
Remerchandising: Increase sales to existing customers	**Improved product:** Improve utility to consumers	**Product life extension:** Add new, similar products based on new technology to serve more customers
New use: Add new segments that can use present products	**Market extension:** Add new segments, modifying present products	**Diversification:** Add new markets with new products developed from new technology

Increasing market newness ↓

THE MAKING OF A MEGA-BRAND

In 1960 Procter & Gamble launched Fairy Liquid on the British market. The launch involved distributing 15 million trial bottles to 85 per cent of the country's homes. The launch had been preceded by extensive research, though the washing-up market was still in its infancy, with only 17 per cent of households using a liquid and the rest using soap powder or soap.

In 1980 the production of Fairy Liquid reached 10 million gallons a year. In 1981 Fairy's market share was 27 per cent, and the actor Nanette Newman was introduced to endorse the product. In 1984–5 the company introduced a lemon variant, and market share increased to 32 per cent. By 1987 this had increased to 34 per cent, with the lemon variant accounting for one-third of sales. In 1988 a new formulation offered '15 per cent extra mileage,' together with better handling of grease.

In 1992 Fairy Liquid was replaced with Fairy Excel, which was '50 per cent better at dealing with grease.' Market share increased to 50 per cent. In 1993 Fairy Excel Plus was launched, with the slogan 'The power of four for the price of one'—claiming that one bottle of Excel Plus would last as long as four bottles of ordinary liquid. Excel Plus was launched simultaneously in Britain, Ireland, Germany, Denmark, Belgium, the Netherlands, Sweden, and Finland.

Consistent themes in the advertising of the product since 1960 have been the mildness of the product, its extra 'mileage', and an unashamed admission that it is dearer but that it is the better-value option. Various interpretations of the mother-and-child theme have also been used. Commercials have concentrated on a 'feel-good' theme, with soft and homely imagery being used—including one in 1994 that used a father instead of a mother at the sink. The jingle used for the commercials has been modified only slightly and is essentially the same as the first one produced in 1960. Procter & Gamble has consistently supported the brand with advertising and some below-the-line promotion.

In 1998, an anti-bacterial variant was introduced and Procter & Gamble reported a market share of 60 per cent in Ireland. In 2001, the Fairy range was repackaged in a transparent plastic bottle.

In 2010, Fairy celebrated its 50th anniversary on the market in the UK and Ireland. Procter & Gamble produced a special 50th anniversary bottle which was based on the original package design.

Source: Alan Mitchell, 'P&G comes clean on brand-new Fairy', *Marketing*, 14 October 1993; *Checkout Ireland*, April 1999; *Checkout*, April 2006.

Marketers do need to exercise caution. The Fairy Liquid case demonstrates how a product was successfully changed and adapted over time; but another leading brand, Persil, found that one of its continuous-development strategies came badly unstuck.

PERSIL POWER TAKES ITS TOLL ON PERSIL

Persil Power was launched in May 1993 as a continuous product innovation. The Persil brand had been around for quite some time, having been introduced in Ireland, for example, in 1909. Persil Power was a new formulation, which promised the consumer an improved cleaning ability. However, tests conducted by the Consumers' Association in Britain showed that the product could damage clothes. The company was forced to admit that launching the product was a mistake and that it would be reformulated.

The immediate impact of the negative publicity was a loss in market share for the brand and a reduction in the parent company's share price. In Britain the brand's market share dropped from 27 per cent before the launch in May to 24 per cent in July and August. In Ireland the brand lost its number 1 position in the market, and it took two years to recover this.

Sources: 'Persil Power takes toll on Persil', *Marketing*, 29 September 1994; *Checkout Ireland*, April 1997.

Reasons for developing a new product

The development of new products has at its core the satisfaction of customers' needs. Consumers' preferences change, and environmental influences may mean that current products no longer meet consumer specifications. In the food and beverage sector, manufacturers have developed low-fat, low-salt, sugar-free, high-fibre, and low-cholesterol products, and other variations of existing products, to meet the needs of an increasingly health-conscious consumer.

In the music industry, where needs may be largely intangible and where there are always opportunities, Polygram felt there was a gap for a new band aimed at the youth market. It advertised for would-be pop stars, and in 1994 it created the group Boyzone, which went on to become an international success. Polygram created another group, called Westlife, in a similar way.

Development also meets a number of organisational needs, including sales and profit growth, adding value, the creation of competitive advantage, responding to competitive pressure, and extending the product life-cycle. HB ice cream in creating the Magnum brand achieved growth in sales and market share; it also prepared the company for increased competition.

New-product development may be a stimulant to business growth, resulting in improved sales, cash flow, and profits. Firms may not be able to expand into new segments or markets without a new product, for example into export markets. In existing segments and markets the firm may wish to use new products to extend its range.

New-product development is part of the value-adding process. Existing products may have more features and benefits added to them. Products that are new to the world may be the result of research and development efforts within the firm, whereby company personnel have added value. The resourcefulness and creativity of company personnel is an important part of the process.

New products are a possible source of competitive advantage. If the firm can bring a superior product or service to the market that has advantages over competitors, it can use this to differentiate itself. Being first on the market certainly has advantages, though competitive advantage will be eroded as competitors enter offering similar or superior products.

Not everyone can be the first on the market with a new product; many firms will be followers and will need to develop new products to do so. Responding to competitors with new products may be necessary to protect the firm's own market position.

New-product development is a necessary part of the product life-cycle; it is the process that creates and that can ultimately extend the life of the product. Many new products are a reaction to declining sales of existing products, which may be replaced or modified to prolong their life.

THE NEW-PRODUCT DEVELOPMENT PROCESS

The new-product development process involves a number of distinct stages, from the original idea to the successful commercialisation of the product. The stages provide a guideline for marketers and indicate the resource and skill requirements necessary for the process.

The idea stage

Ideas can come from a variety of sources. They may come from personnel within the firm, or they may come from the consumer. *Intrapreneurs*—enterprising individuals within the company—may be the source of ideas: they may be marketing, operations, production, or R&D managers or workers. Marketing channel members may also provide ideas. All firms will keep abreast of competitors' activities in the market. While this may involve the firm essentially following competitors, it may also provide the catalyst for it to develop its own unique product or service variation. In 2002, for example, Coca-Cola and Pepsi both launched new product-line extensions in their fight for market share. Coca-Cola introduced a vanilla-flavoured Coke, while Pepsi introduced 'Pepsi Blue', a blueberry-flavoured cola (*Financial Times*, 7 May 2002). In 2006, *Checkout* magazine reported that Baileys were testing both a mint chocolate and a caramel-cream-flavoured version (*Checkout*, February 2006). These flavours proved popular and, in 2008, a coffee variant was added (www.baileys.com).

Consumers may be the source of ideas for new products. Consumer research may emphasise aspects of the product or service that the consumer is dissatisfied with, or may suggest changes to a product and ways in which it can be improved.

Not all ideas will be suitable. Ideas should be screened so that those that are inconsistent with the firm's goals and objectives are eliminated. In general, a number of criteria should be applied when ideas are being screened, including:

- the relationship of the idea to the firm's existing products or services
- the effect the proposed product or service may have on existing sales
- the resource requirements necessary to produce and market the new product
- the segments or markets it will be capable of attracting
- the value-adding that will take place
- the ability of the management to successfully develop and commercialise the product.

These criteria should enable the management to assess the firm's ability to develop the idea. They may point to deficiencies in skills or resources and give the firm an indication of what will be required for it to successfully develop the idea.

Revenue and cost analysis

Revenue and cost analysis will examine the financial implications of the idea. Costs can be estimated, and potential sales income forecast. The analysis will assess the ability of the product or service to achieve the return on investment that may be required. Breakeven analysis will be useful in exploring the relationship between sales and fixed and variable costs.

Costs will also be incurred if a marketer is considering a change in product or packaging. In 1995 Murphy's brewery introduced draught technology into bottled stout; before this it was available only in cans. In conjunction with its parent company, Heineken, and its British distributor, Whitbread, the company spent £8 million on developing a plastic device inserted in the bottle during the filling process (*Checkout Ireland*, August 1997).

The development process

The development process refers to how the firm takes the idea and develops it into a more tangible product concept that can be assessed and tested. The objective of the development stage is to produce a product that meets consumers' needs, is safe, and can be produced by the firm. Regulations regarding copyright, patents, product safety, and consumer law will have to be adhered to.

There are four essential stages in the development process: concept testing, product design, preference testing, and the selection of a brand name.

Concept testing typically involves the use of focus groups of target customers who will be asked to give their views and opinions on the proposed product or service. The researcher may use descriptions, mock-ups, drawings, or illustrations to explain what the product will be or how it will look. Respondents will be asked for their assessment. The researcher will also seek information on consumers' decision-making processes in relation to the product or the general type of product.

Product design follows from concept testing. At this stage designers will prepare detailed designs for manufacture or, in the case of services, outlines of what the service will comprise. They will refer to the research carried out on the concept. Issues such as ease of use, attractiveness, materials used, and ergonomic design may be some of the specific issues to be dealt with at this stage.

Preference testing involves testing consumers' preferences for different levels of product quality or features. Conjoint analysis can be used at this stage, which involves experiments with different price and attribute levels to determine how the consumer differentiates between them.

Selecting a brand name is important not just from the marketing viewpoint but also in ensuring that the name selected is not already in use or that it does not bear too close a similarity to one already in use.

Test-marketing or market simulation

The risk of a new product failing in the market is reduced if market testing is carried out. Test-marketing involves testing the product under typical market conditions. While it may not be possible to replicate all factors in the market completely, for example the response of competitors, it usually gives a good indication of the product's potential.

Test-marketing involves making the product available in selected distribution outlets, supported by marketing communication. Consider the new lager launched by Guinness in 1998.

A NEW LAGER FROM GUINNESS

Guinness began test-marketing a new brand of lager in 1998, its first Irish branded lager since the launch of Harp almost 40 years earlier. The product was called Breó and was classified as a white lager-style beer. This was closer to lager than ale, with a distinctive taste. The product took 18 months to research and develop. Guinness was anxious to develop a new brand in the growing lager market; in 1997 the consumption of lager was up by 6½ per cent. Test-marketing was concentrated at first in selected pubs in Dublin, before a national launch. The brand was aimed at younger drinkers. The product was served slightly colder than other draught beers, at 3° Celsius.

Guinness had consulted a brand name agency when selecting the name. It did not like the ideas, however, and decided to come up with its own suggestions. Breó, based on the Irish word *breo*, 'firebrand', was finally settled on.

Guinness spent €6,350,000 on developing and marketing Breó, and the product remained on the market for two years. In October 2000, however, Guinness decided to withdraw it as it had not achieved a sufficiently large consumer base.

Sources: Paul O'Kane, 'Guinness launches a new lager', *Sunday Tribune*, 19 April 1998; E. Moloney, 'New blond brew proves a fiery mix', *Irish Independent*, 23 April 1998; Christine Doherty, '£5 million blizzard of publicity for Guinness white beer', *Sunday Business Post*, 26 April 1998; Christine Doherty, 'Guinness pulls Breó as punters fail to drink up', *Sunday Business Post*, 29 October 2000.

It was 2010 before Guinness again decided to test a new product in Ireland. On this occasion, it was a black lager and Northern Ireland was chosen as the test market.

GUINNESS LAUNCHES NEW 'BLACK' LAGER

In March 2010 Guinness launched a new product in Northern Ireland, called Guinness Black Lager. This had been developed by Guinness brewers in Dublin and was produced in 330ml bottles. The product targeted younger drinkers and went on sale in selected pubs and off licences. Its price was similar to other premium lagers.

The launch of the product in Northern Ireland was an attempt to increase sales in a difficult trading environment, beer sales had been in decline. Alcohol consumption in Ireland declined by 9.6 per cent in 2009. Northern Ireland also represented a good geographic test market, where Guinness could monitor its success, before launching in other markets.

Source: Éanna Ó Caollaí, 'Guinness launches "black" lager', *Irish Times*, 23 March 2010.

Consumers' response to the new product can be measured, though competitors can intervene and attempt to distort the results by discounting their products or running promotion campaigns. It also gives competitors the chance to see the product or service and start the process of developing their own alternative. If they can replicate the product or service quite quickly they may be able to seize the advantage.

Market simulation involves the establishment of a laboratory test market. This is an artificial means of testing a product, and one that can be expensive. Simulation involves exposing a sample of consumers to advertisements for the new product; they are then given samples of the product to take home and use. Interviews are then held to determine levels of satisfaction and purchasing intention. Repeat purchase levels are measured by offering the consumer the chance to buy the product again. On the results of the simulation, potential sales would be predicted. The main problem with simulated testing is that real market conditions are not replicated; however, it is a good means of testing products where, for competitive reasons, secrecy is important.

Test-marketing and simulation can be used for many products. They may not, however, be easy to implement with some services or industrial products. It would be difficult for a holiday company to test-market a new resort without bringing customers to it. In the case of large industrial purchases, such as ships, the shipbuilder would have to complete the vessel before it would be possible to test it.

In general, test-marketing or simulation can be used to assess how the product is likely to perform in the market. It is a form of research, and it is therefore important to ensure that the product is tested with a sufficiently large sample and that the results are carefully interpreted. There may be a tendency for consumers to express positive opinions about something new, which may not necessarily translate into repeat sales.

Commercialisation

Commercialisation typically involves the full-scale launch of the product on the market. This includes persuading the marketing channel to accept and stock the product and persuading customers to buy the product for the first time. Timing is therefore important. The product will generally have to be in the channel before any form of consumer marketing communication can be engaged in.

Timing is critically important for product launches. The product must be ready for the market, the channel must be able to obtain it easily, and the buyer must be able to get information. Critical factors in the launch include ensuring that the trade press and other appropriate media are aware of the launch, that launch events are well planned, and that communication opportunities are maximised. On occasion, product launches may be accompanied by elaborate hospitality or entertainment, usually directed at the trade and media.

The important issue in a launch is ensuring that the audience with whom you want to communicate is present. This provides an opportunity to explain the new product and the marketing campaign that would accompany it; it also provides an opportunity for questions and feedback. Obviously, large firms may have the budget for large-scale launches; for smaller firms, the launch may have more to do with meeting the trade, providing them with the necessary information, and getting any possible publicity. Sometimes firms will use the services of event managers or public relations companies to assist in the launch.

Success or failure?

Success means that the new product is adopted by a sufficiently large number of consumers, and a proportion of these will become regular users of the product. It is to be expected that some consumers may try the new product once or twice but then revert to their former brand or switch to competitors' offerings, and this has to be allowed for by the marketer. Success is maintained by the marketer staying close to the customer and the marketing channels, communicating with them, ensuring product quality, and ultimately developing the product to its full potential.

Not all new products or services will be commercial successes, as the previous example of Breó illustrated. In 1978 Guinness launched a new product called Guinness Light, a light stout aimed principally at women. It did not achieve the desired level of sales, and it was withdrawn from the market after a few months. Perhaps it was a little ahead of its time. The B&I Line launched a high-speed jetfoil service on the Irish Sea in 1985. The vessel, built by the aircraft manufacturer Boeing, was capable of faster speeds than conventional car ferries. It could only operate successfully, however, in calm seas; when the sea was rough it proved too uncomfortable for passengers. The Irish Sea proved to be unsuitable for successful operation, services were frequently disrupted, and the company ultimately decided to withdraw it. Ten years later high-speed catamaran ferries were being used on the Irish Sea, and these did not experience the same problems as the jetfoil, because of improved technology. Bailey launched a chocolate peppermint cream liqueur, Penny Royal, in 1989. It was more expensive than its existing product and not sufficiently different to guarantee repeat purchases, and it was ultimately phased out. The subsequent launch of Sheridan's liqueur was more successful, the product being significantly different from Bailey's Irish Cream.

Products fail for a variety of reasons. The company may have carried out inadequate market research and analysis, or research results may have been based on an unrepresentative sample, and a sufficient number of consumers may not actually adopt the product. On occasion, new products with defects may make their way onto the market. These may not work properly and may have to be recalled by the manufacturer, inconveniencing the customer and adding to the manufacturer's costs.

Sometimes the costs of developing new products may be higher than expected, and this pushes up the price, which may become unattractive to the buyer. Poor timing can also be a problem: for example, in markets where seasonality is an issue, such as clothing and toys, there is usually a critical period in which anything new must be launched to make sure it reaches the retailer, and ultimately the consumer, in time.

Competitors will certainly play a large part in the failure of many new products. They may be able to produce their own version of the product quickly, or they may use price promotions on their existing products to tempt the consumer away.

The importance of new-product development in the firm

The new-product development process is an important part of the value-adding process in any firm. It implies that the firm keeps its existing product or service range and market developments under review.

The firm should have a procedure for periodically reviewing its new-product development activities. Some have specific research and development departments; others may rely on intrapreneurs to come up with ideas; while in start-up enterprises the process is inseparable from the role of the entrepreneur. The new-product development process demonstrates the importance of market information and research. Formal research exercises may probe specific aspects of the opinions, attitudes or behaviour of consumers or channels. More informal information, such as feedback from channel members or comments, questions or complaints from consumers, may also be the source of ideas.

The new-product development process demonstrates the need for the firm to keep its product range under review. There should be a product development plan for each of the firm's products. This will outline possible development scenarios for the product. If few exist, this may be an indication that the firm should be looking for alternatives to develop. For example, Newbridge Cutlery decided to launch a range of silver jewellery in 1996. This provided a product that could be aimed at new distribution channels in addition to some of its existing outlets.

New-product development may not always come from within the firm. Companies can consider licensing arrangements, mergers or acquisitions as possible sources of new-product development.

Timing market entry

Research has shown that the first firms to develop markets for a new product, known as *market pioneers*, tend to enjoy a long-term competitive advantage over later entrants, reflected in a higher level of market share and profitability. What is not so well understood is whether there is much variation in the experience of later market entrants; in other words, is it better to be an early follower of a pioneer in a still-growing market than to be a late entrant in a mature market? A study by Lambkin (1989) used samples from the PIMS (Profit Impact of Market Strategies) database; the results showed that there were substantial differences both within and between the categories of pioneers, early followers and late entrants with regard to their competitive strategies and performance. From the point of view of later entrants, the evidence suggests that it is better to be early than late into a new market, though the effects of timing are moderated by the choice of competitive strategy. The most successful early followers appeared to be those who manage to leap-frog the market by entering on a larger scale than existing firms and by offering a superior product.

FURTHER READING

de Chernatony, L., and McDonald, M., *Creating Powerful Brands*, London: Butterworth Heinemann 1993.
Fanning, J., *The Importance of Being Branded: An Irish Perspective*, Dublin: Liffey Press 2006.
Hart, S., and Murphy, J., *Brands: The New Wealth Creators*, London: Macmillan 1998.
Urban, G., and Hauser, J., *The Design and Marketing of New Products* (second edition), Englewood Cliffs (NJ): Prentice-Hall 1993.

DISCUSSION QUESTIONS

1. Analyse the different product levels for each of the following:
   (a) O'Brien's Sandwich Bars
   (b) the Gaelic Athletic Association
   (c) Bank of Ireland
   (d) Waterford Crystal
   (e) the *Farmers' Journal*.
2. Comment on how you feel branding will develop in Ireland in the future. Will there be more or fewer Irish brands around?
3. Select some appropriate brand names for each of the following:
   (a) a new range of sun-care products
   (b) a new vitamin-enriched bread
   (c) an Irish-language newspaper
   (d) an electronic printer
   (e) a new environmentally friendly detergent.
4. Discuss the implications of an increased environmental awareness among consumers on the packaging decision. Could consumer products be marketed with less packaging?

5. Outline the stages in the new product development process for:
   (a) a new low-fat range of yoghurts
   (b) an e-business course in a third-level college
   (c) a modern art gallery.

REFERENCES

Benson, C., 'Puffin and Penguin: a step forward for brand owners', *Journal of Brand Management*, June 1997.

Cummins, M., 'Brand positioning: a case history of an Irish whiskey', *Irish Marketing Review*, vol. 1 (1986).

Daly, A. and Moloney, D., 'Managing corporate rebranding', *Irish Marketing Review*, vol. 17 (2005), nos. 1 and 2.

de Chernatony, L. and McDonald, M., *Creating Powerful Brands*, London: Butterworth Heinemann 1993.

Fanning, J., *The Importance of Being Branded: An Irish Perspective*, Dublin: Liffey Press 2006.

Gunin, J., 'Ulster linen brings a touch of Ireland', *Home Textiles Today*, 11 May 1998.

Holt, D. B. 'What becomes an icon most?', *Harvard Business Review*, March 2003.

Kennedy, A., 'The adoption and diffusion of new industrial products: a literature review', *European Journal of Marketing*, vol. 17 (1983), no. 3.

Kohli, C. and Thakor, M., 'Branding consumer goods: insights from theory and practice', *Journal of Consumer Marketing*, vol. 14 (1997), no. 3.

Kotler, P., and Armstrong, G., *Principles of Marketing* (sixth edition), Englewood Cliffs (NJ): Prentice-Hall 1994.

Lambkin, Mary, 'Timing market entry: a key to competitive success', *Irish Marketing Review*, vol. 4 (1989), no. 2.

Lockett, A. and Littler, D., 'The adoption of direct banking services', *Journal of Marketing Management*, vol. 13, November 1997 (no. 8).

Lysanski, S., 'A boundary theory investigation of the product manager's role', *Journal of Marketing*, vol. 49 (1985), no. 1.

MacDonagh, J. and Weldridge, R., *Behavioural Science for Business and Marketing Students*, Dublin: Gill & Macmillan 1994.

Macrae, C., Parkinson, S., and Sheerman, J., 'Managing marketing's DNA: the role of branding', *Irish Marketing Review*, vol. 8 (1995).

Meenaghan, J. and O'Sullivan, P., 'The shape and length of the product lifecycle', *Irish Marketing Review*, vol. 1 (1986).

Mortell, M., 'Design in the product lifecycle: Ballygowan spring water', *Irish Marketing Review*, vol. 6 (1993).

Pratt, Maurice, Proceedings of the National Marketing Conference, MII, October 1994.

Rogan, Donal, 'A Profile of the Early Customer for the Mobile Cellular Telephone in Ireland', MBS thesis, University College, Dublin, 1988.

Rogers, E., *Diffusion of Innovations* (third edition), New York: Free Press 1983.

Romeo, A., 'Brands and competitive strategy', *Irish Marketing Review*, vol. 8 (1995).

8
Pricing

Typically, marketers will be concerned with decisions on setting a price for the product or service and with decisions on the role of price in the firm's competitive strategy. In these decisions, factors such as demand, the nature of the product, the profile of the market, and the profile of consumers and their price-sensitivity will all be considered. Competitors' prices and their pricing strategies will usually have a significant influence.

A number of different approaches are used in calculating price, all of which require an estimate of the costs that will be incurred. The price must produce a satisfactory level of profit for the firm. Price will often form a significant part of promotional campaigns and may become a central aspect of the firm's strategy; for example, Ryanair described itself as 'the low-cost airline'.

Pricing involves putting a value on a product or service. This means that buyers know what they have to pay, and sellers know what they can expect to receive.

Consumer price sensitivity in Ireland was a much debated issue in recent years.

FEELING THE PINCH?

Research carried out in 2008 for Bord Bia by the Henley Centre on the markets in the UK and Ireland concluded that the consumer spending boom of the previous decade was over. House prices and discretionary incomes were falling and inflation was on an upward trend. The Henley Centre felt that the impact of this bleaker landscape on consumer confidence and behaviour would be significant. The research examined consumer anxiety levels and found that:

- Consumers feel negatively about their personal finances, with high proportions becoming more worried over the past year and many expecting the future to be bleak.
- Any action that a company can undertake to help reassure or support consumers in this climate may be appreciated, so long as it is perceived as genuine and in line with the company's brand.
- It was personal, immediate worries that were causing the most anxiety for consumers. For instance, the possibility of a recession or a decline in the stock market is more removed and therefore of less concern than being able to afford the basics of energy and food.

The study identified four segments of consumers, ordered by increasing level of anxiety: the placid, the perturbed, the pressured, and the panicked. In other words, placid consumers are the least worried, while the panicked are extremely worried.

There was a strong correlation between the level of anxiety that consumers feel, the extent of their spending cutbacks in the previous 12 months, and their expected cutbacks in the next12 months.

The most popular money-saving actions for Irish consumers involve using offers and deals, coupons and vouchers, or even switching to a cheaper brand. For the UK, the most popular actions are similar; keeping track of prices and taking advantage of promotions to get products that they are already buying for a lower price. Consumers are prepared to sacrifice convenience if it means that they don't have to compromise the goods and services that they want to consume.

Large proportions of the UK and Irish population are prepared to 'trade down' in the sense that they will choose cheaper brands and cheaper retailers in order to save money. Irish consumers are more likely than UK consumers to do this.

Consumers are willing to give up luxuries, such as shopping for fun, updating goods to keep up with styles and fashions, and eating out. However, these trade-offs only tend to be considered after consumers have saved what they can through price checking and trading down.

Consumers will look to make other cuts in their spending and consumption ahead of cutting their Fairtrade, environmentally friendly, and organic purchasing. Products and services that are perceived to be integral to consumers' life-styles will only be cut as a last resort. It is only really the most anxious who will consider these sacrifices in any significant numbers.

The research concluded that there was also an opportunity for brands to position themselves as helping consumers to maintain their current life-styles.

Source: Bord Bia, 'Feeling the Pinch?': A report on how key trends in Ireland and the UK will be affected by the current economic squeeze', www.bordbia.ie.

PRICING POLICY

Pricing policy acts to guide the business in its pricing decisions. Pricing policy will depend on a number of factors, including the position of the product in its life-cycle, the competitiveness of the industry in which the business operates, and the general strategic thrust of the business.

Pricing policy will also be determined by the other elements in the marketing mix. The price should be consistent with the other elements; a high-value product, for example, communicated with an 'exclusive' image and selectively distributed, will be priced accordingly.

If a new product is being introduced, the company may decide to adopt a *price-skimming* approach, which involves charging the highest price that buyers who most desire the product will pay. If the company wishes to build market share it will typically use a penetration approach, which involves penetrating the market with a low price. This has consistently been the pricing strategy pursued by Ryanair since it entered the airline market in 1984. Pricing was a central aspect of strategy for the other low-cost airlines that were established in Europe in the 1990s.

A company with a mature product may find itself forced to offer price incentives to hold its position in the market. If the product is in decline there may be no alternative but to accept a gradual reduction in price. The business may also have policies in relation to discriminatory pricing, special-event pricing, discounting, and other factors that affect the final price.

In general, the marketer will find it necessary to change or adapt price as demand and competitive conditions dictate.

THE DYNAMICS OF PRICING

Pricing plays a fundamental role in marketing strategy. It is used as a competitive tool in the market and may be emphasised in advertising.

How the marketer reacts to price changes in the market will be a significant aspect of marketing strategy. Some price changes may be the result of competitors' actions; others may be the result of economic influences, such as shortages or shifts in the price of substitute products. Other factors that could influence price changes include regulatory changes: for example, in 1998 Aer Rianta, which was running a campaign for the retention of duty-free sales, stated that the loss of duty-free income in 1999 could lead to increases in landing charges for airlines using their airports. The organisation was asserting that if it lost sales in one area of its business it would have to raise prices in another area to maintain income.

Consumers' perception of price is important, as they may use it to compare competitors' offerings. This applies to many products and especially to services, where intangibility may mean that the consumer uses the price as an indication of the quality of service.

Price promotions may become a significant part of the firm's marketing communication activities. Discounts, rebates, and other price promotions will affect the price the consumer pays. Marketers need to use price promotions strategically: they should not be used as a substitute for advertising or product development but as part of an integrated marketing strategy. They can have a particular role in protecting brands in competitive battles. Price-value promotions, for example, can involve giving extra products at no extra cost, or premiums, such as gifts. There is evidence that these can be used to enhance brand appeal and can help neutralise the competitive effects of retailers' own-label or regional brands (Everett, 1998).

Price will also be used to motivate and give an incentive to marketing channel members. Discounts may be given especially where the channel member increases volumes.

If the marketer is introducing new products to the market, the price charged will be an important influence on the rate of the product's diffusion. It may also determine how quickly the marketer will recoup the costs of developing and introducing the new product. In many new-product introductions the initial price will be high and will be lowered as competitors enter the market.

Price changes may be subject to political or legal sanction. The standard fares charged on public transport services operated by the subsidiary companies of CIÉ can be changed only by ministerial order. Government approval is usually required for some other price changes, such as television licence fees and electricity charges. Pricing practices often come in for public and official scrutiny.

The introduction of the euro in 2002 required consumers to get used to prices expressed in a new currency. When making decisions about purchases, customers will often have acceptable price ranges in mind, within which they evaluate particular products. The introduction of the euro meant they had to convert their existing acceptable price ranges into a new denomination.

PRICE COMPETITION

Price competition will inevitably be a factor in most companies' competitive environment. In addition, consumers will very often use price as the basis for comparing competitors' offerings. Price competition occasionally becomes more intense, when it is usually known as a price war.

Price wars are usually a feature of highly competitive markets; they have included sporadic encounters between the large supermarkets and between airlines. The effect of these battles tends to reverberate in the channels. A research study conducted in 1983, when Dunnes Stores entered the Northern Ireland grocery market and began a price war with the long-established market leader, Stewart's, demonstrated a number of effects (Bell and Brown, 1986). The prices on many FMCGs were cut, and the battle lasted for about six weeks. Every member of the channel felt the effects, and while consumers enjoyed a spell of very low prices, they also suffered from the side effects of overcrowded shops, long checkout queues, and frequent shortages. The only beneficiaries, the research concluded, were the media, especially the *Belfast Telegraph*, which enjoyed a dramatic increase in advertising income.

By the end of the 1980s there was evidence of change (McGoldrick, 1993). Multiple grocers in Britain and Ireland were recording higher profits, had significant power over manufacturers, and were investing in new supermarkets. Their strategy had switched from intense price competition to one of desensitising consumers to price and shifting attention to new types of shops, wider product ranges, and new services.

Price wars can be quite destructive. They can lead to problems in the channels of distribution, and channel members may not like the uncertainty that can result. In extreme cases there can be a shake-out in the market, with some competitors leaving. This happened on the Dublin–London air route in the early 1990s. British Airways was one of the leading airlines on the route, but under extreme competitive pressure the company decided to withdraw, such were the low levels of profit available.

This experience illustrates the worst case for the marketer. It also emphasises the danger of price-based competitive strategies. Low prices need to be accompanied by a low cost base. Ryanair managed to keep its costs low during the 1980s and 1990s by buying second-hand aircraft and providing a 'no-frills' service. Marketers with high cost structures will find intense price competition difficult to sustain.

PRICING AND THE OBJECTIVES OF THE BUSINESS

Businesses exist to make a profit, and their performance will ultimately be evaluated on profitability. Some organisations are non-profit-making but may still be expected to generate income to cover some or all of their costs. Price is therefore the marketing tool that will generate a profit for the business or will generate the income needed to cover costs or to make a contribution towards them. The price charged must generate a profit, and for most businesses this is the primary objective.

All firms incur costs, such as costs of production, staffing, and administration. Marketing activities, such as product development, and research or promotional campaigns, can represent significant costs. The price is the means of recovering costs and generating a profit and is therefore the only element of the marketing mix that actually generates income for the firm.

While the maximisation of income and profit will be the most significant pricing objective, price will also play a role in other aspects of the firm's marketing. Establishing the pricing objectives can be considered the first stage in the pricing process, as fig. 8.1 demonstrates.

Figure 8.1: Stages in the pricing process

1.	Establish pricing objectives
2.	Determine demand levels
3.	Calculate costs
4.	Analyse competitors' prices and pricing strategies
5.	Select a method of calculating price
6.	Consider influencing factors that may determine the final price

ESTABLISHING PRICING OBJECTIVES

Firms will seek to establish the price that maximises sales income and profit. Specific sales and profit targets will usually be established as part of the sales or revenue budgets. In multi-product firms, targets may vary by product category or brand and will take into account such factors as the stage of the product in the life-cycle, promotional campaigns, and competitive market conditions. Oxenfeldt (1973) suggested a number of potential pricing objectives, as illustrated in fig. 8.2.

Price is an integral part of the marketing mix and will be used to achieve particular objectives. If a business is aiming for a significant increase in market share it may decide to charge a lower price than competitors to attract more buyers, the increased number of buyers making up for the lower profits that the lower price will yield.

Competitive market conditions may force the firm to reduce prices, which can cause particular problems if the firm has a high cost structure. If costs cannot be reduced, profits will be. To avoid this profit reduction, promotional campaigns or special offers could be considered in an attempt to maintain income and profitability. In general, marketers will monitor competitive pricing conditions closely.

Some businesses will seek to charge high prices to maximise their present gain. This approach may be adopted for new products where there are few if any competitors and where the firm seeks to recoup the costs of development and market launch. Inevitably, as competitors enter the market, prices will be forced down.

The marketer must have clear pricing objectives and must establish how these relate to the firm's marketing environment.

Figure 8.2: Potential pricing objectives

1. Maximise long-term profits
2. Maximise short-term profits
3. Growth
4. Stabilise market
5. Desensitise customers to price
6. Maintain price leadership arrangement
7. Discourage entrants
8. Speed the exit of marginal firms
9. Avoid government investigation and control
10. Maintain loyalty of middlemen and get their sales support
11. Avoid demands for 'more' from suppliers—labour in particular
12. Enhance the image of the firm and its offerings
13. Be regarded as 'fair' by customers (ultimate)
14. Create interest and excitement about the item
15. Be considered trustworthy and reliable by rivals
16. Help in the sale of weak items in the line
17. Discourage others from cutting prices
18. Make a product 'visible'
19. 'Spoil' the market to obtain high price for sale of business
20. Build traffic

Source: A. Oxenfeldt, 'A decision-making structure for price decisions', *Journal of Marketing*, vol. 37 (January 1973).

DETERMINING DEMAND LEVELS

Economics provides a basis for understanding product demand. The principles of supply and demand and an understanding of price elasticity are fundamental to the pricing decision.

Economic theory provides the general rule of supply and demand. This states that luxury goods that are in short supply will command a higher price than they are perhaps really worth, simply because more people want them than can be supplied. On the other hand, where goods are plentiful, prices will be lower, because people will not pay the higher prices for them. Consider the demand for tickets for the all-Ireland hurling or football finals, and contrast this with the demand for tickets for a local football or hurling match.

The price elasticity of demand gives an indication of the consumer's sensitivity to changes in price. If the price of a product or service goes up or down, demand for it may be affected. Price elasticity gives an indication of how demand will be affected.

Price elasticity can be calculated using the following equation. If the price elasticity of demand equals 1, this implies that demand rises or falls by the same percentage by which the price rises or falls. If the price elasticity of demand is greater than 1, demand rises or falls at a greater rate than that of price change. A price elasticity of demand less than 1 indicates that demand rises or falls at a lower rate than the rate of price change.

$$price\ elasticity\ of\ demand = \frac{percentage\ change\ in\ quantity\ demanded}{percentage\ change\ in\ price}$$

Demand is considered to be elastic if a small change in price changes the quantity demanded; it is inelastic if a small change in price hardly changes the quantity demanded. Price elasticity for the same product may not be the same for an increase and a decrease. Consumer price elasticity must also be assessed in the context of market prices; it will be influenced by how much the price diverges from the average market price. Demand will typically be elastic for products that have close competitors, for example a litre of Avonmore milk as against a litre of Golden Vale milk. Inelasticity may be exhibited in the price paid for a service such as a hairdresser or beautician, where the consumer is more conscious of appearance or the result than of the price they have to pay.

The calculation of price elasticity and research on factors such as consumer sensitivity to special price promotions is of relevance to marketers. One research study in Britain calculated the price elasticities of the five leading brands in a hundred product categories by regression analysis (Hamilton, East, and Kalafatis, 1997). Elasticities were found to be widely spread among product categories, with 19 per cent of them positive. The study also revealed greater price elasticity for new brands and no difference in elasticities between growing and declining brands. Brand leaders were slightly less sensitive to price changes than other brands; and higher advertising expenditure was associated with lower price-sensitivity. These results, while they cannot be considered to provide a general rule, do illustrate the links between price-sensitivity and issues such as whether or not the product is a brand leader, and the relationship between advertising expenditure and price-sensitivity.

Another study, conducted in the United States, used scanner data from a supermarket to investigate the effect of promotional factors on price elasticities in various product categories (Walter and Bommer, 1996). It found that factors specific to the product, such as the brand and its market position, were more significant in affecting elasticities in product categories than promotional factors, such as the frequency and magnitude of the price offer. Promotions on brands with significant market share within a category could therefore have a disproportionate effect.

Marketers need to understand how price-sensitive their consumers actually are. If demand for the product is highly elastic, there may be little scope for increasing the price. Instead the marketer may have to concentrate on ways of reducing the cost or improving the general product offering to maintain profit levels. Generally, companies assess price elasticity on the basis of past experience. This poses a difficulty for marketers who have had little experience of price changes and their consequent effect on demand.

Price elasticity can vary with time. For example, it can be shown to vary over the stages of the product life-cycle. In the beginning it is usually the least price-sensitive consumers, the innovators and early adopters, who adopt new products or innovations; the most price-sensitive consumers tend to be the late majority and the laggards.

CALCULATING COSTS

Costs can be classified as *variable* or *fixed*. Variable costs vary as output or sales vary and typically include raw materials and labour; examples of variable marketing costs include coupon and rebate redemptions. While several thousand coupons may be inserted in magazines or direct-mailed, the cost to the business will depend on the number of coupons or rebates that are redeemed by the consumer. Fixed costs, on the other hand, remain fixed, regardless of output or sales: an example would be the rent the company pays on its premises. An example of a fixed marketing cost would be the salary paid to a marketing manager.

The sum of fixed and variable costs equals total cost. Average cost is total cost divided by the number of units produced. Once the average cost is known, the business can use this as a basis for deciding what the selling price should be and what profit it will make per unit. Broadly speaking, it is the average cost plus the desired profit margin that determines the price per unit that will be charged.

An important consideration is that costs can increase because of inflation. Prices must therefore increase in line with inflation if the business is to maintain its real profits.

ANALYSIS OF COMPETITORS' PRICES AND PRICING STRATEGY

Monitoring competitors' prices and pricing strategies is a continuous activity. In very price-competitive markets, prices and strategies may change regularly; the marketer will need to keep abreast of these changes. Price is used by many firms as their main competitive tool. Competitively, it is flexible, as it can be varied, typically with some form of price promotion. This can be an advantage if there are environmental changes that require a quick response.

In markets with several competitors offering broadly similar products, prices will usually be competitive. The tendency will be for individual competitors to reduce prices to achieve an increase in market share.

The business must also be able to react to changes that competitors may make in their prices. It is wise to carry out some research to determine how buyers perceive price. In perceptual terms, it is a truism that the higher the price the higher the perceived quality of the product, and the lower the price the lower the perceived quality.

Price is a powerful positioning tool. Some firms emphasise quality and service levels and place less emphasis on price. This may be appropriate where buyers are less price-sensitive; in other cases, firms may emphasise price or value for money. For example, Dunnes Stores used the slogan 'Dunnes Stores—better value beats them all' for many years. The company's advertising emphasised this fact.

Firms that pursue strategies based strongly on price competition need to be careful that, in the search for a highly competitive price, the other elements of the marketing mix do not end up turning consumers away from the product. When own-label grocery products were launched on the Irish market, many of the supermarkets concentrated on low prices and neglected quality. The consumer did indeed respond to low prices but was not happy with the quality received. Quinnsworth, for example, introduced its first own-label range in 1977. Approximately 50 imported products were introduced, but consumers perceived the quality to be too low. The company had to change strategy and develop a home-produced range of products, in partnership with Irish manufacturers and distributors (Pratt,

1994). Consumers were used to the quality levels of national brands, and this is what they used in making comparisons.

SELECTING A METHOD FOR CALCULATING PRICES

A number of pricing methods are available to the business, and the method selected can depend on such considerations as the industry in which the firm operates and the type of product or service the company produces. Four main methods can be used: cost-plus, perceived value, breakeven and target profit, and going rate.

Cost-plus pricing involves adding a standard mark-up to the cost of the product, for example taking the average cost of the product and adding a 25 per cent mark-up. Cost-based approaches to pricing are based on the assumption that costs can be identified and calculated. This is a common approach in the retail sector, where products are bought from manufacturers or middlemen and a mark-up is added. The mark-up must take into account the costs the retailer incurs in selling the product and a satisfactory profit margin.

The formula for calculating the mark-up price is:

$$\text{mark-up price} = \frac{\text{unit costs}}{1 - \text{desired return on sales}}$$

Consider a clothing retailer who buys men's suits from a wholesaler. Each suit costs €100, and it is estimated that the cost of selling each suit, in terms of rent, wages, and administration, is €20 per suit. If the desired return on sales is 25 per cent, the mark-up price would be:

$$\text{mark-up price} = \frac{100 + 20}{1 - 0.25} = €160 \text{ per suit}$$

As a pricing method, the cost-plus approach is simple to calculate, and it can be varied to suit different product categories. The mark-up on frozen food, for example, might be higher than the mark-up on canned food, because of the higher costs of refrigeration.

The difficulty with cost-based approaches to pricing, however, is that they may not be able to take into account the demand for a product at different price levels. In the example above, what would happen if the retailer discovered that a close competitor was offering similar suits at €139? A reduction in price will drive down profit, unless costs can be cut. Cost-based methods may not take the demand elasticity of particular segments or competitive conditions into account; they are unlikely therefore to lead to maximisation of profit.

Perceived-value pricing is based on the perception of the buyer, which may need to be researched by the marketer. The research would seek to determine what perceived value the product or service has for the consumer, and how they translate that value into monetary terms. Perceived-value pricing is often used by the marketers of services where the nature of the service is more intangible.

Perceived-value approaches do take market and demand conditions into account. Many airlines, for example, charge different prices according to the time the person wants to travel, the flexibility they require, and how far in advance they book their journey. From experience, airlines know that they can fill a certain proportion of seats with travellers who booked 14 days in advance with APEX, a certain proportion with business travellers who require maximum flexibility on booking and travel times, and a certain proportion with stand-by passengers who turn up on the day. Prices are therefore tailored to suit the demand elasticities of each of these segments and their perception of the value of the fare they receive.

Breakeven and target profit pricing involves calculating a price based on a relationship between cost and volume of sales. The breakeven point is the point where income and costs are equal. Below this point, costs exceed income, and a loss is incurred; above this point, income exceeds costs, and a profit is earned. Breakeven analysis involves estimating how much income is needed to cover the fixed costs of producing a product and at the same time to cover the variable costs.

This pricing technique is particularly useful for pricing new products. Using the relationship between fixed costs, variable costs, price, sales income, and target profit, the marketer can calculate the sales volume required to break even or to achieve a planned level of profit.

Consider the case of an entrepreneur who wishes to establish a small business making jams and marmalades. The fixed costs are estimated at €50,000 per year. The estimated variable costs per unit are €0.50 per jar, and the selling price is to be €1 per jar. How many jars must be sold to break even?

The breakeven point in units can be calculated using the formula:

$$\text{breakeven units} = \frac{\text{total fixed costs}}{\text{unit contribution to fixed cost}}$$

$$\text{breakeven units} = \frac{50{,}000}{1 - 0.50} = 100{,}000 \text{ jars}$$

Therefore, 100,000 jars must be sold to break even. Obviously, the entrepreneur will require a profit. Assuming this is a profit of €20,000 a year, how many units must be sold to achieve this?

This can be calculated by adding the required profit to the formula:

$$\text{target profit units} = \frac{\text{total fixed costs} + \text{desired profit}}{\text{unit contribution to fixed cost}}$$

$$\text{target profit units} = \frac{50{,}000 + 20{,}000}{1 - 0.50} = 140{,}000 \text{ jars}$$

The entrepreneur therefore knows what will have to be sold at this particular price and cost structure to achieve the desired level of profit.

Breakeven analysis can be used to test assumptions, for example whether the sales needed to earn the required profit can be realistically achieved, given the size of the market or competitive conditions. On researching the market for jam and marmalade, the entrepreneur may decide that a higher price can be charged. An examination of costs may reveal that obtaining raw materials from a cheaper supplier can reduce variable costs. Consider how the target profit units would change if the price were €1.10 per jar, the variable costs were €0.40 per jar, and the required profit remained the same. The revised breakeven and target profit is then calculated:

$$\textit{target profit units} = \frac{50,000 + 20,000}{1.10 - 0.40} = 100,000 \text{ jars}$$

In this case a considerably reduced number of units can be sold to make the same amount of profit.

These examples show the benefits of analysing the relationship between price, costs, and sales volume. The marketer should also use experience of the market and market information to supplement this analysis.

Going-rate pricing means pricing according to what competitors in the industry are charging. Industrial marketers, such as steel manufacturers and petroleum producers, often use this approach. In many world commodity markets a going rate is established, though this can change as a result of oversupply or shortages. It is also a fairly common approach in the financial services sector, where interest rates offered or charged tend not to vary very much between different banks or lending institutions.

Going-rate pricing tends to preserve harmony in a particular industry or market. That harmony may be disrupted if some competitors change the rate. It can also be argued that going-rate pricing may be a form of cartel arrangement, whereby manufacturers or service providers have implicitly agreed prices and the consumer ends up with little choice. Such arrangements usually encourage inefficiency.

Selecting the final price

A number of factors can be taken into account before the final price is chosen.

Pricing points are specific points at which products are sold: for example, the price of a litre of milk or of a countline bar are usually standard among most retailers. Any new product coming onto the market has to take this into account. When Irish Biscuits launched Chocolate Kimberly, it was priced in comparison with other countline bars. In the case of many FMCG products, pricing points will vary according to packet size.

Psychological dimensions of the price may be important. Consumers' perceptions of price will be an important determinant in the product evaluation process. Many consumers will use the price as an indication of the quality of the product; they will perceive a direct relationship between the quality of the product and the price charged. Psychologically, prices ending in odd numbers also have significance, as consumers have a tendency to round down prices in their minds. Thus a product that costs €9.99 may be perceived as costing approximately €9, rather than approximately €10.

Discounted prices are a feature of many price promotions; they may also be a feature where the consumer pays in cash or buys large quantities of a product. The marketer must remember that a discount is a cost and so should try to strike a balance between a discount the buyer considers to be worth while and one that does not incur an unacceptable cost for the marketer. Regular customers may expect discounts, and it becomes an incentive in encouraging repeat business.

Loss leaders will occasionally be offered by retailers to encourage shoppers to do their shopping in the particular shop. A number of leading brands may be chosen and promoted at a loss to entice consumers to shop there. The cost of doing this is considered to be a promotional expense for the business.

Special-event pricing typically includes the January sales and other special sale events. Retailers frequently use these as part of their promotional strategy. Under the Consumer Information Act (1978) a product must have been available for at least 28 consecutive days at a higher price before the price can be described as a 'sale' price.

Discriminatory pricing involves offering discounts to specific segments of the market, such as students, unemployed people, or pensioners. Service providers who are anxious to stimulate demand at off-peak times often do this. It takes into account the fact that some groups are more price-sensitive than others and may therefore be willing to be more flexible with regard to time. Discriminatory pricing is widely practised by transport operators, cinemas and theatres, restaurants, and hairdressers.

Discriminatory pricing can also be selectively practised by using promotional campaigns. The marketer may wish to attract consumers in one area or segment without offering the discount to everyone. Discount coupons can therefore be aimed directly at particular areas or segments, which can be redeemed when a purchase is made. In this way the marketer does not end up discounting all sales.

TAXES

In calculating the price to the consumer, the marketer must also consider such costs as value-added tax and any excise duty that may be added on.

DEALING WITH PRICE CHANGES

Inevitably marketers will have to change prices. Price reductions do not tend to cause the same difficulties for marketers as price increases, which will rarely be popular with consumers. Competitive pressures will also be influential. Marketers therefore need to examine carefully the options open to them if they need to change prices.

The price-sensitivity of segments will be an important factor. Some segments may be less resistant to price increases, and it may be possible to charge them proportionately more than other price-sensitive ones. Additional services or augmented aspects of the product may be charged for where previously there was no charge. Minimum order sizes may be increased, or charges may be introduced for additional services, such as repair or servicing. In some cases the marketer may have no option but to make fundamental changes to the product, such as making it smaller or reducing the quality of raw materials.

PRICING AND THE PRODUCT LIFE-CYCLE

The stage the product is at in the life-cycle will affect the price. At the introductory stage, if the product is unique or new to the world, the price charged will typically be high. This will help recover the costs of development and launching. If a business has developed a new product or if a product is protected by patent, a high price will usually be set so as to 'skim' the market. This recognises that the company has incurred costs in bringing the new product to the market and it needs to recover those costs as quickly as possible before competitors enter the market with similar products or close substitutes and force prices down. The first electronic calculator and the first instant camera were launched on the market at high prices, which were subsequently lowered as more competitors launched competing products. If the product is being launched into a market where competitors already exist, the ability to charge higher prices will depend on the product's unique selling points.

As the product moves through the life-cycle, the price will inevitably be forced downwards. This downward pressure will begin to become apparent in the growth phase; competitors will enter the market, substitutes may be developed, and the marketer will face increasing price competition. Pressure on price will require the cost structure of the product to be examined, especially when profits begin to decline. At the mature stage in the life-cycle, price promotions will frequently be used as the marketer seeks to maximise sales volume. Decline may see prices further reduced as the product is phased out of the market.

PRICING STRATEGIES

Pricing strategies will be determined by the firm's pricing policies and objectives, which are determined by general company strategy. Porter's (1980) generic strategies, for example, each yield a different pricing strategy. Cost leadership will be based on penetration pricing approaches. Costs will be kept tightly controlled, so the company can compete on price. Differentiation, where the emphasis is more on quality and added value, may yield more higher priced pricing strategies. With the third strategy, focus, prices will be tailored to the demand levels and market profiles of the chosen segments.

Tellis (1986) suggested a taxonomy of pricing strategies, as illustrated in fig. 8.3. This proposes three broad objectives for the firm and three broad characteristics of customers.

Figure. 8.3: Tellis' taxonomy of pricing strategies

Objectives of firm			
Characteristics of consumers	Vary prices among segments	Exploit competitive position	Balance price over product line
Some have high search costs	Random discounts	Price signalling	Image pricing
Some have low reservation price	Periodic discounts	Penetration pricing Experience curve pricing	Price bundling Premium pricing
All have special transaction costs	Second-market discounting	Geographical pricing	Complementary pricing

The three broad characteristics of customers refer to those who have high search costs. These customers do not know exactly which firm sells the product they want, and they have to search for it. To some the opportunity cost of time exceeds the benefit of a search, so they will be willing to buy without full information. Those with a low reservation price are price-sensitive customers. The third category suggests that all consumers have certain transaction costs, other than search costs, such as travelling costs, risk, or the cost of money.

The pricing strategies suggested by Tellis can be briefly summarised. Where prices are varied between segments, *random discounts* imply maintaining a high cost normally but randomly discounting. Uninformed consumers will therefore be more likely to buy at the high price, while informed consumers will look around or will wait until they can buy at the low price. *Periodic discounts* could apply for transport products: for example, travellers expect to pay higher prices in the peak demand period but can get lower prices if they wait for off-peak times. *Second-market discounting* involves charging lower prices in some segments or markets. The rationale is that as long as the sale generates a price over the variable cost, this will make a contribution to the continuing business. Companies may therefore charge lower prices to students or to pensioners, who may not be in the primary market.

Pricing strategies that are used to exploit competitive position include *price signalling*. This refers to charging a high price for a low-quality product on the grounds that the consumer will perceive the product to be of high quality because of the price. This strategy may not encourage repeat business. *Penetration pricing* involves charging low prices to build market share; while *experience-curve* pricing means that prices can be lowered later in the product's life-cycle as the marketer gains the benefits of the economies of experience. *Geographical pricing* involves charging different prices in different geographical markets.

Product-line pricing strategies are relevant when a firm has a set of related products. *Image pricing* involves the firm bringing out an identical version of its current product with a different name and a higher price; the idea is to suggest quality to uninformed consumers. *Price bundling* involves maximising price yield among a number of products. *Premium pricing* involves charging high prices for quality products, while *complementary pricing* applies in situations where products may require accessories, for example charging a low price for a razor but a relatively higher price for blades.

The anatomy of the relationship between price and quality levels also yields a number of possible pricing strategies, as illustrated in fig. 8.4. There is certainly a strong link between price and perceived quality.

Figure 8.4: Nine marketing mix strategies on price v. quality

| | | PRICE | | |
		High	Medium	Low
	High	Premium	High value	Superb value
QUALITY	Medium	Overcharging	Medium value	Good value
	Low	Rip-off	False economy	Economy

Source: Kotler and Armstrong, 1993.

Consumer perception of the price–quality relationship is significant. If consumers feel that they are being cheated or overcharged they will take action. Such strategies can hardly be considered to be good ethical practice. In other cases, such strategies as offering high value or superb value may be very popular with the consumer but may not yield an adequate return for the marketer.

CONSUMER PERCEPTION AND PRICE

How the consumer perceives price will be critically important for the marketer. This emphasises the need for research on consumers' perceptions. One study demonstrated that price had very little influence over consumer choice (Ehrenberg, Scriven, and Barnard, 1997). It argued that price promotions had a minimal, short-term effect on brand sales and that these generally appealed to a small proportion of existing brand users rather than attracting new customers. It also suggested that these were usually a loss-making endeavour in the long run. The study suggested that consumers had habitual acceptable price ranges for brands they found salient and that price increases of habitual brands lose very few customers, as they generally remain within this acceptable price range. It also noted that price elasticities differed very little between similar brands. In general, it was argued that marketers should concentrate on advertising to build brand saliency and should avoid head-on price competition and price promotions as unprofitable.

This particular study is of interest in that it demonstrates how price is linked to the other elements of the marketing mix. Consumers obviously don't always make their decisions on price criteria alone: their perceptions of brand saliency and the price range that is acceptable to them are also important factors. Marketers could therefore avoid expensive price battles and price-promotional campaigns by concentrating instead on brand salience—in other words, positioning away from price.

Consumers' perception of price is also important in the context of the adoption of new products. The new-product adopter categories can be characterised according to their sensitivity to the price of the new product, with those consumers who adopt the product at earlier stages tending to be less price-sensitive than those who enter the market later.

FURTHER READING

Clarke, P., *Accounting Information for Managers*, Dublin: Oak Tree Press 1995.
Dodge, R. and Hanna, N., *Pricing: Policies and Procedures*, London: Macmillan 1995.
Nagle, T. and Holden, R., *Strategy and Tactics of Pricing* (second edition), Englewood Cliffs (NJ): Prentice-Hall 1995.

DISCUSSION QUESTIONS

1. Select a number of products or services that exhibit elastic and inelastic demand. Explain your choices.
2. Explain why an airline can charge different prices to different customers for the same flight.
3. Can all marketers use discriminatory pricing techniques? Why, or why not?

4. Comment on the relationship between pricing and brand loyalty. Are loyal consumers likely to be impervious to price changes?
5. Explain why pricing decisions must be made in the context of the other elements of the marketing mix.

REFERENCES

Bell, Jim and Brown, Stephen, 'Anatomy of a supermarket price war', *Irish Marketing Review*, vol. 1 (1986).

Ehrenberg, A., Scriven, J., and Barnard, N., 'Advertising and price', *Journal of Advertising Research*, May–June 1997.

Everett, F., 'Price promos can protect brand equity', *Brand Week*, 4 May 1998.

Hamilton, W., East, R., and Kalafatis, S., 'Brand price elasticities', *Journal of Marketing Management*, vol. 13, May 1997 (no. 4,).

Kotler, P. and Armstrong G., *Marketing: An Introduction*, Englewood Cliffs (NJ): Prentice-Hall 1993.

McGoldrick, P., 'Grocery pricing in the 1990s: war or peace?', *Irish Marketing Review*, vol. 6 (1993).

Porter, M., *Competitive Strategy*, New York: Free Press 1980.

Pratt, Maurice, 'Own Brands: The Benefits' (conference paper, National Marketing Conference), *Business and Finance*, October 1994.

Tellis, G., 'Beyond the many faces of price: an integration of pricing strategies', *Journal of Marketing*, vol. 50 (October 1986).

Walter, R. and Bommer, W., 'Measuring the impact of product and promotion-related factors on product category price elasticities', *Journal of Business Research*, July 1996.

9

Marketing Communications

Marketers must communicate with their customers. In the competitive market there will usually be many firms seeking to differentiate their offerings through communication and promotional techniques. Marketers seek to gain attention for their products to remind buyers of the value they can deliver, to promote special offers, and to position their products in the minds of consumers. Different methods of communication, such as advertising, sales promotions, and public relations, are used to achieve this. This chapter explores the nature of communication and the methods of communication used by marketers.

Just as the nature of the product is a broad concept in marketing, so too is the concept of communication. All firms use different media to get their message across.

THE COMMUNICATIONS MODEL

Communication broadly describes the transmission of a message from a sender to a receiver. The communications model (fig. 9.1) is a good basis for explaining the process. As marketers and firms need to communicate to potential and existing buyers and to various publics, an appreciation of the model is a requirement. There are a number of elements in the model, each of which is described below.

Figure 9.1: The communications model

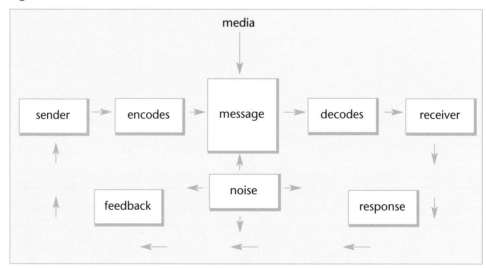

The *sender* is the person or firm sending the message. This could include the marketer of a brand, a charity, or a political party. It is important that the sender is clearly identified so that the receiver is not confused.

Encoding describes the process of putting the message into symbolic form. The sender will use words, pictures, music, images, or any combination of these, to convey the message. The marketer will encode symbols that describe and enhance the product and that convey the desired image. These symbols will relate to the position the marketer would like the product to occupy in the buyer's mind.

The *message* is the actual symbols that the sender transmits. It can be transmitted through a variety of *media*, that is, the possible channels the sender can use. These channels can be person-to-person, such as a sales representative, or can involve the use of press, radio, television, poster sites, events, or other non-personal media.

Noise is anything that can interrupt or disturb the communication process. It can include physical factors that may prevent receivers seeing or hearing the message, the actions of competitors that confuse or cause the message to be ignored, distractions, or other factors in the receiver's environment that impinge on the transmission of the message. Noise can also affect the response and feedback aspects of communication: for example, a buyer may see an advertisement for the marketer's product, decide to buy it, and go to the supermarket; when they are shopping they notice an in-store promotion for a competing brand, which, though it is not their preferred brand, they decide to buy. In this situation the receiver received the message, had a positive evaluation of the message, and did intend to buy, but factors intervened that prevented them doing so. On their next visit to the supermarket they may indeed buy the marketer's brand, but on this occasion the feedback the marketer gets is largely negative.

Large numbers of messages are directed at consumers every day, and this volume of messages can be a source of noise. Receivers cannot pay attention to everything, so some messages will not be noticed. People will generally notice or be receptive to communications about things that are of interest to them; they may remember only small parts of messages, and they can distort messages to suit themselves if they do not like the contents of the message. All these noise factors provide a challenge to the marketer to design messages and use media that will be noticed and that will get the message through.

Decoding refers to the mental process of interpretation and assigning meaning to the symbols transmitted by the sender. It takes place largely in the brain: we see, hear, touch, taste, or smell stimuli, an impulse is sent through the central nervous system to the brain, which interprets and assigns a meaning to the information received. Obviously it is important that clear stimuli are transmitted, so the receiver does not experience difficulty interpreting it. Stimuli that are confusing or difficult to interpret can be ignored or misinterpreted.

The *receiver* is the person or group who receives the message. This could be an individual consumer, a segment of the market, a firm, or any other public. The sender needs to ensure that the message is aimed at an appropriate receiver: for example, if communicating with a firm, it is important to reach the decision-makers or those who influence the decision.

The *response* refers to the receiver's reaction to the message. The response is a rather broad concept, in that it does not necessarily imply immediacy. Consider an advertisement for a fitted kitchen. The receiver may be impressed with the advertisement and decide that they would like to have one, but they may not buy until some time in the future.

A study on listeners' responses to broadcast advertisements in Northern Ireland demonstrated that the accent used in the advertising could have a significant impact (Rahilly, 2004). Northern Ireland listeners were shown to rate southern Irish accents negatively in comparison both to Northern Ireland accents and to those accents whose regional association is initially unclear.

Feedback is the part of the response that is actually communicated back to the sender: thus, if the receiver, having seen an advertisement, decides to buy a product, the marketer receives feedback through an increase in sales. As with the response, feedback is also a broad concept. Sales can certainly be used as a measure of feedback, but there are other possibilities. In the example of the fitted kitchen, the response may be communicated at some future time, perhaps several years away. Some communications attempt to make the receiver more aware of a particular issue, such as environmental awareness, while some may involve several responses, such as road safety.

STEPS IN THE COMMUNICATION PROCESS

Seven essential steps are involved in the marketing communication process, as illustrated in fig. 9.2. These provide a structure for the marketer's communication activities; they emphasise the different stages involved in developing a co-ordinated communication campaign.

Figure 9.2: Steps in the marketing communication process

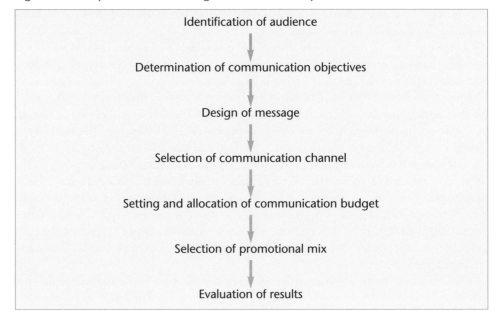

Identification of audience

↓

Determination of communication objectives

↓

Design of message

↓

Selection of communication channel

↓

Setting and allocation of communication budget

↓

Selection of promotional mix

↓

Evaluation of results

Identifying the audience

As with the segmentation decision, marketers do not necessarily want to communicate to everyone. Messages will be aimed at the audience most likely to be receptive and those who are of most interest to the marketer.

Fundamentally, marketers should understand the needs of the target audience. They will therefore specify the characteristics of the target audience according to its background profile, location, interests, attitudes, and opinions. A profile of the target audience will enable the marketer to make decisions about how the message should be structured and how to reach the audience.

Communication objectives

One of the best ways of considering possible objectives is to specify the response that the sender seeks. Responses can be broadly cognitive, affective, behavioural, or a combination of all three.

A *cognitive* response involves putting something in the receiver's mind, for example getting the receiver to consider the benefits of the product or to consider using the product. *Affective* responses refer to positive or negative emotions about the content of the message. The receiver will develop a positive attitude towards the product if they like or are interested in the content of the message, and a negative attitude if they don't. The *behavioural* response involves the receiver engaging in some form of behaviour as a result of the message. In theory, if the receiver considers the message and likes the content, they will be more likely to engage in favourable behaviour.

The AIDA ('attention, interest, desire, action') model (fig. 9.3) is often used to illustrate the objectives of the marketing communication process. Gaining attention is the cognitive stage of the model, stimulating interest and desire is affective, and taking action is behavioural.

The four stages in the AIDA model are sequential, the idea being that the marketer's communications should attract attention, stimulate interest and desire, and obtain action. The AIDA model is a useful basis for any communication activities such as personal selling or advertising.

Figure 9.3: The AIDA model

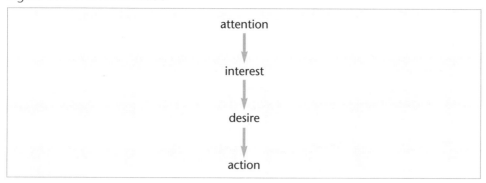

The message

The challenge to the sender is to design a message that will get through the channels and result in a positive response. The sender must decide which symbols to combine into a message; this will largely depend on the nature of the product and on the characteristics of the intended audience. The sender will decide on the appeal of the product.

Figure 9.4:
Rational appeal:
The Big Switch

Figure 9.5: Emotional appeal: Club Energise

Some products have a strong rational appeal, such as the money or time the buyer will save by using a particular brand. A good example of the use of a rational appeal was the campaign developed for Bord Gáis entitled 'The Big Switch'. This received the grand prix at the advertising effectiveness awards in 2010 (fig 9.4). Created by the DDFH&B Group, the campaign was judged successful because of the part it played in getting 300,000 users to switch their electricity supply to Bord Gáis. As a result the judges felt that it gave a tangible return on investment for the brand owner (*Sunday Business Post*, 17 October 2010).

Other appeals will be more subjective and will attempt to stimulate the receiver's emotions. When C&C entered the energy drinks market, it used emotive appeals in advertising the Club Energise brand (fig. 9.5).

Some messages will have a strong moral appeal and will seek to stimulate a sense of right or duty, for example the advertising used to promote road safety (fig. 9.6).

Figure 9.6: Moral appeal: National Safety Council

In general, designing the message requires the sender to consider a number of structural factors, such as what wording to use and the type of illustrations, colours, characters, background, theme, and personalities that might be appropriate. Usually these aspects of design will be taken into account by the creative department in an advertising agency. Marketers will usually require that logos, colours, text, characters, and other factors that have come to be associated with a brand will be maintained but that new themes or situations will be developed. The design of messages that are being sent by interpersonal means, such as through a sales representative, will involve factors such as arguments to be advanced during presentation and what to include in the sales presenter.

Message design will be strongly influenced by the marketing strategy being pursued by the marketer. The launch of a new product will require a message emphasising such aspects as innovativeness or benefits. Some messages will be informative, such as a special promotion or sale, while others will be image-building.

The marketer may want to target a particular audience with a specific message. Consider the example of the RaboDirect advertisement aimed at same-sex couples that was used following the passing of the 2009 Civil Partnerships Act through the Oireachtas (see fig. 9.7).

Figure 9.7: Targeting a particular audience: RaboDirect advertisement aimed at same-sex couples

We do solemnly swear to provide you with access to the most diverse range of funds in Ireland.

To be there for you when you need help or information without the silly jargon.

To be honest at all times, and to not trick you with any hidden catches or sneaky terms.

And to let you start investing at RaboDirect with just €100.

Honest Financial Products From One Of The World's Safest Banks.

Warning: The value of your investments may go down as well as up. Rabobank is licensed by the Dutch Central Bank. Terms and conditions apply.

Message design can give the sender or the creative department tremendous scope for design and creativity. Themes can be amusing, serious, off-beat, evocative, or informative. Consumers in Ireland are accustomed to well-produced, creative, and high-quality advertising campaigns on television and radio, in print, and on posters. Messages that cannot compete in this environment may not be noticed.

Symbolism can be very important. *Semiotics* is the study of the meanings that people attach specifically to non-verbal symbols. Perceptually, pictures are usually considered to be more powerful than words, and marketers are interested in how consumers perceive the symbols they use. Consider the following examples:

- *teddy bear*—tamed aggression
- *penguin*—coolness, refreshment, friendliness
- *tiger*—strong and fearless.

(Source: R. Alsop, 'Agencies scrutinise their ads for psychological symbolism', *Wall Street Journal*, 11 June 1987.)

These three symbols have been used in various advertising and communication campaigns: for example, Bord Gáis has used a teddy bear in its advertising, McVitie uses penguins in its advertisements for the Penguin brand of chocolate biscuits, and Esso has used a tiger in advertising its fuels.

Occasionally a credible source may be used by the sender. Celebrities, sports stars, entertainers, or company personnel may be used to deliver the message and thereby endorse the product or service. The British company, Walkers, engaged the sports presenter Gary Lineker to endorse its crisps.

The use of company personnel in advertising has become more common. Companies may use their senior personnel in an attempt to create an image of authority and to put a human face on the firm. If actors are used instead, the credibility factor may be much lower. In many instances the personnel used have become advertising institutions and are easily recognisable. This has been referred to as the Pygmalion principle: in other words, an unknown talent is transformed into a celebrity (Meenaghan, 1988). The principle has had applications in entertainment and sport but also in the professions and the academic world.

One research study indicated that the consumer has an overall positive attitude towards celebrity endorsements (O'Mahony and Meenaghan, 1997/1998). The study confirmed that consumers expect congruence between the perceived images of the celebrity endorser and the types of products that are endorsed. Celebrities must possess expertise in product categories consistent with their public profiles and their perceived life-styles.

Some messages will be very specific in stating the benefits of the product, describing features, or informing the receiver of special characteristics or offers. Other messages may be more subtle and may concentrate more on visual image than on text. Such messages are usually more effective for well-established brands such as Guinness, where consumers are already familiar with features and benefits.

SELECTING THE COMMUNICATION CHANNEL

There are two choices: using personal or non-personal channels. *Personal* channels include company salespeople, experts, personal influence, and trade fairs or similar events. The firm's sales personnel will spend much of their time communicating about the product to potential buyers, distributors, or retailers. The selling process itself involves presentation and communication, and salespeople will also be involved in customer service and building relationships with customers, all of which involve interpersonal communication.

Experts will occasionally be used to communicate about particular products on behalf of the firm. For example, a dentist might communicate the benefits of a particular brand of toothbrush, or a vet might communicate about the nutritional benefit of a brand of dog food. Sometimes professional bodies or associations will endorse particular products or services; usually, however, such bodies have strict policies on endorsement and will do so only if they believe it will be of benefit to their members or to the wider public.

Personal influence can be a feature of the relationship between a salesperson and a buyer, between an expert and an audience, or between a company manager and decision-makers. It is therefore a broad base for communication. Potentially any sender can have influence over a receiver if the receiver can be influenced. Typically, receivers are more influenced when they have not got the information they need to make decisions, when they have difficult or risky decisions to make, or when they are not experts on the particular subject.

Trade fairs can be used by many marketers as an opportunity for communicating with quite focused audiences. They are particularly useful for industrial marketers: usually the people who attend come from particular industries, and it is therefore an opportunity to communicate directly with potential buyers or decision-makers.

Events are another opportunity for interpersonal communication. Launches of a product to the trade, sponsored events and corporate entertainment are all opportunities for communication.

Non-personal communication channels usually involve using the media. This can be the mass media, such as the national press, radio, or television, or it can be more selective, such as local press and trade or specialist publications. In these channels the message is communicated using symbols, which are broadcast in a non-personal way. The difficulty for marketers in using non-personal channels is that they may not be suitable for complicated products; the receiver is not able to ask questions, and the marketer may not be able to ascertain immediately whether the message was understood. Personal channels, on the other hand, facilitate questions, and the sender is in a better position to determine whether the receiver understands the message.

Most marketers will use a combination of personal and non-personal channels; which one or which combination they select will be determined by their communication objectives, the nature of the product and the message they wish to communicate, and competitive considerations. If competitors are using extensive advertising campaigns to support and position their brands, the marketer may need to do likewise.

There are no hard and fast rules on the use of channels. Some companies have used extensive mass media advertising to build their brands; others use other channels or combinations of channels to reach the target audience. In addition to advertising, Hugo Boss devoted significant resources to the sponsorship of formula 1 racing, while the Body Shop has engaged in social activism, espousing a number of environmental and animal rights issues (Joachimsthaler and Aaker, 1997).

SETTING AND ALLOCATING THE COMMUNICATION BUDGET

Budgets will usually be a limiting factor in the methods and means of communication. Four main approaches are used to determine resources for marketing communication, though many marketers use a combination of approaches.

The *affordable approach* is based on what the firm can afford, after other costs and expenses have been met. This is typical of many smaller firms and business start-ups, where spending on communication may be based on what is left over after other expenditure has been taken into account. The problem with this approach is that communication is relegated to a residual position, and objectives may not be met because the budget is incapable of achieving them.

The *objective and task* approach has more to recommend it. This involves determining what needs to be done and allocating resources accordingly. Specific communication objectives are detailed, and the tasks that need to be carried out are specified. The communicator is forced to specify in detail what it is required to achieve, and this can then be costed and the expense justified.

Sometimes firms base their communication budget on *competitive parity*, which uses competitors' spending and communication activities as the yardstick for their communication budget. They need to be careful, however: if competitors are not spending much on communication, this does not mean that the marketer should automatically follow suit. In many cases the fact that competitors spend little on their communication activities may be an opportunity for the marketer to emphasise and position their product using a communication campaign.

The *percentage-of-sales* method involves relating communications to a unit of activity, namely sales in money terms. This is used by many firms, which spend an annual amount on communication based on their sales. The method is an attempt to link the effects of communication on sales. There are difficulties with the approach for firms that need to communicate but that do not sell anything, for example many non-profit marketers. Care also has to be exercised so that the policy is not applied too rigidly. If sales are falling, this may not mean that communication expenditure as a percentage should also fall.

Factors influencing spending on communication

A firm's communication needs will vary according to the particular situation. New firms or organisations marketing new products may establish awareness as a central communication objective, while another firm operating in a highly competitive environment may need to keep up with the communication activities of competitors. Communication will play an important part in the firm's positioning decision. Establishing a distinctive image in people's minds may be achieved largely through communication activities. Changes in the firm's environment may give rise to the need for a communication campaign, as could changes in role or circumstances.

The problem that many smaller firms can have in making decisions about their marketing communication budget is that financial resources may be limited. However, not all communication has to be bought in. While communication through non-personal channels, such as the use of advertising, may involve direct outlays, other channels may not. Firms should remember that their staff, physical resources, and time are also communication resources. Company personnel can communicate to target audiences in a variety of settings, in-house layout of publications may be more cost-effective than obtaining this service from printers, and events and contacts provide an opportunity for the firm to communicate with receivers.

In deciding on the marketing communication budget, the firm should seek to maximise value. This value will not refer solely to value for money but will include value for time and effort spent, and value for attention or coverage gained or publicity generated.

The promotional mix

The promotional mix refers to the different promotional options available to the marketer. There are four main elements: advertising, sales promotion, public relations, and personal selling. The essential question for the marketer is, which elements or combination of elements are most appropriate?

It is important that marketing communication activities are integrated. While advertising generally remains the most important communication medium for many FMCG companies, greater sophistication and expectation on the part of consumers, new and fragmenting media, and the availability of highly focused communication modes have seen an increase in sales promotion and below-the-line expenditure and a greater use of such instruments as direct mail and sponsorship.

In relation to industrial companies and business-to-business marketers, there is a traditional tendency to use relatively more personal selling than the marketers of consumer goods as a means of communication. Industrial and business-to-business marketers will of course use other forms of communication; the relative mix, as with marketers of consumer goods, will depend on the nature of the product or service.

Above the line and below the line

Above the line is a term generally used to describe advertising; *below the line* is used to describe promotions. In the Irish marketing communication industry, for example, above-the-line suppliers include advertising agencies, media buying specialists, national and regional newspapers, magazines, the broadcast media, mobile advertising, cinema advertising, the internet, and specialist media—in other words, firms involved in the production and transmission of advertising (*Irish Marketing Journal*, 1997).

Below-the-line suppliers include a broad range of companies involved in the creation and implementation of promotional campaigns and activities, such as direct-marketing companies, sales promotion consultants, public relations consultants, conference and event organisers, tele-marketing, in-store promotions and merchandising, press cutting agencies, and promotional merchandise.

Both above-the-line and below-the-line firms use the services of production specialists. The production industry includes a wide variety of companies specialising in such areas as design and graphics, slides, copywriting, typesetting, printing, audiovisual equipment, animation, film and video production, and sound recording.

The distinction between above and below the line is not always clear (sometimes communication that involves a combination of above-the-line and below-the-line activities is known as *through the line*). The broadcasters of many television and radio programmes often engage in programme enhancement. This involves manufacturers providing products or prizes for viewer or listener competitions. Some marketers consider that the subsequent exposure and goodwill is on a par with or greater than the exposure gained through advertising. Product placement on films or television programmes is also a below-the-line activity.

The increase in below-the-line activity by many marketers caused some to suggest that traditional above-the-line advertising would decline in importance (Fanning, 1997). Below the line has certainly increased in importance; other developments—such as direct marketing, new media, a more marketing-aware consumer, and an inability by advertisers to explain the precise effects on sales of a given level of advertising expenditure—have contributed to increased scepticism about advertising. However, advertising power could also be considered to be quite intangible; it can add meaning, add value to products, and create a culture around a brand.

ELEMENTS IN THE PROMOTIONAL MIX

Traditionally the promotional mix includes advertising, promotions, personal selling, and public relations. We will also include sponsorship, which is growing in importance as a communication medium.

ADVERTISING

Advertising can involve the use of the press, publications, poster sites, radio, television, cinema, outdoor advertising, free newspapers, and other advertising media to transmit the message. Advertising is therefore a very public form of communication and is suitable for messages that need to be transmitted to a wide audience. Messages can be repeated several times on press, radio, or television or can be placed on poster sites for long periods. This increases the opportunity for receivers to see or hear the advertisement. The message can be transmitted using words, pictures, music, characters, and a wide variety of symbols.

Advertising campaigns can be easily costed, as advertising rates and audience details are available. The media buying departments in advertising agencies are skilled at obtaining the best rates available. As rates can vary, for instance on television by time of day, the media buying department will seek to obtain the broadcast times that are most likely to reach the intended audience.

In general, television is the most expensive advertising medium. A critical calculation in determining the advertising medium to use will be the *cost per thousand* (CPT): this is the cost of the advertisement per thousand viewers, listeners, or readers. It is calculated according to the time at which the advertisement is broadcast or published and the nature of the viewers, listeners, or readers of the programme or publication.

The annual surveys—Joint National Readership Research (JNRR), Joint National Media Research (JNMR), and Joint National Listenership Research (JNLR)—all provide updated information on the audiences that most of the advertising media reach. In relation to television, the weekly TAM (television audience monitor) ratings give information on the viewership of programmes and commercial break data for the national channels in Ireland and limited data on other channels.

While the power of advertising is significant, Fanning (2004) pointed out that advertising was perceived to be losing its effectiveness—it is not as influential a force in changing people's attitudes and behaviour as it was in the past. The role of advertising agencies is being undermined, partly as a result of the so-called declining force of advertising but also because of the increasing prevalence and relevance of alternative forms of marketing communication.

Advertising models

Advertising models are useful attempts at understanding how advertising works. A number of models that have been developed over time are summarised below. These are known as *hierarchy of effects models*, as the stages are hierarchical and follow on from each other. All the models emphasise the role, awareness or attention at the initial stage; awareness is therefore an important precondition for successful advertising. Other models of advertising concentrate more on the qualitative aspects of the advertisement. These suggest that it is factors such as novelty or the emotive aspects that best explain how the advertisement works.

The DAGMAR model

The DAGMAR model (Colley, 1961) suggests that the consumer or receiver moves through a number of states of mind.

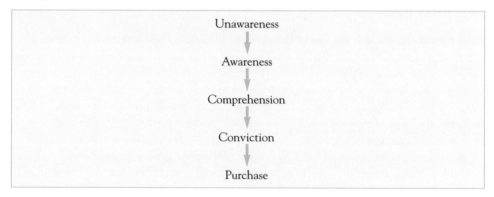

The AIDA model

The AIDA model suggests that the individual goes through a number of stages: cognitive, affective, and conative. Attention requires thought processes to engage; these are cognitive. If interest is stimulated it leads to desire, both of which are emotional or affective states. Finally, if desire leads to action, for example purchase, this is conative.

The Lavidge and Steiner model

This model proposed that—following awareness—knowledge, liking and preference led to conviction. Only when the consumer was so convinced would purchasing take place.

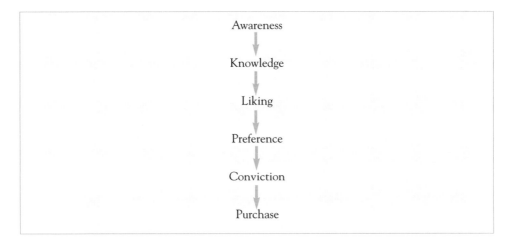

Ehrenberg's ATR model

This model proposed that there are three essential stages and that the principal role of advertising is to create awareness, which would induce trial. This would act as a reinforcer of behaviour.

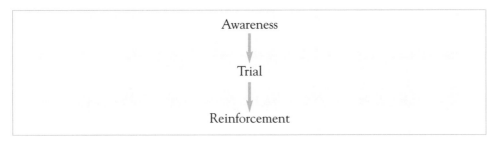

None of the advertising models completely explains how advertising works. Each of them may be shown to work in particular settings or with particular individuals, but they are not all-encompassing.

Perhaps it is easier to examine what advertising can achieve to demonstrate its value and importance. Advertising is fundamentally about communicating information. This can be done with words, pictures, music, and other devices. Advertising can create powerful imagery in support of firms, products, or brands. It can emphasise their unique selling points and in so doing strengthen competitive advantage. Brand personality can be communicated and developed through advertising.

Advertising not only influences consumers' behaviour before purchase but also helps to reinforce post-purchase behaviour. Consumers may look to advertising for reassurance after they have bought the product. Advertising can help reduce the post-purchase cognitive dissonance the consumer may experience; this is the discomfort the consumer may experience as a result of conflicting information, which can be particularly apparent after high-involvement purchases. The consumer may experience dissonance, for example, on the basis of information obtained from a competitor's advertising. One study on the effect of written post-purchase communication (Ward and Turley, 1996) showed that it can be effective in increasing post-purchase customer satisfaction.

There is also a strong role for advertising in marketing channels, where it can influence channel members' perceptions and behaviour. Typically, when products or promotions are being launched to the trade, the marketer will also outline the amount of advertising support that will be provided. This may be influential in the trade member's decision to stock the product or take part in the promotion.

Figure 9.8: Brand advertising: Guinness

TYPES OF ADVERTISING

There are a number of different types of advertising. *Brand advertising* emphasises the features, benefits and image of particular brands. It is important for image-building and will be significant in the decision on brand positioning. In 2008, for example, Guinness used an advert which targeted new consumers in the 20-something age group successfully (2008 IAPI Advertising Effectiveness Awards). Developed by Irish International BBDO, the 'From the Earth' theme was used to relate to the All-Ireland hurling championships and the Irish rugby team (fig. 9.8), which are the two sports that research had revealed Guinness drinkers were passionate about.

Brand advertising is used to create awareness of the brand or to remind consumers to buy. It can be used to stimulate demand for the product or service in general or to encourage selective demand, such as for a special offer or feature.

Co-operative advertising occurs where two marketers decide to combine resources for a joint advertising campaign. Usually they are not in competition but complement each other. Consider the joint campaign by Ryanair and Boeing in fig 9.9.

The microchip manufacturer Intel has also engaged in co-operative advertising with computer manufacturers. The campaign based on the 'Intel inside' message was judged successful and was credited with helping the computer manufacturers Dell and Gateway 2000 in their direct marketing campaigns (Johnson, 1997).

Corporate advertising is used by companies and organisations as a means of building an image and creating a strong corporate identity. This can be important for reinforcing shareholders' confidence in the firm or emphasising particular issues that may be of concern to the firm. It has been argued that corporate advertising is aimed at three specific constituencies: business customers, opinion-formers (investors, politicians, activists, and the media), and employees (*MII News*, May–June 1998). Some companies may use an umbrella corporate advertisement, which is

Figure 9.9: Ryanair and Boeing

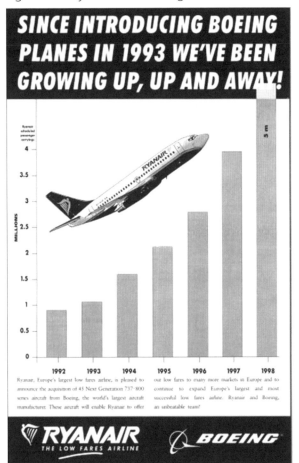

supplemented with additional brand-specific or product-specific advertisements.

Corporate bodies know that their image is much more than a corporate logo or advertisement: the image surrounding the message is just as important as the message itself. Just as marketers seek to develop brand personality and identity, so too should it be examined for the company itself.

The corporate logo is therefore an important feature of corporate image. Symbols such as the Nike tick and the Coca-Cola typeface may be instantly recognisable, but they also require support in the form of the development of an image and personality. Corporate advertising can play a significant role in this. The corporate image may be a determining factor in the firm's ability to extend into new markets or to develop or extend product ranges. Consumers may prefer to buy from a firm that has a good corporate reputation.

Companies will often use advertising material from their archives in attempts to appeal to consumer nostalgia. In 2004, for example, Guinness recycled some of its advertising images in a campaign that launched its extra cold draught in the UK. One of the reasons for doing so was an attempt to change the British beer consumer's preferences. The coldness of beer was not considered to be as important as taste, so very often beer consumed in Britain tasted warm to other palates. By linking the new version of the draught to old advertising images, Diageo hoped consumers would establish a link with the product. Other companies have done the same including Burger King, who resurrected a 1974 tagline 'Have it your way' in 2004, and Volkswagen, who relied heavily on its 1960s advertising when launching the new Beetle in 1998 (*Wall Street Journal Europe*, 21–3 May 2004).

The regulation of advertising

Advertising is generally regulated in most countries, both through public regulation and codes of advertising standards that may be imposed by the advertising profession. In Ireland there is the Advertising Standards Authority, which exists 'to promote and enforce throughout Ireland the highest standards of advertising in all media of communication so as to ensure, in co-operation with all concerned, that no advertising contravenes or offends against these standards having regard inter-alia to the code of advertising standards in Ireland' (Advertising Standards Authority of Ireland, 2007). The code deals with such issues as the legality, truthfulness, decency, and honesty of advertisements. Specific sections deal with advertising to children, comparative advertising, and advertising claims in relation to specific categories, such as health and slimming products, tobacco, and alcohol. The essence of good advertising, as defined in the code, is:

- All advertisements should be legal, decent, honest, and truthful.
- All advertisements should be prepared with a sense of responsibility both to the consumer and to society.
- All advertisements should conform to the principles of fair competition as generally accepted in business.

Each year the Advertising Standards Authority publishes a report on the complaints made by the public or by firms. These complaints are investigated by the authority, and conclusions are drawn. If a complaint is upheld, the authority can request that an advertisement be withdrawn or modified.

ADVERTISING MEDIA

The outdoor sector

The outdoor sector essentially refers to poster sites, which can come in various sizes and are priced accordingly. Sites range from bus shelter sites to larger '48-sheet' and '96-sheet' hoardings and are available throughout the country, enabling marketers to have national campaigns.

The advantages of outdoor advertising are considered to be the number of sites and the fact that posters are on display 24 hours a day. Developments in the sector have included new sizes, illuminated sites, and sites that enable a number of posters to be displayed automatically in rotation.

The top spenders on outdoor advertising in the Republic and Northern Ireland in 2009 are listed in table 9.1.

Table 9.1: Top spenders on outdoor advertising, 2009

Republic of Ireland	€
Vodafone	6,150,764
Heineken	4,401,040
Guinness	4,318,848
Meteor	4,001,504
O_2	3,133,989
Budweiser	3,104,733
Tesco	3,047,736
eircom	3,012,718
11811	2,925,547
Coca-Cola	2,860,704
McDonald's	2,602,130
Coors Light	2,321,984
Lucozade Energy	2,309,763
UPC	2,013,301
3 Mobile	1,989,847
Bulmer's Original	1,936,195
SuperValu	1,918,670
Bank of Ireland	1,834,999
Gum disposal	1,769,418
Carlsberg Lager	1,760,746
Northern Ireland	**£**
KFC	1,835,985
NI Fire & Rescue	1,118,669
Guinness	1,038,100
McDonald's	1,036,095
Coca-Cola	902,998

Harp Lager	826,912
Ulster Bank	724,639
Northern Bank	585,401
Magner's Original	540,930
NI Tourist Board	522,302
Lucozade Energy	496,230
Coors Light	467,433
Spar	455,386
Diet Coke	451,500
Magner's Pear	422,806

Source: PML Posterwatch.

Television

Television provides advertisers with a powerful medium that enables the use of visual imagery as well as sound track and voice overs. Television advertising is available on RTÉ's two channels, RTÉ 1 and RTÉ2, and also on TG4 and TV3.

Advertising on RTÉ television is limited to six minutes per hour, while on radio it is four minutes per hour. TV3 is allowed nine minutes of advertising per hour. Television advertising costs depend on the number of times an advertisement is screened and the time of the broadcast. Generally, advertising during the most popular programmes costs more. The costs of advertising are listed on a *rate card*. The media buying departments in advertising agencies are skilled at buying time for television advertising, based on the number and profile of viewers watching at particular times of the day. Media buyers typically negotiate advertising packages with the television stations to ensure that advertisements are broadcast at the times when they are most likely to reach the target audience.

In addition to running its two channels, RTÉ pays a subvention to TG4 as part of the national station's public service broadcasting obligations.

In Northern Ireland the main terrestrial channels are BBC1 and BBC2, Ulster Television, and Channel 4. Advertising is not available on BBC but is available on Ulster Television, which was received by 74 per cent of Irish homes in 1998. Some advertisers in the Republic use UTV for this reason. Channel 4, along with other channels, such as MTV, Sky, and NBC Europe, have London bases and have various levels of penetration in the Irish market. One channel in Britain, Tara TV, is directed at people of Irish descent living in Britain.

The main challenges in the television industry in the late 1990s and the early years of the new century were the launch of TV3 and the impact of digital television.

TV3 pays an annual rental to RTÉ for the use of its transmission system. Originally established by a consortium of investors, it was sold in 2001 to the British company Granada. TV3 is aimed primarily at the 15–44 age group.

Digital television

Digital television is essentially the combination of telephony, computing, and television technology. The result is an interactive television that will completely replace existing analogue technology. It is likely to begin to have an impact in the early years of the century (Carter, 1996). There are four main digital broadcasting alternatives: digital terrestrial transmission (DTT), digital cable transmission (DCT), digital satellite transmission (DST), and digital microwave transmission (DMT). Fig. 9.10 illustrates how these can be broadcast to the home.

Figure 9.10: Digital signals in the home

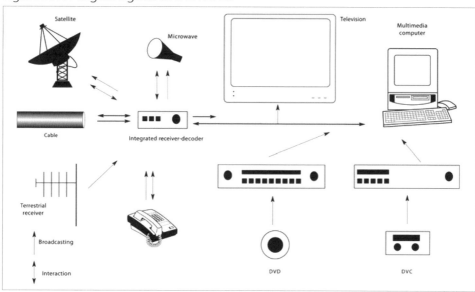

Source: U. Reimers, 'Digital broadcasting: the future of television', *Physics World*, April 1998.

As the following report indicates, it would be 2012 before digital TV would be available in the Republic.

RTÉ PUSHES ON WITH SCALED-DOWN DTT

Questions still remain over the digital terrestrial television project, on which RTÉ is working alone. In a statement to the Oireachtas Communications Committee in July 2010, RTÉ made clear that DTT—which is a key issue for a million Irish people—is definitely on the way, but will offer a more limited choice of channels than had been envisaged and will come at an as yet unspecified cost for householders.

What was new was the revelation that, for a small minority of households—those unable to receive analogue TV signals at present—a free view satellite option will be on offer at a estimated cost of around €200 for a satellite dish. RTÉ said this signal should be live by the second quarter of 2011.

RTÉ said the satellite signal would also provide a backup service 'in the event of an emergency and/or catastrophic failure of the DTT system'.

RTÉ suggested that the service had commercial potential since broadband operators might wish to use the platform to offer free-to-air TV and broadband packages.

This would be good news in advertising terms for RTÉ, providing a shield from competitors. RTÉ also promised technological advances, such as a more high definition television services once DTT is fully advanced in 2013. Before then, DTT will offer a partial 'HD Light' service on RTÉ2.

The projected cost of setting up the new transmission network has dropped by more than 50 per cent from original estimates to a total of €70 million, largely because the service no longer has to accommodate a commercial DTT service as well. RTÉ set out a tight timetable for delivery of the full service, starting in October 2010, when, in theory, a DTT signal will be in place that covers 94.5 per cent of the population, the same as TV3.

Most households will need to buy a set-top box to access DTT. In Britain, the cheapest set-top boxes cost around £100, while top brands sell for around £250. The timetable finishes in the fourth quarter of 2012, by which time RTÉ has promised that DTT will replicate the analogue signal with 98 per cent coverage.

RTÉ's submission, however, has raised a large number of complex issues that have yet to be resolved. These include the question of how the analogue switch-off process will be managed and financed; when precisely it will happen; and the funding of the financial subsidy that will be needed to help elderly people and other low-income citizens pay for the service.

The question of the specifications for set-top boxes also remains open, as well as finalisation of content for the public service DTT (RTÉ has mooted several new channels, such as a news service and children's TV, but has not made a firm commitment to any of them).

There is also the outstanding issue of when a pay TV DTT service can be appended to RTÉ's DTT, and who will provide it. Until then, all that viewers will be able to access will be RTÉTV and radio services, plus TV3 and 3e.

It also remains unclear who will fund and manage the considerable public information campaign and marketing campaign that will be needed to tell people what DTT is, and the retailer training campaign that will be needed as soon as the set-top boxes are being sold.

Source: Catherine O'Mahony, 'RTÉ pushes on with scaled down DTT', *Sunday Business Post*, 18 July 2010.

Digital television is expected to bring dramatic changes to the content and infrastructure of broadcasting. At the most basic level it enables there to be many more channels. Lower production costs will mean that regional and local content becomes cheaper to produce. Additional services to the viewer will include near video-on-demand, multimedia and interactive television, more sophisticated home shopping, and internet access.

Digital television has a number of implications for marketers. There will be a number of opportunities but also threats. If viewers can have a keyboard attached to their television they will be able to respond online to advertising, special offers, or competitions. Marketers will be able to use this interaction to build databases on viewers: for example, those with special interests could be specifically identified. Interaction means that direct response to advertising may become easier. When advertisements are being shown, for example, an icon could appear on the side of the screen inviting the viewer to click on it and get more information on the product. Advertising for a particular brand could incorporate price promotions, with the viewer again being invited to click on an icon leading to their frequent-shopper card being automatically credited with a discount the next time they buy the product in the supermarket (Branagan, 1997).

There will also be threats. Digital television will mean more choice of channels for the viewer, but the fragmentation that may result could mean that advertising to a national audience may become more difficult. It will also mean more widespread pay-per-view television: in other words, particular programmes or televised events, may be available only to subscribers. While in principle this means a more focused audience for an advertiser, it may be a smaller audience if pay-per-view leads to a reduction in the total number of viewers.

Radio

The JNLR/Ipsos mrbi research into radio listenership in 2010 showed that 85 per cent of Irish adults listened to the radio every day. A total of 15,400 people were surveyed, 58 per cent tune in to a local or regional station and 46 per cent listen to a national station. On average, Irish audiences listen to radio for almost four hours per day, during the hours from 7 a.m. to 7 p.m.

Looking at the various regions throughout the country, national radio holds the majority share position in Dublin and the north-east/midlands area while local/regional radio is in the majority in all other regions. Among the younger, 15–34-year-old audience across the country, local/regional radio holds the national majority share position at 61 per cent versus 39 per cent for national radio. In particular, this party has a very strong share position among this age group in Dublin (71 per cent), Cork (65 per cent), north-west (63 per cent), and the multi-city region (66 per cent).

Local radio is a strong performer in the individual radio markets across the country – in many areas reaching more than 40 per cent of the local adult population daily. In particular, on the criterion of share of minutes listened during the prime 7 a.m. to 7 p.m. time, Highland Radio, Tipp FM and Radio Kerry hold the majority share position in their franchise areas.

Digital audio broadcasting (DAB)

Digital audio broadcasting may become a replacement for conventional radio signal transmission. The technology it uses means that listeners will have a greater choice of stations and it will be able to transmit text and pictures. In 2006 there were about 30 digital-only radio stations in the UK, including the dedicated Smash Hits pop station, a Virgin classic rock station, and BBC7, which airs archive material. RTÉ planned to introduce DAB but by 2006 no agreement had been reached on which type of DAB broadcast system to use (*Sunday Tribune*, 9 July 2006).

Press and magazines

The Joint National Readership Survey (JNRS) is used by media buyers to calculate the most cost-effective way of spending print advertising budgets. Readership figures for the publications covered in 2010 are given in table 9.2.

The importance of regional newspapers—almost half the population read one weekly—should not be underestimated.

Table 9.2: National Readership Survey results, 2009–2010

Sample: 6,918. Universe: 3,522,000

	Figures (in 000s)	Percentage
Morning titles		
Irish Independent	560	15.9
The Irish Times	359	10.2
Irish Examiner	204	5.8
Irish Daily Star	410	11.6
Irish Daily Mirror	204	5.8
Irish Sun	285	8.1
Irish Daily Mail	144	4.1
Any daily	1,928	54.7
Any morning	1,821	51.7
Evening titles		
Evening Herald	260	7.4
Sunday titles		
Sunday Independent	992	28.2
Sunday Tribune	167	4.7
Sunday World	843	23.9
Sunday Business Post	193	5.5
The Sunday Times	422	12.0
Irish News of the World	533	15.1
Irish Sunday Mirror	146	4.2
Irish Mail on Sunday	332	9.4
Irish Daily Star Sunday	213	6.1
Weekly newspapers and magazines		
Irish Farmers Journal	259	7.3

Source: Millward Brown Lansdowne.

Public transport

Advertising on all CIÉ property is handled by a company called Bravo Outdoor. It can provide advertisers with sites on public transport vehicles, as well as poster sites. A separate company, JC Decaux Ireland, handles advertising on the Luas system.

Cinema advertising

The cinema enjoyed a renaissance in the mid- to late 1990s and by 1998 Ireland had the highest rate of cinema attendance in Europe (*Euromonitor*, March 1998). In 1988 cinema admissions were 6 million; in 1997 the figure was 12 million; and by 2009 there were 17.7 million admissions. The importance of cinema advertising increased as a result, with many marketers using it as part of their advertising mix.

Carlton Screen Advertising is the agent for 86 per cent of cinemas in the Republic. The top 10 cinema advertisers in are listed in table 9.3.

Table 9.3: Top 10 cinema advertisers

	2010	2009	2008
1.	O_2	O_2	O_2
2.	Fáilte Ireland	Vodafone	Coca-Cola Ireland
3.	Diageo	Unilever	McDonald's
4.	Coca-Cola Ireland	Coca-Cola Ireland	Unilever
5.	Cadbury Ireland	Heineken Ireland	Cadbury Schweppes
6.	Kellogg's	Cadbury Schweppes	Vodafone
7.	Nokia	Nestlé	An Post
8.	Meteor	BSkyB	RTÉ
9.	Red Bull	Red Bull	C&C
10.	Glaxosmithkline	Britvic Ireland	Beamish & Crawford

Source: Carlton Screen Advertising.

The growth in cinema attendance has been attributed to the age profile of the population and the arrival of multiplex chains. The 15–34 age group tend to be the most frequent cinema-goers. Cinema advertising can be booked on a screen-by-screen basis; many firms have taken advantage of this and advertise on screens in their local area.

The internet

The internet was originally developed in the United States for military purposes but is now a series of linked networks spanning the globe. It can be used by companies and individuals for sending e-mail messages, transferring files, advertising products and services, and carrying out other transactions. As a result its marketing applications are widespread, particularly for research, communication, promotion, and sales transactions. The introduction of digital television means that television sets can be interactive, which is a potential threat to the internet.

The use of the internet is considered to have a number of advantages for marketers (Paul, 1996). It presents international communication opportunities, is becoming more accessible as consumers and businesses become more familiar with personal computers, and enables the user to interact with the marketer online. The main problem has been security;

the possibility that transactions, such as the consumer giving a credit card number, can be intercepted by someone else has probably reduced its attractiveness.

The possibilities of the worldwide web for marketers include corporate sites, marketing sites, service sites, and commerce sites (O'Brien, 1997). Corporate websites can provide basic information about the company, such as financial reports or contacts. The marketing site will usually contain more detailed product information or details of promotions and therefore can be used as an aid to interactive selling. Service websites could provide the customer with the facility to download programs, provide detailed technical information, or enable the customer to track the progress of their order. Commerce websites enables commercial transactions to take place, which will involve a financial transaction; banks have been using such sites for international financial transactions.

With the growth in the internet as a communications medium there has been a corresponding growth in the number of internet specialists. These provide a variety of services, including the design of web pages, programming, training, and other internet support services. Websites are an important link with consumers; some people argue that they can reduce the traditional problem of advertising waste because they are accessed by people who are directly interested in the company (Heinen, 1996).

Many firms began developing websites in the late 1990s. A number of issues are important in the design of pages. Websites can perform a public relations role; they can therefore contain information about the company, its staff, and its products. Some firms place press statements or news updates about the company on their website. Sites can also be used for database capture: for example, market research information can be obtained from people using the site. Pre-sales activities, such as requests for information or detailed specifications, can be entered, while post-sales activities, such as feedback on product performance, can be received online.

Websites can also play a role in customer loyalty schemes: for example, airlines or supermarkets can provide information on special offers aimed at members. With products such as Waterford Crystal, where customers may become collectors of particular suites or ranges, websites can be used to communicate with potential customers and with customers who have a special interest in the brand. This is particularly so for customers in the United States, who may like to be kept up to date on new items added to the range or on limited editions that are available. Similarly, airlines have been developing websites for their frequent fliers to provide them with up-to-date information and offers.

Developing a strategy for the worldwide web

The use of the internet as a communications medium should be considered in the context of a company's general business strategy. The internet may have a role in achieving particular marketing objectives. This will depend on the nature of the product or service: for example, the internet may be especially good for reaching market niches. Customers' computer access and proficiency will be important factors; it will also be important to monitor what competitors are doing on their websites. Websites need to be maintained and updated; users will become frustrated if information is out of date.

As with advertising, marketers can be creative in the design of websites, which will help differentiate them from competitors.

Other advertising media

Additional advertising media range from posters mounted on the back of lorries and vans to light aircraft pulling advertising banners. These services are usually supplied by specialists or by promotional companies.

EVALUATION AND EFFECTIVENESS OF ADVERTISING

Obviously, sales can be used as a test of the effectiveness of advertising. This is not, however, the only measure. Since the objectives of advertising can be quite broad, the measure of effectiveness must be similarly broad. Advertising research will therefore be important, and it may concentrate on measuring recall, perceptions, or attitudes.

If the objective of an advertising campaign is to change attitudes, these should be measured before and after the campaign to determine whether the advertising has had an influence. Some advertising campaigns attempt to include an interactive element. There has been an increase in the number of advertisements that include a phone number that the viewer can ring for more information (*Marketing*, 26 March 1998).

Consumer behaviour emphasises the difference between high-involvement and low-involvement decision-making. The level of involvement can have practical implications for advertisers. One study (Fanning, 1987) suggests that low-involvement theory means that the consumer passively processes advertisements, rather than consciously evaluating them. Behaviour that is often triggered by association of the advertisement with the product at the time of purchase precedes change of attitude. This theory was considered particularly relevant for fast-moving consumer goods. The advertising practitioner may not therefore need to concentrate on bringing the consumer through the traditional hierarchy-of-effects model: instead, the creative role of advertising becomes more important, the hope being that by differentiating and entertaining, people will associate the advertisement with the product. In other words, the more creative the advertising, the more effective it may be. To some extent, advertising in the 1990s moved away from a strict statement of unique selling proposition to an approach that sought out inherent consumer needs and appealed to these needs in an entertaining manner.

With regard to research, the main implication of low-involvement theory was the swing away from the use of quantitative measures of advertising, such as recall measures, towards more qualitative approaches, such as focus group discussion. Quantitative measures, such as percentage recall, can measure only one dimension of the effectiveness of advertising: qualitative measures of perceptions or attitudes can yield additional, perhaps more insightful, information.

DEVELOPMENTS IN ADVERTISING

Given the competition for the receiver's attention from different advertisers using different media, there will always be an interest in developments that may attract more attention. In recent years much interest has been expressed in the internet and its use as an advertising medium. In the outdoor sector, new technology has created poster sites that can incorporate several advertisements that change in rotation, and sites with three-dimensional features.

It is probable that there will be increased competition in the television market. New integrated media will develop. Internet, satellite, and digital technologies will become more important, providing new challenges for conventional television providers. Direct-response television and pay television are also likely to be significant.

THE ROLE OF THE ADVERTISING AGENCY

Advertising agencies are essentially service providers who specialise in media buying and scheduling, the creation of advertising, and providing advice to their customers on their marketing communications. Many advertising agencies have become more integrated and in addition to their traditional role in above-the-line have also become engaged in below-the-line activities. This enables them to offer a more integrated service. In 1998 there were just under 80 advertising agencies in Ireland.

The specialist skills of the agency are in getting the best possible exposure for their clients with creative and attention-getting advertisements. The agency plays an important role in the development of brands. Many brands have been successfully built with advertising support.

SALES PROMOTION

Sales promotion involves the use of incentives to encourage purchase or sales. As a communication activity it is designed to create a sense of immediacy by offering reasons for purchase in the short term. It is therefore useful for stimulating sales. Typical forms of consumer sales promotion include samples, coupons, rebates, price reduction, banded offers, premiums, and competitions.

Promotions may involve product give aways, and marketers often co-operate in joint promotions. Sales promotions can be aimed at the retailer or other channel members. These may include buying allowances for specified orders, samples, free goods, co-operative advertising support, or sales competitions. Sales promotions are also possible on industrial products and may also involve financial incentives, samples, and competitions.

Sales promotion has become a growth area in marketing practice, with many marketers using it to complement their advertising activity, while for firms with limited resources for advertising it can be an effective means of communication. The principal uses of promotions include attracting new users for the product, rewarding loyal users, and increasing purchasing frequency among occasional users. Sales promotions may help differentiate the product offering and can be used to counteract competitors' activity.

Marketers launching new products or relaunching existing products may find sales promotions useful. Consider the example of the launch of round tea bags by Lyon's Tetley, where in the short term, at least, sampling coupled with a price promotion did increase market share.

DEVELOPING A ROUNDER TEA

In the mid-1980s Lyon's Tetley was examining the tea market in Britain. At the time it was the number two brand, after PG Tips, and it was losing market share to own-label products. Research established that brands of tea bags were being differentiated according to personality. The company began researching potential physical differentiation of the product. A large number of new ideas were generated, and a shortlist of the better ideas was qualitatively researched.

This resulted in the identification of round bags as a concept worth developing. Research on the concept was carried out that involved giving respondents traditional square tea bags to test for one week and then round bags to test for another week. Both square and round bags contained exactly the same quality and amount of tea. The result of the test was a significant preference for round bags, which were perceived as better-tasting and having a stronger flavour.

Further research was undertaken, and by 1989 the company decided to launch the round tea bag. The Tetley brand was relaunched in the southern half of England in July 1989, when 6½ million samples were delivered to households, consisting of 16 tea bags and a 20p coupon. Almost immediately the brand share in southern England began to rise sharply, with Nielsen research showing that Tetley's market share, which had been 11 per cent in the summer of 1989, increased to 15 per cent by the end of the year.

Source: A. Phillips, J. Parfitt, and I. Prutton, 'Developing a rounder tea', *Esomar*, 1990.

The Tetley example shows how price coupons and free samples can be combined to encourage the trial of a new product. Other consumer promotions can involve the use of coupons inserted in newspapers, magazines, or other publications, coupon booklets, on-pack coupons, or direct-mail coupons. *Price packs* typically involve extra quantities of the product, such as '25 per cent extra free,' or blister packs that may comprise two packs together for a special price. *Cash rebates* could involve the consumer collecting tokens on the product and redeeming them for cash. *Banded offers* might include a free toothbrush on a packet of toothpaste. *Advertising gifts* may involve gift items that the buyer can send away for: thus a brand of breakfast cereal might offer buyers a bowl with its logo on it, or a coffee brand might offer a mug. Promotions can also involve the use of point-of-purchase displays or merchandising that emphasises the nature of the promotion and the offers that are available. *Competitions* for holidays, cars, or other prizes may be used to promote the product and create a sense of excitement.

The effectiveness of sales promotions

As with any form of communication, the marketer needs to assess the effectiveness of sales promotion efforts. Promotions represent a cost to the business, in some cases involving significant price discounts. It is important that promotional campaigns are planned and that specific objectives are set. One study (Wickstrom, 1987) found that the regularity in the consumption of a product group, a product or a brand will determine what type of effects will result from a promotion. Another study (Lambkin and O'Dwyer, 1994) explored the nature of couponing and coupon redemption; it found that coupon redemption rates are influenced by a variety of factors, including the company's promotional strategy, the method of coupon distribution used, the value of the coupon, and the effort and timing of the coupon drop.

Poor planning and wastage were found to be significant problems in the implementation of promotions. Evidence was presented that instant point-of-purchase coupons were more suitable for receiving higher redemption rates, and that ideally coupons should offer a discount of 15 to 20 per cent on the value of the product.

Sales promotion agencies

Just as with advertising, there are a number of sales promotion agencies that design and implement promotional campaigns for marketers. These may come up with creative ideas for promotions; they may also undertake the administrative aspects, such as sending out gifts or cash rebates. Other companies specialise in providing personnel for in-store promotions, such as product tastings.

Fulfilment companies specialise purely in the administrative aspects of sales promotion. Consumers may send tokens or coupons to them in exchange for gifts, samples, or rebates. Fulfilment companies should provide the marketer with *top-line reporting*, which involves updates on the proportion of coupons redeemed, gifts despatched, monetary value of the rebates sent out, and stock levels remaining. Profiles of respondents may be possible if some background information has been obtained. Top-line reporting is required if the marketer is to judge the effectiveness of the promotion, and will be required as a financial control where cash rebates are involved.

Planning sales promotions

Sales promotions should be attractive to the consumer, but the marketer needs to avoid the pitfall of discounting sales too heavily, and promotions that have higher costs than benefits. The domestic appliance manufacturer Hoover discovered this to its cost in 1993, when a very successful promotion cost the company more than it expected.

An issue that the marketer should consider when designing promotional campaigns is the long-term effects they may have on sales. The Hoover promotion, for example, had a long-term negative effect on sales of vacuum cleaners.

There is a danger inherent in promotions that the consumer will stockpile when the product is on promotion. One research study (Mela, Jedidi, and Bowman, 1998) suggested that stockpiling behaviour has changed over the years. The increased long-term exposure of households to promotions has reduced their likelihood of making category purchases on subsequent shopping trips. The study found an increasing tendency among consumers to 'lie in wait' for especially good promotions. This change could affect profitability in product categories.

Trade promotion is a feature of many marketers' activities. Distributors and retailers may expect buying allowances, free products, advertising and promotional support, contests, or prizes. Business conventions or trade shows may be used to communicate the promotion to the trade, or sales representatives may communicate the promotion directly. Trade promotions will often be undertaken in advance of consumer promotions: marketers may need to communicate to the trade to encourage them to stock the product or to participate in a particular promotion.

A SUCCESSFUL PROMOTION, BUT AT WHAT COST?

In 1993 the Hoover company began a promotion in Britain. Consumers who spent £100 or more on a Hoover vacuum cleaner were entitled to a voucher for two free transatlantic air tickets. The company calculated that redemption rates on the coupons would be low and that the cost would be more than covered by increased sales of its products.

The promotion worked well, and sales of vacuum cleaners increased substantially—so much so that the manufacturing plant in Scotland went on 24-hour production. Problems emerged, however, when customers began looking for their tickets. So many applied that Hoover's seat allocation with the airlines was quickly used up; complaints began when the company was unable to offer seats. The news media took up the story, and Hoover had to hastily arrange additional seat allocations, at a higher cost. Not enough seats could be secured, and the company was criticised in parliament, by the Consumers' Association, and in the media. It had not intended to mislead or disappoint but had been over-ambitious in its promotional planning.

In addition to the costs incurred in running the promotion, sales of Hoover vacuum cleaners declined immediately after the promotion ended. The small ads in local newspapers featured many advertisements offering unwanted new vacuum cleaners.

A similar promotion was run in the Irish market but was limited to a particular product in the Hoover range and involved the customer being able to buy two flights for the price of one.

Source: S. Dibb, L. Simkin, W. Pride, and O. Ferrell, *Marketing: Concepts and Strategies*, New York: Houghton-Mifflin 1997.

PERSONAL SELLING

Personal selling covers a wide variety of areas, including delivery, order-taking, building goodwill, educating customers, and providing technical support. Traditionally it involved interpersonal communication and was therefore useful for dealing with complicated products, where the receiver can ask questions. Usually, consumers are involved in very little direct selling; but there are exceptions. When Daewoo launched its cars in Britain and Ireland it sold directly to customers, using advertising to provide them with the necessary contact information (Simms, 1997).

Increasingly the internet is having an important role in selling. This does not involve the same level of interpersonal contact, but it does enable for interaction. One of the large computer multinationals, Dell, differentiates itself by selling directly to customers using the internet. In 1998 the company was recording worldwide sales of $4 million per day using the internet (O'Dwyer, 1998). The advantages to the company were considered to be a better ability to service and support customers, the ability to build to order, the elimination of unnecessary mark-ups in the distribution channel, a reduction in the time taken to get the product to the market, and a reduction in stock-carrying costs.

It remains to be seen what precise impact electronic sales will have on the personal selling process. It will certainly be an aid in selling products, but it may not be a complete replacement for personal selling. The process itself involves a number of stages, and these are described in the following section.

SETTING THE OBJECTIVES OF THE SALES FORCE

Objectives will vary between companies, but the sales force will usually be expected to perform a number of tasks. These should be specified and might include:

- finding and developing new accounts
- communicating information about the company's products or services
- presenting products
- answering questions
- providing service or support to the buyer
- gathering market intelligence
- preparing sales reports
- involvement in the planning of sales budgets
- dealing with customers' complaints or difficulties.

The objectives of the sales force can therefore be quite broad and are usually much more than simply selling the product, and it is important that sales personnel have a clear understanding of them. The objectives emphasise the importance of the role of the sales force in relationship marketing.

Sales force strategy

The essential element of sales force strategy must be understanding the customer's buying process, which can be quite complex in business-to-business selling. A variety of sales approaches are possible: for example, the salesperson can be an account manager, managing the relationship between company and buyer; other approaches may involve teams of sales people being responsible for different products or territories. The sales force will usually be expected to engage in identifying new business and in developing existing accounts.

Structure of the sales force

Three main approaches are used in designing the structure of a sales force: territorial, product, and customer.

1. **Territorial structure.** Each salesperson is assigned a geographical area. This is quite a common approach. The salesperson is then responsible for this area and can build close contacts with buyers.
2. **Product structure.** Salespeople specialise in particular products from the company's range. This is commonly used for technical or industrial products.

3. **Customer structure.** Where salespeople sell to specific customers or industries, the sales force may be assigned to particular customers. This can also be a feature of business-to-business selling.

The structure chosen will depend on the nature of the company, its products, markets, and buyers.

Size of the sales force

The size of the sales force will depend on a number of factors, including the number of accounts, number of sales calls expected per day, or type of account. A formula can be used to calculate the required size of a sales force, based on call frequency, the number of customers, and the average number of calls that can be made:

$$N = \frac{1}{K} \times [F1(C1) + F2(C2)]$$

where N = desired number of salespeople
Fn = call frequency required
Cn = number of customers
K = average number of calls the salesperson can make per year.

Suppose a marketer has two groups of customers, supermarkets and TSNs. There are 50 supermarkets and 400 TSNs that salespeople need to call to. Supermarkets require a sales call every two weeks, while TSNs require a weekly call. The average number of calls a salesperson can make per year, given distances to be covered and other factors, is 1,400:

$$N = \frac{1}{1,400} \times [26(50) + 52(400)] = 16$$

In a research study carried out by the UCD Marketing Department in 1991 on the top thousand firms in Ireland it was found that the most common sales force size was between five and ten people (Lambkin and de Búrca, 1993). There were no significant differences between consumer, industrial and service companies in this regard. The average number of calls made by a sales representative was 28 per week. The ratio of sales managers to sales representatives was 1 to 4.

Sales force pay

Generally the pay for sales representatives involves a basic salary together with a mix of other rewards, including company car (including tax, insurance, and fuel), commission or bonus, allowances for entertainment, and other expenses. In most cases salespeople will have sales quotas or targets set for them. These are considered to be motivational and may be the basis for calculating sales bonuses. Quotas or targets should be realistic and fair. If sales are declining, raising the target for salespeople may not be the answer; in many cases declining sales are more a marketing problem than a sales issue.

Sales force selection

Typically there are a number of personality traits that companies will look for in their salespeople: persistence, enthusiasm, attention to detail, initiative, self-confidence, and honesty. As the salesperson will be a communication medium, communication skills will also be important. The UCD research established the selection criteria used by the companies surveyed, and these are listed in table 9.4. Usually when companies are recruiting salespeople, personality tests will form a large part of the assessment.

Table 9.4: Selection criteria for sales force

	Mean score
Personal characteristics	4.6
Ambition or potential	4.5
Sales experience	3.9
Knowledge or experience	3.8
Education level	3.7
Personal mobility	3.8
Age	3.4

Source: 'Profile of a Salesforce', UCD.

A salesperson should be able to demonstrate competence in six basic areas: business knowledge, industry knowledge, company knowledge, product knowledge, sales skills, and attitude (Denny, 1988).

The selling process

There are a number of steps in the selling process.

1. Prospecting and qualifying

Prospecting involves identifying potential customers, for example using trade directories or phone calls to arrange initial meetings. *Qualifying* means screening out poor prospects, for example on grounds of their size, location, or specific needs. This ensures that the salesperson does not waste time prospecting for customers that the company cannot realistically serve.

2. Pre-approach

Pre-approach involves learning as much as possible about potential customers before meeting them. The use of secondary research will be particularly useful here. It is important that the salesperson be familiar with the target customer's markets, business, and environment. Secondary research may provide profiles of the business or changes that have taken place in its environment. A salesperson needs to be well informed about these issues, not least because they may identify where sales opportunities exist.

3. Approach

The approach stage involves meeting the potential customer for the first time and getting off to a good start. It is important to build up a professional rapport with potential customers; salespeople should remember the adage that first impressions last. The salesperson should be on time, be dressed appropriately, and have with them all the documents and other material they may require.

4. Presentation and demonstration

The salesperson will usually be given the opportunity to make a presentation. From a communication point of view this is critically important. Use should be made of well-designed and illustrated presentation aids. *Sales presenters* may be used: these have illustrations of the product, variations, and details of price and other specifications. With the advent of multimedia technology, sales presentations can be quite sophisticated. The presentation should be tailored to the potential customer or audience and can be used to emphasise the benefits or features of the product. If using videos or multimedia technology the salesperson should make sure they can obtain access to the required equipment; if not, they will need to bring it with them and allow for setting-up time.

The demonstration stage may be required if the salesperson needs to show how the product works. This may involve the use of the product itself or a demonstration using video or multimedia. Demonstrations may even involve inviting the potential customer to another location.

5. Handling questions

This stage involves clarifying issues about the product and answering any questions the customer may have. If, for some reason, it is not possible to answer the questions on the spot, the salesperson should undertake to provide the answer at a specified time. It will become apparent at this stage whether the potential buyer is interested in the product. This stage gives the salesperson an opportunity to provide more information and to engage the potential customer in a more detailed discussion about the product.

6. Closing the sale

Closing the sale involves asking the customer for an order. The salesperson must ask for an order; this creates a sense of immediacy. Details of special incentives or promotions that may exist can be included. Prices should be clearly specified, and the buyer should be made aware of the payment terms or options.

7. Follow-up

The objective in selling anything is not just the sale itself. It is important that the salesperson verifies that the order was successfully processed and delivered. Follow-up with the customer is extremely important, especially for building a base for repeat business.

Technology and selling

Direct selling has, over time, been influenced by developments in communications technology. The introduction of the postal service in the 19th century and the telephone in the 20th century enabled marketers to sell directly to more customers. Developments in telecommunications have continued, with telemarketing and internet marketing becoming more important. Many firms have established telemarketing centres to serve the domestic and international markets.

The internet is also taking on an increasingly important role in sales. As with telemarketing, selling is only one dimension of the internet, but it is likely to become more important. The interactive nature of the internet enables the sales prospect to look at illustrations of the product, in many cases in virtual reality form. Prospects can request information about the product and even create a virtual product on their computer screen. Products can be ordered and feedback provided on line. To the extent that use of the internet becomes more widespread among firms and consumers, its role in selling will increase.

Relationship marketing and selling

Given the nature of the salesperson's job, their direct contact with customers will mean that they will play an important role in developing relationships with those customers. Salespeople should therefore be familiar with the concept of *relationship marketing*. There are a number of implications. While all customers are important, some may require more time or sales effort. Significant customers may require more contact and special care. The salesperson will therefore have to identify prospects and customers who are most important with regard to relationship effort.

Salespeople also need to build up a rapport with their customers. We rarely buy from people we do not like. Personality clashes between a salesperson and customer, for example, can be avoided by attempting to match the salesperson with the particular customer.

Salespeople should not be required to manage too many relationships. The sales manager or other manager should supervise the relationship. Salespeople could provide updates on the quantity and quality of their interactions with customers, and customers could be surveyed to assess their satisfaction with the relationship. In general, salespeople should be encouraged to actively develop relationships with customers. Taking initiatives such as anticipating the customer's needs or problems, keeping them informed or thoughtful gestures may be appreciated and help build the relationship. If the customer perceives the salesperson as someone who only reacts and does not initiate, they may have a less favourable impression.

PUBLIC RELATIONS

Public relations broadly describes attempts to achieve favourable publicity for the product, service, or firm. It can involve a variety of aspects, including press relations with the news media, obtaining publicity for the product, for example for a product launch, internal and external corporate communication, lobbying decision-makers, and advising the company management on public issues and media relations.

Specific tools that are used include press statements to the news media and specialist media, speeches by executives or the company management, special events such as conferences, openings, and photo opportunities, written materials such as annual reports, company profiles, brochures, articles or newsletters, corporate videos, and social or charitable activities. All of these provide communication opportunities and are a means of communicating the message.

The press statement

Press statements are used by firms to convey information to the media. Many of the activities of firms are newsworthy, such as new investment, job creation, the launch of new products, sponsorship of events, management appointments, or marketing activities. Some activities will be newsworthy to the general news media, such as the publication of an annual report or accounts, while other activities will be of more interest to specific media, such as the trade press. Press statements facilitate the media, as they communicate newsworthy items directly, which saves journalists time in investigating or obtaining material; they can be used to fill space in newspapers, magazines or the trade press and will usually be welcomed by journalists. Needless to say, the information in the press statement must be factual and accurate, otherwise journalists will not use it.

A number of factors should be noted when preparing press statements.

- The statement should be relevant and useful to the publication that receives it.
- The statement may need to have a time embargo placed on it if it is not to be published immediately. For example, the firm may want to issue advance information to the press about a forthcoming product launch or event.
- The statement should begin with a suitable headline. This should describe the general theme of the information and should attract attention.
- The main details should be set out in the first paragraph. The publication may not have space to publish all the information in the statement, and so the most relevant information should be communicated at the beginning.
- The statement should be structured in distinct paragraphs.
- The information in the statement should emphasise facts rather than opinion.
- The style used should be plain and concise. Exaggerated statements should not be made.
- Direct quotations should be used if possible.
- The statement should indicate where further information can be obtained. Usually company stationery will be used, giving the address, telephone number, and fax number, or the website address.

In a study on the evolving role of public relations in Ireland, O'Dwyer (2005) concluded that the public relations function had evolved from being a line management to a management function. This would indicate that public relations was being viewed as an integral part of corporate decision-making rather than just a communications function. The study, which was conducted in 2003, involved a survey of the top 300 Irish firms and compared the evolution of the public relations function with the results of a similar study on the same 300 firms conducted in 1993.

For public relations to be considered a management function there are seven prerequisites:

1. The presence of management support and understanding.
2. Public relations practitioners with broad interests and perspectives.
3. The use of those perspectives to identify key needs, problems and issues affecting the organisation.
4. Public relations practitioners who are good managers as well as skilled practitioners.
5. Participation in the dominant coalition (in other words key decision-makers in the organisation must be involved).
6. The public relations function model (which ranges from public relations being used for simple information provision to it being used as an integral part of corporate marketing communication strategy).
7. The public relations practitioner roles—either expert prescriber or the problem-solving process facilitator.

Measuring the effectiveness of public relations

As with any communication exercise, it is important that objectives are set for a company's public relations activities. Equally it is important to measure the results of campaigns. There are no definitive measures of performance. Firms may quantify the amount of positive publicity or coverage they have received; these, however, will give only one dimension of effectiveness. To measure effectiveness more comprehensively, research on perceptions, attitudes or opinions before and after a public relations campaign would be desirable.

It is important that the marketer establishes objectives for the public relations campaign at the outset and that this is used to measure performance. The evaluation of public relations activities can be difficult, given their sometimes intangible nature. The public relations industry has been searching for a standard of measurement, but such a universal system is unlikely to solve the problems of evaluation (Marshall, 1997). One approach (Dubin and Farrell, 1997) suggested tying in a response mechanism to PR activities. This included fine-tuning objectives, making sure news statements actually contain news, being objective in communications, incorporating response mechanisms in PR activity, and reaching out directly to communities. Tying in PR with other marketing activities was also considered important.

The impact of negative publicity

Negative product publicity can be a nightmare for marketers. It almost always leads to a loss in market share; however, there is much evidence to suggest that the way in which the marketer handles the publicity can limit the damage. Typical problems that have faced marketers include the contamination of a product, environmental damage, accidents, or tampering with a product. Faced with such situations, the firm should remember that it is the customer who must come first.

One American study (Weinberger and Romeo, 1989) looked at the negative publicity that surrounded four companies: Ford, Dodge, Procter & Gamble, and Johnson and Johnson. In the case of Ford and Dodge the negative publicity arose because of safety problems. Both companies lost market share, and in Ford's case the product was ultimately withdrawn. In the case of Procter & Gamble the results of negative publicity involved an entire product class and affected the brand's market share. The Johnson & Johnson case involved tampering with the product. This did affect market share, but the company's response, involving the recall of 22 million bottles of the product (Tylenol), ultimately restored the brand to the position it held before the crisis.

Marketers want to encourage positive word-of-mouth publicity, but the effects of negative word-of-mouth can be disastrous. Public relations can play a strong role in a crisis, when it is important to communicate to consumers, the media, or other relevant publics. The way in which the crisis is handled can determine how much damage is done to the company and its products.

Advertising can play an important role in post-crisis situations also. Following a contamination scare in 1990, the Perrier brand of mineral water was completely withdrawn from the market. When new stock was on the shelves, the company began an advertising campaign with the line 'Helleau again'. One year later the brand was back as the number one mineral water in Britain.

Relations with the media are also important. The media should be considered as customers, and therefore getting to know them and building relationships with them will be important (Matthews, 1994).

SPONSORSHIP

Commercial sponsorship has been defined as an investment in cash or in kind in an activity in return for access to the exploitable commercial potential associated with that activity (Meenaghan, 1994). Sponsorship can have many forms and has grown in importance in marketing communications.

Sport and sporting events have always been strongly associated with sponsorship activities, and these continue to be important. One research study examined the Guinness sponsorship of the All-Ireland Hurling Championship.

Sports are not the only form of sponsorship activity. Firms may become involved in the sponsorship of individuals such as athletes, events such as concerts, and causes such as the environment or charity. Television programmes may also be sponsored.

GUINNESS SPONSORSHIP OF THE ALL-IRELAND HURLING CHAMPIONSHIP

Guinness began its sponsorship of the All-Ireland Hurling Championship in 1995. Guinness as both company and brand, while global in marketing terms, has always been synonymous with Ireland and 'Irishness'. The company's flagship brand, Guinness stout, began to encounter a more competitive and changing marketplace in the mid-1990s. This was due to changing alcohol preferences in its major markets and additionally in the Irish market. Some further market difficulties arose from the changing demographic structure, which involved a younger population profile who were more resistant to the appeal of Guinness in light of more fashionable and 'younger' alternatives. Against this backdrop, the marketing strategy was to appeal to younger drinkers for brand recruitment purposes while simultaneously seeking to reassure older, brand loyal consumers who were responsible for the bulk of brand volumes.

Hurling as a sport dates from early Celtic history and is regarded as the quintessential Irish sport, being rightly labelled as the fastest field sport in the world. Its brand values are hinted at in the description by one commentator who suggested that the game involved 'a beautifully balanced blend of silken skills and fierce man-to-man combat'. In the 1990s hurling was also facing a difficult competitive environment arising from the globalisation of sport via new media platforms and the growth of soccer in particular.

Against these twin backgrounds Guinness selected the hurling championship as suitable for sponsorship on a number of levels:

- *organisational level*—in terms of Guinness and the GAA
- *brand level*—in terms of the association of Guinness stout with hurling and its reservoir of desirable brand values
- *market level*—in terms of Guinness customers and hurling fans.

The objectives of the sponsorship from a Guinness perspective were to:

1. make an emotional connection with and thus build affinity with the loyal Guinness drinke
2. build a strong association with the property, which could articulate the desired brand values of Guinness
3. give the brand a property, which would provide a 'life-style backdrop' against which it could 'talk' to its loyal customers.

The target market for the sponsorship was the loyal Guinness drinker in both the 18–25 and 35–55-year-old segments, with a bias towards the latter group, and who were overwhelmingly male.

EXECUTION AND EXPLOITATION

Over the duration of its involvement from 1995 to 2003, Guinness invested some €25 million in the sponsorship programme. The media used focused primarily on television, press and outdoor with special marketing and advertising campaigns being created approximately every two years as the sponsorship focus evolved. The creative execution initially sought to build and contemporise the hurling brand with considerable success. More recent creative executions sought to derive value for Guinness by building brand affinity with fans.

OUTCOME AND EVALUATION

In conjunction with this sponsorship campaign, Guinness undertook an extensive and ongoing research programme involving both qualitative and quantitative research.

Three examples of this effectiveness measurement were the results achieved for sponsorship awareness/association; the delivery of brand values; and brand affinity.

Sponsorship awareness/association

The scores achieved on these dimensions indicate almost universal levels of association of sponsor and event. For example, prompted awareness scores for the total population, 35–55 and 18–34-year-old target markets were 60 per cent and 80 per cent respectively in August 2001.

Delivery of brand values

In order to verify the selection decision, determine consumer reactions, and examine the image benefits of the sponsorship association, Guinness commissioned qualitative research in 1997. This indicated that the desired image values were being created. It also revealed that the support advertising for the sponsorship had contributed to a perception that the sponsorship had helped, promoted, and sustained the game itself.

Brand affinity

Strong affinity scores for Guinness are linked to the sponsorship. In other words, 54 per cent of 35–55-year-olds and 60 per cent of 18–34-year-olds felt closer to the Guinness brand as a result of the sponsorship.

Source: This is an edited version of T. Meenaghan, 'From sponsorship to marketing partnership: the Guinness sponsorship of the GAA All-Ireland Hurling Championship', *Irish Marketing Review*, vol. 15 (2003), no. 1.

Sponsorship is usually used in addition to other forms of marketing. The Bailey's brand is supported by worldwide advertising and promotion, but the company also sponsored the world figure skating championships.

BAILEY'S GOES ON ICE FOR £5 MILLION

In 1994 R. and A. Bailey signed a five-year sponsorship deal with the International Skating Union to sponsor the world and European ice skating championships. While ice skating is a minority sport in Ireland, women's figure skating ranks as the second most popular sport in the United States, after American football. Bailey had been advertising its product using a 'Bailey's and ice' theme for several years and believed that the sponsorship would be synergistic. It was also considered appropriate, as ice skating was very popular in Eastern Europe, which at the time was an emerging market for the product.

To assess the value of the sponsorship, the company carried out a media audit. This involved estimating how many people the brand reached through sponsorship. In 1994 it was estimated at 230 million people in 15 countries; in 1995 it was 320 million people. All of these were people who had watched a significant number of hours of the championships. The Bailey logo and signage were available for 60 per cent of the time.

The sponsorship has given the brand inroads into markets that are difficult to penetrate. The 1994 world championship was held in Japan, an expensive market in which to advertise. However, with the logo prominently displayed around the skating rink, the brand enjoyed its highest sales in Japan immediately after the event.

Sources: *Sunday Business Post*, 16 January 1994, 19 March 1995.

Sponsorship is usually used by firms as part of their general communication strategy. As the following panel illustrates, Eircom, which has been a sponsor of the Special Olympics for over 25 years, consider its involvement to be a cross-over between sponsorship and corporate social responsibility.

EIRCOM AND THE SPECIAL OLYMPICS

In June 2010 Irish Special Olympics for intellectually disabled athletes took place in Limerick. The event involved 1,900 Irish participants, backed by around 3,000 volunteers. Among these were hundreds of Eircom employees, a number of whom have been involved with the Special Olympics since the telecoms firm first signed up as its sponsor in 1985. Eircom is the event's premier sponsor, Accenture sponsors one of the game's programmes and official suppliers include Kia Motors, Ulster Bank, Snap Printing, Sportsfile Photography, and Stagetek.

Eircom's core practical role is to supply phonelines, broadband, and computers, but the company also offers support in other ways, including helping with marketing, fundraising, and athletes' organisations. In 2010 for example, staff raised €750,000 in the process.

To mark the company's 25 year backing of the event, one leg of the Special Olympics torch run set off from Eircom's headquarters in Dublin. Eircom was also behind a virtual torch run that took place on Facebook, aimed at getting 25,000 people to pass on a virtual Special Olympics torch.

For Eircom, the Special Olympics association represents a cross-over between commercial sponsorship and corporate social responsibility (CSR). Chief executive Paul Donovan, whose family hosted a group of Honduran athletes during the event in 2003, said he was proud of the company's association with the games.

'We're very pleased to have been associated with the Special Olympics for such a long time. The Special Olympics is something that I think you only appreciate when you come in direct contact with it. You always think about the 2003 World Games and how that captivated the nation, but it's not just about that, it's what happens month in, month out, all over the country. The World Games was a tremendous experience and across corporate Ireland, a spirit of volunteering sprang up—which is the very essence of what makes the games work.'

'They survive on the basis of people giving their time.' Matt English, chief executive of the Special Olympics, said Eircom's support was critical. 'Twenty-five years ago we had 700 volunteers; today we have 27,000 across the country. Some of our most vocal supporters are from Eircom. It's a true partnership and it has helped us to redevelop our programme and achieve growth since the 2003 games. We now have 432 clubs throughout the 32 counties.'

Padraig Corkery, Eircom's head of sponsorship, said the association enjoyed 98 per cent awareness among Eircom's staff. At that time, awareness among the general public was less than 50 per cent, but he said this would rise after the Limerick event.

'The Special Olympics [sponsorship] is a little bit different from us sponsoring the Irish football team or Meteor sponsoring *The Apprentice*,' said Donovan. 'These are commercially driven to drive brand awareness and saliency. The Special Olympics is a cross between sponsorship and CSR. As part of our CSR agenda, we believe it's very important that we give something back to communities, that our employees understand it and they feel good about it. We think it's good business, it's also very good for our own staff morale and further underpins our sheer ubiquity in the country. Eircom is everywhere and Special Olympics is absolutely everywhere as well.'

2010 marked the Special Olympics' first major foray into social media (though the organisation already has a presence on Facebook). The virtual torch run targeted the online community; Eircom publicised this drive via its own website and through banner ads elsewhere. The 2010 phone books also featured images of the Special Olympics.

Source: 'Eircom holding a torch for its Special relationship', *Sunday Business Post*, 30 May 2010.

As with all forms of marketing communication, it is important that the marketer evaluates sponsorship activities. In the case of R. and A. Bailey, sponsorship gave it access to viewers that it would have found difficult to reach otherwise.

Only a limited amount of research has been carried out on sponsorship. One study (Hoek, Gendall, Jeffcoat, and Orsman, 1997) did compare sponsorship and advertising within the context of Ehrenberg's awareness-trial-reinforcement model of advertising. It found that while both advertising and sponsorship stimuli evoked responses consistent with the model with regard to unprompted recall, attitudes, and purchasing probabilities, sponsorship may generate higher levels of awareness and may lead to the association of a wider range of attributes with the promoted brand. Another study, conducted among financial institutions in Britain, sought to identify the contribution of sports sponsorship to achieving particular objectives, and this yielded the results illustrated in table 9.5.

The same study also examined influences on the choice of sponsorship activity. These are illustrated in table 9.6.

This research illustrates the role sponsorship can play as part of the firm's communication effort. It also emphasises the need for marketers to establish clear objectives for their sponsorship activities and to evaluate the results. Common forms of evaluation include establishing the number of mentions made of the sponsor, the amount of broadcast time given, or the number of column inches printed. With regard to the quality of the publicity, it is probable that the marketer will need to consider perceptual and attitudinal research.

While evaluation measures such as awareness levels will be important, it is also necessary that sponsorship be assessed on the broader issues of its effect on brand, product or company image. The planning of sponsorship activities is also important. This list illustrates the lack of exclusivity that a sponsor can enjoy and the competition that exists between sponsors, particularly for large-scale events. Given the amount of money that companies invest in sponsorship, it is important that planning and forms of evaluation exist.

Table 9.5: Contribution of sports sponsorship to achieving objectives

	Mean
Increased corporate awareness	5.9
Increased media attention	5.1
Community involvement	4.9
Corporate hospitality	4.2
Increased sales	4
Change of corporate image	3
Increased product awareness	3
Increased new-product awareness	2.7
Change of product image	2.2

Source: D. Thwaites, 'Corporate sponsorship by the financial services industry', *Journal of Marketing Management*, vol. 10 (1994), no. 8.

Table 9.6: Influences on choice of sponsorship activity

	Mean
Sponsor's name can be linked to event	5.9
Event has a clean image	5.5
Sole sponsorship is available	5.3
Provides a good fit with brand or corporate positioning	5.1
Audience profile can be determined	5
Audience size can be measured	4.8
Television coverage is available	4.5
Can be incorporated in mainstream advertising and promotion	4
Little dialogue is necessary with organisers	3.5
Represents a new event	3.2
Contract is available for three years	3.1

Source: D. Thwaites, 'Corporate sponsorship by the financial services industry', *Journal of Marketing Management*, vol. 10 (1994), no. 8.

FURTHER READING

Advertising Standards Authority of Ireland, *Code of Advertising Standards for Ireland*, Dublin: ASAI 2007.

Medcalf, P., *Marketing Communications in Ireland*, Dublin: Gill & Macmillan 2005.

Meenaghan, T. and O'Sullivan, P. (eds), *Marketing Communications in Ireland*, Dublin: Oak Tree Press 1995.

Discussion questions

1. Outline the components of the communication model that would apply for each of the following:
   (a) Tayto crisps
   (b) Bord Fáilte
   (c) Wavin drainpipes.
   In your answer you should detail each of the components of the model.
2. Explain how you would design appropriate messages for each of the following:
   (a) a new brand of fruit juice
   (b) a holiday resort for over 55s
   (c) a campaign to discourage litter.
3. Prepare a press statement for each of the following:
   (a) Eircom's sponsorship of the Irish Special Olympics
   (b) Bord Gáis's successful 'Big Switch' advertising campaign.
   In each case you should indicate the appropriate media for your statement.
4. Can sponsorship be used by marketers *instead of* advertising and other forms of communication, or is it complementary to them?
5. Discuss the pros and cons of marketers such as Kellogg's, Guinness and Unilever using internet advertising.

References

Advertising Standards Authority of Ireland, *Code of Advertising Standards for Ireland*, Dublin: ASAI 2007.

Branagan, P., 'Is digital TV good for the advertising industry?', *Irish Marketing Journal*, April 1997.

Carter, M., 'Digital: the future of TV', *Campaign*, 5 July 1996.

Colley, R., *Defining Advertising Goals for Measuring Advertising Effectiveness*, New York: Association of National Advertisers 1961.

Denny, R., *Selling to Win*, London: Kogan Page 1988.

Dubin, S. and Farrell, J., 'Direct response through "direct public relations"', *Direct Marketing*, May 1997.

Ehrenberg, A., 'Repetitive advertising and the consumer', *Journal of Advertising Research*, 14, 1974.

Fanning, J., 'Perspectives on the new advertising', *Irish Marketing Review*, vol. 2 (1987).

Fanning, J., 'Is the end of advertising really all that nigh?', *Irish Marketing Review*, vol. 10 (1997), no. 1.

Fanning, J., 'Irish advertising—bhfuil sé or won't sé', *Irish Marketing Review*, vol. 16 (2004), no. 2.

Heinen, L., 'Internet marketing practices', *Information Management and Computer Science*, vol. 4 (1996), no. 5.

Hoek, J., Gendall, P., Jeffcoat, M., and Orsman, D., 'Sponsorship and advertising: a comparison of their effects', *Journal of Marketing Communications*, March 1997.

Irish Marketing Journal, *Guide to Marketing and Advertising Services, 1997*, Dublin: Marketing Information and Communication 1997.

Joachimsthaler, E., and Aaker, D., 'Building brands without mass media', *Harvard Business Review*, January–February 1997.

Johnson, B., 'Intel-ligence inside', *Business Marketing*, August 1997.

Lambkin, M. and de Búrca, S., 'Sales force management in Ireland', *Irish Marketing Review*, vol. 6 (1993).

Lambkin, M. and O'Dwyer, M., 'Couponing and coupon redemption: problems and perspectives', *Irish Marketing Review*, vol. 7 (1994).

Lavidge, R. and Steiner, G., 'A model for predicting measurement of advertising effectiveness', *Journal of Marketing*, 25, October 1961.

Marshall, S., 'A wordy cause?', *Marketing Business*, November 1997.

Matthews, W., 'Do unto media as you shall do unto your customers!', *Communication World*, August 1994.

Meenaghan, J., 'High visibility: celebrities, marketing and image-making', *Irish Marketing Review*, vol. 3 (1988).

Meenaghan, J., 'The role of sponsorship in the marketing communications mix' in M. Lambkin and J. Meenaghan, *Perspectives on Marketing Management in Ireland*, Dublin: Oak Tree Press 1994.

Mela, C., Jedidi, K., and Bowman, D., 'The long-term impact of promotions on consumer stockpiling behaviour', *Journal of Marketing Research*, May 1998.

O'Brien, B., 'Harnessing the new interactive tools', *Decision*, April 1997.

O'Dwyer, A., 'Perspectives on Developments in Electronic Media and their Implications for Marketing Practice', presentation to conference of Irish Marketing Teachers' Association, National University of Ireland, Cork, May 1998.

O'Dwyer, M., 'The evolving role of public relations in Ireland', *European Journal of Marketing*, vol. 39 (2005), no. 7/8.

O'Mahony, S. and Meenaghan, T., 'The impact of celebrity endorsement on consumers', *Irish Marketing Review*, vol. 10 (1997/1998), no. 2.

Office of the Director of Telecommunication Regulation, *The Future Delivery of Television Services in Ireland*, Dublin: ODTR 1998.

Paul, P., 'Marketing on the internet', *Journal of Consumer Marketing*, vol. 13 (1996), no. 4.

Rahilly, J., 'Advertising in Ireland: accents and attitudes', *Irish Marketing Review*, vol. 16 (2004), no. 2.

Simms, J., 'A driving force', *Marketing Business*, February 1997.

Ward, R. and Turley, D., 'The effect of post-purchase communication on consumer satisfaction', *Irish Marketing Review*, vol. 9 (1996).

Weinberger, M. and Romeo, J., 'The impact of negative product news', *Business Horizons*, January–February 1989.

Wickstrom, Bo, 'Analysis of the effects of special retail promotions in a consumer perspective', *Irish Marketing Review*, vol. 2 (1987).

10

Marketing Channels

The *marketing channel* is the external, contractual organisation that the management operates to achieve its distribution objectives. A *distribution system* is an essential element of the marketing channel; this is the network of people, institutions, or agencies involved in the flow of a product to the customer, together with the informational, financial, promotional, and other services associated with making the product convenient and attractive to buy and rebuy.

Physical distribution is only one part of marketing channel activities. This chapter explores the nature of marketing channels and the decisions required for the effective flow of the product to the buyer.

The marketing channels selected will play a critical role in the success of a product. Changes in marketing channels in Ireland in recent years have included the arrival of new retailers such as Lidl and Aldi in the grocery sector.

ALDI: EXPANSION IN THE IRISH MARKET

In 2008, Aldi announced plans for an additional 17 stores in Ireland, all of which were due to open within a year.

It had first entered the market in 1999. The new stores would cost about €200 million and would employ 255 people. In addition, the firm also planned a new distribution centre in Mitchelstown costing €100 million and providing another 160 jobs.

Aldi considers that the recession will cause more Irish consumers to switch to low-cost retailers. It was also keen to support Irish producers, it sourced about 40 per cent of all goods sold from Irish suppliers, higher than the amount sourced by its rival Lidl. Aldi had been engaging with Irish suppliers in a series of seminars hosted by An Bord Bia.

Aldi had 59 stores in Ireland (the expansion would bring this to 76), compared with Lidl's 98 and Dunnes Stores 120.

In July 2008, data from the TNS Worldpanel research gave Aldi and Lidl a 7.6 per cent share of the Irish grocery market, this was expected to rise. Aldi, which was formed by brothers Karl and Theo Albrecht in 1946, operated 7,600 stores worldwide.

Source: Tom Lyons, 'Aldi ramps up retail war with new stores', *Sunday Times*, 9 November 2008.

The marketing channel comprises a number of different flows that provide a useful framework for understanding the scope of channel management.

- **Product flows** are the physical movement of the product from the manufacturer to all parties who take physical possession of the product.
- **Negotiation flows** represent the interplay of the buying and selling functions associated with the transfer of title of the product: for example, retailers will seek to negotiate with manufacturers to get preferential prices or promotional deals.
- **Ownership flows** are the movement of the title of the product as it passes through the channel.
- **Information flows** consist of information exchanged by channel members on all aspects of the product: pricing, order sizes, technical details, and other issues.
- **Promotional flows** include the involvement of promotional agencies, such as advertising agencies, sales promotion agencies, and public relations consultants. In relation to many communication campaigns, the marketer may have to rely on the co-operation of channel members: for example, retailers who are expected to redeem coupons or to stock promotional items may need to be encouraged to do so.

THE ROLE OF MARKETING CHANNELS

Marketing channels perform a number of different roles, all of which involve delivering value to the marketer, the channel members, and the customer. Five roles in particular can be identified: the creation of purchase opportunity, communication, service, cost reduction, and control.

Creating purchase opportunity

One of the primary roles of the channel is to make the product readily available and easily accessible to buyers. Marketing channels therefore create place utility for the buyer. Marketers cannot always achieve this on their own, so they rely on channel members to provide their products at appropriate locations and with the necessary support.

Communication role

The channel facilitates the flow of information about the product. Channel members may be asked for advice by buyers, and they may approach potential buyers and be involved in demonstrations of the product. Specific promotional campaigns may be implemented by channel members, which may mean they are expected to stock promotional items, to redeem coupons, or to give rebates.

Service role

Marketing channels involve a service role, whether this means giving advice on using and maintaining the product, providing for repair and spare parts, providing credit, or simply a friendly greeting. Obviously some products will require more service, but in many cases it is the channel member who will be relied on to provide it.

Cost reduction

For many marketers it may be more cost-effective to use 'middlemen' than to establish their own distribution channels. Firms use middlemen because they themselves lack the financial resources to have their own distribution system, and because a middleman who is a specialist in distributing, wholesaling, or retailing may be more cost-effective.

Channels can be expensive to establish and maintain. In many cases where marketers have had their own distribution system they may decide to change or adapt it.

Control

Marketers will generally be concerned about the control implications of channel management. The more members there are in the channel the more difficult it can be to maintain control over such factors as distribution coverage, communication, and price.

One of the main disadvantages of using a middleman for distribution is that the company may lose control, and this is why many companies consider it a strategic advantage to have their own distribution system, or to exercise as much control as possible in the channel. Distribution arrangements are protected vigorously.

DEFENDING THE DISTRIBUTION CHANNEL FOR HB ICE CREAM

The HB brand, now owned by the multinational Unilever, has been Ireland's market leader in ice cream for several decades. The company's distribution system was based on supplying retailers with a freezer, which HB owned, stocked, and serviced. Retailers were supplied with a freezer on condition that it was stocked only with HB products. This distribution policy gave HB a strong measure of control in the channel.

In 1990 the Mars range of ice cream products was launched and began to appear in many of the HB-owned freezers. HB reacted by getting a High Court injunction to stop Mars putting products in its freezers. Masterfoods, the owner of the Mars brand, took the case to the European Commission, which took the view that some aspects of HB's practices were anti-competitive.

A compromise was reached, with Unilever agreeing to give rebates to retailers who owned their own freezer and who sold a minimum of €825 worth of HB ice cream a year. This allowed retailers to buy their existing HB freezer cabinet or to buy a new unit from HB in instalments, with the obligation to stock it exclusively with HB products ending when the last payment had been made.

By 1996, however, Mars was still pursuing the case, claiming that Unilever had not done enough to open the market to competition. In February 1997 the European Commission appeared to support this view when it informed Unilever that rules banning retailers from stocking rival ice creams were illegal and in breach of EU competition rules. Inspections had taken place in the market, and the commission was unhappy with Unilever's pledge not to tie retailers to them.

Sources: *Sunday Business Post*, 9 March 1995; *Irish Times*, 15 October 1996; *Examiner*, 22 February 1997.

FUNCTIONS OF MEMBERS OF THE MARKETING CHANNEL

The firm relies on members of the marketing channel to perform a number of different functions. **Research** information should be available from channel members: for example, retailers meet customers face to face and may be a source of feedback to the marketer who does not have this level of personal contact.

Communication and promotion campaigns may be implemented by channel members; they may be the medium through which the marketer communicates.

Consider the company relying on its distributors in overseas markets, where it may not have the resources to engage in direct advertising campaigns. Channel members will make **contact** with buyers and potential buyers and will be involved in **matching** supply and demand. **Negotiation** may be carried out by channel members on behalf of the marketer, and the physical aspects of distribution, such as **transport and storage**, may be performed by them. **Finance** may be arranged by channel members: for example, car dealers may arrange packages with financial institutions, and they may take the buyer's old car as a trade-in or in partial payment for a new car.

Channel levels

The term *channel levels* refers to the number of possible levels that can exist between the marketer and the consumer. A level 0 channel means that there is no middleman between the marketer and the consumer, while other channels can comprise a number of levels, as shown in fig. 10.1.

Figure 10.1: Levels in marketing channels

0: marketer ....customer	
1: airline ....travel agent ....customer	
2: manufacturer ....wholesaler ....retailer ....customer	
3: manufacturer ....export agent ......importer ....retailer ....customer	

The number of levels in the channel is determined by the nature of the product and by market conditions. Many products—some services, for example—cannot be distributed through middlemen, while other channels are highly structured and involve several levels, for example hardware. In some cases exporting can involve the use of extra channel members, such as an export or an import agent.

Technological developments have enabled many marketers to reach the customer directly, for example direct banking and insurance services. Customers can get quotations over the phone, transfer funds, or pay for the service with a credit card. These activities were traditionally carried out in the branch or through an agent or broker.

Logistics

Logistics refers to planning, implementing and controlling the physical flow of materials and goods from points of origin to points of use. This is a function of the marketing channel.

There are a number of fundamental components in a logistics system. *Transport* involves physical movement. *Materials-handling* refers to the placement and movement of products in storage areas; while *order-processing* is a significant component at different levels in the distribution channel. *Stock control* attempts to strike a balance between holding the lowest levels of stock and the customers' demands. *Warehousing* involves the storage of raw materials or products.

In addition to these factors, *packaging* affects the other components of the logistics system: for example, it may not be possible to transport some products in their consumer package, and they may need to be transported in bulk or in protective packaging.

A detailed review of each component is beyond the scope of this book; in the following section an overview of the components of the logistics system is given.

THE COMPONENTS OF THE LOGISTICS SYSTEM

Transport

There are a number of different modes of transport, each being particularly suitable for different types of products. In general, air transport has advantages for low-volume, high-margin products, such as flowers or crystal glassware, while rail and water suit higher-volume, low-margin products, such as timber or cement. Road transport will invariably be used for many inter-modal transfers, in addition to being a direct mode.

Ireland's island location means that air or sea must be used for the export and import of most tangible products, while for internal movement road and rail are the main modes. Transport may involve the movement of freight or it may be an element of the product itself, for example a flight to a holiday destination.

Materials-handling

Materials-handling comprises the range of activities and equipment involved in the placement and movement of products in storage areas. The principal objectives are to minimise the distances over which products are moved within the storage area, to minimise damage, and to maximise efficiency. Mechanical equipment, such as conveyor-belt systems, computer-aided systems, and fork-lift trucks, may be required. Materials-handling is required at ports, airports, railheads, warehouses, and production plants.

Order-processing

A firm's order-processing system is an important feature of customer service. The principal objective is to minimise the *order cycle time*, which is the time it takes from the customer giving the order to delivery. An important consideration is accuracy. Electronic data interchange (EDI) has been a significant development; this involves the direct transfer of structured data from one firm's computer system to another. If one firm wishes to order from another, the order can be transmitted by electronic data transfer, provided the information can be exchanged to agreed specifications. The same system enables the firm to track a shipment during transport and to get electronic proof of delivery. The more integrated the system, the more advantages firms can derive from it.

Stock control

The main objective of stock control is to hold the lowest level of stock that will enable the firm to meet demand from customers. Stock-carrying costs, such as storage, insurance, and damage, can be quite high. The ideal position is where the firm can keep stock at the lowest possible level while at the same time placing orders for goods in large quantities; this is because average stock costs rise in direct proportion to the level of stock, while order costs decrease in proportion to the size of the order. A trade-off point must be established between these two costs to find the optimum levels for both, and this point is known as the *economic order quantity* (EOQ), which can be calculated by using the formula:

$$EOQ = \sqrt{\frac{2AS}{i}}$$

where

A = annual usage
S = order set-up cost
i = stock-carrying cost.

For example, if a manufacturer uses 2,000 units of product A in a year, each costing €20, and each order set-up cost is €100 and the carrying cost of stock is 25 per cent, the EOQ is:

$$\sqrt{\frac{2 \times 2,000 \times 100}{20 \times 0.25}} = 283 \text{ units}$$

The main problem with the EOQ formula is that the reorder quantity it yields means that more stock is carried than is actually required per day over the complete order cycle (except on the last day). This represents a cost to the business. To overcome this, Japanese industries developed the 'just-in-time' (JIT) approach, whereby small shipments are made frequently to meet the precise time requirements of the user.

Developments in information technology, such as EDI, have facilitated the JIT approach. A retailer, for example, could order on line as demand warranted and could be supplied with the appropriate amount of the product. This eliminates the need to hold stock. Just-in-time approaches obviously need to be supported by an efficient and cost-effective logistics system.

Warehousing

Warehousing describes the holding or storage of products until they are ready to be sold. An important consideration is the location of warehousing facilities, convenient to the road network, ports, airports, or railheads. Many warehouses are equipped with materials-handling systems, which minimise movement of the product through the warehouse and reduce the risk of damage to stock.

Packaging

In general, air cargo packaging costs can be lower than for rail or road, because there is less risk of damage. Special packaging may be required for transport: for example, liquids may be transferred in bulk containers to bottling plants, where they are packed into consumer packages. A significant development in the 1960s and 1970s was the introduction of ISO (international standard) containers. These are manufactured to precise dimensions and are the same throughout the world. They can be carried by road, rail, or water, and variants are used to carry liquids, dry goods, and frozen or refrigerated goods.

DEVELOPING AND MANAGING THE MARKETING CHANNEL

Channel distribution strategy

Channel distribution strategy refers to how resources are deployed to build a channel linking the producer to the consumer. The marketer will be required to make decisions on how the distribution channel will fit in with general organisational strategy and how it may become a strategic tool for the firm.

Fig. 10.2 illustrates the stages in the development and management of the marketing channel.

Figure 10.2: Developing and managing the marketing channel

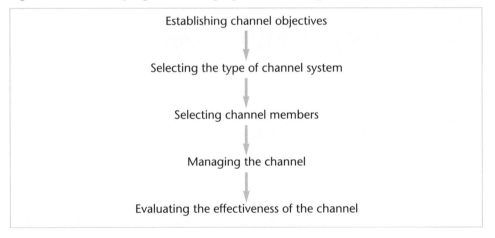

Channel objectives

In general, the marketer will want to choose the most efficient system possible. Channel objectives will be influenced by general company objectives, the role of distribution in the marketing mix, the channel design, the profile of channel members, and their performance.

The push-pull approach

If the marketer is relying on the *push* approach, this involves the channel members, such as wholesalers or retailers, 'pushing' the product towards the consumer. Incentives may be used to encourage channel members to achieve sales targets, and they may be encouraged to prospect for new business in the market.

The *pull* approach, on the other hand, involves using advertising and promotion to 'pull' the consumer towards the product. The idea is that if consumers have a positive reaction to the advertising and promotion they will be drawn towards the distribution channel to obtain the product. In general, most marketers will use a combination of push and pull approaches; it may be dangerous to rely on one approach alone.

Customer shopping preferences

Consumers have preferences with regard to factors such as time, convenience, availability, price, and the location of distribution outlets.

Consumers' shopping preferences vary by product and service but are important considerations in designing channels. It is also important to remember that the atmosphere and image of the outlet should be in line with the customers' self-image. Consumers may prefer to shop where they feel most comfortable and where they feel the outlet reflects something about themselves. The growth of shopping centres in urban areas and the increase in the number of British retailers that have extended their operations to Ireland, such as Debenham's, Boots, and Argos, have catered for changed preferences in location and variety.

Image

The distribution channel must be consistent with the image projected by the rest of the marketing effort.

While image is important, retailers must concentrate primarily on customer satisfaction. One study examined the relationship between shop image, shop satisfaction, and shop loyalty (Bloemer and de Ruyter, 1998). It found a positive relationship between shop satisfaction and loyalty but no evidence of a direct effect of shop image on loyalty.

Services offered

Members of the marketing channel may have to offer services such as finance, credit, delivery, technical advice, or maintenance and repair. Depending on the nature of the product or service, these services may be quite extensive and may involve high levels of technical expertise. Some outlets offer a limited service, such as supermarkets or discount stores, though several supermarkets have sought to differentiate themselves by using customer service.

The development of new technology—in particular, the internet—has provided opportunities for channel members. This new form of retailing has been referred to as 'e-tailing'.

E-tailing in Ireland

Electronic commerce can provide new sales channels for traditional retailers, but one study in the early 2000s revealed that many of them had been slow to embrace the new technology. Scott, Golden and Hughes (2003) found that while the cyber-retailing market in Ireland was vibrant and growing, the majority of retailers examined did not have the facility to support online sales. Their study of 25 of the country's top retailers found that the majority had a web presence but technical functionality and sophistication was low. Only 40 per cent of the 25 retailers offered online sales and of these 60 per cent did not optimise their sales functions to take advantage of technologies that increase online purchase rates. In spite of this they concluded that there were positive business and consumer attitudes to the internet and there were high satisfaction levels with online purchases.

Some businesses had increased their electronic distribution significantly: in 2006, for example, Aer Lingus reported that 71 per cent of its sales in 2005 were online (*Aer Lingus Annual Report* 2005).

Irish retailers had yet to follow the example of the German company Metro, which had created an almost completely electronic store.

TECHNOLOGY RULES FUTURE STORE

Germany's Metro AG, the third largest retailer in Europe and the fifth largest worldwide, has been experimenting with computers and transmitters to monitor shoppers and track sales. At an experimental store in the north-western city of Rheinberg, portable computers guide shoppers to sale items, big video screens offer specials and tiny transmitters keep track of thousands of products. Metro hoped that the Future Store's technology, supplied and co-sponsored by 39 companies including SAP AG, Intel Corp and Cisco Systems Inc., will help lower operating costs.

It is no accident that this experiment is taking place in Germany, one of the world's most difficult retail markets. German retail sales had stagnated. In the US, private consumption remains a powerful factor in the economy, accounting for about 70 per cent of gross domestic product. In Germany, laws limiting shopping hours, discounts and competition, plus a general social unease about consumption, discourage people from buying even in good times. As a result private consumption plays a smaller role in the economy, making up about 56 per cent of the country's GDP.

A rise in consumer spending would have helped Germany to jump start its economy by increasing economic activity outside of exports, traditionally the mainstay of German economic growth.

Metro believed that innovation would lead to more efficiency. A journey through the future store began with the keyboard-sized computers stacked up outside the entrance. Swiping a Metro customer card through the device generates lists of items the customer purchases frequently and alerts him or her to special offers. Fitted with a touch screen and a barcode scanner, it also rings up purchases as the customer shops, eliminating the need for a trip through a central checkout.

Central to the concept is the quarter-size radio transmitters called RFID tags that are attached to individual products, tracking their movement from storeroom to shelves to shopping trolley. These tags, which consist of a tiny wire antenna coiled around a microchip, are used only on a few products like DVDs, Gillette razor blades and Philadelphia cream cheese. Each transmitter costs €0.50, but the plan is to reduce this so that they eventually appear on all products, replacing barcodes. The tags alert the store's central computer when shelves need to be restocked or trigger commercials on one of the store's video screens. For example, if a shopper picks up a bottle of paint stripper, a video might come on showing how to use it and how to clean up afterwards. The tags also enable the retailer to track which customers pick up which products and then put them back, which items they buy together and in what order.

Despite optimism about the future store, there are risks. Another German retailer, Rewe, built a similar store in 2000 but found that shoppers preferred to interact with people, not computers.

Source: Annick Moes, 'Technology rules future store', *Wall Street Journal Europe*, 19 June 2003.

Competition

The firm's strategy may require using the same distribution channels as competitors, so that consumers can make their selection from the different competitive offerings. In most supermarkets and groceries in Ireland, competing brands within product categories can be found in close proximity. Ensuring that the marketer's products are available in the same locations and through the same outlets as those of competitors may be a significant aspect of positioning strategy. In other cases the marketer may find it more effective to seek non-conventional distribution channels: in the cosmetics market, for instance, Avon has tended to avoid department stores and pharmacies and has concentrated on direct selling and distribution. The houseware manufacturer Tupperware has done likewise.

Type of product

The type of product will be a determining factor in the design of distribution channels. If the product is a convenience product, for example, it should be widely available; thus marketers such as Cadbury and Nestlé distribute their confectionery products through TSNs, supermarkets, petrol stations, cinemas, restaurants, and vending machines. In cases where products are more expensive or specialised they may be distributed less extensively. Many services and industrial products are distributed directly from the provider to the customer.

Defensive flexibility

If a manufacturer is to have influence in the channel, the channel must value the manufacturer's business. The stronger the value placed on the manufacturer's business, the easier it is to manage the channel.

Trade marketing has taken on added significance as channels become more competitive. Many firms have appointed trade marketing managers to develop and maintain relationships with the trade. Trade members are encouraged to be loyal through a range of marketing activities, such as rebates, price promotions, incentives, and offers.

Channel enslavement

'Channel enslavement' can occur when members make demands for discounts, better margins, or preferential treatment and the marketer is obliged to meet these demands because the channel members have sufficient power. Enslavement is obviously something that the marketer should avoid, but it can happen in channels where the balance of power is in the hands of channel members.

Cost

Channel alternatives must be ranked according to costs. These costs refer not just to transport and distribution but also to costs associated with the management of the channel. Channel members will require a margin on sales, which becomes part of the cost structure of the product. If the marketer attempts to reduce the margin, difficulties within the channel can emerge. This was well illustrated in 1997 by the case of the airline Ryanair when it reduced the commission on sales of its tickets through the travel trade.

RYANAIR AND THE TRAVEL TRADE

In 1997 Ryanair announced that it was reducing the commission it paid travel agents on the sale of its tickets, from 9 to 7½ per cent. This provoked an immediate response from the travel agents, who began a national advertising campaign condemning Ryanair's action. Many agents began to refuse to sell Ryanair tickets.

In the fiercely competitive air market, Ryanair's decision was motivated by a desire to cut costs. The company had also established a call centre where customers could make bookings directly, thus avoiding the middleman and saving the airline the commission that would have to be paid.

The Competition Authority took legal proceedings against the Irish Travel Agents' Association as a result of its campaign against Ryanair. The authority was acting under section 4 of the Competition Act, which deals with collusion by traders to keep prices up or charges down. The association denied that it had promoted collusion, stating that it was common for traders to take their custom elsewhere when prices fell below a certain level.

The case against the ITAA was the first such case taken by the Competition Authority under new powers it received in July 1996. These require the authority to enforce competition law. It can act on complaints received from a company or a member of the public; it can also act on its own initiative.

Sources: D. Crowley, 'Travel agents face legal action over alleged Ryanair campaign', *Sunday Business Post*, 12 April 1998; Paul O'Kane, 'Travel agents face court', *Sunday Tribune*, 12 April 1998.

SELECTING THE TYPE OF CHANNEL SYSTEM

After establishing the general channel objectives, the marketer needs to consider the type of channel system required. There are a number of alternatives, ranging from direct selling to more indirect channels.

Direct selling

Direct, face-to-face selling is suitable if a high level of pre-sales and post-sales service is required, if the product is complex, or if order size is large. This will be the case for many industrial products. Airbus Industries, the European manufacturer of aircraft, has a team of sales executives and technical sales personnel who sell directly to airlines around the world. They can provide the potential buyer with comprehensive information on their range of aircraft and on features ranging from different seating configurations to fuel consumption.

Direct selling is also widely used by service providers. Where the service is inseparable from the person providing it, for example consultancy or advice, the marketer will usually sell directly. Other service providers, such as airlines, use a combination of direct selling and sales agents.

Few marketers of consumer goods use direct selling; the majority tend to use middlemen. The impact of the internet could change this, however, and many marketers are investigating using the internet to sell directly. In the United States several companies use the internet to sell products directly, and as the use of the internet increases in Ireland this may also happen here.

Direct marketing

Direct marketing involves the use of various media to interact directly with carefully selected customers. Generally the customer is expected to make a direct response; direct marketing can therefore be a combination of focused communication and distribution. It includes mail order, telemarketing, invitations to events or launches, free phone advertising, and marketing on the internet. It is gradually becoming more widely used by marketers. To be successfully implemented it requires accurate databases of potential targets. The main types of direct marketing include direct mail, catalogue marketing, telemarketing, and shopping channels on television.

Technology has had an impact, in the form of CD-ROMs, the internet, and the use of promotional videos. The internet in particular will take on added significance in direct marketing.

The increased use of credit cards by consumers means that payment can be made easily, even by phone, and this has facilitated direct marketing activities.

A number of direct marketing techniques are widely used. Direct mail is useful for letters, samples, or promotional material, which can potentially be sent to every private and business address in the country, An Post operates the 'Postaim' service to facilitate this.

The main difficulty with direct mail is the 'junk mail' tag with which it has come to be associated. This is probably due to poor targeting as much as anything else, with many direct mail campaigns amounting to nothing more than large-scale leaflet drops.

Catalogue marketing has traditionally been limited in Ireland to companies such as Family Album, which offer a range of clothes, footwear, and household items. The British company Argos has also established a number of catalogue stores. Customers select items from a catalogue, and these are obtained from a warehouse. Items are not usually displayed in the shop, which eliminates the need for large areas of shelving and display.

Telemarketing, which involves direct contact with individuals or organisations, has become a growth area, not least because the Industrial Development Authority began to identify the sector as a potential generator of jobs in the 1990s. Several multinational firms established their telemarketing centres in Ireland: for example, American Airlines opened its European call centre in Dublin in 1996, which it used to handle reservations, enquiries and sales to several European countries (*Sunday Tribune*, 17 March 1996).

A related concept is *teleshopping*, which first came to prominence in the 1970s. It was thought that it would pose a serious challenge to retailers, and many companies investigated it or began teleshopping activities in the 1980s. While some early entrants did not appear to do very well, others, such as Télétel in France and the Home Shopping network in the United States, prospered (Reynolds, 1990–1).

Owned outlets exist where manufacturers own the retail outlet. These can be good for control purposes: for example, airlines often have their own sales outlets or reservation centres in shopping districts, as has the handmade chocolate manufacturer Butler. Few firms rely on their own outlets exclusively: airlines, for example, will also sell tickets through travel agents and the internet, and Butler's products are available in supermarkets and duty-free shops. Other companies that distribute some of their products through owned outlets in Ireland include Sony and Levi's.

SELECTING CHANNEL MEMBERS

Given that few manufacturers or service providers own their own distribution outlets, most will use middlemen. The selection of middlemen is an important decision and will be influenced by a number of factors, including the type of product, the amount of service or support required, location, financial security, and willingness to participate in marketing activities. Selection will also be influenced by the degree of exclusivity of the product or the number of outlets actually available to stock it. For many specialist products in a small market like Ireland, there may be only a small number of possible sales outlets.

General criteria for the selection of channel members are:

- market coverage
- customer service ability
- stock and efficiency in order handling
- credit facilities
- value of the product to them
- willingness to co-operate in marketing activities, for example sales promotions
- ability to provide additional services, for example repair.

The marketer will apply these criteria when assessing individual channel members. They will also be important factors in the development of relationships between the marketer and channel members.

There are different types of channel members. In the following section we examine three broad types, under the headings wholesaling, retailing, and franchising. The criteria listed above can be used in assessing individual members in each case.

Wholesaling

Wholesalers typically function as middlemen between manufacturers and retailers. They store products, deal directly with manufacturers or importers, and provide a range of services to retailers.

The main function of the wholesaler is to buy in bulk from manufacturers and then sell smaller quantities to retailers. In some sectors, such as clothing, where there are many small retailers, the wholesaler is still a strong element in the marketing channel. In other markets, such as the grocery market, the number of smaller retailers has declined and the wholesalers' importance has declined also. Manufacturers and retailers increasingly deal directly, bypassing the wholesaler. Strategically, wholesalers have had to adapt to these changes in the channel system. Some, such as Musgrave, engaged in forward integration by buying the L&N chain of supermarkets in 1995 (*Checkout Ireland*, May 1997); in addition to forward integration in Ireland, Musgrave has also made acquisitions in the United Kingdom.

MUSGRAVE

Musgrave owns the SuperValu and Centra chains and is also the biggest grocery wholesaler in the country. Ireland's grocery market is estimated to be worth €7 billion per annum. The company perceives that the expansion of Tesco and Dunnes represents a significant challenge. Tesco, for example, has begun opening Tesco Express outlets in smaller towns, which would traditionally have been the bedrock of Musgrave's retail operations.

Another challenge would come from the abolition of the Grocery Prices Order: it was expected that this would lead to a 3–4 per cent reduction in grocery prices.

The company has expanded into the UK, where it purchased the Londis and Budgen's chains. Budgen's is based in the south-east of England, but Musgrave believes that it is capable of becoming a national brand.

Source: Ciaran Hancock, 'Musgrave's big push', *Sunday Times* 5 March 2006.

Retailing

Retailing is the selling of goods or services to the final consumer. Retailers are marketing institutions, members of the marketing channel, and they play an important role in the positioning of the product or service. The value and volume of retail sales in Ireland continued to rise until the year 2007, since then both rates have declined (fig. 10.3). In 2009 retail sales value dropped to 134 and volume to 118.

The retail sector has undergone considerable change in recent decades. Grocery retailing, for example, is concentrated in the hands of a small number of multiples.

In recent years a significant trend in Irish retailing has been large-scale expansion. In the DIY market B&Q opened a number of large-scale outlets in Ireland and the Swedish retailer Ikea opened a new outlet in Dublin following a government decision to scrap a regulation that capped the size of retail outlets (*Irish Times*, 3 May 2005).

Figure 10.3: Retail Sales Index

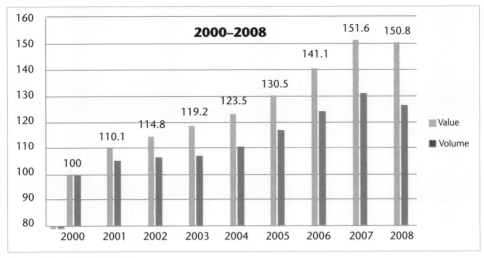

Source: Central Statistics Office

Similar large-scale expansion has been a feature of retailing in the United Kingdom. A report on the future of British retailing forecast a difficult future for the independent sector in grocery retailing. The report predicted that by 2015 there would be a significant reduction in the number of independent retailers in the United Kingdom and that grocery retailing would be dominated by the larger multiples (*Checkout*, March 2006).

Tesco had the largest market share in grocery retailing in Ireland.

TESCO

In 2010 Tesco was the market share leader in the Irish supermarket sector with a market share of 26.7 per cent. Its nearest rival was Dunnes Stores which had 24 per cent of the market. In the grocery market in Ireland, each point in market share is worth about €80–90 million in sales.

Tesco launched in Ireland when it acquired Quinnsworth/Crazy Prices in 1997: these had a market share of 20 per cent of grocery sales. It began an expansion programme, opening new supermarkets and refurbishing existing ones. A low-price own-label 'value' range was launched to target price-sensitive customers, while at the other end of the market it launched an own-label 'finest' range of premium products.

Some companies had left the market, for example Roches Stores (which had 2 per cent market share), while the main new entrants were the German discounters Aldi and Lidl.

When Tesco arrived on the Irish market, few supermarkets opened on Sundays and late opening was confined to the end of the week and the run-up to Christmas. By 2005, 13 Tesco stores were open 24 hours a day every day, and another 19 were open 24 hours a day Monday to Friday.

In addition to its Irish and British operations Tesco was also expanding internationally. Between 1996 and 2006 it expanded its operations in 11 countries in

Eastern Europe and Asia. Expansion into China began in 2005 and in 2006 it announced it was opening a convenience store chain in California.

In June 2003 Tesco had agreed to acquire the Japanese retailer C Two-Network. The acquisition was part of Tesco's strategy to grow internationally in order to balance its mature UK market.

C Two-Network is a small retailer that focuses on the lower end of the market; it had 78 stores, mostly in and around Tokyo. The acquisition provided Tesco with a low-risk way to gain some insight into the €315 billion Japanese retail market, the second largest in the world. Tesco has pursued a strategy of expanding internationally to balance slow growth in the UK market, where it is the leader. In 2003 it earned 8 per cent of total company sales in its Asian operations from stores in South Korea, Taiwan, and Thailand. It had been looking to break into the Japanese market since 2000.

Foreign retailers have, however, found it very difficult to break into the Japanese market. After more than a decade of economic stagnation, consumer prices have been falling for four consecutive years, progressively reducing profit margins. Many foreign chains have failed in their attempts to apply business models designed elsewhere to Japanese shoppers' fastidious tastes.

In 2001 another UK retailer, Boots PLC, pulled out of a joint venture after three years. It failed to attract customers from smaller pharmacy chains. The US-based chain, Office-Max Inc., an office supply retailer, withdrew from Japan in 2000. Still, the sheer size and fragmentation of the Japanese market continue to lure retailers with global ambitions. French supermarket chain Carrefour SA opened in Japan in 2000 and was operating three stores in 2003. In 2002 Wal-Mart Stores Inc., the US retailer, purchased a controlling stake in the Japanese chain Seiyu Ltd. Wal-Mart did not immediately implement its strategy of low-priced volume sales as Japanese customers tend to buy small quantities of merchandise in more frequent shopping trips.

Tesco planned to bring to C Two-Network its expertise in supply chain management, private label development, customer loyalty schemes, and real estate management. It planned to open 10 to 20 new stores a year in Japan.

Tesco's success in Ireland has been attributed to price cuts and an aggressive advertising strategy. In 2010 it announced a €113 million expansion, promising to open new stores and create around 750 jobs around the country. Tesco maintains that its annual contribution to the Irish economy is €2.5 billion; it buys €655 million of Irish food and drink products which are exported to its international stores.

Sources: Paul O'Kane, 'Tesco closer to becoming an Irish institution', *Sunday Tribune*, 17 April 2005; Deborah Ball and Jason Singer, 'Tesco agrees to acquire Japanese retail chain', *Wall Street Journal Europe*, 11 June 2003; *Sunday Times*, 5 March 2006; John Ruddy, 'Irish shoppers show no sign of falling out of love with Tesco', *Sunday Tribune*, 18 July 2010.

Functions of the retailer

In addition to making products or services available to the market, retailers are a source of market information, they play a role in the legal transfer of title, and they implement promotional activities on behalf of marketers. Increasingly, retailers are competing directly with national brands by developing ranges of own-label products.

The development of own-label or retailer brands has been of particular significance in the grocery market. Quinnsworth (now Tesco) was the first supermarket chain in Ireland to introduce own-label brands. It did so to offer a cheaper high-quality alternative to its customers, to enhance its price-perception and price-competitiveness, and to improve its profitability (Pratt, 1994). Retailers may be involved in delivery, offering repair or adjustment services, packaging, or arranging finance.

In the 1990s many retailers concentrated on attempting to differentiate through customer service. One study (Sparks, 1990–1) examined what retailers could do to establish a service strategy, drawing an analogy from the value chain. It looked at the experience of an American retailer, Nordstrom, which had managed to become synonymous with customer service. The lesson for retailers was clear: they could improve customer service by adding value. This could be done by being more responsive to customers' needs, through shop layout and design, staff training, and complaint-handling procedures, and providing services such as children's play areas or home delivery.

INFORMATION TECHNOLOGY IN RETAILING

One of the concepts that many retailers concentrated on in the 1990s was efficient consumer response (ECR). This involved a number of applications that retailers could use to improve service-stock management by constant maintenance of stock levels and increasing the range of goods available. It also involved data warehousing and mining, which concentrates on consumers' preferences and selects specific groups with product or service offerings.

In-store modifications, such as self-scanning and electronic shelf edge labelling, which improved the shopping environment and made more information available to customers, also came under this heading (*Checkout Ireland*, December 1997). Scanning systems had been widely introduced by retailers. These had the advantages of improved stock control, reduced labour costs, increased speed, and improved customer service. These benefits could be reinforced by linking the scanning equipment to head office computers, which can then provide the latest sales and stock figures. Stock control could be implemented for all products, or simply for high-value stock, depending on which option offered the retailer greater added value.

Electronic data interchange

Electronic data interchange (EDI) has had a significant impact on channel relationships. EDI is the transfer of structured data by agreed message standards from computer to computer (Nelson, 1990). In retailing it involves the transmission of orders by means of a computer network from the retailer to the supplier. Large suppliers, such as Musgrave and BWG, have been using this method; every retail unit in the SuperValu chain, for example, is linked to head office through an EDI system. Order confirmations arrive to verify the delivery.

EDI technology can also be used for invoicing, for notifying retailers of price changes or new products, and for payment. It is essential for suppliers who want a central billing facility for all the products they deliver.

Developments in computer systems enable more accurate sales forecasts, more focused promotions, and comparative analysis with similar products. When combined with sales-based ordering or a continuous replenishment programme, such systems will increase the precision with which demand is estimated and stock ordered. This will reduce warehouse storage time, lower stock costs, and improve customer service.

It is also possible for manufacturers to manage the retailer's stock directly. This would largely depend on the closeness of the relationship between the manufacturer and the retailer.

Improved delivery efficiency can be achieved with hand-held terminals, which can be used by delivery drivers. The driver has a programmed terminal containing customers' details, which calculates the amount and any outstanding balance for cash sales. This can be linked to a printer, which can produce a cash invoice or delivery note for credit customers. At the end of the day the delivery information is downloaded to the supplier's computer, and the deliveries made can be checked against remaining stock.

In-store changes

The changes that will have the most immediate effect on customers are advances in in-store technology, including electronic, shelf-edge pricing. This involves an LCD screen built in to the shelf, which can be altered instantly by the in-store computer by means of infrared or radio frequency transmission, with the checkouts receiving the information simultaneously to give full price agreement. With in-store price changes quite common, such a system would achieve labour savings. The LCD display could also show information on nutrition, unit value, and special offers, and these could be updated easily.

Self-scanning involves giving customers a hand-held scanner, which they can use to scan items as they move through the supermarket. When they reach the checkout, the scanner prints the bill. Self-scanning reduces queuing time. Superquinn has tested these systems among members of its loyalty club. Some supermarkets in Britain have experimented with self-service checkouts, which allow shoppers to scan, bag and pay for groceries using a system that incorporates an ATM.

Computerised in-store information kiosks can provide information on special offers, new products, or brands in stock. Bookshops could find such systems beneficial. Other developments include what has been referred to as 'micro-marketing', with electronic screens on trolleys, which can even broadcast personal messages to specific customers. This development may be some years away.

Loyalty schemes

Retailers in the 1990s enthusiastically embraced the concept of loyalty schemes. Loyalty cards certainly play a role in holding on to customers; they also provide an information database on the customer's shopping behaviour. Online systems mean that points can be recorded or redeemed instantly. (The implications of loyalty schemes for consumers' behaviour are discussed in chapter 6.)

Retailers and the internet

Shopping on the internet will probably grow in importance as use of the internet increases. Some retailers have developed websites to expand their retailing activities.

The main drawbacks of the internet have been making secure payments and the slowness of downloading information. Improvements in telecommunications technology and improved security software have been developed in an attempt to overcome these problems.

CLASSIFYING RETAIL OUTLETS

Retail outlets can be classified in a number of ways, ranging from self-service to full service and from speciality shops to vending machines. Some outlets are specialist, for example a fishing tackle shop, which specialises in product lines within a particular category. Other outlets, such as supermarkets, convenience stores, and department stores, stock wide ranges of products in many categories. The nature of the product and the customers' requirements will dictate the type of retail outlet used.

Franchising

A franchise is a contractual agreement under which the franchisor sells certain rights to market specified goods or services to the franchisee. Many international franchises have developed their operations in Ireland, especially in the fast-food sector, but there are also some Irish examples, as the following panel shows.

DUDS 'N' SUDS

Duds 'n' Suds is a franchisor in Derry specialising in the franchising of launderettes. By 1997 a number of franchises had been established around the country. The estimated total start-up cost of each is €127,000. The franchise itself costs €19,000, and the franchisor assists with the negotiation of leases, purchase of machinery, training, and business advice. Franchisees pay a fixed proportion of turnover each year to the franchisor.

The basics of the business range from offering self-service washing and drying facilities to a full service that includes cleaning, dry-cleaning, drying, and ironing. Clothes are docketed and washed separately according to colour and temperature; a single customer's washing may require the use of five separate machines.

Source: *Examiner*, 10 May 1996.

Franchising was also chosen by the O'Brien's sandwich bar chain.

O'BRIEN'S SANDWICH BARS: SUCCESS THROUGH FRANCHISING

The O'Brien's sandwich bar chain has successfully expanded its business through franchising. Initially it was established with three outlets; by 2006 the company had almost 300 outlets in 13 countries. The largest number—150—were in the United Kingdom. There were 30 outlets in Asia and 15 in Spain, the Netherlands, South Africa, Saudi Arabia, and Australia. The company had also franchised outlets in the United States but following losses decided to pull out.

In 2009 O'Briens had 85 outlets in Ireland, however, the chain experienced difficulties partly because of the recession and partly because of its structure. Unusually for a master franchise, O'Briens held the head leases on most of the 85 stores around the country; it then subleases out the locations to its individual franchisees. However, a number of stores struggled to pay their rents, leaving the main holding company exposed. The firm went into examinership, but the fast food entrepreneur Graeme Beere put together the finance for a rescue package.

Beere, the businessman behind the Abrakebabra and Bagel Factory franchises, agreed to team up with Brody Sweeney, the founder of the O'Briens chain, to bail out the business. As part of the deal, creditors were asked to write off a significant portion of what they were owed by O'Briens. The investment by Beere was authorised by Bank of Ireland, the main creditor of O'Briens.

Through their holding company, Abrakebabra Investments, Beere and his business partner, the concert promoter Denis Desmond, control a range of food franchises. As well as Abrakebabra and Bagel Factory, they include the Gourmet Burger Kitchen, Yo! Sushi, and Chick King. Beere plans to work with Sweeney to develop the O'Briens brand, which employs more than 800 people in Ireland, and restore it to profitability.

Other chains have also thrived in Ireland, including Insomnia, Café Sol, Perk and West Coast Coffee.

The sandwich and takeaway coffee sector is one of the fastest growing areas in the food and beverage market. Takeaway sandwiches account for about 14 per cent of all eating out.

O'Brien's uses well-known specialist Irish producers to supply it with food products, such as Darina Allen's Ballymaloe relish and Lily O'Brien's handmade chocolates which, according to Mr Sweeney, 'complement the ambience of the O'Brien's concept', and ensure consistency across the franchise.

Mr Sweeney considered that economic growth in Ireland helped the success of the business. In addition, there has been exponential growth in the sandwich–coffee-bar sector across the world. One aspect of the franchise that has caused some difficulties is the name. Using a family name like O'Brien's has been difficult to copyright.

The franchise arrangement involves franchisees paying 9 per cent of sales turnover to the franchisor. The main barriers to growth in Ireland were identified as the availability of good-quality properties and the acquisition of staff.

Sources: J. Kaminski, 'Bread and butter man', *Irish Times*, 8 October 1999; N. Callanan, 'Sandwich bars eat up available rental space', *Sunday Business Post*, 14 April 2002; Siobhán Creaton, 'Cafe market is expanding worldwide', *Irish Times*, 30 October 2004; Colm Keena, 'US Failure costs O'Brien's €500,000', *Irish Times*, 20 January 2006; Ian Kehoe, 'Beere to ride to the rescue of embattled sandwich chain', *Sunday Business Post*, 6 September 2009.

Franchisors can be classified in a number of ways. Manufacturer-sponsored franchisors exist where manufacturers grant franchises to dealers or retailers. This is common in the motor industry. Manufacturer-sponsored wholesale franchisors include companies such as Coca-Cola, which give franchises to bottlers. Service-sponsored retail franchises include international operations such as McDonald's and Burger King, and the Duds 'n' Suds example described above. There has also been some growth in retail-to-retail franchises: for example, the Body Shop chain in Britain has expanded through franchising new retail outlets in various parts of the world.

With most franchises the product or service will have proved itself in the market before franchising gets under way. The franchisee must have the capital to get the operation off the ground, and the system must be properly supervised. The franchisor must have a continuing interest in the franchisee's success and must give advice and help to the franchisee.

Typically, franchise agreements permit the franchisee to carry on a particular business under a specified name or using a process or equipment belonging to the franchisor. It entitles the franchisor to exercise control over the manner in which the franchisee carries out the business, and it obliges the franchisor to provide the franchisee with assistance in carrying out the business. The agreement obliges the franchisee to pay sums of money periodically in consideration for the franchise.

The benefits of franchising to the franchisor are an expanded distribution system without the need for large-scale capital investment, a guaranteed income—which can range from 5 to 15 per cent of the franchisee's turnover—and the onus on the franchisee to run the franchise smoothly (MTS, 1992). In some cases franchisors charge a fixed annual fee or royalty, though in other cases financial arrangements vary.

Franchisees usually pay an advertising levy, which can vary between 1 and 6 per cent of turnover. In return the franchisee has the benefit of advertising and promotional campaigns that would cost them more if they were financing them on their own. The franchisee will get the benefit of the support and assistance of the franchisor, a proven product or service, and the benefits of the franchisor's research and development. Usually a high level of interdependence will develop between the franchisor and the franchisee. Business failure rates for franchisees in start-up ventures may therefore be lower.

Channel management

Relationship marketing plays an important role in marketing channel management. Relationships should be mutually beneficial. Relationships may also be influenced by the level of power held by the marketer or a channel member.

If a manufacturer or marketer is to give a lead to co-ordinating channel members, they must possess and exercise the requisite amount of power. The essence of power is having access to resources needed by others. Leadership in a channel results if the marketer can command the loyalty of the channel members. Power can have a number of bases:

1. *Coercive power*—the ability to harm the interests of the other party in the relationship, for example, the manufacturer could slow down deliveries to retailers.
2. *Reward power*—the ability to withhold or bestow some material reward on the other party in the relationship, for example price discounts.

3. *Legitimised power*—the extent to which the commands of a particular member of the channel are obligatory, for example under contract.
4. *Manipulative power*—resourcefulness in the use of credibility and attractiveness.

A source of high credibility convinces, while a source of high attractiveness persuades.

The different power bases can have varying degrees of effectiveness. Coercive power is generally the least effective, in that it achieves minimal compliance. People do not like being coerced, and coercion tends to fuel resentment. This is not a basis for developing channel relationships.

Reward power gets results in line with the magnitude of the reward. Reward power in channels will usually be based on the profitability of individual products or the volumes ordered. The more sales effort expended by the channel member the higher the potential reward. The difficulty with reward power arises when competition or other environmental forces limit the channel member's ability to achieve the reward. Successfully achieving rewards encourages the tendency to expect more and better rewards the next time. Marketers have not got unlimited resources with which to reward channel members.

Legitimised power generally results in no higher level of performance than is formally needed to signify compliance. In other words, channel members may fulfil their contractual obligations and no more.

Manipulative power is regarded by many as the most effective. The power of persuasion can deliver the desired results. This may be a feature of developing relationships.

Motivating channel members

Motivation of channel members will be an important part of the channel management process if channel relationships are to be maintained. There are many ways in which to motivate, and the way chosen will depend primarily on the needs of the channel member.

The use of power in the channel will also be important. Support can be offered to channel members in the form of co-operative arrangements, partnerships, and strategic alliances. In addition, some firms use distribution programming. This has been defined as a comprehensive set of policies for the promotion of the product through the channel (Bucklin, 1970); a frame of reference for it is illustrated in fig. 10.4.

Figure 10.4: Frame of reference for distribution programming

Manufacturer's marketing goals
Based on careful analysis of:
- corporate capability
- competition
- demand
- cost-volume relationships
- legal considerations
- reseller capability

and stated in terms of:
- sales (cash and unit)

- market share
- contribution to overhead
- rate of return on investment
- customer attitude, preference, and 'readiness-to-buy' indices.

Manufacturer's channel requirements

Reseller support needed to achieve marketing goals stated in terms of:
- coverage ratio
- amount and location of display space
- level and composition of stock investment
- service capability and standards
- advertising, sales promotion, and personal selling support
- market development activities.

Retailer's requirements

Compensation expected for required support stated in terms of:
- managerial aspirations
- trade preferences
- financial goals
- rate of stock turnover
- rate of return on investment
- gross margin (cash and percentage)
- contribution to overhead (cash and percentage)
- gross margin and contribution to overhead per pound invested in stock
- gross margin and contribution to overhead per unit of space
- non-financial goals.

Distribution policies

- price concessions
- financial assistance
- protective provisions.

Source: Bucklin, *Vertical Marketing Systems* (1970).

In addition to distribution programming, co-operative arrangements might include co-operative advertising, in-store promotional materials, coupon-handling allowances, prizes for competitions, training, research, and discounts. The principles underlying partnerships and strategic allowances will be fundamentally based on the principles of relationship marketing (these are described in chapter 15).

Assessing the effectiveness of channel members

Rosenbloom (1995) recommends that firms conduct periodic and comprehensive performance audits of channel members. Criteria that could be used to measure effectiveness include sales performance, stock maintenance, attitudes of channel members, competition, general growth prospects, and other relevant criteria, such as the channel members' financial status, their reputation, and the quality of their service. To a large extent these criteria derive from the criteria used in the initial process of selecting channel members. These criteria can be developed into a weighted credit system for evaluating each member's performance, as shown in table 10.1.

Table 10.1: Weighted credit method for assessing performance of channel members

Criteria	Criteria weights (A)	Criteria scores (B) (out of 10)	Weighted score (A ×B)
Sales performance	0.5	7	3.5
Stock maintenance	0.2	6	1.2
Selling capability	0.15	6	0.9
Attitudes	0.1	5	0.5
Growth prospects	0.05	3	0.15
Overall performance rating			6.25

The marketer can therefore assess each channel member using this system. The relative weightings indicate the importance attached to a particular criterion: thus sales performance is judged to be the most important in the table above. The weighted credit method is one way to assess performance. It is useful as it provides an overall rating; low scores on individual criteria can be examined in further detail.

FURTHER READING

Berman, B. and Evans, J. R., *Retail Management: A Strategic Approach* (seventh edition), Englewood Cliffs (NJ): Prentice Hall 2004.
Christopher, M., *Logistics and Supply Chain Management*, London: FT Pitman 1992.
Rosenbloom, B., *Marketing Channels: A Management View* (fifth edition), Hinsdale (IL): Dryden Press 1995.
Stern, L., el-Ansery, A., and Coughlan, A., *Marketing Channels*, Englewood Cliffs (NJ): Prentice-Hall 1996.

DISCUSSION QUESTIONS

1. While the internet offers marketers many opportunities to redesign channels, consumers appear slow to adopt it. Comment on the reasons for this.
2. Profile the marketing channel components for each of the following:
   (*a*) O'Brien's Sandwich Bars
   (*b*) Blaupunkt televisions
   (*c*) Apple personal computers
   (*d*) Dulux paint.
3. Can you identify any franchising opportunities in Ireland that have not yet been exploited? Please give some examples.

4. Explain the reasons why customer service has become more important to consumers.
5. Outline how relationship marketing principles can be used in the management of marketing channels.

REFERENCES

Bloemer, J. and de Ruyter, K., 'On the relationship between store image, store satisfaction and store loyalty', *European Journal of Marketing*, vol. 32 (1998), no. 5–6.

Bucklin, L. (ed.), *Vertical Marketing Systems*, Glenview (IL): Scott Foresman 1970.

MTS, *Franchising in Ireland Survey*, Dublin: Bank of Ireland 1992.

Nelson, C., *EDI: The Key to Business Success*, Dublin: Eirtrade 1990.

Pratt, Maurice, 'Own Brands: The Benefits' (paper presented to National Marketing Conference), *Business and Finance*, October 1994.

Reynolds, J., 'Is there a market for teleshopping?', *Irish Marketing Review*, vol. 5 (1990–1), no. 2.

Rosenbloom, B., *Marketing Channels: A Management View* (fifth edition), Hinsdale (IL): Dryden Press 1995.

Scott, M., Golden, W., and Hughes, M., 'E-tailing in Ireland: a review of Ireland's top 25 retailers', *Irish Marketing Review*, vol. 16 (2003), no. 1.

Sparks, L., 'Retailing in the 1990s: differentiation through customer service?', *Irish Marketing Review*, vol. 5 (1990–1), no. 2.

JACOB FRUITFIELD FOOD GROUP

Introduction

The Jacob Fruitfield Food Group was established in 2004 when Fruitfield Foods took over W&R Jacob, the company that owned the Jacob's and Boland's biscuit businesses in the Republic of Ireland. W&R Jacob had belonged to the French Groupe Danone and Fruitfield paid them around €70 million to acquire it.

Fruitfield Foods itself had only been in existence since 2002 when it bought Nestlé's food manufacturing plant in Tallaght in west Dublin. Nestlé planned to focus on its international brands and had decided to sell its Irish brands, including Chef sauces, Fruitfield jams, Little Chip marmalade, Silvermints, and Double Centres. This presented an opportunity for Michael Carey, who, along with a number of other investors, made a bid for the company and formed Fruitfield Foods. This business was loss making at the time of the acquisition and Carey acquired it for around €8 million.

The 2004 purchase of W&R Jacob meant that the Jacob Fruitfield Group, had a total turnover of €100 million and net assets of €94 million. The group reported pre-tax profits of €4.6 million in the five months after its acquisition of W&R Jacob.

Over the next few years the company set about investing in its brands and building sales. The market for its food products was becoming more competitive, especially as the multiple supermarkets began to introduce more own-label products. By 2008 the food group needed to restructure its business to be more competitive. A decision was taken to close the manufacturing facility in Tallaght, with the loss of 220 jobs. Manufacturing was outsourced to the UK and Portugal, with smaller facilities in Drogheda and Cork being retained. The firm maintained its sales and marketing management in Tallaght meaning that total employment in the group was 100.

Marketing Challenges

In addition to restructuring its manufacturing, Jacob Fruitfield needed to develop its brands in what was becoming a fiercely competitive market. The company had brands in a number of product categories including biscuits, jams, and sauces.

THE BISCUIT MARKET

Jacob Fruitfield estimated that 24,000 tonnes of biscuits are consumed in Ireland each year. It had around one third of the market. The main competitors were McVities, Fox's, and supermarket own-label brands. Since 2008 the market has become much more price competitive, although the recession did mean that consumers were buying more biscuits. Price reductions and the fact that people were staying at home more, meant an increase in biscuit sales.

Figure 10.5

JAMS AND PRESERVES

This comprised the Fruitfield jams and preserves (originated in 1853) and Old Time Irish and Little Chip marmalade. Fruitfield had a 50 per cent share of the Irish marmalade market. The main competitors were Chivers, Folláin, Bonne Maman, and own-brand labels. Overall, the jam and marmalade market had experienced a decline in both volume and value terms. Household sizes were getting smaller and the quest for healthier life-styles also had an impact. With less bread being consumed in general by the population, bread toppings were also suffering. The overall number of private label offerings was on the increase.

SAUCES

These were marketed under the Chef brand and included brown sauce, tomato ketchup, and mayonnaise. Also included were condiments, such as beetroot and pickles.

The market leader in the sauce category was Heinz, while the Hellmans brand dominated the mayonnaise category.

The Chef brand was originally introduced in 1921, in 2007 its packaging was revamped and a television advertising campaign which was based in the Gaeltacht was used to promote the brand (see www.jacobfruitfield.com website to view the ad).

Challenges

As he surveyed his brand portfolio, Michael Carey was aware of a number of significant challenges, including:

*   marketing a range of mature products in a highly competitive grocery market
*   budgeting for sufficient marketing expenditure to support a large portfolio of brands
*   the abolition of the Groceries Order in 2006 which meant less restriction on price promotions
*   the expansion of discount retailers Lidl and Aldi
*   a much more price-conscious consumer
*   changing consumer dietary habits.

Mature markets are generally characterised by competitors having excess production capacity, this leads to increased price competition and in some cases to a 'shake-out' whereby some competitors are forced out of the business. Success in mature markets is usually dependent on a company differentiating its products more successfully than competitors or becoming a low-cost producer. Michael was aware that his options included trying to sell more product to existing customers (increased penetration), trying to increase the company's sales coverage both nationally and in international markets (new geographic segments), developing new product options, for example new flavours or ranges (related diversification), and improving existing products.

Budgeting for increased marketing expenditure would be difficult. In addition to supporting older products, marketing expenditure would be required for new introductions. Typically, companies marketing grocery brands spend 2–3 per cent of their sales on marketing. For a company such as Jacobs Fruitfield whose annual turnover was €100 million this would imply a marketing spend of €2–3 million spread over three categories of brands.

In March 2006 the Groceries Order (1996) was formally abolished. This order had prevented below-cost selling and had been designed to protect smaller retailers who did not have the same purchasing power as the larger supermarkets. It was predicted in the grocery sector that the demise of the order would lead to the larger supermarket chains cutting prices on selected items for promotional reasons. Following the demise of the order, the supermarkets put pressure on manufacturers to offer lower prices, while many smaller retailers who purchased much smaller volumes saw their sales decline.

The German retailers Lidl and Aldi had just had a very successful decade in Ireland. Their strategy was to offer a range of mainly own-label products at lower prices than national or international brands. The concept proved popular with Irish consumers and, by 2010, they had almost 8 per cent of the Irish grocery market. Most of the products they sold were sourced outside Ireland and this was especially so for their biscuits, jams, sauces, and condiments. Both retailers had expressed an interest in sourcing products in Ireland, especially those that could be sold in their shops across Europe. Such products would have to suit consumer tastes in these markets.

Consumer tastes in Ireland were changing. Products that were perceived to be healthier, such as those with low fat, sugar, additives, preservatives, and salt content, were performing well and there was an increased interest in organic products, premium products, and functional food products. In the biscuit category, for example, a number of manufacturers had introduced ranges of low fat/low sugar products. Cereal bars, for example Kellogg's Nutrigrain, were also popular and were often perceived as biscuit substitutes by consumers.

In some product sectors there were also increased opportunities for niche products. In the jam market, for example, a number of smaller manufacturers such as Folláin had entered the market with ranges of premium-quality products while in the condiments market, the cookery expert Darina Allen had launched a range of premium chutneys and relishes.

Changes were also apparent in people's eating habits, consumers were more willing to experiment with new types and flavours of food products. Functional foods, which were foods that provided additional health or medical benefits, were also becoming popular.

The Challenges Ahead

In assessing these challenges Michael Carey was aware that his range of mature brands would face not only increased price competition but could also appear to be old fashioned or out-of-date when compared to newer ranges and flavours. Repackaging, new introductions, increased advertising and promotion had all helped but this would need to be continued. In October 2010 for example, two new television adverts which had been created by the agency DDFHB were screened. These were for the Fig Rolls brand and the theme was: 'Your taste buds want them'. The ads cost €200,000 to make and Jacob Fruitfield planned to spend €800,000 airing them. Advertising was an expensive medium, but necessary for brand awareness and positioning. As he reflected on his other brands, Michael wondered how his marketing budget would stretch to give them the support they needed.

Sources: Michael Murray, 'Sweet job for ex-Kellogg's man', *Sunday Business Post*, 7 July 2002; Catherine O'Mahony, 'Fruitfield product range gets a chance to shine', *Sunday Business Post*, 7 September 2003; Barry O'Halloran, 'Fruitfield move for W&R Jacob takes the biscuit', *Irish Times*, 13 August 2004; Arthur Beesley, 'Fruitfield makes profits of €4.6 million', *Irish Times*, 2 February 2006; Ciarán Hancock, 'Loss of 22.3 million for Jacob Fruitfield after restructuring', *Irish Times*, 29 October 2009; Siobhán O'Connell, 'Jacob's hoping new biscuit commercials will be foolproof recipe for success', *Irish Times*, 7 October 2010; www.jacobfruitfield.com.

DISCUSSION QUESTIONS

1. Outline the reasons for the success of the Jacobs Fruitfield group to date.
2. How would you deal with the challenges faced by Michael Carey? Outline the marketing actions that you would take.

DONEGAL CATCH NETS SPECTACULAR PROFIT

This is an edited and adapted version of this case study. The full version can be found at: www.iapiadvertisingeffectiveness.ie/cases/cases08/donegalcatch.pdf.

Irish International BBDO

This case study describes the development and execution of an advertising campaign that earned its creator Irish International BBDO, a grand prix at the 2008 advertising effectiveness awards. Irish International BBDO, which forms the advertising arm of the Irish International Group, holds an array of clients from a diversity of sectors with one unifying philosophy: the creative work comes first. Quite simply, it is the work that gets talked about in shops, bus stops, pubs, and clubs, it is the work that remains after the briefings, workshops, presentations, and discussions have long passed, and it is the work upon which all agencies are judged.

Introduction and Background

The original brief to Irish International in 2003 was to create a compelling advertising campaign around three individual products: one existing—Chunky Cod—and two new introductions—Salmon with Pesto Crust and Cod with Mediterranean Vegetables.

The agency responded with an advertising idea to cover all three, an idea which proved so enduring that it survived the withdrawal, three months later, of the two new products (for manufacturing reasons) and the removal from the campaign of their associated TV executions. In the period pre and post the first airing of 'Filing cabinet' in 2003, ex factory sales of Chunky Cod increased by 11 per cent. Interestingly, sales of Donegal Catch Breaded Fillets, a separate product line, which constituted 38 per cent of volume sales but featured nowhere in any of this, or previously aired, advertising, rose by 10 per cent during the campaign period.

The agency had created a big Donegal Catch brand campaign idea which, through one execution alone, would benefit all products within the range between 2004 and 2007. Two new TV executions, launched in January 2008, have further amplified the campaign's success. Irish-made advertising campaigns that speak so directly to our very particular narrative tradition, local dialects, and sense of humour are rare. What's even rarer is for them to be so commercially successful.

Between 2003 and 2008, Donegal Catch's absolute profit rose by 600 per cent, resulting in a corresponding six-fold rise in the fish business.

Marketing Objectives

As brand leader, the marketing objective for Donegal Catch in 2003 was to grow value sales. It has to justify its 20–25 per cent premium versus own-label and cut through the clutter of Birds Eye's higher media spend. Between 2005 and 2008, the cost of sourcing fish like cod, haddock, whiting, and salmon increased by 6 per cent, 15 per cent, 18 per cent and 10 per cent respectively (source: Northern Foods Procurement). This meant that Donegal Catch has had to pass on a 6 per cent price increase to consumers each year since 2006 without losing any volume sales.

While it's true that people want to eat more fish, it's fresh fish they are prepared to pay a premium for, not frozen, which accounts for a much smaller value share of the total fish market, down from 45.1 per cent in 2006 to 39.4 per cent in 2008 (source: TNS Worldpanel Ireland).

Since the downturn in the Irish economy began in 2008, retailers are demanding heavier brand promotions in return for shelf space, for example the Young's brand of frozen seafood was selling at a 50 per cent discount in Tesco supermarkets. Between 2006 and 2008 retailers have grown their own-label volume share of frozen fish from 32.3 per cent to 34.6 per cent and discounters have increased their penetration within frozen fish from 25.4 per cent to 34 per cent (source: TNS Worldpanel Ireland).

Communication objectives (2003–2008)

INCREASE BRAND SALIENCE

Given the low involvement of the frozen-fish category and breadth of the Donegal Catch range, when people think frozen fish, they need to think Donegal Catch, whatever species or format they are looking for.

REINFORCE BRAND CREDENTIALS

Donegal Catch only uses natural fillets of fish, not fish that has been formed into fillets. The skin and bones are removed without compromising the integrity of the fish so it offers consumers both convenience and authenticity. The brand's Irish provenance signals premium quality and freshness.

PROMOTE PRODUCTS AND BRAND

New news is the key to driving brand reappraisal of Donegal Catch as being relevant and contemporary.

The task

GROW VALUE SALES

The net effect of increasing the price of Donegal Catch will only be positive if volume sales don't decline. Price promotions fly in the face of growing value sales, so the agency was aware that there was a need to reduce the proportion of Donegal Catch volume sold on discount, while, at the same time, recognising that a minimum level of promotional activity will always be required to keep retailers sweet.

INCREASE BRAND SALIENCE

Frozen fish is shopped for on autopilot, so if Donegal Catch is not a 'destination purchase' or top of mind at point of purchase, it's unlikely to be chosen on impulse. This is where retailers can, and do, use the allocation of freezer cabinet space to their advantage.

REINFORCE BRAND CREDENTIALS

Despite product innovation, Donegal Catch is still primarily associated with breaded fish, which does little to reinforce the premium or natural aspect of its brand offering. Meanwhile retailers and other brands are attempting to 'steal Donegal Catch's clothes' by reinforcing their own 'fresh', 'natural', 'quality', and 'Irish' credentials. The presence of a fresh fish counter in many multiples has prompted some customers to buy own-label, pre-packaged fish to freeze themselves, under the mistaken belief that it is fresher than Donegal Catch.

Naturalness has been the mainstay of Birds Eye's master brand advertising strategy. An advertising campaign for 'wild salmon', was just one of a range of new products designed to boost its quality perceptions and focus on its naturalness, and, while Bird's Eye can't claim to be Irish, in the way Tesco can, it localises its advertising wherever possible. Also worth noting is that, in the UK, Young's has a similar brand positioning to that of Donegal Catch in Ireland. It has tried to leverage this fact by airing a TV commercial that sells itself on its local Grimsby provenance and authenticity. In the period 2003–2008, Bird's Eye spent six times the amount on advertising compared with Donegal Catch.

PROMOTE PRODUCTS AND BRAND

The difficulty of using a single product commercial to do an overall branding job from 2004 to 2007 cannot be underestimated.

The strategy

The agency set out to find a platform that was true to the Donegal Catch provenance but also capable of showcasing existing or new products in a compelling, relevant, and accessible way to Irish people.

It knew from qualitative research conducted in 2002 that Donegal Catch's provenance was strong when prompted, but not top of mind, and largely inferred from its signature blue foil packaging with its prominent trawler image. From informal discussions with Irish people, the company knew people wanted to eat more fish but felt too intimidated to go to the fishmongers or cook it themselves. They disliked handling raw fish and were afraid of skin and bones. It also discovered that housekeepers tended to cook the same meals everyday of the week to make catering and shopping less of a chore. So it defined the target audience as 'convenience cooks' who are sold on fish in theory but lack the know-how to work it into their weekly repertoire of meals. To them, Donegal Catch is a back-up meal that stays at the back of the freezer. They equate the brand with breaded fish, not its healthier, more sophisticated offerings.

The strategy was to help them 'make friends' with Donegal Catch as the first step on their ladder of fish appreciation.

The product had to be pivotal to the advertising narrative but in a way that would drive overall brand affinity and sales.

Our communications idea was 'real fish from real fishermen'. Who better than three fishermen from Donegal to vouch for the brand's fresh, natural, and intrinsically Irish brand credentials? Three characters were created—Donal, Connor, and 'wee' Eoin—to win over hearts and minds by 'walking the product talk'.

Figure 10.6: Images from the 'Filing cabinet' television advert

The creative work was qualitatively tested in 2003. Both the idea and its execution resonated with Irish consumers. It was felt to capture the essence of the brand and they loved the way the three characters interacted with each other like family members. Their banter was focused on product specifics but still managed to be entertaining and memorable.

Communications activity

MEDIA STRATEGY

The media brief was to focus on housekeepers with children as the key decision-makers when it came to brands which made it onto the weekly shopping list. In 2003 the budget didn't enable a multimedia campaign. TV was deemed necessary to create a multi-dimensional picture of the fishermen's characters, whose on-screen performance would be key to the advertising's success.

Outline of character portraits

Donal is the captain, a big man in every sense of the word, part father to his crew and part enforcer. His word is law. He is willing to hear the others' points of view and is equally willing to dismiss them. He's been on boats since he was a boy. Fishing is his life.

Connor is Donal's right-hand man and can't understand why he's not in charge. One day he'll take over; it's only a matter of time. He resents, respects, and fears Donal in equal measure. He is opinionated and dismissive of the fancy folks who live on land and knows everything there is to know about fishing.

'Wee' Eoin is younger than the other two and about as bright as the bottom of a very deep hole. Naïve but lovable, women can't help but want to mother him. However, he's also shockingly handsome so this maternal instinct quickly degenerates into a desire to devour him whole!

The thinking in 2003 was that as people became more familiar with these characters in different media, they might eventually, over time, evolve into bona fide spokesmen on Irish life. So a suitably philosophical sounding end line—'Another world altogether'—was chosen to refer not just to the fish they endorse and the life they lead, but also the values they represent. However, with only one TV spot surviving from the original three and limited support in the intervening years, it became clear that the characters should be thought of as 'product'-oriented brand ambassadors. Thus the 2008 end line—'It's all about the fish'—was used to emphasise the dedication, expertise, and fruits of their fishing vocation.

Advertising activity

The brand idea first manifested itself in three TV executions between 15 October and 3 November 2003, at a weight of 1,050 TVRs (television audience ratings) and a cost of €149,725: 'Filing cabinet' (Chunky Cod), 'Finn McCool' (Salmon with a Pesto Crust), and 'Girlfriend' (Cod with Mediterranean Vegetables).

Due to the withdrawal of Salmon with Pesto Crust and Cod with Mediterannean Vegetables, the corresponding TV spots also had to be shelved, which meant that only one ad, 'Filing cabinet' was on air between 18 February and 8 March 2004 at a weight of 1,050 TVRs and a cost of €354,097. In 2005 this ad went back on air between 2 and 29 May, 12 and 25 September, and 10 and 23 October with a combined weight of 1,545 TVRs. This was supplemented by a radio campaign also featuring the fishermen extolling the virtues of Donegal Catch Battered Cod and Fish in Sauce.

The total media spend for the year 2005 was €360,098. In 2006 'Filing cabinet' was aired between 16 January and 5 February at a weight of 430 TVRs and a cost of €130,372.

In 2007 with a media budget of €81,308, the agency decided to air 'Filing cabinet' between 7 May and 4 June at a weight of 340 TVRs and to invest the remainder of the budget in a summer print and outdoor campaign for the BBQ range of Donegal Catch products.

In 2008 two new TV campaigns were launched featuring the fishermen. These promoted 'prawns' and 'salmon'. The first burst ran between 28 January and 17 February at a weight of 310 TVRs and the second one between 7 and 27 April at a weight of 250 TVRs. Total media spend to end of June 2008 was €161,144. In 2008 it was planned to add seabass and hake as additional variants. Television, radio and outdoor advertising would be used to create consumer awareness for these.

The results

Donegal Catch's performance is measured against all Irish people aged 25 to 60. The figures quoted below are from an Ipsos ASI online survey amongst a nationally representative sample of this group from April to May 2008. Respondents were asked to indicate the strength of agreement with a number of image statements.

RECALL

Altogether 74 per cent of respondents claimed to have seen Donegal Catch advertising versus 70 per cent for Bird's Eye, whose spend in 2008 was five times higher.

TAKE-OUT

Of the 74 per cent who claimed to remember the advertising, 61 per cent recalled executional elements and 22 per cent specific messages around fresh from sea, natural product, good quality, and local/Irish.

Donegal Catch's relative image strengths mirror its communications objectives as shown in the following image statement table.

Image Statements	Donegal Catch	Bird's Eye
Originates from Ireland	80	13
Has a wide choice of products	78	45
Cares about good food	71	49
I would recommend to friends	69	43
Captures fish's natural goodness	68	41
Goes to extra lengths to make quality products	65	42
Best tasting	64	31
Innovative	63	35
Frozen fish expert	60	49
Makes frozen fish that taste as good as fresh fish	58	31
Takes health into consideration	55	41

Seventy-three per cent of respondents claimed to have purchased Donegal Catch in the previous three months compared to 58 per cent for Bird's Eye. This figure is higher (79 per cent) for recognisers of the Donegal Catch ad than for non-recognisers (56 per cent). Sixty-eight per cent claimed they were likely to purchase Donegal Catch in the following three months compared to 57 per cent for Bird's Eye. Again this figure is higher (74 per cent) for ad recognisers than for non-recognisers (50 per cent).

Since 2003 ex factory sales of Donegal Catch have trended consistently upwards and the peaks have coincided closely with the timing of media spend. Comparing 2007 with 2008, Donegal Catch successfully grew value sales by 14 per cent, bettering total market growth by 5 percentage points during a period when the value sales of its closest rival, Bird's Eye, actually declined by 12 per cent (source: TNS Worldpanel Ireland).

It managed to achieve this in spite of a price rise of 11 per cent versus a market average of 6 per cent and Birds Eye's smaller 1 per cent increase.

CONCLUSION

Donegal Catch advertising worked in a very special way connecting people emotively to the brand and justifying a price premium of 20–25 per cent against own-label in the process.

Most importantly, however, it has directly increased the value of the Donegal Catch business to Northern Foods by a factor of six and created a substantial intangible asset for the company, at a fraction of the media spend of its biggest competitor.

PART 4

Marketing Applications

11

The Marketing of Services

Marketing theory has developed mainly on the basis of product marketing. However, a significant share of the economic activity of most industrialised countries is accounted for by services. Services marketing has increased in importance as marketers come to operate in an increasingly competitive services environment.

The same basic principles of marketing products apply also to the marketing of services, but the characteristics of services imply that some adaptation in marketing practice is required. This chapter explores the nature of services and examines how they are marketed.

THE NATURE OF SERVICES

A service is any activity or benefit that is largely intangible in nature. While products are physical things, objects, or devices, services tend to be deeds, efforts, or performances. Berry (1980) argued that three broad characteristics of services distinguish them from products: they are more intangible than tangible; they are more likely to involve simultaneous production and consumption; and they are less standardised and uniform.

If a person flies from Dublin to London, they buy not just a flight but a bundle of benefits, including the time they save by flying, the in-flight service, and the comfort and convenience of the flight. These can be quite intangible. To avail of the flight the customer has to be physically present: the service is therefore produced and consumed simultaneously. While every passenger on the plane has bought a transport service, some may be travelling business class and may therefore have bought a more customised service in the form of a flexible ticket and in-flight service.

A service customer may therefore experience a number of elements of the service. If any one element gives rise to dissatisfaction, this can influence the customer's general perception of the service offering. The challenge for the service marketer is to ensure that all the elements of the service are consistent with the customer's expectations.

Obviously, a product marketer can experience similar challenges. However, the highly intangible nature of many services implies that service marketers have to adapt their marketing mix in an attempt to manage intangibility.

Services in general can be considered to be intangible, inseparable, perishable, and variable. As we have seen, *intangibility* refers to services being deeds, performances or efforts rather than tangible things. *Inseparability* means that many services cannot be separated from the person providing the service—for example a visit to a hairdresser; we rely on the skills and ability of the person performing the service. Services are *perishable* if they cannot be stored: for example, if a flight takes off with empty seats, the opportunity to sell those seats is gone for ever. Given that many services are dependent on humans, the outcome can be more *variable* than if machines are involved. Thus in the case of visiting a hairdresser, if the person is not concentrating on their work the result may not be satisfying to the customer.

REASONS FOR GROWTH IN SERVICES

New services to meet new needs

Changing consumer and organisational needs contributed to the growth in services. Consumers' consciousness of the importance of health and leisure meant an increase in demand for associated services. Increased leisure time was spent on travel, eating out, health clubs, and fitness. Firms require new computer systems and programs, while training and retraining needs also increased.

Increased world trade and investment contributed to the demand for financial services. The growth in electronic commerce also required creation and support services. Any increase in commercial activity usually means an increased demand for business-to-business services, such as the marketing services provided by advertising agencies and market research companies. In some cases old service ideas are resurrected, such as the Luas light rail or tramway system in Dublin. (Trams had been a feature of public transport in Dublin from the 19th century, but the network had ceased operations by 1959.)

Social trends

More women in the workforce, increased leisure time, and increased consumer sophistication have all contributed to increases in the demand for services. Services such as child-minding, 'ethnic' restaurants, and home delivery all increased in importance. Increased travel means increased use of transport, accommodation, and associated agency services. More emphasis is being placed by consumers on convenience, and in many cases it is more convenient to use a service than to do the work oneself.

Demographic trends

Increased life expectancy, lower marriage rates and smaller family sizes mean that people are living longer and have more disposable income. In industrialised countries, when people have more money to spend they will be more likely to buy non-essential items, and many services have benefited as a result.

CHARACTERISTICS OF SERVICES

Intangibility

Products are physical objects that can be seen, touched, heard, or smelled. Services, on the other hand, are intangible and are more likely to involve feelings or emotions. The degree of intangibility can vary, as demonstrated in fig. 11.1.

Figure 11.1: Relative tangibility and intangibility

While many product marketers try to attribute intangible aspects to their products in order to differentiate them from competitors' offerings, service marketers often try to attribute tangible aspects to their service so that the customer can relate to them. For example, credit card companies that are providing consumers with the benefits of flexibility, convenience, and an interest-free credit period relate these to a small plastic card.

Customer involvement in production

Customers are more likely to be involved in the production of a service than in the production of a product. A customer who visits a hairdresser or self-service restaurant has to take part physically in the production of the service; in all such cases the customer must be present. This is not so for most products, where the finished product can be selected from the shelf, without the customer becoming involved in the production process.

Quality control

Many services are produced and consumed simultaneously. Unlike products, where quality control techniques are used before they leave the factory, services can have a variable outcome, which can be difficult to control. This is so because for most services the marketer is relying on people to deliver the service. The variability in service quality can occur for many reasons, including poor training, poor communication, and the mood of the service provider.

A marketer needs to make sure that service quality is consistent, otherwise the consumer may not return. As people are an integral part of the production of the service, quality control must be through people. An interesting research study in Britain examined how service quality could affect blood donations (Newman and Payne, 1997). The study examined the motivations for giving blood, the reasons why people stopped giving, and the reasons why the majority of people eligible to donate don't do so. It concluded that there were important customer service and service quality issues to be addressed.

The benefits to firms of improving service quality are well documented. They include greater customer satisfaction, customer retention and improved company profitability as direct benefits, and attracting new customers as well as inducing customers to increase their use of the service (Danaher, Rust, Easton and Sullivan 1996). One Irish study (Carson and Gilmore, 1993) examined how the ferry company Stena Sealink enhanced service quality on its Ireland–Scotland route. The result was a significant reduction in the number of complaints by customers.

Another study (Quinn, 1994) proposed the 'PROMPT' approach to service quality. This provides managers with a guide to improving service quality. It has six components:

- prioritising customers' needs
- reliable and fast delivery of service
- organising for customers
- measuring customers' satisfaction
- personnel training
- technology focusing.

The PROMPT approach involves establishing what customers' needs are and giving priority to the most important ones. Reliable and fast delivery of the service is considered to be crucial. Firms need to be organised around the customer, not around particular managers.

The chief executive of Scandinavian Airlines, Jan Carlson, recommended the inverted pyramid as the basis for organisation design (Carlson, 1987). When a company is being organised it should be borne in mind that personnel who come in contact with the customer are more likely to interact with the customer than higher level management.

Customer satisfaction can be measured using research techniques. If a company is seeking to improve customer service, measurement means that comparisons can be made before and after. The training of people is obviously part of the process, as is the use of technology that can provide faster, more efficient or more reliable service.

One technique for measuring service quality that became widely used was 'Servqual' (Parasuraman and Berry, 1986). The model measured consumers' perceptions of five areas of service: tangibles, reliability, responsiveness, assurance, and empathy. *Tangibles* refers to the appearance of physical facilities, equipment, personnel, and communications. *Reliability* is the ability to perform the promised service dependably and accurately. *Responsiveness* requires the service provider to be willing to help customers and to provide prompt service; while *assurance* is the knowledge and courtesy of employees and their ability to convey trust and confidence. *Empathy* refers to the service provider's ability to be caring and to provide individualised attention to customers.

Quality or, more specifically, *quality management* became a much-researched and documented topic from the 1980s. *Total quality management* (TQM) developed to become a significant influence on product and service organisations in the 1990s. The process of introducing TQM in a service industry requires the management to be conscious of service gaps that may emerge (Candlin and Day, 1993). Service gaps may come about from not knowing what customers expect, having the wrong quality standards, service performance not living up to expectations, or promises not being met. A conceptual model of service quality is illustrated in fig. 11.2.

Quality, whether of products or services, became an important differentiation tool.

Stock

In general, services cannot be stored easily, if at all. Staff and equipment can be held in readiness to produce the service, but unused capacity—for example one empty seat on an aircraft—is lost for ever. An important task for the service marketer is to smooth demand levels to match supply. The marketer must establish what the patterns of demand are and then adopt strategies that attempt to change these patterns to make them more favourable. Price is often used as a means of achieving this, for example offering reduced prices at times when demand is lowest to encourage people to change their usage patterns of the service.

Distribution channels

Typically, services are distributed through people—for example a solicitor or a dentist—rather than through physical distribution channels. There are exceptions: some services, such as cash lodgment and withdrawal, are now highly mechanised through ATMs. Developments in technology, such as the internet and EDI, are having an increased impact. Information services can be easily accessed on the internet, and orders, reservations, and payments can be made. In general, the distribution channels for services will be shorter and will not involve as many levels as those for products.

Figure 11.2: Conceptual model of service quality

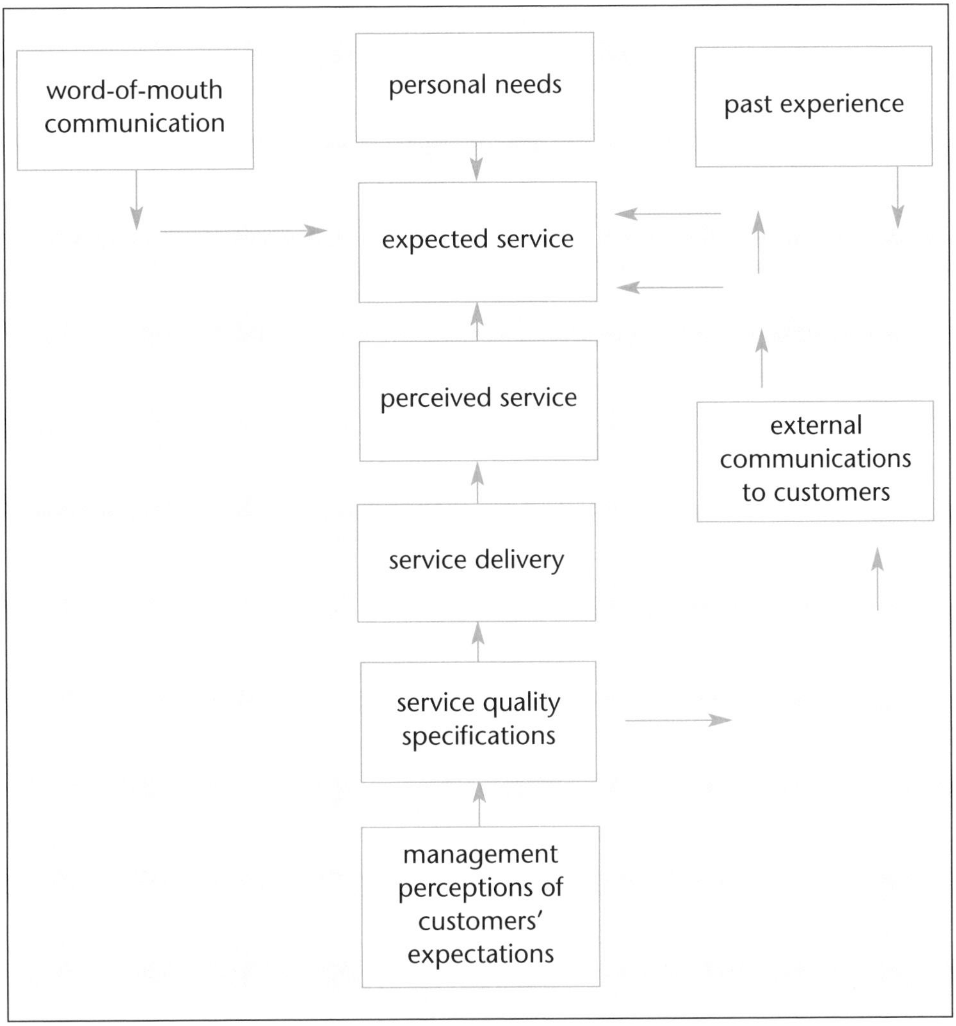

Source: V. Zeithaml, L. Berry, and A. Parasuraman, 1990.

THE SERVICES MARKETING ENVIRONMENT

The services marketer will have to monitor continuously the micro and macro forces in the environment that affect the business and to react by providing a competitive service that meets the needs of the customer.

In the 1990s there were many indications that such elements in the service environment as speed, quality, price-competitiveness, and reliability were the main factors used by customers to judge service offerings. Society became more convenience-oriented, presenting opportunities for service marketers. This had been forecast by the Henley Centre of Ireland (1992), which had predicted an increase in demand for ready meals, for example, and a growing demand for delivery to the home. It was also expected that consumers would spend more on services and leisure following trends in more affluent countries.

THE SERVICES MARKETING MIX

The marketing mix for services is basically the same as that for products, namely product, price, promotion, and place. Many marketing theorists would argue, however, that the traditional 'four Ps' framework needs to be expanded for services so as to include an additional P: people. Certainly the provision of services is normally people-intensive; in many cases the service cannot be separated from the person providing it. We will include people as a fifth P in the services marketing mix. Other theorists consider that additional Ps, such as *process* and *physical evicence*, should be included. These are also considered in context.

Product

In relation to services, *product* is used broadly to describe the offering that is being made to the customer. The service product will have *core*, *actual*, *augmented*, and *potential* features.

Consider the following panel, which examines the levels of Ireland's tourism product.

IRELAND: A TOURISM PRODUCT

Tourism is one of Ireland's most important economic activities, accounting for over 60 per cent of the country's exports of services. At the core, visitors to Ireland are buying a number of benefits. Their visit is an experience that can include a wide variety of elements: relaxation, excitement, peace of mind, friendship, and a different pace of life. Tourists are attracted by the country's greenness, clean air, pure water, and unspoilt landscape as well as the activities they can engage in, such as golf, water sports, and angling. These, as well as accommodation, food, and drink, are all part of the tangible aspects of the product.

When they are here, visitors have expectations about the augmented aspects of the tourism product. They expect to get value for money and good-quality service and to have a guarantee that any problems or difficulties that might affect their enjoyment of a visit will be sorted out satisfactorily. The *potential product* describes what Ireland could possibly become from a tourist point of view. This would include the development of particular attractions or facilities that are different from or enhance the existing product offering.

One of the main considerations for the marketer is the degree of intangibility involved in the service. The marketer may try to associate something tangible with the service so that the consumer can relate to it or can easily recognise what the service will offer.

Branding may play a part by giving the service added value and providing a recognisable cue for the consumer. Many service marketers have invested substantially in their brands; McDonald's, Jury's, and Golden Discs are all recognisable brands regarding whose quality, value, and standards of service the customer has definite expectations. As with the marketing of products, the services marketer can use branding to differentiate the service offering.

Price

The relationship between price and quality can have great significance in the marketing of services. Price will form the cue the consumer uses to compare different service offerings. Given the intangibility of services, the consumer may use the price of the service as an indication of the level of quality they can expect. It is important therefore that the services marketer has a clear idea of what the consumer's perception of the price actually is.

Berry and Yadav (1996) recommended three broad strategies for service pricing. *Satisfaction-based pricing* could include, for example, a guarantee that if the customer is not happy they will receive a refund. *Benefit-driven prices* would depend on the benefits the buyer required from the service—the more benefits, the higher the price—while *flat-rate pricing* would involve the same price being charged to everyone for the same service.

Costing a service can be more difficult than costing a product, because of its intangibility. How do you price the services of a medical specialist? It is inherently difficult to place a value on something intangible. The tangible costs incurred in providing the service—for example the materials or equipment used—can be computed, but the value of time or advice is more difficult to calculate. A cost-plus pricing approach may be used where the tangible costs are computed. A cost is added for the intangible aspects, such as time, and then a mark-up is added.

In many cases service providers will price on a *going-rate basis* or on what they estimate the market will bear. A *rate of return* approach may also be used: for example, an airline that has a large investment in aircraft and ground equipment might use a pricing approach based on a target rate of return on its investment.

Price is an important tool for the services marketer, as it can be used to influence the patterns of demand for the service. This will be especially relevant where demand reaches peaks at certain times but is lower at other times. In off-peak times, price will be reduced in an attempt to stimulate demand: thus cinemas offer reduced rates for afternoon showings, and transport companies offer reduced fares at off-peak times.

Promotion

The general objectives in promoting services will be much the same as in the promotion of products. The principles of the communication model (chapter 10) should be adhered to. The marketer should identify the audience, determine what the promotional objectives are, develop the message, and decide which element or combinations of elements of the promotional mix should be used.

The nature of the service may sometimes limit the type of promotional activity that can be undertaken. Unless something tangible can be associated with the service, the consumer may have difficulty visualising it. Promotion may therefore have to emphasise tangible cues.

All the elements of the promotions mix can be used by the services marketer. Advertising is widely used and is good for creating a strong visual image. Organisations like Tourism Ireland rely heavily on television and print advertising to create an impression of what Ireland has to offer; similarly, financial services companies use television, radio, and print to inform and in many cases explain what can be quite complicated products. Many services marketers like to use images of their staff in advertising or promotional materials, for example, fig 11.3 shows one image that was used by Aer Lingus. The airline uses its own staff so that the consumer gets an impression of what to expect.

Personal selling is particularly important for services because of the high involvement of people in delivering the service. As with products, the person selling the service will be seen to represent the service provider and will therefore create an image in the mind of the customer. Personal selling is good for explaining the nature of the service, answering questions, and learning about customers and their needs. It is widely used by financial services companies, as it enables them to explain the range of options available, and customers can ask questions about what can be quite complicated products.

Figure 11.3: Aer Lingus

Source: BFK Design (www.bfk.ie).

Sales promotion can be used to provide incentives to buy. Discounts or special offers can be used to encourage trial or repeat purchases. Given the importance of price as a means of attempting to change demand patterns for services, sales promotions involving special prices are quite common.

Public relations can be a useful medium for newsworthy aspects of the service. The use of press statements, or coverage of conferences or sponsorship events, can help to communicate a message about the firm. Banks use public relations opportunities to communicate, among other things, the strength of their financial performance. They will usually place particular emphasis on the publication of their annual report and results.

In general, direct sale is the most common method of service distribution. Channels are therefore short:

service provider ——▶ consumer

Intermediaries can be involved: for example, airline and holiday services can be sold through travel agents. Franchising has also been used successfully by many service providers, ranging from fast food and launderettes to printing and financial services.

The service may be distributed totally through people, but technological changes have presented more opportunities to marketers. Information-based services, such as Aertel (on television) and Weatherline (delivered by phone), provided new distribution channels. The growth in use of the internet increased the possibilities considerably and improved marketers' ability to provide interactive services.

Place

The location of the service provider can vary in importance according to the nature of the service. For a car breakdown service, location is not important, as the customer will use a phone to summon help; in the case of a restaurant, however, location will be very important.

Modern telecommunications technology and data transfer mean that the location of the service provider may be irrelevant. The IDA has identified international telemarketing as a new service that could be established, using Ireland as a base for marketing products to consumers in other countries by phone. A good telecommunications network and low-cost international phone calls are the main considerations for these companies. Several companies were attracted to Ireland during the 1990s, one such being American Airlines, which established its European call centre in Dublin in 1996, creating 220 jobs (*Sunday Tribune*, 17 March 1996). By 1997 the IDA had attracted 43 companies, and 3,600 were employed in the sector (*Sunday Business Post*, 16 February 1997). The fact that costs were 30 per cent lower than alternative sites was considered to be Ireland's competitive advantage.

Ireland is well placed to compete in international service markets, as one indigenous enterprise, the Foreign Exchange Company of Ireland, has demonstrated.

THE FOREIGN EXCHANGE COMPANY

The Foreign Exchange Company of Ireland (FEXC), was established in Killorglin, County Kerry, in the early 1980s and began by operating a number of foreign exchange bureaus around the country. The opportunity for this business had been spotted by the company's founder and managing director, Brian McCarthy, who had previously worked as a bank official. He noticed that tourists were frequently frustrated at the limited opening times of the banks, so he applied for a licence from the Central Bank to operate exchange bureaus. This business developed, but the company was keen to exploit its opportunities, and did so with Cashback.

Cashback was established to process and refund VAT payments to overseas visitors, who are entitled to claim back the VAT they have paid on purchases made while in Ireland. At the time, the processing was being done by retailers, who found it costly and time-consuming. Cashback took over this task and provided a service whereby visitors were able to claim their refund directly, or have it forwarded to them; retailers in turn paid Cashback for the service. The business relied on the development of data-processing technology and good telecommunications, which enabled the company to process potentially millions of claims at its premises in Killorglin. Location was not a disadvantage, and Cashback expanded rapidly, selling its service to practically all the large retailers in Ireland. In Britain, retailers such as Harrod's use the service, and Cashback has expanded to corner a significant share of the market.

Fexco expanded rapidly and, by 2010, had 1,300 staff, about 900 of whom were based in Ireland. The firm's expansion was based on identifying new opportunities beyond the original foreign exchange and cash back services. By 2010 it was organised into four broad business areas:

- *merchant services*—dynamic currency conversion (DCC), multi-currency pricing, credit card processing, global treasury solutions, gift and prepaid spending solutions, bureau de change, and consumer tax solutions.
- *business services*—payment, customer service, and administration services).
- *consumer services*—stock-broking and asset finance.
- *international services*—Prudential Investment Company of Australia, Fexco Pacific, and Western Union European Call Centre.

Fexco customers included Bord Gáis for whom it provided customer service support, the Irish government (administration of the prize bonds scheme), and Sustainable Energy Ireland, for whom it administered grants and customer service for the home energy improvement scheme.

Sources: T. Harding, 'Fexco plans VAT refund service', *Sunday Business Post*, 8 February 1998; *Sunday Tribune*, 13 November 2005; www.fexco.ie.

Many service providers, including airlines, financial service providers, hotels and retailers, have used the internet as a means of conducting transactions and providing information. Customers benefit from 24-hour availability, while service providers can reduce staffing costs.

People

People are an important part of the services marketing mix, as in many cases the service cannot be separated from the person providing it. The problem for marketers is that it can be difficult to ensure uniformity in the quality of service. With manufactured products, uniformity can be achieved with quality control techniques, which in many cases can be highly mechanised. In the case of services, quality control can be achieved through supervision, motivation, and training, and these need to be carefully organised to ensure that the consumer gets the level of service they expect. Many service marketers, for example airlines, banks, and hotels, use the quality of their staff as part of their promotional campaigns.

Increasingly, service providers are coming to recognise that competitive advantage can be gained through the quality of their staff. This implies a need for adequate training, especially for those who come in contact with customers. Service strategy can be seen as a combination of a firm's marketing and human resource strategies. This can be categorised as either a *relationship-based marketing* strategy, which emphasises customers' loyalty to the firm, or, in contrast, a *transaction-based* strategy, which emphasises volume, resulting in lots of customers with no expectation of loyalty (Dearick, McAfee and Glassman 1997). It is possible to consider a mixed strategy, for example taking a transaction-based approach with customers and a relationship-based approach with employees, or vice versa. Determining which strategy to pursue will depend on the nature of the customers, the type of service or product, and the firm's ability to attract and retain competent employees.

A service company's corporate culture should be supportive of staff and should help to motivate them to provide the best service possible. The firm's culture refers to the shared experiences, beliefs, and actions that characterise the firm. All employees of the American airline Delta are expected to help get the job done; if passengers' luggage is delayed, managers are expected to help out in physically dealing with the problem. The core policy is that the customer should not be inconvenienced and should receive the best possible service.

Internal marketing means applying the marketing policy to people within the firm so that they come to appreciate the importance of the customer and of how the performance of their job is directly related to customer satisfaction. Internal marketing should be practised by all firms, but service marketers need to be especially aware of its benefits. Internal marketing can contribute to the firm's corporate culture by facilitating a positive spirit in the company, and this in turn will affect the attitudes and motivation of employees.

The recruitment and training of staff are important elements. At the recruitment stage, such factors as the aptitude and personality of the applicant must be taken into account: the company needs to make sure that the people being recruited are capable of delivering the service in the desired manner. They will be trained to deliver the service, to dress in the required manner and to deal with people but also to appreciate the importance of service quality.

Many service companies have recognised the importance of involving their employees in decision-making. The Scandinavian airline SAS believes that its frontline staff need to be empowered to make decisions. Individual customer requirements imply that staff need to be able to react quickly to a situation and make decisions that are in the best interests of the customer.

DELIVERING CUSTOMER SERVICE

Customer care

The role of marketing is not just to create customers but also to initiate and develop a relationship with those customers from the first stage of contact and throughout a series of different transactions. Customer relationships are a marketing asset, to be cultivated and maintained.

One study, which examined how a customer care improvement scheme was developed by Northern Ireland Electricity (Carson and Gilmore, 1989), set out a model for customer care and examined the quantitative issues involved, such as speed of delivery, and the qualitative issues, such as courtesy. The study suggests that rules and procedures are common for the former but that in the qualitative or psychological areas it is the perceptions, attitudes and behaviour of staff who come into contact with customers that are important. Obviously these are areas where marketing managers can have an impact or can implement improvements.

Increasingly, consumers are demanding higher levels of service and have expectations about the quality of service they expect. Service marketers can use this to advantage by seeking to deliver these standards and by differentiating themselves on the basis of their service quality.

Among the factors that should be taken into account when considering customer service are the following:

- customers' enquiries and questions should be dealt with as comprehensively as possible.
- customers' orders should be accepted, processed, and delivered in an efficient manner.
- time deadlines should always be met.
- all complaints, comments, or suggestions should be dealt with.
- service providers should seek to understand their customers' requirements and seek to add value in their dealings with the customer.

In his book *Crowning the Customer*, Feargal Quinn, the owner of Superquinn supermarkets, stated that customer service would be the competitive battleground for business in the 1990s. He described some of the policies and practices that helped make Superquinn a successful business and a recognised provider of good customer service, including getting a feel for the market, listening effectively to the customer, and the use of consumer panels.

High-contact services

High-contact services are those where there is a high degree of contact between the service provider and the customer, for example in health care. The quality of the service is therefore inseparable from the service provider. Marketers need to be sure they have the right service personnel to provide the level of service the customer expects. They must also devote resources to the training and development of their service personnel.

Understanding what motivates people is important for all firms; the service marketer, who must rely on people to deliver the service, must be especially aware of this. Service companies can find, for example, that because demands for the service can vary during different periods of the day, they can introduce flexible working hours for employees.

Employees may therefore feel that the company is accommodating them in allowing them to work their preferred working hours, and their attitude to the employer may therefore improve.

Internal marketing is also important for service providers. The services marketer needs to remember that they must market the job to the employee before they can expect the employee to market it to the customer.

The physical services environment

In cases where the production and consumption of the service happen simultaneously—for example in a restaurant or a dentist's surgery—the physical environment is important, as this will convey an image of the service provider to the customer. In many restaurants the customer can see the food being prepared behind the counter, and so the kitchen area must be well maintained. The layout of the seating area, the cleanliness of toilets, and the facilities for children will also be noted by the discerning customer. Banks, which traditionally provided their service across counters lined with metal bars or thick glass, have changed their layouts, and in many cases business is now conducted without physical barriers, so that customers do not feel intimidated. In the waiting areas of doctors' and dentists' surgeries some have started to provide play areas for children. Retailers pay particular attention to shop design and layout and to providing added value in the form of someone to pack the shopping at the checkout, someone to help the customer to their car, or simply the umbrellas that are kept at the checkout for customers to borrow.

All these examples illustrate attempts by service providers to improve their physical environment and to create a distinctive image for themselves.

Reshaping supply and demand

This may be required because of fluctuating demand patterns for the service. Demand can be reshaped using price incentives to encourage people to use the service when demand is normally lower.

Reshaping supply can take the form of using part-time staff to cater for the increased demand at peak times or having employees do more than one job so that they can be moved to other jobs as demand for the service requires. It is possible to automate some services, for example food and beverage dispensers or cash-dispensing with ATMs.

Services marketing strategy

All marketers will have to adjust and adapt strategy to take into account changes in the marketing environment. Some marketing environments, such as the environment for airlines, are prone to rapid environmental changes. This was the case for Aer Lingus.

AER LINGUS: OPERATION GREENFIELD

Operation Greenfield was the name given to a cost-reduction programme launched by Aer Lingus in 2010. The objective was to restore the airline to profitability, from the losses it had incurred in 2009 as a result of a difficult recessionary environment. The cost-reduction programme required the airline to reduce costs by €97 million. The main areas where costs were reduced included:

- withdrawing from unprofitable routes
- reducing flight frequencies on other routes
- deferral of new aircraft delivery from Airbus
- reduction in staff numbers (including 40 per cent fewer managers)
- a pay freeze for all employees.

The airline would seek to reposition itself as 'Ireland's civilised airline'. The key elements of this repositioning strategy were:

- a target audience of leisure and business travellers (87 per cent of its passengers travelled for leisure reasons)
- a quality core product with benefit driven à la carte paid options (e.g. seat selection, in-flight food and drink)
- positive engagement with customer
- seeking to satisfy 'medium' customer expectations
- use of the internet for distribution, but other channels used as appropriate (e.g. travel agents can still be important in some markets)
- a brand image that was professional but affordable
- appropriate connectivity at selected hubs (e.g. allowing passengers to connect with airline partners at Heathrow (British Airways), New York (Jet Blue), or Chicago (United)). Aer Lingus also entered an agreement with Aer Arann resulting in the creation of the Aer Lingus regional brand. This covered flights mainly on regional routes from Irish airports to regional airports in the UK.

Sources: Aer Lingus Investor and Analyst Day, London, 26 January 2010; www.aerlingus.com.

DISCUSSION QUESTIONS

1. Ireland has witnessed growth in many service sectors in recent years. Where do you think new growth opportunities will emerge?
2. Outline the elements in the service marketing mix for each of the following:
   (a) Ryanair
   (b) Butler's Chocolate Cafés
   (c) Bank of Ireland
   (d) an advertising agency.
3. Many service providers have found the internet a particularly useful marketing tool. Outline the advantages of an interactive website to a service marketer.

4. Given that many services are inseparable from the person providing the service, what role can internal marketing play in assisting service marketers with quality assurance?
5. Outline the advantages of loyalty programmes to service marketers. Why do you think so many service providers use loyalty programmes?

FURTHER READING

Palmer, A., *Principles of Services Marketing* (fourth edition), Maidenhead: McGraw-Hill 2005.

REFERENCES

Berry, L., 'Service marketing is different', *Business Magazine*, May–June 1980.

Berry, L., and Yadav, M., 'Capture and communicate value in the pricing of services', *Sloan Management Review*, summer 1996.

Candlin, D. and Day, P., 'Introducing TQM in a service industry', *Quality Forum*, September 1993.

Carlson, J., *Moments of Truth*, Cambridge (MA): Ballinger 1987.

Carson, D. and Gilmore, A., 'Customer care: the neglected domain', *Irish Marketing Review*, vol. 4 (1989), no. 3.

Carson, D. and Gilmore, A., 'Enhancing service quality: the case of Stena Sealink', *Irish Marketing Review*, vol. 6 (1993).

Danaher, P., Rust, R., Easton, G., and Sullivan, M., 'Indirect financial benefits from service quality', *Quality Management Journal*, vol. 3 (1996), no. 2.

Dearick, D., McAfee, R., and Glassman, M., '"Customers for life": does it fit your culture?', *Business Horizons*, July–August 1997.

Henley Centre of Ireland, *Planning For Social Change: Report*, Dublin: Henley Centre of Ireland 1992.

Newman, K. and Payne, T., 'Service quality and blood donors: a marketing perspective', *Journal of Marketing Management*, August 1997.

Parasuraman, A. and Berry, L., *Servqual: Multiple Item Scale for Measuring Customer Perceptions of Service Quality Research*, Cambridge (MA): Marketing Science Institute 1986.

Quinn, F., *Crowning the Customer*, Dublin: O'Brien Press 1990.

Quinn, M., 'Winning service quality: the PROMPT approach', *Irish Marketing Review*, vol. 7 (1994).

Zeithaml, V., Berry, L. and Parasuraman, A., 'Five imperatives for improving service quality', *Sloan Management Review*, summer 1990.

12

International Marketing

This chapter explores the nature of international marketing and the adaptations to marketing practice that may be required when a business operates in more than one country. International marketing is of particular relevance to Ireland, because of its high dependence on trade; Ireland is one of the most trade-dependent countries in the world.

Between the 1960s and 1990s the Irish economy was transformed. It went from being largely agricultural, with only 22 per cent of merchandise exports consisting of manufactured goods, to a technology-based economy, with manufactured goods accounting for 70 per cent of merchandise exports.

The main difference between marketing in the home country and in international markets is the marketing environment. In international markets the environment can be less certain; and the more international markets the business is involved in, the greater the potential uncertainty.

Uncertainty arises for many reasons, not least the fact that international markets can be physically and culturally removed from the home market. These differences may require adapting the marketing practice for different markets.

INTERNATIONAL TRADE

Countries trade because few, if any, can be completely self-sufficient. Generally, countries will concentrate their productive effort on the products they can produce best and that give them a competitive advantage.

International economic activity takes place in a number of ways.

1. **International trade**: Imports and exports of goods and services have steadily increased. Among wealthy, developed countries the share of world merchandise exports in 2007 was 71 per cent, with developing countries having 29 per cent. In 1995, the equivalent figures were 82 and 18 per cent respectively (World Bank Development Indicators, 2008).

   Trade is especially important for Ireland. As table 12.1 illustrates, the country's balance of trade surplus declined after 2002, but increased in 2009. The increase was due to a significant reduction in imports.

Table 12.1: Balance of trade, 2000-2009 (in € million)

Year	Imports	Exports	Trade surplus
2000	55,909	83,889	27,980
2001	57,384	92,690	35,306
2002	55,628	93,675	38,047
2003	47,865	82,076	33,211
2004	51,105	84,409	33,304
2005	57,465	86,732	29,267
2006	60,857	86,772	25,915
2007	63,486	89,226	25,740
2008	57,585	86,394	28,810
2009	45,061	84,239	39,178

Source: Central Statistics Office

2. **Foreign direct investment**: Investment by firms in operations in other countries. As barriers to investment have lowered, global flows of foreign direct investment have more than doubled relative to GDP. In 2007, high income economies received about 75 per cent of global foreign direct investment flows (World Bank Development Indicators, 2008).

3. **Capital market flows**: This takes place when savers include foreign assets such as shares, foreign bonds, or loans in their portfolios or when borrowers use foreign sources of funds.

The World Bank tends to favour a reduction in barriers to trade or foreign direct investment as a means of stimulating economic development and reducing poverty. It is less enthusiastic about liberalising the global capital flows market because these markets tend to be highly volatile and can experience boom-and-bust cycles. This can have serious destabilising effects on economies as happened in South Asia in 1997–8.

The international marketing environment

International marketers have to take into account conditions in the different marketing environments in which they operate. While some conditions, such as physical proximity or language differences, may be quite apparent, others may be less so and will need to be researched before a company enters that market. As in the home market, the company must keep abreast of environmental changes and their implications.

Before examining the individual forces in the international marketing environment it is necessary to consider the broad nature of globalisation.

Globalisation

Globalisation is a term that has sparked one of the most highly charged debates of the past decade. It has been the subject of several books and the cause of demonstrations in Europe and North America. There is no agreed definition of globalisation. Levitt (1983), who was one of the first academics to write on the subject, described it as a trend for companies to have a presence in more of the world. He argued that globalisation would become an important force because consumers would be willing to sacrifice preferences in product features, functions and design for lower prices and higher quality. In other words, it would be driven by lower costs.

According to the Economist Intelligence Unit (1991) globalisation was stimulated by cheaper air travel, rising incomes, instant communication, increased use of credit cards, erosion of national barriers, financial deregulation, and shifting international cost structures. The trend towards globalisation seems set to continue.

Young (2001) argued that the international business environment was changing under the influences of globalisation, the information technology revolution and the new economy. He felt that the main debating points as a result of this would be the benefits of free trade and investment, the rise of non-governmental organisations (NGOs), and the role of multilateral institutions.

While free trade had benefited many economies, it had also caused inequality and exclusion in some of the world's poorest nations. Many non-governmental organisations, for example pressure groups, have argued against liberal trade policies and advocate protectionism. Multilateral institutions, such as the World Trade Organisation and the European Union, have been criticised for not adequately addressing issues of poverty and global inequality. The new economy referred to industries that fuel the development of or participate significantly in electronic commerce or the internet, develop and market computer hardware or software, or develop any form of telecommunications services (Mullins, Walker, Boyd and Larréche, 2005).

As time has moved on, the term globalisation has been used in cultural and political contexts in addition to its economic meaning. The fact that in the past two decades an increased amount of economic activity in the world has been taking place between people who live in different countries would suggest that it is principally an economic phenomenon.

While the term globalisation may suggest a sense of global inclusion, for many poorer and less developed countries it is something from which they are effectively excluded. During the 1990s the less globalised countries had negative growth rates on average while the more globalised developing countries increased their per capita growth rate from 1 per cent in the 1960s to 5 per cent in the 1990s.

Globalisation is not a new phenomenon; economic theorists can point to the late 19th century when it can be argued that a form of economic globalisation took place. This corresponds with the growth in colonialism by mainly European powers at that time. These powers were driven by a combination of economic and political motives to colonise less developed parts of the world. The result was increased international trade and investment. The end of the First World War (1914–18) ushered in several decades of political and economic instability and protectionism, in addition to the rise of fascism. After the Second World War (1939–45) it took several decades before globalisation was once more a significant part of the world order. The establishment of the United Nations and institutions such as GATT (General Agreement on Tariffs and Trade) were important in resolving international political and commercial issues respectively. Other factors that contributed to the increase in importance of globalisation have included:

- the collapse of communism in the USSR and the establishment of a Confederation of Independent States
- the ending of Soviet domination in Eastern Europe
- China's economic reform and increased international trade and investment
- the Uruguay round of the GATT in 1994 and subsequent agreements that saw many developing countries participate for the first time in international trade agreements
- the enlargement of the EU so that by 2007 it comprised 27 member states
- the advent of new technologies, especially in the areas of telecommunication and information processing.

These factors caused an increase in the pace of global economic integration, especially in the 1990s when many barriers to international trade and investment were removed or reduced.

The critics of globalisation argue that it has caused exploitation in developing countries, has led to job losses and has given large firms more control of international trade and markets. They argue that it encourages standardisation throughout the world and therefore reduces consumer choice. Quelch and Hoff (1986) argued that 'the decision on standardisation is not a rigid either/or decision between complete standardisation or adaption but rather there is a wide spectrum in-between and that there are degrees of standardisation'. Their argument would indicate that strategy choice could be viewed as a continuum between highly uniform to highly adapted.

Levitt did indeed argue that globalisation would lead to a standardisation of international marketing behaviour and practices for consumer products based on:

- an international equalisation of relative income levels
- increased personal consumption
- a convergence of ownership patterns of durable consumer products
- increased and better information and communications
- convergence in consumer tastes and values due to the importance of young people who express much more converged tastes than older people.

He also suggested that technology in transport and communication would enable more people to travel and experience more of the world. People who lived in isolated places would become more informed about the world around them and would desire the new products and life-styles that they became aware of.

While globalisation has presented many opportunities for brands such as Bailey's and Jameson there are also several examples of Irish firms that have been initially successful in seeking to develop their international operations.

IRISH FIRMS TARGET GLOBAL GROWTH

The retail climate in Ireland is the toughest shop owners have seen for many years, as consumers tighten their purse strings. But many Irish retailers have broadened their horizons in recent years and are pursuing opportunities in new markets. Fashion chain A-Wear is the latest Irish retail name to set its sights on international expansion, with its entry into Britain.

Irish shoppers are well accustomed to British and international retailers opening in Irish thoroughfares, but travellers in Britain and Eastern Europe will have noticed local names like O'Brien's Irish Sandwich Bars and Lifestyle Sports in foreign cities. Mark Stafford, chairman of Lifestyle Sports, said that the Czech Republic, Slovakia, and Poland were the firm's focus for the next two to three years. The company acquired a Czech chain in 2007 and was to open its first operation in Slovakia in 2008.

Although Britain might seem like an obvious first stop for Irish retailers, Lifestyle has stayed away from the market due to the intense competition among sports retailers there. Also, British retail has been suffering from negative consumer sentiment for some time. 'We knew that, even though we're a relatively small Irish player, we are actually quite a big customer for the key brands, given the fragmented nature of the sports retail market on an international level,' Stafford said.

The company focused on Eastern European countries with good macro-economic growth stories, assuming that spending on sportswear would grow, as has happened in Ireland. The company acquired 25 stores in the Czech deal, closing a number of these and opening others, giving the company 23 outlets there at present. Lifestyle plans to open 10 more over the next six months. All are wholly owned by the Irish parent.

In Slovakia, Lifestyle has done a deal to run a store in a high-profile location for a major sports brand, and it will take a Lifestyle unit in this new centre also.

Aisling Walsh, marketing manager with Butlers Chocolates, said that the café's concept was first franchised into New Zealand in early 2007 and a second outlet there opened later in the year. In 2009 café outlets were opened in the US and Britain. She said research was key to any expansion plans, with distribution channels and costs being particularly important.

'While the product might be fantastic and positioned at the right retail price, if the distribution strategy is not thought through and executed properly, the ultimate success of the product may well be threatened,' said Walsh.

Source: Samantha McCaughren, 'Irish firms target global growth', *Sunday Business Post*, 31 August 2008.

The economic environment

The economic strength of the particular country or market will dictate such factors as wealth and disposable income. The economies of countries can be classified as subsistence, raw-material-exporting, industrialising, and industrial. *Subsistence economies* are those of countries such as Ethiopia or Somalia, where the majority of the population subsist on very low levels of income; the consumer market will therefore be relatively undeveloped. *Raw-material-exporting countries*, such as Nigeria, typically have natural resources such as mineral ore, oil, or food commodities that account for the bulk of their exports. These may be exported in their raw state without any further processing or added value in the country of origin. There are usually low levels of industrial and commercial development, and consumers have low levels of disposable income. *Industrialising countries*, such as Egypt, are attempting to build up an industrial base. This may involve attracting internationally mobile investment by means of tax incentives and low labour costs. Consumers may have higher levels of disposable income. In *industrial countries*, significant value-adding activities take place, and consumers have the highest levels of disposable income.

The classification of an economy is based on income; and how income is distributed in a particular country is an important economic indicator. It is also a determinant of the size and nature of the consumer market.

The political and legal environment

Ireland and other member states of the European Union have seen significant developments in the harmonisation of laws and regulations. A fundamental principle of the 1957 Treaty of Rome is the free movement of products, people, and capital between member states. Many of the directives issued by the European Commission have been aimed at the removal of laws or regulations that hinder the free movement of goods or trade between states. As a result, it is easier for Irish companies to do business in Europe, and, similarly, the Irish market has opened up to more competition.

In relation to trade outside the European Union, regulations, tariffs, and quotas may govern whether and how much trade can take place between Ireland and other countries. Members of GATT, for example, agree tariffs and quotas; these then determine how much trade can be done between states.

Political and legal considerations may determine whether any trade can take place. The United Nations may impose trade sanctions against particular countries. Such sanctions were imposed against Iraq in 1990, which affected a number of Irish companies that had been involved in exporting food products and medical services to Iraq. Similar sanctions were imposed against Libya in the past, and this also affected Irish companies doing business there.

While trade barriers are being lowered around the world, there are still many countries that may not have positive attitudes towards foreign marketers. These attitudes may be based on a desire to protect the market for indigenous suppliers, or they may be based on political, social, or religious grounds. The result can be laws or regulations that prevent or limit the activities of foreign marketers.

Regulations and bureaucracy are an inevitable part of exporting. In the European Union efforts have been made to reduce aspects of regulation and bureaucracy that had the effect of slowing down or hindering the movement of products. Regulations exist governing, among other things, how products are to be transported between countries, safety issues, and the components and ingredients of products. These exist to prevent disease, accidents, and contamination. Customs examination, which usually takes place at the point of entry, involves administration and may lead to delays. Monetary regulations may prevent the marketer repatriating profits, while exchange controls may place limitations on the financial transactions associated with trade.

Political stability is important for trade to flourish; instability creates uncertainty and increases the risk associated with exporting. In general, industrialised countries tend to be politically stable; difficulties tend to emerge in countries where there is significant political or social unrest.

The cultural environment

The way in which foreign consumers think about certain products must be clearly understood. Cultural conditions can influence whether or not the product will be considered by consumers in the overseas market. Not all products or services are cross-cultural, though several, such as Coca-Cola, Levi's, and McDonald's, are sold virtually throughout the world. Irish products such as Waterford Crystal and Bailey's Irish Cream also have cross-cultural characteristics.

In a globalised business environment, cultural factors play an important role in determining management practices and strategies. Differences in national culture have been shown to influence firm's entry modes into international markets (Shane, 1994) but also the perceived difficulty surrounding the integration of foreign personnel into the organisation (Hofstede, 1980). Cultural differences will also be an important consideration in any marketing strategies in international markets. Rugman (2001) argues that there is no such thing as a single world market with free trade and that therefore businesses need to think local and act regional.

Understanding cultural differences is an important prerequisite for international business success. Swift and Lawrence (2003) pointed out that, traditionally, the majority of cross-border relationships were based on exchange relationships, such as those that exist between a goods manufacturer (seller) based in the country of export and the importer (buyer) of the goods based in the importing country. Such relationships imply a comparatively low level of manufacturer involvement with, and knowledge of, the foreign market. In many cases, knowledge of the local language, culture, and the market requirements is assumed to be the responsibility of the importing agent or distributor. The advent of globalisation, however, means that companies have to develop cross-cultural business relationships. To be successful, companies have to operate within a cultural framework dictated by the market environment; a lack of understanding of this may put the company at a competitive disadvantage.

Factors that influence how a product is perceived in a particular cultural setting include the nature of the product and the needs and motives of buyers. Language differences can also affect how the product is communicated in the market. In less developed markets, consumers may have little or no familiarity with certain products or the concepts underlying them. The rate of literacy may be low, and pictures or symbols may therefore be more important than text; this can have implications for packaging and advertising.

Understanding cultures in international markets is vital. This enables the firm to determine whether there are opportunities in the market. In recent years, many firms have found opportunities in China, as the following example illustrates.

KFC IN CHINA

The American company Kentucky Fried Chicken expanded rapidly in China as Chinese life-styles became geared towards speed, convenience, and choice. Between 2000 and 2003 it opened 1,000 restaurants in China, most of them located near new workplaces, housing developments, and shopping centres. The menu was adapted to suit Chinese tastes, while restaurants also open for breakfast, something that does not happen in the United States.

KFC did not pursue their normal franchising strategy in the Chinese market. All but 10 outlets are run either directly by KFC or as joint ventures. Franchising proved difficult because of the lack of managers who understand franchising, the early difficulties in establishing a supply chain, and government restrictions.

The company sources about 95 per cent of its ingredients in China, creating entirely new markets for products such as iceberg lettuce that are not normally grown by Chinese farmers.

Source: Richard Mc Gregor, 'KFC leads China's new appetite for fast food', *Financial Times*, 20 January 2003.

For other firms, the Chinese market may represent more of a challenge. The Kerrygold brand, which had annual global sales of €260 million in 2005 and an international marketing budget of €20 million, has targeted the Chinese market as a growth opportunity. The growth may, however, be slow as average dairy consumption in China is only 13kg per capita, compared with the EU figure of 200kg. In China the brand is known as Jin Kai Li (*Sunday Tribune*, 12 March 2006).

According to the *McKinsey Quarterly*, there are a number of significant things to remember about building brands in China.

BUILDING BRANDS IN CHINA

- Chinese shoppers love brand names.
- Salespeople in China have tremendous sway over consumers' decisions. Point-of-sale promotions can be an effective way of addressing last-minute switching and getting products into the hands of consumers.
- Compared with developed markets, messages that focus on functional features can be more important in China, since many product categories are new. This will change as consumers become more experienced.
- Consumers in China have strong national pride, so multinational companies could lose important segments by seeming too foreign.

The French retailer Carrefour has become the largest chain of hypermarkets—giant outlets offering everything from consumer electronics to groceries under one roof—in China since it opened its first outlet in 1995. By 2006 it was operating 73 hypermarkets in 29 cities with turnover in 2005 of $2 billion. It expected its sales in China to grow by 25–30 per cent per annum between 2005 and 2010.

Source: www.mckinseyquarterly.com.

Many international marketers have discovered that what works in some markets will not work in others. Consider the experience of some international marketers in India.

MARKETING IN INDIA

India is one of the toughest markets for international marketers. Marketers such as Pepsi and McDonald's have discovered that it is important to play down the fact that they are foreign. Advertisers say that India's colonial past has left a profound mistrust of foreign brands.

When Coca-Cola returned to the Indian market in 1992, having been thrown out in the late 1970s, it acquired Thums Up, the local cola market leader, as a means of eliminating its biggest competitor. Indian consumers responded negatively when Coca-Cola tried to replace Thums Up with Coke. Coca-Cola realised that it would have to promote Thums Up rather than compete with it. Coke is third after Pepsi and Thums Up in the $1,200 million Indian cola market.

Pepsi's success derived from its joint processing venture with the government of Punjab and an agreement that it would be a net exporter, earning India foreign currency. Pepsi exports products such as chillies and basmati rice to its subsidiaries. It was therefore perceived to be supportive of employment and the Indian economy.

McDonald's spent six years studying the Indian market prior to entry. It expected to have about a hundred outlets in India by 2003. In a country where 70 per cent of the population does not eat beef and where half the population is vegetarian, McDonald's could not simply replicate what it did in the rest of the world. Vegetarian dishes are offered and the 'Big Mac' equivalent is made from chicken and local spices.

Source: Edward Luce, 'Hard sell to a billion consumers', *Financial Times*, 25 April 2002.

Cultural change can present opportunities for marketers. In China, government policy has limited families to one child each. The result was the creation of a generation of young people who were well educated and prosperous, materialistic, and accepting of western culture (Barnathan, Comes, Roberts, Einhorn, Roy and Moore, 1994). This group of younger consumers were described by some marketers as 'the little emperors' (Wei, 1997).

Foreign retailers have, generally, found it very difficult to break into the Japanese market. After more than a decade of economic stagnation, consumer prices had been falling for four consecutive years, progressively reducing profit margins. Many foreign chains have failed in their attempts to apply business models designed elsewhere to Japanese shoppers' fastidious tastes (Ball and Singer, 2003). In 2001 another UK retailer, Boots PLC, pulled out of a joint venture in Japan after three years. It failed to attract customers from smaller pharmacy chains. The US-based chain Office-Max Inc, an office supply retailer, withdrew from Japan in 2000. In 2002 Wal-Mart Stores Inc, the US retailer, purchased a controlling stake in the Japanese chain Seiyu Ltd. Wal-Mart did not immediately implement its strategy of low-priced volume sales as Japanese customers tended to buy small quantities of merchandise in more frequent shopping trips.

Technological environment

Technology is a possible source of competitive advantage; in international markets, technology developed in one country may give it an advantage over other countries. Consider the example of Bantry Bay Mussels, which developed process technology to give it an advantage in selected export markets.

Products do not necessarily have to represent the most advanced technology in order to compete in international markets. What is considered a low level of technology in a developed market may well be high technology in a developing market.

BANTRY BAY MUSSELS

Bantry Bay Mussels, established in 1991 to harvest fresh mussels, has patented a process for producing frozen vacuum-packed mussels for export. France became the company's largest market, accounting for 70 per cent of sales; the remainder went to Italy, Germany, and Britain.

In addition to supplying fresh produce, the company began to investigate the production of processed mussel products to boost sales. These would have the advantage of a longer shelf life. The result was the development of a process for freezing and vacuum-packing the mussels, which the company has used successfully, as well as licensing the technology to other mussel producers. Other value-added products include the development of mussels frozen with a variety of sauces so that they will keep for 18 months.

In 1996 the company was awarded the AIB Capital Markets Export Award. According to the judges, the company had developed an intimate knowledge of its target market and adapted the product range accordingly.

More awards followed, including an exporter of the year award in 2003.

The firm employs over 120 people and can produce 50 tonnes of product per day. New markets have been developed in Austria, Belgium, Denmark, Holland, Iceland, Latvia, Lebanon, Romania, Russia, Spain, Sweden, and the United States.

In 2005 the firm entered a joint-venture with a Chilean company Masato S.A. This resulted in the construction of the largest mussel farm in Chile and the launch of a new brand on the market there called Blue Shell.

Sources: *Irish Independent*, 31 October 1996; *Sunday Business Post*, 23 February 1997; www.bantrybayseafoods.com.

Competitive environment

A profile of competitors in the overseas market will be required, with information on who they are, what range they offer, how widespread their distribution coverage is, and how they promote their products.

If competitors enjoy the benefits of protection in the foreign market, this can be a significant disadvantage for a company trying to establish there. Marketers will seek to create a competitive advantage over rivals in the market, as Waterford Wedgwood did with the development of the Marquis range of glassware, which it used to widen its product base.

Waterford Wedgwood's strategy in developing this product, which was obtained from other European countries, such as the Czech Republic, was to fill the gap in price segments it had vacated when it had increased the price of its classic hand-cut range. In the crucial American market the product achieved sixth place in sales in higher priced crystal (Galvin, 1993).

MARKETING DECISIONS IN INTERNATIONAL MARKETS

Research

Research is vital for making decisions, especially if the decisions are being made on markets with which the business has little familiarity. The research process will be the same for international markets as for the home market. Enterprise Ireland, which provides assistance to Irish business, has a market information library, which provides various profiles, reports, and figures on overseas markets.

The benefits of conducting international market research were demonstrated by the experiences of Tyrone Crystal in the Japanese market (Bell and Brown, 1989). The research showed that there were few official impediments to entering the market but that many of the design qualities prized in other markets were incompatible with prevailing Japanese tastes. In spite of this, the study identified some concrete opportunities within specific market segments.

Research carried out on European teenagers in 1997 resulted in the identification of a number of distinct segments.

The researchers argued that these clusters could be applied in seeking to understand media and brand selection. They felt that increased use of the internet and the expansion of digital television would make it easier for marketers to tap into these teenage cultures.

EUROPEAN TEENAGER SEGMENTS

In 1997, Euroquest, a research company, carried out a survey of teenagers in Europe. Ten thousand 11- to 19-year-olds were interviewed in Germany, France, the Netherlands and Britain—four countries that accounted for two-thirds of teenagers in the European Union. The study covered use of and attitudes to media (television, radio, press, cinema and the internet), use of around 150 different products and a wide range of attitudinal data.

The results identified six clusters or segments:

- *Dreamers* (15 per cent) are enthusiastic children who are media and technology fans and are curious about everything. They are confident and have dreams that they believe they can fulfil—becoming another Bill Gates or a famous footballer, for example. They are social and have friends, while living happily within their families. They spend their money on computers, music, sports, and entertainment outside the home. Dreamers are heavily into television and watch almost seven hours more each week than other teenagers.
- *Big babies* (15 per cent) also have good family relationships, but have much more limited horizons than the dreamers. They tend to be more insecure and shelter behind the world of school and home. Studying and family are important to them, and their leisure time is spent mostly at home, though the amount of time spent

watching television or listening to radio is quite low. They spend their money mainly on gifts for others, on clothes and CDs.

- *Good kids* (16 per cent) are every parent's dream—they are in harmony with their families, able to think intelligently for themselves and well equipped to deal with the real world. They have lots of interests and friends but maintain their individuality within friendship groups. They have ideals and ethics but also know how to enjoy themselves, and their spending includes music, clothes, sports, and books. They tend to come from higher social-class backgrounds.
- *Independents* (14 per cent) are less in harmony with their families. They are more likely to be female and to be working. Consequently their life-style is quite free, with family having little influence or authority. They have the highest personal income of all six groups and their focus is on entertainment and fun. They spend money on clothing, entertainment, and music, and their values tend to be materialistic rather than idealistic.
- *Searchers* (20 per cent) are more in conflict with the adult world as they seek to create a 'different' life from that of their parents. Their orientation is more towards peer group than family; they are eager to explore and have many interests. Their emphasis is on experimenting and experiencing new things. Music is very important to them; they have the highest cinema and internet usage of all groups.
- *No-hopers* (19 per cent) are in conflict with the adult world as they seek to escape from real life. They are more likely to be male. There is little communication at home but they have few interests outside the home and do not tend to have many friends. They are not interested in the future and have an attitude of waiting to take whatever life brings. They are unenthusiastic consumers.

Source: R. Ford and A. Phillips, 'Targeting European Teenagers', *Admap*, June 1998.

Developing the product for international markets

A classic example of the development of a product for international markets comes from the 1960s and the development of the Kerrygold brand.

IRELAND IS KERRYGOLD COUNTRY

In 1961 the Irish Dairy Board was established as the central export marketing organisation of the dairy industry. In 1962 the British market was the successful launching pad for Kerrygold butter. A number of factors can be attributed to the success of the launch, such as product quality, distinctive packaging, a higher priced pricing policy, and a television campaign that presented strong visual images of the green pasturelands of Ireland.

The strategy for the launch of the product in the German market in 1972 echoed the British formula, namely providing a high-quality butter tailored to consumers' tastes. Once again the advertising emphasised the country of origin, the green island with the clean and unspoilt nature. '*Das gold der grünen insel*' was the theme with which the advertising would become associated for 20 years.

With the success of Kerrygold butter the logical progression was to capitalise on brand awareness and to extend the range to include 'light' butter and a range of natural cheeses.

The key to developing Kerrygold branded sales in Belgium has been the role played by the board's subsidiary, IDB Benelux, which imports and distributes products from eight European countries, including Ireland. This has given Kerrygold improved access to the Belgian trade and a greater presence in retail outlets for both butter and Kerrygold cheddar in blocks and pre-pack form. Support for both product categories ranges through television and press advertising and sales promotions directed at the trade and the consumer. IDB Benelux also developed a successful 'Green Flag' brand for a range of higher priced European fine foods, including Irish smoked salmon, breakfast bacon, and salmon spread and the Greek speciality tzatziki, as well as a range of pre-packed convenience foods.

In Greece, Kerrygold was the first branded cheese on the market in 1980, and Kerrygold Regato became the largest cheese brand in the country. Again the brand was supported by a significant expenditure on advertising and promotion. Television commercials demonstrated the versatility of the cheese by incorporating it in traditional Greek recipes as well as in new, imaginative dishes.

The Irish Dairy Board attributes the success of the Kerrygold brand around the world to a number of factors:

- All the products marketed under the Kerrygold brand are of the highest quality, and many are demonstrably superior to the competition.
- The board has a total commitment to branding in the long term and a heavy investment in achieving national distribution, including maximising consumers' awareness through above and below-the-line support.
- An attractive brand name is enhanced by the positive image towards its country of origin: 'Ireland, the food garden of Europe.'
- Regular innovation enables the board to capitalise on the Kerrygold brand name with a complementary product line.

Notwithstanding the fact that the different countries demand marketing tactics to suit their various individual requirements, the core communication values of Kerrygold remain constant in all markets served by the board. In that regard Kerrygold has become a Eurobrand and will, through time, become a truly international brand.

Source: Caroline Palmer, 'Irish Dairy Board', *European Marketing Confederation Gold Book*, 1994.

The development of the Kerrygold brand demonstrates some of the prerequisites for success in international markets. Another significant Irish success has been Bailey's Irish Cream, which has become a leading world brand in the drinks market.

BAILEY'S IRISH CREAM:
THE WORLD'S TOP-SELLING LIQUEUR

Since it was launched in 1974 on the Irish market and in 1975 on the international market, Bailey's Irish Cream has become an international brand success story. It created a completely new market where no products had existed before and is number nine on the list of top spirit brands in the world. Bailey's is sold in 180 countries and requires the 275 million litres of Irish milk to product the cream required for the product. Irish whiskey is sourced from the old Midleton distillery in Cork.

Bailey's ranks seventh in the international league of top-selling global premium spirits brands, it is the world's best-selling liqueur brand. In 2009 6.7 million 9-litre cases of Bailey's were sold, accounting for over 50 per cent of Ireland's spirits exports.

The top 10 markets for Bailey's are:

- North America (including Canada)
- Great Britain
- global duty free
- Spain
- Italy
- Germany
- Russia
- Australia
- France
- Ireland.

Sources: Paul O'Kane, 'Bailey's tops world sales chart', *Sunday Tribune*, 22 February 1998; *Sunday Business Post*, 16 March 1997, 13 July 1997; *Irish Times*, 27 February 2002; www.baileys.com.

There are three distinct categories of global brand: long-term international brands, such as Ford or McDonald's; brands created for the global market, such as the Sony Playstation; and exported brands (Byfield and Caller, 1996). It is probably true to say that Bailey's Irish Cream is Ireland's main global brand. Most of Ireland's international efforts have been concentrated on exported brands. Two-thirds of Irish exports are to other EU member states.

While brands like Kerrygold have been very successful in many markets, there are of course many other products and services that may be less well known but have been successfully marketed in many overseas markets. The successful development of a product or service for the international market must take account of the needs of buyers in those markets, and there must also be a competitive advantage.

New ranges may need to be developed to suit changes that have taken place in international markets.

Not all products can be successfully internationalised. Exporting the product that is being supplied to the home market is not always possible, and adaptation of the product may be required. The existing product may have to be adapted to the particular tastes and needs of the overseas market, or a completely new product may have to be developed.

In some cases a product developed for the international market may ultimately be launched on the home market. For many years the Kilkenny brand of ale, developed by Guinness for the international market, was available only outside Ireland, but it was subsequently launched on the home market.

The home market may provide a good testing ground for the product before its international launch. Waterford Wedgwood launched the John Rocha range of crystal on the Irish market in 1997. Inspired by the dress designer John Rocha, the range was designed to bring the Waterford brand to a younger, more contemporary market that had not previously been buying Waterford. The range, which included bowls, glasses, and vases, was designed to be more simple than traditional Waterford.

Some companies try to have a standard product for all markets. In 1988 the Ford Motor Company made a strategic decision to launch a global car. Similarities between the various markets were growing as legislation reached new levels of harmony; car buyers in various continents found their motoring needs less different than they had been in the past. The company spent over $6,000 million on the development and manufacture of the Mondeo, an international design team having carried out extensive research into customers' needs, desires, and aspirations (Nolan, 1993). In 1998 Ford began to implement a value-engineering programme designed to eliminate excess cost from the Fiesta, which was a popular European brand. The company found that it was making 27 million differently specified Fiestas: there were 132 different door trims alone. The scheme had as its target a reduction to about 10,000 different specifications (*Sunday Times*, 18 January 1998). Obviously such drives to simplify production, reduce manufacturing costs, and create a globally competitive product cannot be at the expense of product quality.

Products and culture

A product has both tangible and intangible features. Much of the importance of the intangible benefits is attributed by the values and customs within a culture, and it is important to understand how consumers will perceive products or communications about them in international markets. One successful export in the 1990s was the 'Irish pub', which had tangible and intangible aspects. Guinness had a pivotal role in the concept, along with firms such as the Irish Pub Company, a Dublin design and building firm. Irish-themed pubs spread throughout Europe, and a number were also established in Asia (Prystay, 1997; Jones, 1997).

The semiotics of the product or the message may dictate a need for change or modification. The personalities, colours, settings, characters, and advertising copy used will all need to be scrutinised to make sure they cannot be misinterpreted or misunderstood. In China, alphanumeric brand names are popular with consumers, because of the impact of Chinese lucky and unlucky numbers (Ang, 1997).

Some cultures are very receptive to products and brands from other countries. In many markets there is widespread consumer acceptance of and desire for American brands (Taninecz, 1997). Irish marketing organisations such as Tourism Ireland and An Bord Bia attempt to build on the positive perceptions of Ireland as a holiday destination and as a source of quality food products. Enterprise Ireland attempts to build a positive perception of Ireland as a country in which to invest.

The country of origin of a product can affect consumers' evaluation of it. One research study (Schafer, 1997) evaluated the potential impact of British consumers' age, sex, and socio-economic background on the magnitude of the effects of country of origin on the purchase of lager and sparkling wine. It found that older consumers in particular showed stronger effects for country of origin. The AB socio-economic group had stronger effects for sparkling wine, while the C1C2 group had stronger effects for lager. The sex of the respondents had no impact on the magnitude of effect. The image of the country of origin may therefore be linked to brands. This has probably benefited brands such as Bailey's Irish Cream.

One study (Kim and Chung, 1997) emphasised the importance of international marketers taking country image into account in their competitive analysis. Another research study, conducted among industrial buyers in Britain and Germany (Corrigan, 1994), ranked Ireland fourth and second, respectively, in 'environmental friendliness'. To the extent that this is considered an important purchasing criterion, this was a significant finding.

Sometimes products can take time to be successfully adopted in overseas markets. The rate of diffusion will be affected by such factors as age and income but also by familiarity with the product concept, communication, and distribution.

Promotion

In the development of an effective promotional strategy for international markets, the same principles apply as for the home market. However, the same promotional mix or the same content may not be appropriate. Cultural factors will be important here.

Marketers need to be particularly careful with the language used. A small number of companies, such as Coca-Cola and Pepsi, use global advertising campaigns. Most marketers have to adapt campaigns at a basic level to incorporate different language voiceovers and, at a more advanced level, to have completely different campaigns for individual markets.

Global advertising and promotional campaigns have the advantage of being more cost-effective than developing separate campaigns for each market. British Airways unveiled a new corporate identity in 1997, incorporating 50 world images, which would be incorporated in its signage, stationery, and aircraft (Marsh, 1997). Some of the images were commissioned from designers; in other cases the company held competitions in different countries to select a suitable image.

If market or competitive conditions dictate, separate campaigns will have to be used. In some cases the same product is known by a different name in different markets.

The imagery used may also be very different. Tourism Ireland has developed an image of Ireland that, while not radically different, has subtle differences in different markets. Advertising standards and the rules governing the promotion of products can vary from country to country, and advertisements may have to be modified accordingly.

Marketers may encounter restrictions on the type of marketing activities they can undertake in particular markets, as the following example shows.

ADVERTISEMENTS YOU CANNOT SEE ON FRENCH TELEVISION

Internet retailer Amazon.com Inc. can't advertise on French television. Furniture store Ikea can, supermarket giant Carrefour SA can't, fast-food chain McDonald's can. Make sense? Not to Amazon and a host of other retailers, ad agencies and media that are fighting a 40-year-old French law banning TV advertising by retailers. In a filing in

2000 with the European Commission, these groups sought to overturn the French law, arguing that it runs counter to EU rules.

The battle began with e-tailers like Amazon which argued that they weren't traditional retailers with a network of stores, so the ban should not apply to them. The push snowballed and quickly broadened into a demand for a complete overhaul of the law. The pro-ad groups have formed a committee called 'Comité Pourquoi', or the 'why committee'. Aside from retailers and ad agencies, the campaign also includes newspapers such as Le Monde, La Tribune, and Les Echoes. That's because under legislation confirmed as recently as 1992, four sectors are excluded from advertising on TV: retail, cinema, books, and the press. McDonald's and Ikea are regarded in French law as manufacturers and can therefore advertise on television.

While the ban remains, retailers such as Carrefour have become heavily involved in sponsoring TV shows such as Who Wants to be a Millionaire? Leroy-Merlin, the do-it-yourself retail chain, sponsors a daily five-minute home-improvement show, while the electronic appliances retailer Darty is the official partner of weather forecasts. Carrefour has also engaged in sponsoring the Tour de France cycle race.

Source: M. Richter and K. Maxwell, 'Ads you can't see on French TV', *Wall Street Journal Europe*, 21 February 2001.

Advertising regulations also vary in different countries. In the European Union, Sweden has campaigned for a ban on advertising to children under 12, as the following panel illustrates.

SWEDEN SEEKS TO BAN ADVERTISING TO UNDER-12s

A move to prevent images of products such as Furbies, Gameboys, or Smarties from appearing on European television screens was launched by Sweden during its presidency of the EU in 2001. The Swedes would like to ban television advertising aimed at children under 12.

This has prompted senior figures from the television and advertising worlds to form an alliance called the Children's Programme, which will try to convince MEPs of how important these ads are to their revenue. Based on a study of TV stations in 12 states, the European Group of Television Advertising has calculated that the gross annual revenue collected by its EU-based members from child-oriented advertising amounts to €320 million. An estimated 94 per cent of this is reinvested into children's programmes. As most of this is used to buy programmes from European audio-visual companies, the EGTA believes that banning such ads would have a disastrous effect on this sector. If deprived of this advertising revenue, EGTA argues, commercially run television stations will decide to remove children's programmes, make them less prominent in their schedules or import cheaper programmes.

Similar views are held by the Association of Commercial Television in Europe (ACT). It points out that children's television is one of the few areas where it is viable to produce programmes that can be watched across the EU. Adults may change channels when they see the opening credits to a foreign language film (either dubbed or subtitled) but research has shown that children will happily watch cartoons from another country provided that they have been dubbed with simple dialogue they understand.

The ACT argues that the experience in Sweden, where a national ban on child-oriented advertising has been in place since the early 1990s, is that commercial TV stations plough fewer resources into children's programmes than their counterparts in other EU states. They have also decided to show children's programmes at breakfast time rather than after the children come home from school.

A spokesperson for the Swedish representation at the EU said it was anxious that advertising should not target children under 12. 'They are simply not capable of understanding the message.' Sweden planned to promote greater debate of the issue.

Although few expect that an EU-wide ban will be introduced in the short term, the three subsequent holders of the EU presidency are known to be sympathetic to the Swedish position. The Greeks have already banned toy adverts, primarily to protect their national manufacturers from imports.

The EGTA also argues that child-directed ads already have to meet strict guidelines—for example, sponsors must not influence programme content; ads for alcohol cannot target underage drinkers; and ads must not encourage children to pester parents.

Source: David Cronin, 'EU row brews over children's advertising', *Sunday Tribune*, 10 September 2000.

As with the product decision, a vital question in international promotion is whether a standardised promotion strategy can be developed for all international markets or whether it is necessary to customise to meet needs in different markets. Language will certainly play a part. One American study (Ueltschy and Ryans, 1997) investigated the extent to which standardised advertising could be effectively employed in the United States and Mexico. The research concentrated on consumers' attitudes to different versions of print advertisements designed to test the impact of language and cultural differences. The conclusion was that respondents in both countries preferred total customisation of the advertisement.

Many marketers are interested in developing pan-European advertising campaigns. There are difficulties, however, in getting pan-European media that will deliver the audience the marketer requires. Television channels such as MTV and Eurosport do reach pan-European audiences, but they have their limitations. MTV has lost some of its position, because countries such as Britain and France are launching competitive domestic channels; and Eurosport has a predominantly male audience (Barrett, 1997).

Language is also an issue. Consistency in advertising campaigns may not come from words but rather from a consistent image. This may mean that direct translations, which can sometimes be unfortunate, can be avoided. It was found that Wrigley's Spearmint gum, for example, would have a direct translation in some Eastern European markets as 'shark's sperm', while Mitsubishi realised it could not launch the Pajero brand in Spain, where this word would have an offensive meaning (Barrett, 1997).

This demonstrates that it is not easy to develop standardised promotional campaigns. There are few marketers that can successfully promote their product in the same way in all markets.

Pricing

When the price of the product to consumers in the overseas market is being calculated, it must be remembered that there are additional costs to be taken into account when marketing in international markets. Such costs as transport and the margins required by middlemen have to be included in any cost calculations.

Some companies adopt a variable-cost pricing approach, which means they cost goods on the basis of the marginal or incremental cost of production: they do not include any fixed costs in their calculations (these fixed costs are covered by sales in the home market). The danger with this approach is that the business can be accused of dumping and could face anti-dumping penalties. Products will therefore be costed on a full-cost basis, which means that each product will bear a portion of the fixed and variable costs incurred in its production.

Other important factors that have to be taken into account are exchange rate fluctuations, inflation, and VAT or local taxes.

Distribution

Distribution channels can be longer in international markets, as illustrated in the diagram. Indeed some markets may have many more levels than the five illustrated.

manufacturer → exporter → importer → wholesaler → retailer → **consumer**

An important aspect of the distribution of the product is the assessment of middlemen in international markets. Prospective middlemen should be assessed according to the same factors used in the home market but bearing in mind the unique features of the overseas market. The difficulty for the marketer is that control can become more difficult in international channels. Many international marketers have used franchising as the means of expanding into international markets and alleviating the control problems. Whatever the nature of the distribution channel, a formal agreement or contract is desirable. Considerations that should be taken into account in assessing international channel alternatives include productivity or volume, financial strength, market coverage, managerial stability and capability, and the nature and reputation of the business.

Customer service issues, such as the availability of information, spare parts, and a procedure for handling complaints, also need to be addressed.

EXPORTING

Exporting is one aspect of international marketing, concerned with the supply of finished or semi-finished goods from one country to one or more foreign countries. It is therefore an operational aspect of international marketing. The principal objective in exporting is to get goods or services from the manufacturer or service provider to the market with the minimum cost and delay and the maximum efficiency.

A good example of a company managing to keep its export costs down was the deal secured by Tayto to supply supermarkets in Shanghai.

TAYTO EXPORTS TO SHANGHAI

He's already been to Moldova and to Libya and now Mr Tayto is set for a six-month trial in China. Ray Coyle's Largo Foods has secured a listing in 1,200 stores in Shanghai, including French chain Carrefour.

Two containers of crisps will be shipped from Ashbourne each week as Coyle dips his toe in the world's biggest consumer market.

Ironically, the shipping costs are almost the same as sending a consignment to London. 'There's loads of containers going back to China empty so we can get them for about €1,400 or €1,500. If you go to London it would cost you €1,250. There's a great opportunity there for us.'

Back home, Coyle says Tayto's volumes this year are slightly up, but the increase is mostly accounted for by discounted bulk-buying in supermarkets rather than 'impulse' buying.

Source: 'Largo Foods bags tasty crisp deal for Shanghai stores', *Irish Times*, 25 June 2010.

Exporting can be direct, through the firm's own channels or through middlemen; it can also be indirect, for example using a professional exporter or trading house.

The principal issues in exporting

As countries are keen to keep statistics of imports and exports, products are classified, with each product given a tariff code number, in the Irish case by the Central Statistics Office. This enables them to maintain records and to produce quarterly trade statistics. Tariff codes are useful when market research is being conducted, as they give details of the quantities of the product exported or imported.

Export controls may exist in the home country: in Ireland, for example, export licences are required for certain agricultural products and for works of art. Import controls in a country may limit or place restrictions on the amount of a particular product that can be imported. As part of the GATT, for example, quotas and limits were negotiated and agreed between participating states.

Some goods may have import duties imposed on them, and these are usually payable at the point of entry. The valuation for duty can vary: for alcoholic products, for example, the duty is calculated on the percentage alcohol content; thus the duty on wine is usually lower than on whiskey. Whether the goods are delivered *free on board* (FOB) or with *cost, insurance and freight* (CIF) paid will also determine how much duty is to be paid.

Exporting requires familiarity with any regulations that may exist. Some of these may be temporary: some countries imposed a temporary ban on the importing of Irish beef, for example, following the BSE outbreak in the 1990s. Typically there are regulations governing the exporting of dangerous goods, drugs and medicines, and foodstuffs. Regulations require that the product's origin be clearly stated. This is particularly important if the product has come by way of a third country. Other regulations govern product samples and weights and measures.

Exporting involves several risks, not least when there are difficulties in receiving payment. Generally *letters of credit* or *bills of exchange* are considered the safest method. The bill of exchange is an unconditional order in writing, signed by the person giving it, requiring the person to whom it is addressed to pay a sum of money on demand or on a specified date. This will be underwritten by a bank or financial institution, thus minimising the risk. Banks or financial institutions may *discount* the bill of exchange, thus providing a source of finance to the holder. Other methods of payment, such as *cash against documents* or *open account*, may be more risky or difficult to administer.

Exporting may also involve dealing with special packaging requirements. It may not be possible to transport the product in its retail pack, and therefore a transit pack may be required. This provides maximum protection during transport. On arrival, the product can be packaged for sale in the market.

Entering international markets

Direct export involves the company establishing its own export division, selecting and managing the channel, and possibly engaging in advertising and promotional activities in the market. This is an expensive option, which may require significant investment. *Indirect exporting* usually involves using professional exporters or trading houses. The company supplies the product to them and they manage the channel and the marketing activities.

Large companies or existing multinationals typically use *wholly owned subsidiaries* or *foreign direct investment*. Foreign direct investment may involve the establishment of manufacturing facilities in other markets: for example, Guinness established breweries overseas in countries such as Nigeria and Malaysia.

Licensing and royalty agreements reduce the cost of owned subsidiaries or direct investment. Typically the licenser will sign an agreement with a local manufacturer, which may involve the licensing of patents and will involve the payment of royalties, disclosure fees, and possibly payments for management or technical assistance. The licenser is therefore guaranteed an income and typically a certain proportion of turnover, without the risk of investment. In the early 1970s Waterford Co-operative signed a licensing agreement with a French company, Sodial, to produce Yoplait yoghurt in Ireland; this subsequently became the market leader in the sector. Franchises are a common form of licensing agreement and have been used extensively by firms to expand into international markets.

Contract manufacture involves arranging for a manufacturer to produce the product in the overseas market. This may enable a speedy entry to the market but must be tightly controlled to ensure that quality levels are maintained. Waterford Wedgwood produces the Marquis range of glassware using contract manufacturers in Eastern European countries; and the frozen food manufacturer Bird's Eye has used contract manufacture to produce some of its range in Ireland.

In joint ventures the firm may identify suitable local partners and develop the market jointly with them. This may or may not involve the purchase of an interest in the company. Joint ventures will be governed by an agreement on such issues as the allocation of dividends and commercial policy. In 1997 Ballygowan entered a three-year agreement with Scottish Courage, the largest brewing company in Britain, to consolidate its position in the British licensed trade (*Deadline*, November 1997). The company already had a similar agreement with Bass breweries in Britain. The concept of joint venture has been extended to include strategic alliances and partnerships.

Which market to enter?

The ultimate decision in international marketing may be which market to enter. Most businesses have limited resources, therefore the most attractive market should be picked.
Target markets should generally be assessed according to:

- estimates of the existing market potential
- estimates of future market potential and risk
- forecasts of sales potential
- forecasts of sales and profit for five years
- estimates of the rate of return on investment.

Markets should be thoroughly researched before a decision is made. Given development costs associated with entry to a market, it can be several years before a company realises a return on its international markets. A commitment to international marketing is therefore required.

FURTHER READING

De Burca, S., Fletcher, R., and Brown, L., *International Marketing, an SME Perspective*, Englewood Cliffs (NJ): Prentice-Hall 2004.
Jeannet, J. P., and Hennessey, D., *Global Marketing Strategies* (sixth edition), New York: Houghton Mifflin 2004.

DISCUSSION QUESTIONS

1. Pick an Irish product that has been successfully internationalised, such as Bailey's Irish Cream, and describe the environmental forces it must contend with in its international markets.
2. Identify an Irish product or service that is not internationally traded as present but has the potential to be. Give reasons for your choice.
3. Explain why an understanding of cultural differences is important for the international marketer.
4. Do you think there is a potential for more global brands? Give some examples to illustrate your answer.
5. Describe how relationship marketing can be relevant to international marketers. What role can strategic alliances play in this?

REFERENCES

Ang, S., 'Chinese consumers' perceptions of alpha-numeric brand names', *Journal of Consumer Marketing*, vol. 14 (1997), no. 3.
Ball, D. and Singer, J., 'Tesco agrees to acquire Japanese retail chain', *Wall Street Journal Europe*, 11 June 2003.
Barnathan, J., Comes, F., Roberts, D., Einhorn, B., Roy, E., and Moore, J., 'China's youth: a new generation leaves tradition behind', *Business Week*, 14 July 1994.
Barrett, P., 'Abroad-minded', *Marketing*, 24 April 1997.

Bell, J. and Brown, S., 'Tyrone Crystal: striking out in Japan', *Irish Marketing Review*, vol. 4 (1989), no. 2.

Byfield, S., and Caller, L., 'Building brands across borders', *Admap*, June 1996.

Corrigan, J., 'How a green image can drive Irish export growth', *Greener Management International*, October 1994.

Economist Intelligence Unit, *Marketing 2000: Critical Challenges for Corporate Survival*, London: EIU 1991.

Galvin, P., 'The Turnaround at Waterford Crystal', National Marketing Conference, October 1993.

Hofstede, G., *Culture's Consequences: International Differences in Work-related Values*, Cross-cultural Research and Methodology Series, Vol. 5, Thousand Oaks (CA): Sage Publications Inc., 1980.

Jones, A., 'Éire apparent', *Marketing Week*, 7 February 1997.

Kim, C. K., and Chung, J. Y., 'Brand popularity, country image and market share: an empirical study', *Journal of International Business Studies*, second quarter, 1997.

Levitt, T., 'The globalisation of markets', *Harvard Business Review*, vol. 61 (1983).

Marsh, H., 'Why BA has designs on a global brand', *Marketing*, 12 June 1997.

Mullins, J., Walker, O., Boyd, H., and Larréché, J.-C., *Marketing Management* (fifth edition), New York: McGraw-Hill 2005.

Nolan, E., 'Launching a New Product in a Hostile Environment', National Marketing Conference, October 1993.

Prystay, C., 'Betting on the luck of the Irish', *Asian Business*, July 1997.

Quelch, A. J and Hoff, J .E., 'Customising global marketing', *Harvard Business Review*, vol. 64 (1986), 59–68.

Rugman, A., 'The myth of global strategy', *International Marketing Review*, vol. 18 (2001), no. 6, 58–8.

Schafer, A., 'Do demographics have an impact on country of origin effects?', *Journal of Marketing Management*, November 1997.

Shane, S., 'The effect of national culture on the choice between licensing and direct foreign investment', *Strategic Management Journal*, vol.15 (1994), 506–20.

Swift, J. and Lawrence, K., 'Business culture in Latin America: interactive learning for UK SMEs', *Journal of European Industrial Training*, 27/8 (2003), 389–97.

Taninecz, G., 'Global grocers', *Industry Week*, 17 March 1997.

Ueltschy, L. and Ryans, J., 'Employing standardised promotion strategies in Mexico: the impact of language and cultural differences', *International Executive*, July–August 1997.

Wei, R., 'Emerging lifestyles in China and consequences for perception of advertising, buying behaviour and consumption preferences', *International Journal of Advertising*, vol. 16 (1997), no. 4.

Young, S., 'What do researchers know about the global business environment?', *International Marketing Review*, vol. 18 (2001), no. 2.

13

Business-to-Business Marketing

usiness-to-business marketing covers all activities involved in the marketing of products and services to firms that use them in the production of consumer or industrial goods and services. The fundamentals of marketing are essentially the same; however, there are a number of important distinguishing aspects of business-to-business marketing. In this chapter the nature of business-to-business marketing is reviewed and examples of business-to-business marketing practice are given.

THE NATURE OF BUSINESS-TO-BUSINESS MARKETING

Industrial markets are relatively concentrated. As a result, individual orders can be quite large. Consider the world airline market, where there are a small number of producers and where individual orders from airlines can be very significant.

The concentrated nature of business-to-business markets means that relationship marketing is important. Marketers in business-to-business markets may have a smaller number of customers to develop relationships with, a significant advantage when compared with many consumer marketers.

As with many services, distribution channels in business-to-business markets tend to be shorter, and in many cases products are sold without intermediaries. For many Irish companies, however, additional levels will be added in international markets, as Unilokomotiv of Galway found.

UNILOKOMOTIV

Unilokomotiv is a Galway manufacturer of rail shunting vehicles, which are used to move railway wagons around marshalling yards and industrial complexes. The limited potential of the home market—its only Irish customer being Tara Mines—means that it had to develop export markets. In addition to European markets, the company has built export markets in Pakistan, China, Malaysia, and Bangladesh. It competes in international markets with producers from Germany, Italy, and the United States.

The firm's brand is Unilok and its main advantages are that it can carry out the same shunting tasks as locomotives that are four to five times heavier. This is much cheaper for railway operators. More than 2,000 Uniloks have been produced.

Source: www.unilok.ie.

The company concentrated on developing a network of local agents in its export markets, estimating that it took nine months to appoint an agent and a further six months before there were any tangible results. Bureaucracy was certainly an issue. When tendering for contracts, the company had to supply bid bonds; and when it was awarded the contract, performance bonds had to be obtained. When the vehicles were being prepared for delivery, guarantee bonds had to be issued. All of these required a lot of paperwork and an appropriate level of financial backing. Unilokomotiv built a close relationship with its bankers, which was necessary in order to have access to bond facilities and international sources of credit.

Local agents gave the company the advantage of being able to conduct business at the right pace. It also ensured that due attention was paid to social norms. Gaining knowledge of what might appear to westerners to be more complex social structures within Far East markets was also important.

Sources: M. Downes, 'Galway firm wins £500,000 orders', *Sunday Business Post*, 9 May 1993; E. Hughes, 'Local agents: key to eastern markets', *Sunday Business Post*, 3 November 1996.

Ultimately, the demand for business-to-business products and services is derived from the consumer. If consumers' demand for a product or service increases, then the demand for the raw materials, services, and equipment necessary to produce and deliver that product or service will also increase. This is known as *derived demand*. The concept of derived demand means that the business-to-business marketer has to monitor trends in the consumer market. Opportunities may present themselves from doing so: for example, Moffett Engineering spotted an opportunity to develop an innovative fork-lift truck as the distribution industry increased in importance.

MOFFETT ENGINEERING

Moffett Engineering was a family-owned business, established in the 1940s to manufacture and repair agricultural machinery. The company was innovative in product development, which culminated in the development of the Moffett Mounty, a truck-mounted fork-lift, which became the company's main product line. Orders for the product increased in line with increases in the distribution sector.

Moffett Engineering had been run by Carol Moffett, who had taken control of the company at the age of 19 on the death of her father. The company established a strong customer base among co-operatives and had built significant export markets, the Mounty being sold in 30 countries.

The firm was acquired by the Finnish company, Cargotec.

Source: Richard Curran, 'Ms Moffett's bread and butter', *Sunday Tribune*, 14 September 1997; Paul O'Kane, 'Powerscreen consolidates its Irish market', *Sunday Tribune*, 14 September 1997.

The Moffett Engineering case has an interesting postscript, as the company's former engineering manager went on to establish a new business called Combilift, which ultimately began to market a new forklift design jointly with Moffett.

COMBILIFT

Combilift was established in 1998 by Martin McVicar, the former engineering manager of Moffett engineering, and Robert Moffett. In 2006 it agreed to market a new truck mounted forklift called the Combilift with Moffett engineering and, in 2009, the 10,000th unit was sold.

Combilift is sold in 50 countries and a range of designs are offered to suit customer needs. The product is designed for safer handling and operation; it has a unique four-way steering system that enables the unit to travel sideways with long loads, it can also operate both indoors and outdoors.

Figure 13.1: Before Combilift

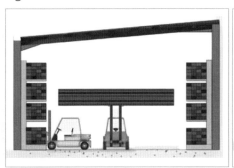

Figure 13.2: After Combilift

Source: www.combilift.com.

The firm has also developed a number of new products, including the Straddlecarrier, which can be used to lift containers on and off lorries and eliminates the need for a crane.

Figure 13.3: The Straddlecarrier

Source: www.combilift.com

Myopia

Industrial marketers can be especially prone to 'marketing myopia' if they become too caught up in the technological aspects of their product and forget about customers' needs. This can be compounded by the nature of derived demand if they lose sight of the needs of the ultimate consumer.

Many industrial companies are very product oriented. One research study conducted among manufacturers in Scotland (Donaldson, 1995) suggested that many industrial companies were not following the principles of customer service for their business customers. It recommended that managers become more customer-driven by concentrating on three central issues: business vision, service implementation, and a commitment to quality.

A good example of a business-to-business firm that was not myopic is Kerry Die Products.

KERRY DIE PRODUCTS

Kerry Die Products was originally a manufacturer of a range of pellet mill dies and rolls, mainly for use in animal feed and associated industries. The company was established in 1980 and its background in the manufacturing of pellet mill dies was to provide an impetus for a change in business direction in the 2000s.

Around 2000 the firm decided to concentrate its production on wood pellet systems, for which there was growing consumer demand. These are used to fuel pellet burners and stoves. Manufacturers of wood pellets had been using manufacturing equipment that had been developed for animal feed pellet production, but Kerry Die had noticed that this equipment was not entirely effective as the wood pellet manufacturing process is more complicated than animal feeds, mainly due to the different types of wood that can be used.

Kerry Die undertook a research programme with two universities in Austria and Sweden and, after three years, derived a completely new approach to the manufacture of the pellets. The research was used to develop state-of-the-art wood pellet manufacturing systems which have been sold to several manufacturers.

European demand for wood pellets is expected to increase from 10 million tonnes per annum in 2010 to 100 million tonnes in 2020, so the firm expects growing demand for it manufacturing systems.[body text ends]

Source: www.kerry-die.com.

Differences between consumer and business-to-business markets

There are a number of broad differences between business-to-business and consumer markets, as illustrated in fig. 13.4. These differences demonstrate the ways in which marketing practice and activities may need to be adapted to suit the type of product or service being marketed.

Figure 13.4: Broad differences between business-to-business and consumer markets

	Business-to-business	Consumer
Market structure	Concentrated; fewer buyers; e.g. Irish airline market	Dispersed mass markets, e.g. Irish lager market
Buyer behaviour	Functional involvement, e.g. production manager	Family involvement, e.g. housewife
	Rational or task motives, e.g. packaging machine	Social or psychological motives, e.g. after shave
	Technical expertise, e.g. technical manager	Less technical expertise, e.g. child operating video
	Interpersonal, e.g. technical sales representative	Non-personal, e.g. vending machine
Decision-making	Distinct or observable stages, e.g. management meetings	Unobservable or mental stages, e.g. 'black-box' decision-making
Products	Technical or complex, customised, e.g. drilling equipment	Standardised, e.g. television set
Distribution channels	Short and direct, e.g. car ferry	Longer and less direct, e.g. breakfast cereal
Promotion	Personal selling, e.g. Moffett Engineering	Advertising, e.g. Calvin Klein
Price	Technical or complex, customised, e.g. drilling equipment	Standardised, e.g. television set

The nature of industrial buying

The buying process in business-to-business markets can be more complex than in consumer markets. Consumers can of course face highly involved decisions; and levels of involvement will vary for different products and buying situations. In business-to-business markets there will typically be more functional involvement in the purchasing decision. If a company is considering a purchase, different people will usually have influence. This influence is usually determined by their position within the company.

Business-to-business buyers tend to be well informed and highly organised. This is, after all, their job. They are unlikely to buy on impulse, as in consumer markets, and will pay particular attention to the detail of product and service specifications and quality. Sophisticated buying techniques, such as value analysis, may be used to assess products; this involves the systematic appraisal of an item's design, quality, and performance requirements in an effort to minimise costs. It includes an analysis of the extent to which the product can be redesigned, standardised, or processed using less expensive production methods.

Cost analysis will also be part of the process. This seeks to determine what it costs a supplier to produce the item, and the results may be used to obtain more favourable prices from suppliers.

Given that it is the business that is making a purchase, multiple influencers will usually exist, offering different points of view on the purchasing decision. An analogy can be drawn with family buying, where different family members have different relative amounts of influence. In the business-to-business setting, different personnel may perform different buying roles and have different amounts of influence.

There are, typically, five buying roles: *decider, influencer, user, buyer,* and *gatekeeper*. These roles may be performed by different individuals in the firm, or an individual may have more than one role. The marketer or salesperson needs to determine who precisely performs these roles.

One of the principal tasks the marketer or business-to-business salesperson has to determine is who is in the *decision-making unit* in the prospect firm. The buying roles will determine the amount of influence or decision-making ability an individual possesses. The most important or primary decision roles will usually be the deciders and influences, while the users, buyers, and gatekeepers may be considered to have secondary roles.

Users are those in the firm who will actually use the product: for example, the operator of a packaging machine may have some influence on the purchase of a particular type of packaging material used.

Influencers are those who provide information on the product and who have a particular expertise. The information will be used in the evaluation of the product; influencers will therefore have a technical or professional expertise, as for example a technical manager or cost accountant.

Gatekeepers control the flow of information to others. The gatekeeper could therefore be a secretary or personal assistant who arranges meetings for their superior, or a purchasing or functional manager.

Buyers are those who actually buy the product: for example, most of the multiple supermarkets have specialist buyers in different product categories. The buyer's influence depends on the amount of decision-making autonomy they enjoy. In some cases their influence may be limited by specifications or organisational requirements. Most public service organisations are required to seek tenders for purchases.

Deciders are those who have the power and authority to make decisions. In most companies this describes the board of directors or senior managers. Naturally, the senior management or directors will not be involved in every organisational purchasing decision: responsibilities will be devolved to others.

The buy grid model

One model that has been developed to illustrate the buying process in industrial markets is the 'buy grid' model, illustrated in table 13.1. This model proposes that three broad buying situations face the industrial marketer. *New task* means that the product has not been bought before; *modified rebuy* means that modifications are required to a product that has been bought before; *straight rebuy* is a simple repeat purchase.

The model proposes that there are eight stages through which the buyer may progress. The speed of progress and the number of stages will depend on the nature of the buying task. Thus in the new buy situation it is probable that more time will be spent and that each stage will be gone through. The modified rebuy usually occurs where the need remains unchanged but there is a desire to modify the buying task because of quality or price, for example. In the straight rebuy situation the search, analysis, evaluation, and selection stages may be skipped.

Table 13.1: The buy grid model

	New task	*Modified rebuy*	*Straight rebuy*
1. Need recognition	✓	✓	✓
2. Determine quantity	✓	✓	✓
3. Describe quantity	✓	✓	✓
4. Search for quantity	✓	✓	
5. Analysis of proposals	✓	✓	
6. Evaluation	✓	✓	
7. Selection	✓	✓	
8. Performance feedback and evaluation	✓	✓	✓

Source: P. Robinson, C. Faris, and Y. Wind, *Industrial Buying and Creative Marketing*, Boston: Allyn and Bacon 1967.

The influence of purchasing on buyer behaviour

Material requirements planning (MRP) refers to the co-ordination of purchasing with production scheduling. Raw materials, sub-assemblies, parts, and components should be available to be incorporated in the production process. The purchasing department or manager will liaise with the manufacturing or production department to plan purchasing requirements.

A significant influence on MRP has been the 'just-in-time' approach developed by

Japanese industry, based on the idea that wherever possible no activity should take place in a system until there is a demand for it. This should eliminate the need to hold stock, which ties up working capital. The just-in-time approach can therefore have implications for business-to-business marketers if customers require products and services just in time to be incorporated in their production process.

Just-in-time operations require careful co-ordination. They can also lead to the development of closer relationships between the marketer and the customer. The use of new technology, in particular electronic data interchange (EDI), will usually have a significant role.

In attempting to sell to the purchasing department in a firm, the marketer or business-to-business salesperson should be familiar with the reporting relationships and the level of involvement that individuals have in the purchasing decision. The purchasing manager may perform the buying role described on page 362. It will be important to determine whether they perform any of the other roles. It is necessary to determine who performs the buying decision roles so that communications can be aimed at them.

MARKETING RESEARCH

The principles of conducting marketing research will be the same for business-to-business products and services. If these have a technical orientation, that will be reflected in the research. The concentrated nature of business-to-business markets may mean that there is also concentrated access to information. If, for example, research was being conducted among cement producers, there are only three possible companies that could be interviewed: Irish Cement, Seán Quinn Group, and Blue Circle Cement. The small population size in business-to-business research may also affect respondents' willingness to participate. Respondents may fear that their views or opinions could be easily identified when the population of interest is so small.

The research techniques used will also be determined by the size of the population. In the case of research on cement production, for example, it is probable that personal interviews with particular people would be sought, rather than using a postal questionnaire. In this case personal interviews would be feasible with regard to timing: the researcher would have to alleviate respondents' fears of identification.

Technical research may need to be conducted by specialist researchers. Respondents will expect the researcher to understand the research topic.

SEGMENTATION VARIABLES

The basis for market segmentation may be different in business-to-business markets. Consumer markets are very often segmented according to demographic or psychographic variables. Factors such as life-style, for example, may have little relevance in a business-to-business context. It is more probable that the following bases would be used:

- *industry*—for example agriculture, mining, light engineering
- *organisational characteristics*—for example number of employees
- *plant characteristics*—for example assembly, finishing
- *location of plant*

- *customers' industry*—for example freight v. passenger transport
- *purchasing*—for example centralised in the company's head office or decentralised at branch level.

THE BUSINESS-TO-BUSINESS MARKETING MIX

Product

The industrial or business-to-business product may be more technically complex than many consumer products. However, factors such as branding, quality, and the development of product extensions will be just as important.

Branding can be as much a source of competitive advantage to business-to-business marketers as to consumer marketers. One research study (Mudambi, Doyle, and Wong, 1997) suggested a conceptual framework for brand value in industrial markets. This comprises four performance components: distribution, the product, support service, and the company itself. This demonstrates a number of salient considerations for business-to-business marketers. Relationship marketing will be important in managing the marketing channels and the provision of support service. Product quality will be an important prerequisite, and the reputation of the business will be strongly linked to the brand.

Another study (Thompson, Knox, and Mitchell, 1997–8) concluded that business-to-business branding was a potentially powerful differentiation and communication tool. It considered that business-to-business branding could play a strong role in an environment where there were changing work practices, globalisation, and new technology.

The role of packaging may vary somewhat for business-to-business products. Products may be transported in bulk, and the main functions of the packaging used will be protection and economy rather than promotion. Specialist packaging or containers may be required to transport the product.

Given the technical nature of many business-to-business products, new-product research and development activities may be more technical in orientation. New consumer products may also be developed from technical research; but many new consumer products have been based on the development of less technical factors, for example the change from square to round tea-bags. Such innovations may be less apparent with many business-to-business products.

MARKETING COMMUNICATION IN BUSINESS-TO-BUSINESS MARKETS

The principles of communication apply regardless of product or service type. In business-to-business markets the relative use of components of the communication mix can vary. In general, specialist media rather than general consumer media will be used, and there tends to be a greater emphasis on personal selling than there is in consumer markets.

Advertising

Business-to-business marketers tend to use specialist advertising media, such as trade magazines and journals. They rarely use consumer media, though marketers such as Airbus have advertised in consumer media, as fig. 13.5 shows. Such advertising can be considered important for corporate image and identity. In the case of Airbus, the brand is sold directly to consumers. By advertising directly to the consumer the company may have hoped to build awareness levels for the product and to stimulate demand in the ultimate market.

Figure 13.5: Airbus Industries

Business-to-business advertising can appear in general business and trade publications. Trade directories, such as Kompass directories, are also used. Generally, advertising for industrial products emphasises factors such as technical description and detail rather than life-style or image, which is more common in consumer advertising. There can be exceptions, of course, but advertising will usually be a reflection of the product it seeks to portray. A purchasing manager in a target firm may be more interested in cost and quality than in image.

Business-to-business branding is of course important, and advertising can play a role in support of this.

Sales promotion

Sales promotion may be a feature of business-to-business communication, though the type of promotion will vary from those used by consumer marketers. In-store promotions will not usually be significant if the channels used are direct. Price promotions are often used and may be a feature of competitive strategy. These are typically related to sales volume: the bigger the order, the higher the promotional discount.

Direct marketing

Direct marketing and communication has also had an impact. Most business firms are used to being selected by telemarketers and may be less suspicious than consumers, who are much less likely to be the target. Developments in the internet and in multimedia offer significant opportunities for business-to-business marketers. It is possible to show diagrams or even products in virtual reality form and to give detailed specifications online.

Sponsorship

Sponsorship has been used by some business-to-business marketers as a means of building a profile, associating the product with particular causes and events, and developing corporate image. Some sponsorship activities have been at local level, for example the sponsoring of local sports teams. Television programmes have also been sponsored: the American comedy series *Frasier* was sponsored on British television by Ericsson, which, in addition to consumer products, is a significant business-to-business marketer. In Ireland a number of GAA county football teams were sponsored by largely business-to-business firms, including the meat-processors Kepak (Meath) and the engineering company Sperrin Metal (Derry). Business-to-business marketers also appear as sponsors in large-scale international events: for example the stockbrokers NCB sponsored a yacht, *NCB Ireland*, in the round-the-world yacht race in 1994. Sponsorship events may also be used by business-to-business marketers to entertain corporate customers.

Trade shows

Trade shows are widely used by business-to-business marketers, as they reach a relatively large and specialised audience. Usually trade shows are organised by particular industries or professions; the audience is therefore quite focused and specialist. A trade show may reduce the number of sales calls the firm has to make, especially if it attracts large numbers of home and overseas sales prospects.

Participation in trade shows can be expensive. Costs usually include floor space and rental of the stand, the provision of presentation and audiovisual equipment, catalogues, leaflets, staffing costs, and entertainment expenses. Overseas trade shows will be more expensive when travel costs are added to this.

If participating in a trade show, marketers must set clear objectives. The trade show is an opportunity to communicate with a target audience; it is therefore vital to follow the stages in the communication model. It is also important to measure and evaluate the trade show as a communication activity. Typical objectives for participating in a trade show include:

- reaching new sales prospects
- selling the product
- launching a new product or brand extension
- distributing promotional material
- publishing a new or updated catalogue
- conducting research among those attending
- entertaining existing or potential customers
- enhancing corporate image
- introducing new personnel to the trade
- the opportunity to update the company's database
- publicity opportunities in general or specialist media.

While selling the product may be an objective, it may not actually happen at the trade show if buyers need time to evaluate or discuss the product within their own firms. Sales leads generated at the trade show should be followed up.

If clear objectives have been set, methods of evaluation should follow. The marketer should seek to measure the response they obtain. If sales have been an objective, these can be measured. If selling is an objective, sales personnel should realise that they may have limited time to engage people attending the show (Kaydo, 1996).

Attempts should be made to measure the quality of communication at the show. Simply handing out publicity material may not be enough; engaging people who attend the show, seeking opinions or inviting questions will yield more information. It is important therefore that the company personnel manning the stand are good communicators, can answer questions, and can gather market intelligence (McCune, 1993). In measuring the effectiveness of trade shows, activities that could be evaluated include pre-show promotion, the size and prominence of the stand, and the number of staff on the stand. In addition, the type of show and size of show should also be evaluated (Dekimpe, François, Gopalakrishna, Lilien and van den Bulte 1997).

Trade shows also provide an opportunity to monitor what competitors are doing. The presence of competitors also emphasises the comparisons that people attending the show will make. If the business is considering international markets, the trade show can be used as a means of gaining access to market information and to decision-makers in those markets (O'Hara, Palumbo and Herbig 1993). It can also be used to find potential distributors or other channel members.

Planning for international shows should involve studying the criteria for selecting which shows to attend. It is recommended that the planning process begin at least a year before the show (Vanderleest, 1994). Enterprise Ireland provides advice and assistance to companies planning or preparing for overseas trade shows.

The trade show is like a shop window or shelf: poor presentation may lead to the prospect passing on to the next stand or to a competitor. In many industries the annual trade show may be the most significant marketing communication event. It is important to plan and evaluate carefully (Blythe, 1997). Developments in technology have provided more communication alternatives for trade shows: for example, the use of interactive technology on stands or displays can augment other forms of communication (Shaw, 1994).

Public relations

Public relations may not be as widely used in business-to-business marketing, but it can be useful in developing corporate image and identity, media and press relations, and product launches and other events. Business-to-business marketers should consider public relations opportunities in the context of their general communication plans.

Pricing

Pricing decisions for business-to-business marketers will be based on the same process that applies to consumer marketers. The nature of demand, price elasticity, cost calculation, competitors' prices, and environmental influences will all be taken into account in the pricing decision. Pricing methods will also be the same. Less emphasis may be put on concepts such as loss leaders or special-event pricing.

If the business-to-business product or service is to be incorporated as a component cost, issues such as operational costs will be significant. The customer may judge on the basis of keeping operational costs optimised. The benefits of the product or service, such as its functional or design features, may play a significant role in price positioning. These may be assessed relative to the price and corresponding price-benefit ratios calculated.

The nature of derived demand means that there may be a more indirect relationship between price and quality. The buyer of a piece of production machinery, for example, will know that the quality of the finished product will be partly determined by the machine and its features.

If marketers are buying in large quantities they will calculate the economies of scale from doing so. The price per unit may therefore be lower if larger amounts are ordered, and this will have an impact on the total cost of production.

The close interpersonal relationships in business-to-business markets can lead to greater co-operation, which may mean reduced costs. It is not uncommon for suppliers to attempt to show customers where they can reduce costs; in some cases this may mean that the customer ends up buying less of the product. While this may not appear very sensible from the sales point of view, from the point of view of building a relationship and demonstrating that the marketer has the customer's interests at heart it may make a lot of sense. Will the customer perceive a difference between someone who identifies where they can cut costs and someone who tries to sell them more?

MARKETING CHANNELS

The channels used by business-to-business marketers tend to be more direct than those used by consumer marketers. The same product, information, ownership, and promotional flows will take place. The smaller number of larger customers that may exist means that it is easier to design more direct channels. It also facilitates the development of relationship marketing. Where middlemen or intermediaries are used, the same selection and management criteria will apply.

If business-to-business channels are more direct, the need for wholesalers and retailers may be eliminated. There can, however, be business-to-business wholesalers and retailers. There are several building materials wholesalers; and many of the franchised printing services, such as Prontaprint and Snap, count many businesses among their customers.

Information technology, such as the use of EDI and the ability to transfer data directly from the marketer to the business-to-business customer, has had an impact on channels. EDI could be used by purchasing managers, for example, to transfer data and to receive information from suppliers. Advances in EDI technology enable such transactions to be conducted over the internet, and this reduces investment requirements and running costs (Stafford-Jones, 1997). EDI can play an important role in making possible just-in-time ordering and supply.

As with all technology, marketers need to carefully assess the implications of using EDI. One study (Banfield, 1994) found that the companies they researched had to make radical changes to their own systems in order to implement an EDI system with the retailers they served.

Franchising can also be a feature of business-to-business contexts. Franchising can apply to processes as well as to products and services; it is possible for the franchisee to franchise the know-how for producing a business-to-business product or service that may be incorporated in the production or operations of their customers.

FURTHER READING

Brierty, E., Eckles, R., and Reeder, R., *Business Marketing Management* (third edition), Englewood Cliffs (NJ): Prentice-Hall 1998.

DISCUSSION QUESTIONS

1. Using fig. 13.4, describe how marketing practice may differ for each of the following:
   (*a*) a motorway construction company v. Cadbury
   (*b*) Tetra Pak (suppliers of packaging machines to the food and beverage industry) v. Jury's Doyle Hotels
   (*c*) Boeing v. O'Brien's sandwich bars
   (*d*) Unilokomotiv v. Kerrygold.
2. Is decision-making for business-to-business products more involved than that for consumer products? Give reasons for your answer.
3. Does business-to-business branding differ from consumer branding? Give reasons for your answer.

4. Why is relationship marketing so important to business-to-business marketers?
5. A business-to-business marketer has asked you to advise on the relative benefits of trade shows v. advertising. Outline the pros and cons of each.

REFERENCES

Banfield, J., 'Implementing EDI', *Logistics Information Management*, vol. 7 (1994), no. 1.

Blythe, J. 'Does size matter?: objectives and measures at UK trade exhibitions', *Journal of Marketing Communications*, March 1997.

Dekimpe, M., François, P., Gopalakrishna, S., Lilien, G., and van den Bulte, C., 'Generalising about trade show effectiveness: a cross-national comparison', *Journal of Marketing*, vol. 61 (1997), no. 4.

Donaldson, W., 'Manufacturers need to show greater commitment to customer service', *Industrial Marketing Management*, October 1995.

Kaydo, C., 'Don't waste a minute', *Sales and Marketing Management*, November 1996.

McCune, J., 'On with the show!', *Management Review*, May 1993.

Mudambi, S., Doyle, P., and Wong, V., 'An exploration of branding in industrial markets', *Industrial Marketing Management*, September 1997.

O'Hara, B., Palumbo, F., and Herbig, P., 'Industrial trade shows abroad', *Industrial Marketing Management*, August 1993.

Shaw, R., 'Trade shows "go interactive"', *Business Marketing*, January 1994.

Stafford-Jones, A., 'Electronic commerce: the future with EDI', *Logistics Focus*, November 1997.

Thompson, K., Knox, S., and Mitchell, H., 'Business to business brand attributes in a changing purchasing environment', *Irish Marketing Review*, vol. 10 (1997–8), no. 2.

Vanderleest, H., 'Planning for international trade show participation: a practitioner's perspective', *SAM Advanced Management Journal*, autumn 1994.

14

Social and Not-for-Profit Marketing

S ocial marketing is a perspective of marketing theory which places emphasis on social responsibility and the needs of society or individual communities. It is an emerging field in contemporary marketing theory, having been first elaborated in the 1970s. Social marketing describes the use of marketing principles and techniques to influence a target audience to voluntarily accept, reject, modify, or abandon behaviour for the benefit of the individual, groups, or society as a whole (Kotler and Lee, 2008). Kotler and Levy (1969) were the first to talk about social marketing which they saw as a way of broadening the concept of marketing. Andreasen (1995) defined social marketing as the process for developing social change programmes, which often relate to issues such as obesity, drugs, anti-social behaviour, health, and welfare.

The principles of marketing are equally applicable to non-profit-making organisations. Non-profit organisations typically include charities, museums, art galleries, and other bodies where it is not expected that a profit, in the accepted business sense, will be made. They can also include large commercial organisations, such as the Voluntary Health Insurance (VHI) Board, which is involved in the health insurance business.

In recent years many non-profit organisations have become more marketing-oriented, with many employing full-time managers or organisers. Many non-profit organisations are substantial businesses and are subject to the same environmental forces as profit-making concerns.

THE MAIN DIFFERENCES BETWEEN SOCIAL MARKETING AND COMMERCIAL MARKETING

Social marketing
- selling behaviour change
- competitors difficult to identify
- emphasis on individual or societal gain

Commercial marketing
- selling products and services
- emphasis on profit (corporate)
- competitors easy to identify

Andreasen (2002) identified six benchmarks for identifying genuine social marketing programmes:

1. Behaviour change is the benchmark used to design and evaluate interventions (e.g. consuming less alcohol).

2. Audience research is undertaken to: (i) assess the needs of the target group; (ii) pre-test the programme materials and ideas; and (iii) monitor the ongoing implementation of the programme.
3. Segmentation principles are applied.
4. The intervention strategy creates attractive motivational exchanges within the target group.
5. The intervention strategy attempts to use all 4 Ps of the conventional marketing mix.
6. Careful attention is placed on the competition faced by the desired behaviour.

Source: Adapted from Andreasen, A.R., 'Marketing social marketing in the social change marketplace', *Journal of Public Policy and Marketing*, 21 (1) (2002), pp. 3–13.

TYPICAL PROBLEMS FACED BY NON-PROFIT ORGANISATIONS

In many cases, non-profit marketers do not see themselves as business activities. As a result they may be slow to adopt marketing or management techniques. In some cases the organisation may be run completely by volunteers, so that there is no full-time marketing or administrative staff.

With regard to mission, many non-profit organisations are based more on good intentions than on good organisation. The organisation may have been established to support a worthy cause or to campaign on a particular issue, and these become the central objectives. If, however, there is poor organisation, this may lead to inefficiencies and make the organisation less effective.

Some non-profit organisations may look on the notion of being a business with disdain: they do not want to be tainted, as they might see it, by commercialism. They would rather concentrate on their activities, for example the arts, for the sake of art alone. One study on charities in Britain (Balabanis, Stables and Phillips, 1997) identified a reluctance among larger charities to adopt a strategy based on market orientation, largely for ideological reasons.

Given the voluntary nature of many non-profit organisations, there may be a poor knowledge of marketing. Marketing may be associated purely with selling or advertising; they may not appreciate its role in understanding the nature of the exchange process in which they are engaged. The principles of relationship marketing may not be applied. One research study (Lindsay and Murphy, 1996) found that the donors to a British charity, the National Society for the Prevention of Cruelty to Children, were confused about its work. It suggested that the charity could learn from the theory of relationship marketing and should place greater emphasis on product attributes and brand image.

Political interference can be a problem for some non-profit organisations and may impede or prevent them carrying out their functions. Many relief agencies have found that in attempting to assist victims of famine or war in certain countries they ran into difficulties with the political authorities.

A perennial problem for non-profit organisations is securing adequate funds for their work. While other marketers produce continuously a product or service that is priced and sold, yielding a steady income stream, non-profit organisations may not have this continuous income flow. They may be reliant on sporadic donations or sponsorship and as a result find it difficult to plan and budget. Many smaller charities and charities in less attractive areas, for example those dealing with drug abuse, can find the fund-raising task even more difficult (Hirst, 1997).

Non-profit organisations may take up causes that society pays little attention to or chooses to ignore. Children of Chernobyl is an organisation that sought to provide medical care, relief, and support to children who suffered the effects of the nuclear accident at Chernobyl in 1988. The organisation exists because of a lack of resources to deal with the after-effects of the accident.

Given the number of volunteers who may be involved, there can be too many committees in some non-profit organisations. This can slow down or even prevent decision-making. While committees can be essential, they must also be effective. The problem can be alleviated if the principles of organisation typically used in commercial firms are applied.

Some non-profit organisations are dominated by older people, who may not encourage the involvement of younger volunteers, managers, or organisers. This can pose a threat to the organisation's survival.

Sometimes organisations that are based on noble intentions may not have a coherent strategy or direction. As with all organisations, there should be a mission and objectives, and these should translate into specific strategies and plans.

Marketing management issues

According to Shapiro (1973), four principal business concepts provide the basis for marketing thought and action in the non-profit environment: self-interest, the marketing task, the marketing mix, and distinctive competence. The *self-interest* aspect describes the nature of the exchange, whereby both the buyer and the seller believe they are receiving greater value than they are giving up. The *marketing task* is to satisfy the customer's need; and the *marketing mix* consists of the tools that the non-profit marketer will use to achieve the marketing objectives. The *distinctive competence* describes what the organisation does best. These four factors are of course central to any marketing, whether for profit or not, but may need to be emphasised to the non-profit marketer.

According to Shapiro, the principal tasks for the marketing manager of a non-profit organisation will be attracting resources, allocating resources, and persuasion.

Attracting resources

The main issue in attracting resources is determining the correct appeal. Guilt, fear, and pride tend to be the dominant themes. Attracting resources implies a need to examine issues such as seeking sponsorship, using advertising and public relations, and personal selling.

Donors and potential donors can be segmented. A school or university might segment on the basis of:

- *graduates*—appealing to a sense of pride or loyalty
- *parents of present-day students*—interested in better facilities and profile for the university
- *business or industry*—interested in skilled graduates, tax advantages, and making a contribution to society.

Allocating resources

The resource allocation decision will be analogous to product policy. In other words, resources will be allocated on the basis of the business in which the organisation is engaged. The organisation therefore needs to define its business or area of operation, for example: an orchestra may be in the entertainment business, but it also exists to promote and preserve particular types of music; and the Irish Heart Foundation exists to educate the public about heart disease and to promote a healthy diet and life-style.

Persuasion

Persuasion involves persuading donors or buyers; it may also involve persuading people to use the non-profit service or product. Sometimes this involves convincing them to do something that the organisation desires but that makes no direct contribution to the organisation itself, for example anti-litter campaigns, or campaigns to encourage people to put themselves on the electoral register, to go for cancer screening or cholesterol testing, or avoid contracting HIV.

THE MARKETING MIX

The following section describes the principal elements of the marketing mix for non-profit organisations. The elements of the mix are broadly similar to the marketing mix for any product, but, given the importance of people in non-profit organisations, as with the services marketing mix, we will include people as a separate element.

People

In marketing services, a lot of emphasis is put on the people element of the marketing mix. It is equally important for many non-profit organisations. Many non-profit bodies have found that they cannot be effectively run by part-timers, and therefore full-time administrative and marketing staff are required. The Irish Heart Foundation and Crumlin Children's Hospital, Dublin, have full-time marketing and support staff to implement marketing plans and activities. There will still be a good deal of reliance on volunteers: indeed voluntary effort helps keep the administrative costs of the organisation low. Volunteers may have plenty of enthusiasm—an important trait—but they may also require some training. The training of volunteers may concentrate on skills such as responsibility, participation, decision-making, and accountability. These will be important where volunteers are required to take responsibility for aspects of the organisation's work and where they have access to donations or the organisation's funds.

Many non-profit organisations rely on people to deliver the benefit, for example counselling or guidance. For an organisation like the Samaritans the training and support given to its volunteers is very important. The service cannot be separated from the person providing it, who needs very special psychological skills and a strong ability to empathise with the caller.

The role of people is particularly relevant, given the importance of personal selling to many non-profit bodies, whether from door to door, in street collections, or in approaches to businesses for donations. They will need communication and presentation skills and to be able to explain clearly the nature of the organisation they represent.

The product

The non-profit organisation may need to have two sets of product policies, one for donors and one for beneficiaries. In both cases non-profit marketers should seek to define the different product levels they are marketing (see chapter 7).

The product from the donor's viewpoint

The definition of the product from the donor's viewpoint can be quite loose, for example personal satisfaction, a sense of belonging or pride, a sense of right or duty, or a sense of involvement. It is probably not surprising that many appeals to donors concentrate on moral or public-spirit grounds. Lindsay and Murphy (1996), for example, recommended that charities should engage in 'relationship fund-raising', in other words lead donors through a life-cycle from small donations to larger donations to ultimately leaving the charity a legacy.

In relation to corporate donations, there are strong financial and marketing advantages to be derived from giving. Non-profit marketers can use this in selecting and convincing corporate donors. The financial advantages derive largely from the tax relief a company can obtain from donations to charitable causes. Consider the example of the advertisement placed in the business press by the Society of St Vincent de Paul (fig. 14.1).

The marketing advantages derive from being associated with a cause and being perceived as a good corporate citizen. Corporate philanthropy has been defined (Carrigan, 1997) as an investment of support (financial or otherwise) for an event or activity where the returns are primarily expected to society but are of ultimate long-term value to the company itself. The non-profit marketer needs to be aware that companies can have different reasons for getting involved in corporate philanthropy and should monitor and evaluate it and make contributions in different ways.

Needless to say, it is not just non-profit bodies that may be beneficiaries: corporate philanthropy may extend to encouraging enterprise development, as is the case with the Plato programme and First Step (see chapter 2). If the non-profit marketer can present reasons why they could develop a mutually beneficial relationship with a corporate body, this may be a significant part of the augmented product.

In some cases the activities of non-profit organisations are designed to encourage consumers to engage in a particular behaviour. Organisations such as Oxfam, for example, sell products under the Fair Trade label. These have been obtained from suppliers who guarantee that producers and workers have been paid a fair price and that the products have been produced in an environmentally responsible way. The difficulties with the Fair Trade approach appear to be a lack of recognition by consumers and a lack of extensive distribution channels (Strong, 1997).

Figure 14.1: Society of St Vincent de Paul

PUT A SMILE ON THE FACE OF THE TIGER

Tough times - but good - in the
land of the Celtic Tiger.
For some.
Now thanks to a change in Tax law,
your company can help put a smile
on faces who've only seen the tough.

Give to our work and then deduct what
you give from your profits -
anything between £250 and £10,000.

You pay less tax. We raise more funds.
We know where the need is greatest.

Act now. Talk to your tax adviser.
For smiles all round.

Society of St. Vincent de Paul, 8 New Cabra Road, Dublin 7. Tel: (01) 838 4164 / 838 0527. Fax: (01) 838 7355

The product from the recipient's viewpoint

The product provided to recipients can be quite simple, for example meals on wheels or financial support, or more complex, for example advice, guidance, or counselling. The Irish Cancer Society is involved in a number of activities, including financing research into cancer and cancer treatment, providing information to the public and to specialist publics such as the medical profession, raising funds from the general and corporate public, and lobbying decision-makers or influencers. There may therefore be a need to organise priorities. Funds will not be unlimited, and this will dictate where resources can be allocated.

In relation to product policy it may also be important to associate something tangible with the intangible. The Irish Cancer Society, the Irish Heart Foundation and the Irish Kidney Association use tangible symbols in the form of artificial daffodils, heart badges, and forget-me-nots. These have come to be associated with particular days or weekends during the year. Other symbols have taken on an international significance, such as the red ribbon for World AIDS Day.

Institutions such as museums and art galleries could consider themselves as being in the business of selling an experience to the visitor. Consider the example of the National Museum of Ireland at Collins Barracks, Dublin.

THE NATIONAL MUSEUM OF IRELAND AT COLLINS BARRACKS

In November 1997 the National Museum of Ireland opened a new museum in the former Collins Barracks, Dublin. This became the third part in a trio of museums, which includes the National Museum in Kildare Street and the Natural History Museum in Merrion Square. The museum is operated by the Heritage Service under the Department of Arts, Heritage, Gaeltacht, and the Islands.

Collins Barracks positioned itself away from its sister museums as offering something new and different from traditional museums. Many of the displays have never been seen in public before, and the visitor experience is meant to be more informal and accessible than is usual in museums. Computer technology is used so that the visitor can obtain information on the displays. These include tools and utensils and a collection of craftwork over the years from 1600 onwards.

As with the other national museums, admission is free, on the grounds that as a national institution it should be accessible to everyone. The museum relies principally on state financing, though it also plans to develop a Friends Society to encourage sponsorship, and corporate and private donations.

Creating awareness of the museum's location is probably one of the most significant issues to be tackled in initial communications. Emphasising the uniqueness of the museum and its collections to tourists and natives alike will be a continuing communication strategy.

Source: Based on A. Fitzgerald, C. Graham, and C. Toolis, 'A Report on the Marketing of an Irish Non-Profit Organisation', term report, Institute of Technology, Tallaght, May 1998.

Pricing

In a profit-making organisation, price links the allocation of resources to resource attraction. If the product is no longer in demand, or if demand is declining, resources will usually be diverted to other, more profitable products or activities. This may not be the case for non-profit organisations: for example, a counselling service may need to be provided whether there is a handful of users or many users.

Some non-profit organisations do charge for their services, in most cases to reach a breakeven point. Credit unions, for example, charge interest on loans but, as the following panel illustrates, do not charge for services in the way that banks and other financial service providers do.

THE CREDIT UNION MOVEMENT

The Credit Union Act (1997) granted substantial new powers to credit unions, including the right to lend money for longer periods. It also provided the movement with a platform for expanding beyond its traditional savings and loans services.

A credit union is a financial co-operative owned and democratically controlled by its members. It exists to serve its members, not to make a profit. Members can invest in savings or shares, which earn them a dividend; and only members may get a loan. Credit unions do not impose charges for operating accounts, but interest on loans is charged at 1 per cent per month on the outstanding balance; any surplus made is ploughed back into the credit union.

The credit union movement in Ireland grew rapidly from the 1950s and 1960s and became very strong among communities, occupations, and associations. In 1998 there were 536 autonomous credit unions in Ireland, and it was estimated that 34 per cent of the population were credit union members. Sixteen thousand volunteers were involved in the movement, in addition to the 1,800 administrative staff. Annual growth in the 1990s was 25 per cent.

Credit unions are supervised by the Registrar of Friendly Societies. The registrar has various powers under the act, including the power to give directives on credit union advertising.

The 1997 act allowed credit unions to get into new markets, such as insurance, credit cards, and mortgages. They will also be allowed to offer support to small and medium-sized businesses. It was probable that one effect of the act would be the emergence of credit unions as a more competitive force in the banking market. Some credit unions had begun offering ATM services, facilities for electronic funds transfer, and foreign exchange services. Banks are often criticised for their perceived anti-consumer bias, but no one has ever lost money through a credit union. The strength of the movement has been that it is based on a common bond and is operated on a non-profit basis.

Source: A. Coffey, 'Credit unions: banking's biggest threat', *Business and Finance*, 16 April 1998.

Some non-profit organisations receive state subvention, for example relief agencies at times of disasters, but must still carry out fund-raising activities to keep going.

Important considerations in pricing are both monetary and non-monetary. Monetary considerations include donations, admission charges, or charges for the service provided. The factors affecting the pricing decision outlined in chapter 8 will be relevant. The non-profit marketer will have to be aware of the nature of demand, the costs associated with providing the product or service, consumer price elasticity, and pricing methods.

Non-monetary pricing considerations include such factors as time, advice, friendship, and support. These intangible aspects may be difficult to cost, and in this regard there are strong similarities with the costing decision faced by services marketers. Intangibility is difficult to cost.

With regard to pricing policy, many of the non-profit bodies that introduced fund-raising activities around special badges charge a fixed price of £1 per badge. The introduction of the euro was a source of concern for many charities as it was felt that the equivalent price in euro (€1.27) would be impractical, and raising the price—to €1.50, for example—could meet with resistance. This not only presents the contributor with the opportunity to support a cause for a relatively small amount but also guarantees a price per unit and is an aid to stock control. The non-profit organisation can readily assess sales on the basis of the number of units sent out to collectors and on the income and unsold units returned.

MARKETING COMMUNICATION

Most non-profit marketers use a variety of marketing communication tools. The main difficulty they have is typically a lack of resources to finance sustained communication campaigns. Many organisations may not be able to spare scarce resources for any media-based campaigns. Whether the organisation has the resources or not, the principles of communication will still be important; indeed it may be possible to have someone else finance the costs of communication.

Advertising

Some non-profit organisations and social marketers use the mass media fairly extensively, for example the 'Power of One' campaign (fig 14.2). The Irish Blood Transfusion Service Board (fig. 14.3) is a statutory service provider that needs to be concerned about social altruism; it uses advertising to position its service and to encourage the public to give blood donations.

Advertising for many non-profit organisations, such as relief agencies, tends to veer towards a strong moral appeal, attempting to appeal to the receivers' sense of right. Other appeals can be more rational, while the poster advertisement for the National Museum at Collins Barracks in fig. 14.4 seeks to inform and differentiate.

The use of databases and newer means of communication, such as the internet, can have a significant role in the communication of the non-profit organisation's message. Data can be compiled on previous donors, and this can be used in direct marketing campaigns. Similarly, the development of a website enables the organisation to communicate and interact with potential donors or specific targets.

Other means of communication, such as direct mail and magazines or newsletters for members, can also be used. It is important for the non-profit marketer to stay in touch with previous donors, and this is fundamental to the development of a relationship with them.

Figure 14.2: Power of One

Figure 14.3: Irish Blood Transfusion
Board

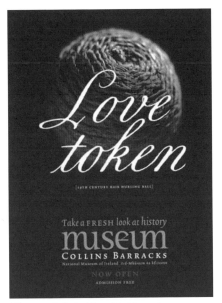

Figure 14.4: The National
Museum at Collins Barracks

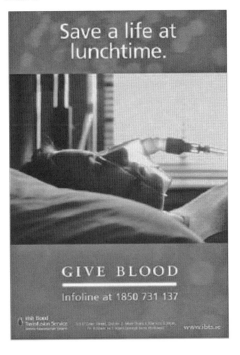

In some cases the use of public figures to endorse the organisation will be emphasised in advertising: for example, the broadcaster Gay Byrne has endorsed the Irish Cancer Society, and the actor Geraldine Plunkett has endorsed the Special Olympics.

Personal selling

Personal selling can be quite important for many non-profit marketers. The main difference between personal selling in the profit and non-profit worlds is that the non-profit marketer may have to rely heavily on volunteers to do the actual selling. Personal selling will cover everything from selling lines or badges to selecting large organisations to ask for donations.

Personal selling is highly suitable for a small target audience, such as seeking donations or sponsorship from the corporate sector. In this case the stages in the selling process described in chapter 9 will be relevant.

Sponsorship

As described in chapter 9, sponsorship is becoming a more significant element of marketing communication. It can be particularly important for non-profit marketers, especially where they are aiming at the corporate sector for funds or support. Sponsorship of a non-profit organisation, cause or event will be considered by companies on a number of grounds. There may be a genuine desire to support a worthy cause, but there will also be marketing advantages from being seen to do so. As a result, companies will assess their sponsorship activities to find those that best meet their criteria. This may mean that there can be competition between non-profit organisations for the corporate sponsor.

Public relations

Public relations can be especially important for non-profit organisations. The chance to obtain publicity, to publicise a particular cause or issue to the media or to gain coverage for an event or launch should not be missed. Public relations has played an important part in the case of Goal, the relief and development agency, as the following panel illustrates.

EFFECTIVE USE OF PUBLIC RELATIONS

Goal is a non-profit organisation involved in relief and development projects. It was founded by John O'Shea, who was a sports journalist. Not surprisingly, many well-known figures in the sports world, including Jack Charlton, Stephen Roche, Seán Kelly, and Niall Quinn, have endorsed the organisation's work and appear at charity events and fund-raisers. This helps guarantee media coverage. John O'Shea himself is well known and accessible to the media, which helps gain coverage for the organisation's activities, including its annual St Patrick's Day collection, when it sells shamrock pins.

The work the organisation has done to alleviate poverty and provide relief is well recognised. In 1994 the organisation received a strong public endorsement by the President of Ireland, Mary Robinson.

The 1990s also witnessed the development of 'telethons', when television channels devoted considerable time to particular causes. In Ireland the annual 'People in Need' telethon was televised on RTÉ; this involved various television presenters and members of the public raising funds for worthy causes. Many organisations seek to be associated with the event by giving donations or products, both for philanthropic and publicity reasons.

Channels

The marketing channels for non-profit organisations serve the same broad functions as channels for other marketers. They may involve different levels, although, like services and business-to-business channels, they tend to be short. The channels should facilitate provision of the service, facilitate donations, and facilitate volunteers.

Provision of the service

The non-profit organisation may distribute its service in a set place, such as a museum or art gallery, or it may involve the provision of a service that the consumer can gain access to anywhere, for example telephone helplines. If a fixed place is used the consumer may need to be made aware of its location and how to get there. If the organisation operates a telephone helpline, important criteria will include emphasising awareness of the number and possibly arranging for the provision of a 24-hour service.

Facilitating donations

It should be easy and convenient for people to make donations. This may mean having donation points in many places, for example shopping centres, door-to-door collections, or dedicated telephone lines where credit card donations can be made. In the case of nationwide appeals or campaigns this may require the involvement of thousands of individual collectors. The Irish Heart Foundation selects retailers, pubs, restaurants, factories, and other business premises, using point-of-sale displays. Stocks of heart emblems are provided, together with a collection box, which can be placed on the counter or beside the checkout.

Facilitating volunteers

The facilitation of volunteers is analogous to the sales territory decision. Volunteers can cover their own localities, which is not only convenient but is also important for trust and credibility. People will be more likely to give to or support someone they know.

PLANNING AND STRATEGY

Drucker (1989) in his research into non-profit organisations in the United States found that the most successful had a clear mission statement. He also found that some of the organisations had much better management structures than their profit-making counterparts. The mission statements Drucker came across include:

- Salvation Army: 'To turn society's rejects, alcoholics, derelicts and convicts into citizens.'
- Scouts and guides: 'To help young people become confident and capable, to respect themselves and others.'
- Nature conservancy: 'To preserve the diversity of nature's flora and fauna.'

The benefits of strategic planning for non-profit organisations were emphasised by the World Wildlife Fund, which introduced strategic planning in 1978 (Medley, 1988). In the following nine years, as the result of planned actions, cohesive teamwork, and clear objectives, the organisation increased its net funds by a factor of five and its productivity by a factor of six. It simply followed the planning process, carrying out a SWOT analysis (see chapter 15), developing strategies and action plans designed to achieve and implement the strategies.

Distinctive competence

Shapiro (1973) drew attention to the importance of non-profit bodies establishing what their distinctive competence was and sticking to it. Generally, the competitive system in free-market countries means that companies prosper when they meet customers' needs but fail when they do not. In other words, they establish a competitive advantage; if this disappears or is eroded, they may disappear.

This self-regulating mechanism is not as significant for non-profit organisations, for a number of reasons. Many needs are so great that people cannot choose between competitors: they have to take what is available, for example counselling. Demand for the products or services often exceeds supply. For many non-profit organisations, financial viability depends on the attraction rather than the allocation of resources. Market forces may not prevail in the allocation of resources; they may be allocated to highly intangible projects, for example the preservation of historic buildings, which will not be judged by criteria such as market share leadership.

Many non-profit organisations do evaluate the service they give, and co-operate with each other to ensure that no two organisations are seeking to serve the same need. There can still be duplication—a criticism that is often levelled at the charities involved in development aid and disaster relief, with several organisations competing for donations from the public for the same relief effort.

The launch of the National Lottery in 1986 had an impact on many charities. As a certain proportion of the lottery's income goes to such causes, many people perceived that they were in effect giving to charity by buying a lottery ticket. Some charities noticed a decline in donations. Many, however, responded in kind; and it is no coincidence that the number of organisations promoting the sale of £1 badges on particular days of the year has increased: these were priced at the same price as a lottery ticket or scratch card.

FURTHER READING

Hannagan, T., *Marketing for the Non-Profit Sector*, London: Macmillan 1992.

DISCUSSION QUESTIONS

1. Compare and contrast marketing practice in profit-making companies with that of non-profit-making organisations.
2. Do you think people can become apathetic about the marketing activities of charities or cause-related organisations? Give reasons for your answer.
3. Comment on the reasons why many non-profit organisations are reluctant to take marketing principles into account. Is there an inherent contradiction in their reluctance?
4. Describe the elements of the marketing mix for each of the following:
   —GOAL
   —the Blood Transfusion Service
   —Bord na Gaeilge
   —the Royal British Legion in Ireland.
5. Explain why many large corporations engage in philanthropy. How can this benefit non-profit-making organisations?

REFERENCES

Andreasen, A. R., *Marketing Social Change: Changing Behaviour to Promote Health, Social Development and the Environment*, San Francisco: Josey-Bass 1995.

Balabanis, G., Stables, R., and Phillips, H., 'Market orientation in the top 200 British charity organisations and its impact on their performance', *European Journal of Marketing*, vol. 31 (1997), no. 8.

Carrigan, M., 'The great corporate give-away: can marketing do good for the do-gooders?', *European Business Journal*, vol. 9 (1997), no. 4.

Drucker, P., 'What business can learn from non-profits', *Harvard Business Review*, July–August 1989.

Hirst, J., 'Charities with attitude', *Marketing Business*, June 1997.

Kotler, P. and Lee, N., *Social Marketing: Influencing Behaviours for Good* (third edition), Thousand Oaks (CA): Sage 2008.

Kotler, P. and Levy, S., 'Broadening the Concept of Marketing', *Journal of Marketing*, vol. 33, January 1969.

Lindsay, G. and Murphy, A., 'NSPCC: marketing the solution not the problem', *Journal of Marketing Management*, November 1996.

Medley, G., 'Strategic planning for the World Wildlife Fund', *Long-Range Planning*, February 1988.

Shapiro, B., 'Marketing for non-profit organisations', *Harvard Business Review*, September–October 1973.

Strong, C., 'The problem of translating fair trade principles into consumer purchase behaviour', *Market Intelligence and Planning*, vol. 15 (1997), no. 1.

JAMESON IRISH WHISKEY

The Jameson brand has enjoyed considerable success in world markets; in 2010 it was still the most successful Irish whiskey brand and was defying the prevailing economic recession by continuing to increase its sales. The brand's success is due to a combination of factors, including growth in demand for premium whiskeys, increased penetration in a number of markets, and the successful positioning approach adopted by Irish Distillers Ltd in international markets.

Research by Datamonitor in 2010 predicted that Irish whiskey sales would grow in the United States by 9.4 per cent per annum until 2014, compared to 2 per cent growth per annum in the overall whiskey market (which includes US, Canadian, and Asian brands), and a 0.2 per cent growth for Scotch whiskey. The majority of whiskey drinkers in the US are aged over 55, but the typical Jameson consumer is a much younger, professional male. In 2008, for the first time, total Irish whiskey sales in the US were 1 million cases.

The success of Jameson in the US has demonstrated that the brand can appeal to a non-traditional market segment; could this success be replicated across other markets?

Company history

The Jameson brand originated in 1780 when John Jameson secured a licence to establish a distillery. The company remained independent until the 1960s when it merged with John Power Ltd and the Cork Distillery Company to form Irish Distillers Ltd. In 1988 the French firm Pernod Ricard acquired Irish Distillers and, in 2005, Pernod Ricard merged with Allied Domecq, another large global competitor.

Pernod Ricard operates as a federation, with a small headquarters in Paris that lets its local subsidiaries get on with production and formulating marketing plans. The acquisition of Irish Distillers was significant for the Jameson brand as Pernod Ricard decided it was a brand it wished to develop in international markets. Consequently a considerable marketing effort was devoted to Jameson, including the development of markets in Europe, the Far East, and the United States.

In 2005 Jameson sold 2 million cases and, by 2010, this had increased to 3 million cases per year. In 1988 when Pernod Ricard took over, Jameson's sales had been 400,000 cases.

Whiskey production

In marketing whiskeys, distillers tend to place significant emphasis on the nature of the production process, the length of maturation and the quality of the oak casks used to age the product. Whiskey connoisseurs pride themselves on their ability to distinguish different brands on the basis of taste, and a significant market has been established in premium-priced, mature whiskey as a result.

The production process requires three basic ingredients: malted barley, unmalted barley, and water. These are combined to produce a low-strength alcohol, or wash.

Distilling creates new whiskey from the wash, the wash is heated in traditional large copper-pot stills and Jameson is created after three separate distillations, which results in a smoother taste. The product is then matured in seasoned oak casks for at least three years. The casks are manufactured by a cooperage at Jerez in Spain, before being used for whiskey they are used to mature sherry for two years.

An expert blender then blends a variety of whiskey types that have matured in these oak casks. Finally the whiskey is put into vats where the blends are allowed to marry before being bottled as Jameson. Jameson is considered a premium whiskey brand, given the quality of the production process and the time taken to distil it. Lower priced whiskeys tend to have been distilled using cheaper raw materials and for shorter time periods of time.

The global whiskey market

The global market for blended whiskey was estimated by the research firm Research and Markets in 2010 to be 130 million cases (each case contains 12 bottles). Scotch whiskey dominates the market with about 60 per cent market share. Irish whiskeys have about 3 per cent market share, with the remaining market being accounted for by US, Canadian, and Asian producers.

Competition

Until 1987 Irish Distillers had a monopoly on the distilling of whiskey in Ireland. In that year Cooley Distillery PLC had been founded by John Teeling and production had begun in Louth on the Cooley Peninsula; this was the only independent distillery to be set up in Ireland in over a century. In the same year Cooley had acquired the assets of the old Kilbeggan Distillery, which had ceased production in the 1950s. This brought about the revival of a lot of old Irish whiskey brands such as Kilbeggan, Tyrconnell, Millars, and Connemara, which had disappeared from the market.

Initially Cooley's strategy was to generate cash flow through a number of own-label Irish whiskeys for supermarket chains in Britain (Tesco and Sainsbury's) and France (Intermarche and Carrefour). This cash flow helped facilitate the development of a whole range of Irish whiskey products, such as single malts, single grains, and blends. This strategy enabled Cooley to innovate its product offerings so as not to compete directly with the market leader and to ensure its survival as

an independent. However, low margins prompted them to announce in 2002 that they planned to reduce this aspect of their business to concentrate on premium brands.

Cooley also pursued the strategy of aligning itself with a strong partner for the development of private label Irish whiskeys. While Cooley had the production capabilities, they lacked the sales and marketing expertise. Through this route to the market, Cooley could compete with other multinational companies.

On St Patrick's Day 2006, Cooley Distillery launched Michael Collins Whiskey, in both blend and single malt varieties, in the USA. In joint partnership with Sidney Frank, the company planned to sell 38,000 cases (7,000 of which would be single malt). Sidney Frank, a company that had propelled the Grey Goose premium vodka brand and Jagermeister to a spectacular performance in a few years, was viewed as a perfect partner for Cooley.

The Michael Collins whiskey was aged in Bourbon casks and both the single malt and the blend contained some 10- and 12-year-old whiskey. The bottles, which were sourced in China, were similar in shape to champagne bottles and had a long gold cap.

Cooley's target market for the Michael Collins brand was 21–24 year olds who were 'young, educated and savvy'. An advertising campaign used Irish-American publications such as *Irish Voice*, but also ran in more mainstream publications such as *Forbes*, *USA Today*, and *Business Week*.

The global drinks industry is dominated by large companies that own several brands. One of Pernod Ricard's main global competitors is Diageo which owns brands such as Guinness and Bailey's. Diageo were also the owners of Bushmills Irish Whiskey, which had originally belonged to Pernod Ricard. In August 2005 Pernod Ricard sold the Bushmills brand to Diageo as an incentive to keep it from bidding for Allied Domecq, another global drinks giant that Pernod Ricard ultimately took over. Diageo paid €293 million for Bushmills and immediately began to increase its marketing spend, especially in the US where it had an estimated one third of the market for Irish whiskey. Commenting on the extensive distribution that Diageo enjoyed in the US market in 2010, Global Research Inc. stated that 'it is only a matter of time before it uses that distribution clout to establish Bushmills to a greater extent'.

The main source of competition to Irish whiskeys on international markets is from Scotland where there were 28 distilleries producing a large number of brands.

SCOTLAND

The earliest documented record of distilling in Scotland occurs in 1494 when reference was made to monks distilling 'aqua vitae'. Scottish whiskey is sold in over 200 countries and, in 2009, shipments were worth £2.7 billion. Sales to the European Union (excluding the UK) accounted for 40 per cent of shipments. Blended Scotch whiskey is the most popular product sold in global markets, with approximately 82.5 million cases sold per year. The top 10 Scotch blended brands in 2010 were:

1. Johnnie Walker
2. J&B
3. Buchanan's
4. Chivas Regal
5. Ballantine's
6. Famous Grouse
7. Teacher's
8. Cutty Sark
9. Dewar's
10. Grant's

Source: Research and Markets, *The Global Market for Whiskey*, 2010.

In addition to these, there are probably about 100 well-known brands of Scotch whiskey, but there are countless others, many of which are produced in small quantities and sold locally and some that are only sold to private clubs or individuals. Production of Scotch has been steadily increasing since 2005. The top markets for Scotch whiskey in 2009 were:

Market	Sales value (£million)
1. USA	418.8
2. France	406.7
3. Spain	315.8
4. Singapore	167.5
5. Venezuela	115.8
6. South Korea	112.5
7. South Africa	108.2
8. Germany	103.2

Source: Scotch Whisky Association.

To be termed a Scotch whiskey, the spirit must mature in oak casks in Scotland for at least three years. The majority of Scotch whiskey is consumed in blended form; this means that a combination of grain distilled whiskey is blended with malt distilled whiskey.

A growing segment of the market is single malts, which can be the product of only one distillery, and which account for 5 per cent of world whiskey sales. There are several single-malt brands, the most significant of which, in sales terms, is Glenfiddich, the largest selling, single-malt scotch in the world, which is produced by William Grant & Sons Ltd, an independent distillery. The best selling single malt in Scotland is the brand Glenmorangie. As mentioned earlier, Cooley was the only producer of Irish single-malt whiskey.

Consumption tastes vary in different parts of the world. In Britain whiskey is usually consumed with a little water, in Spain it is typically consumed with cola or club lemon, while, in Japan, a lot of ice and water is used.

Scotch whiskey differs from Irish in that the unmalted barley is usually dried over peat fires, the smoke from the peat penetrates the barley, giving the whiskeys their distinctive smoky taste. Irish whiskey is produced from barley that is dried in closed ovens, so there is no contact with smoke. In addition, Scotch whiskey is usually distilled twice whereas most

Irish whiskey is distilled three times. This triple distillation increases the purity and smoothness of the whiskey.

GLOBAL COMPETITORS

The merger of Pernod Ricard and Allied Domecq in 2005 brought together two of the world's biggest whiskey producers. The other significant competitor is Diageo. Between them, the three companies accounted for approximately 60 per cent of global whiskey sales.

The Diageo Group owns a number of whiskey brands including two of the world's best-selling whiskeys, Johnnie Walker and J&B. Diageo has categorised all its brands, including whiskey, into three groups. The first group are the 'global priority' brands refer to those brands that are critical to Diageo's global market presence, this would include the Bailey's liqueur brand, for example, as well as the whiskey brands, J&B and Johnnie Walker. Diageo developed a global campaign for Johnnie Walker using the theme 'keep walking'. In the US, for example, one advert featured the actor Harvey Keitel and placed emphasis on his personal journey through life. In China where collective success rather than individual achievement is important, Diageo showed groups of young men toasting each other with scotch and making a collective pledge to 'keep walking'. Worldwide, Johnnie Walker sold 14.3 million cases in 2009.

The second group are the 'local priority' brands are those that do not have a global presence but are important in local markets, thus the Buchanan's brand is important in Latin America and Bells is important in Britain. Bushmills was categorised as a local priority brand. The final group are the 'category management' brands which are not critical growth drivers for the company and will not be significant value creators in the future, the Vat 69 brand is included in this category.

The other significant Irish brand is Tullamore Dew, which had belonged to the Cantrell and Cochrane Group, but was sold in July 2010 to the Scottish distiller William Grant & Sons. In September 2010 the new owner announced the opening of a global marketing office in Dublin, one of the priorities of which was to develop the brand across several markets, including the US where its triple blended characteristics would be emphasised.

In 2010 Tullamore Dew was the top-selling Irish whiskey in Germany, Sweden, Poland, Denmark, the Czech Republic, Bulgaria, Latvia, Lithuania, and Estonia. William Grant owns a number of Scotch brands, such as Glenfiddich and Grant's, and these continue to be marketed from its London office, with the Dublin office also leading global planning and innovation.

The initial plans were for an international television, press, and poster campaign to support the brand.

A number of other countries have significant whiskey production, notably Canada and the United States

CANADA

The biggest distiller in Canada in terms of market share is Corby's whose three brands—Lot No. 40, Pike Creek, and Gooderham & Worts Ltd—have 41 per cent of the market. Canadian whiskey has an estimated share of 12 per cent of the United States whiskey market.

THE UNITED STATES

The most familiar whiskey product is bourbon, which must be made from at least 51 per cent maize and distilled in a combination of column and pot still. Legally it must have matured for at least two years. Bourbon is produced in a number of states and is especially associated with Kentucky, Pennsylvania, Maryland, and Virginia. The Jim Beam brand of bourbon, produced in Kentucky is one of the largest sellers, while the Southern Comfort brand is, basically, peach-flavoured bourbon.

Other types of whiskey include rye whiskey, which must be made from at least 51 per cent rye, and sour mash, which is associated with Tennessee. Sour mash gets its name because the production process involves adding the residue from one fermentation into the next to create continuity in taste. Sour mash is filtered through sugar-maple charcoal, a process that takes 10 days and results in a sweet-tasting whiskey. Possibly the most famous sour mash whiskey brand is Jack Daniels, a brand that has been increasing its sales in international markets.

International Advertising

The success of Jameson in international markets has been due to several factors, not least of which was the initial advertising campaign developed by the Dublin-based agency, McConnells. Entitled 'Rush hour', this campaign came about as part of a global marketing strategy that reflected the brand's international success. The advertising featured stylish young people in fashionable locations enjoying Jameson in an oasis of calm surrounded by a streaming rush of others in a hurry (IAPI, 2002). The importance of people finding time to enjoy themselves with friends was emphasised, as was the presentation of the product as a dynamic and stylish international spirit for men and women (in itself unusual in the whiskey market). The advertising was designed for use on television, magazines, and poster sites.

The 'Rush hour' campaign won an Institute of Advertising in Ireland (IAPI) advertising effectiveness award for McConnells in 2002. The campaign was judged to have been successful in breaking the older more conservative values associated with whiskey and recruiting younger drinkers in the 25–35-year-old category. In qualitative research conducted by Behaviour and Attitudes in 2002, this campaign was seen to be 'motivating and engaging', communicating successfully the core image values of the brand, sophistication, cosmopolitanism, warmth, and camaraderie. The fact that Jameson had already become an international brand helped its position considerably in the Irish market.

In addition to the United States and France, most of the growth in demand for Jameson in recent years has come from the Mediterranean markets of Spain, Portugal, Italy, and Greece; however, the 'Rush hour' campaign was not used in France or Spain. In France, regulations regarding the advertising of alcohol meant that it could not be used, as advertisements cannot feature people drinking and cannot feature people and alcoholic drinks in the same picture.

In Spain, Jameson was a relatively new brand on the market and the 'Rush hour' campaign was not considered suitable. Spain has one of the highest consumption levels of whiskey in Europe, but Scotch dominates the market. In

1997 Pernod Ricard purchased the Spanish distributor Larios and this has enabled them improve their distribution in Spain. An advertising campaign, separate from the 'Rush hour' campaign was developed to create awareness for the Jameson brand (see example of Spanish advertising above). The leading brand in the Spanish market is the Scotch Ballantines which has a 16 per cent share. In Spain, 65 per cent of consumption takes place between midnight and 4 a.m., suggesting that the product is popular with younger clubbers. Growth in the Spanish market was triggered by Spain's accession to the EU in the 1980s when trade barriers came down.

In December 2002 the advertising agency Cawley Nea was successful in its bid to handle the global advertising for the Jameson brand, an account that was valued at €45 million (*Irish Times*, 12 December 2002). It developed a number of campaigns, and, in 2008, launched the 'seriously playful' advert in international markets, the idea was to show the brand as a contemporary, iconic spirit, without losing its appeal to more traditional drinkers.

In 2009, *Advertising Age*, judged Jameson to be a recession-proof brand as it had increased sales by successfully targeting young male consumers who were less price conscious and more adventurous. It considered that Jameson was using what it described as a 'premiumisation' strategy, which meant that it was attracting consumers who were willing to pay more for the same volume of alcohol, by providing them with a product and brand attributes that fit with their desire to improve their lives or their perception of their lives.

Sponsorship

In addition to advertising Jameson is involved in the international sponsorship of film festivals. Festivals sponsored include Dublin, Cannes, Berlin, and Venice. Irish Distillers felt that this sponsorship reached into the consciousness of trendy thirtysomethings and was therefore very much in keeping with its target market.

Sponsorship is quite a common method of marketing communication among whiskey producers. Brands such as Johnnie Walker and Suntory are associated with international golf competitions, the Famous Grouse was sponsor of Scotland's international rugby team and the Black and White brand was associated with a pub of the year competition.

Visitor centres

In the early 1990s, Irish Distillers opened a visitor centre at the Midleton Distillery, which receives over 200,000 visitors per year. It was marketed as a tourist attraction and provided visitors with displays and audio-visual presentations that explain how whiskey is made and offers a chance to taste the products. A similar centre was opened at Smithfield in Dublin on the site of the original Jameson distillery and, by 2002, it was attracting over 400,000 visitors per year.

Visitor centres have also been important for Scottish distilleries attracting 1 million visitors per annum.

Trends in the market

According to *Business Insights* (2010), these are some key trends relevant to global whiskey producers in the period 2010–2020:

- Over the next 10 year period, 1.2 billion people in Asia-Pacific will be born into or move into the global middle-class, representing the largest single expansion in consumer spending power ever recorded.
- Using unique flavors and ingredients has become a focus area for differentiating products and adding perceived value, as they can enhance a drink's positioning of authenticity, heritage, quality, or exclusivity.
- Increasingly consumers want to know the story behind a brand, as part of the discovery that sets them apart from others and giving them 'insider' status into a perceived exclusive world.
- As consumers seek out 'masstige' products due to the challenging economic environments, manufacturers, and retailers are looking beyond price to image, packaging, and marketing to deliver an affordable premium experience.

The Future

The global market will continue to be highly competitive and Irish Distillers are aware that the success of Jameson in the US means that competing brands Bushmills, Cooley, and Tullamore Dew will all be paying particular attention to this market. It is also aware that there were other markets, especially emerging markets such as China, where whiskey consumption is increasing. Scotch producers have been successfully targeting the Chinese market and, in 2009, had sold £80 million worth of whiskey there. Irish Distillers has also been targeting China and has enjoyed some success, but the market is dominated by Scotch. Jameson is also doing well in South Africa where the whiskey market has increased, for example, in 2007 it increased by 16.2 per cent.

All marketers of whiskey were aware of the success of the premiumisation strategy and this was being reflected in their advertising and promotional campaigns. In the US Jameson had a market share of about 60 per cent of Irish whiskey sold; it was determined to hold on to this. As management considers its plans for the brand's future, they were conscious that they needed to keep telling the story behind the brand.

ADDITIONAL SOURCES

Coffey, Á., 'Spirit of Michael Collins flies whiskey flag in the US', *Sunday Tribune*, 15 January 2006.

Datamonitor, 'Market Watch: Drinks', January 2010.

Datamonitor, 'Jameson Case Study: Targeting the 'recession resistant' consumer', May 2010.

Dermody, J., 'Global boost for Irish whiskey as Scottish Distillery opens Dublin office, *The Examiner*, 8 September 2010.

Global Market Research Inc, 'Global Market Review of World Whiskeys – Forecasts to 2014', March 2010.

Islay, C., 'Whiskey Business', *Time Europe*, 25 November 2002.

Kiley, D., 'Scotch makers roll out a new barrel', *Business Week*, 12 January 2009.

Miley, M., 'Jameson 'speaks' out to public', *Advertising Age*, 1 December 2008.

Mark P., 'Whiskey Galore', *Sunday Times*, 4 September 2005.

Mulcahy, N., 'Jameson Mixes in the Big League', *Business Plus*, March 2003.

Mullman, J., 'Jameson', *Advertising Age*, 16 November 2009.

Sonne, P., 'As world develops a taste, Scotch whiskeys pour it on', *Wall Street Journal Europe*, 7 June 2010.

Useful Websites
www.jameson.ie
www.scotch-whiskey.org.uk
www.diageo.com
www.cooleydistillery.com

DISCUSSION QUESTIONS

1. Elaborate on the reasons for the success of Jameson in international markets.
2. Explain how cultural values may affect how this brand is marketed.
3. What will be the challenges for Jameson in coming years?

REFERENCES

Business Insights, 'Premiumisation Strategies in Alcoholic Drinks', June 2010.

IAPI (Institute of Advertising Practitioners), Advertising Effectiveness Awards, 'Jameson: The Rush Hour Effect', 2002.

PART 5

Marketing Strategy and Planning

15

Marketing Strategy and Planning

A *strategy* provides a logic that integrates the different functions of the business and points them in the same direction. A strategy is simply what you do to achieve your objectives.

Firms cannot afford to adopt a trial-and-error approach to planning—in other words, continuing with schemes that seem to be working and eliminating those that are not. Rapid environmental change means that this approach can be costly in the form of missed opportunities, and it means that the business may be unprepared for the future.

Planning does not mean that the future becomes any more certain, nor does it mean that future events or developments can be predicted with certainty. What it does do is force the business to consider its future and how it will achieve continued success.

STRATEGIC PLANNING

There are four distinguishing features of strategic planning: an external orientation, a process for formulating strategies, methods for analysing strategic alternatives, and a commitment to action (Day, 1984).

An external orientation

Having examined the forces in the marketing environment (chapter 3), we should not be surprised to learn that firms need to look continuously outwards at what is happening in the environment. The changing environment presents both opportunities and threats; the business must monitor trends and prepare for change. Consider the example of the market for bottled mineral water. Companies in the sector that monitored changing consumer tastes and distribution channels found opportunities for the development of new products and channels.

CHANGES IN THE BOTTLED MINERAL WATER MARKET

Up to the mid-1980s the Irish market for bottled mineral water was very much a niche market, served by imported brands such as Perrier. With the arrival of the Ballygowan brand, the market increased considerably in size. This growth was principally due to life-style factors: consumers became more interested in the health benefits of drinking water; it also became socially more acceptable to drink water than alcoholic drinks. To some extent the Irish market was just catching up on consumption levels in other

European countries, though, as the table below shows, in 2003 consumption was lower than several other European countries.

Table 15.1: European bottled water consumption per capita

	Litres	2003
Italy	144.0	
France	119.8	
Belgium	113.8	
Germany	99.3	
Switzerland	86.4	
Spain	77.8	
Greece	37.0	
United Kingdom	35.0	
Ireland	22.0	

Sources: *Checkout* Ireland, May 1997; *Checkout* May 2006, June 2005; www.ballygowan.ie.

The market in Ireland has grown and it was estimated that it would be worth €145 million in 2007.

Table 15.2: Bottled water market size 1997–2003

Year	Literage (in millions)	% Change
1997	47	+18
1998	54	+15
1999	66	+22
2000	86	+30
2001	98.5	+14.5
2002	107	+9
2003	119	+11

In the early years almost three-quarters of sales were sparkling water, but over the years this position was reversed. In addition, flavoured waters were introduced and there was an increase in the size of the market for water coolers.

Ballygowan had been the first Irish entrant to the market in 1981, and over the years it was followed by several others. Its market share declined as a result but in 2010 it had a 22 per cent share in the grocery market, 50 per cent in licensed trade, and 44 per cent in the water cooler segment. The brand had also been extended with new flavoured variants.

Sources: *Checkout* Ireland, May 1997; *Checkout* May 2006, June 2005; www.ballygowan.ie.

The danger for companies that did not monitor these changes was that they would fail to innovate and would get left behind. An external orientation implied monitoring the changes and taking action. Ballygowan, the market leader, offered both still and sparkling variants, flavoured waters, and dispensers for offices and other locations.

A process for formulating strategies

The process for formulating strategies implies that the marketer has a structured planning process. From this, a clearer picture of what strategies are appropriate should emerge. The process consists of four principal stages:

1. Assessment:
   * present business position
   * environmental situation
   * analysis of competitors.
2. Strategy generation:
   * strategic options
   * sources of competitive advantage.
3. Strategy selection:
   * rewards and risks
   * objectives
   * allocation of resources.
4. Implementation:
   * programme
   * budgets.

Situation assessment

The situation assessment will involve a thorough review of the firm's present business position, the forces in its environment, and an analysis of competitors. A useful tool for assessing situational variables is the SWOT analysis.

The SWOT analysis

The SWOT analysis (an acronym for 'strengths, weaknesses, opportunities, and threats') is fundamental to the formulation of strategy. It can be used in situation assessment as an analytical tool.

Strengths and weaknesses will be identified in any internal analysis conducted by the company. Strengths typically derive from skills and capabilities that enable the firm to develop and implement strategies. Weaknesses will exist where a lack of skills and abilities prevent the company from achieving its objectives.

Opportunities and threats exist in the external environment (chapter 3 described the forces in the environment). Opportunities and threats analysis will be based on an external environmental analysis. Opportunities may exist to develop markets or segments or to produce new products or variations of existing products. In other words, opportunities are phenomena or events that, if exploited, may improve the firm's performance.

Threats are the opposite: they are phenomena or events that may make it difficult or impossible for the firm to achieve its objectives. Porter (1980) suggested that in any industry the opportunities and threats can be analysed according to the 'five forces': the level of competitive rivalry, the power of suppliers, the power of consumers, the threat of substitutes, and the threat of new entrants. The higher these are, the more threats in the industry there will be.

Consider the example of the SWOT analysis conducted by Tesco after its decision to re-enter the Irish market.

TESCO SWOT ANALYSIS

Tesco first acquired stores in the Irish Republic in 1978 when it purchased a chain of discount stores. The company then became a discounter, but due to a lack of emphasis on the Tesco brand, the venture was unsuccessful and the stores were sold in 1986.

An example of a SWOT analysis conducted by Tesco in 2001 is given below.

INTERNAL ANALYSIS OF TESCO IRELAND

STRENGTHS

* one of the leading supermarket retailers
* accelerating sales growth
* Clubcard providing information about the customer
* extensive market research
* Tesco Local developed after requests for a small store with as full a range as possible
* financial status—able to bid high for sites on which to build
* experienced in building large stores with a range of food and non-food items
* all Tesco stores being refurbished and upgraded with wider aisles, better shopping trolleys, faster checkouts, in-store bakeries, in-store customer assistants and improved car parking
* good relationships with local contractors and suppliers
* regional support office for Northern Ireland stores
* employing local people, therefore gaining respect from consumers
* centralised distribution of fruit and vegetables—reducing the time taken to get produce to the supermarkets
* distribution centre solely for Northern Ireland
* aims to bring about price equity—lower prices for Irish customers.

WEAKNESSES

* have wasted time and money finding out the needs of consumers, e.g. the removal of multimillion pound Premium Choice brand
* bad image following advertisements that the company was only buying British beef
* the unsuccessful launch of Catteau in France proves that the Tesco approach cannot necessarily be replicated overseas
* accused of a very arrogant approach to retailing in Ireland
* airmiles have withdrawn its incentive scheme from Tesco in favour of Sainsbury's
* own brands suffer from a cheap and nasty image.

OPPORTUNITIES

* most recent figures suggest a 20 per cent increase in turnover through outlets established for one year or more in Irelan
* close trading links between the UK and Ireland

- buoyant Irish economy
- both countries are English-speaking, making relations easier
- the Irish have similar tastes to their UK counterparts
- a large number of successful UK businesses operating in Ireland
- the Irish retail market is underdeveloped and expanding
- good growth area in wine houses in Ireland.

Threats

- large Irish stores such as Superquinn and Dunnes
- the Irish government is very much against large superstores
- stores must sell a large number of Irish products
- Irish consumers are extremely sensitive and unsure about UK supermarkets
- short-term difficulties have been brought about by the strength of the pound
- continual expansion of major supermarkets into Ireland such as Safeway and Sainsbury
- legislation to prevent low-cost selling.

Source: C. Vignali, 'Tesco's adaptation to the Irish market', *British Food Journal*, vol. 103 (2001), no. 2.

Strategy generation

In generating strategic alternatives, it is useful to examine the work of Porter (1980) and Miles and Snow (1978). Porter described three generic strategic options available to firms at the business level: *differentiation*, *cost leadership*, and *focus*. Miles and Snow developed a typology of four broad business-level strategies: *prospector*, *defender*, *analyser*, and *reactor* (fig. 15.1). Porter argued that firms should choose one of these three strategies and concentrate on implementing it.

Figure 15.1: Porter's generic strategies

	Definition	Examples
Differentiation	The business seeks to distinguish itself from competitors through the quality of its products or services	Rolex watches; Cross pens; the Westbury Hotel; Lir Chocolates; Waterford Crystal
Cost leadership	The business attempts to gain a competitive advantage by reducing its cost below the costs of competing firms	Ryanair; Dunnes Stores; credit unions; Budget Travel
Focus	The business concentrates on a specific regional market, product line, or group of buyers	Macardle's ale; regional newspapers; Beamish stout; Superquinn

The Miles and Snow typology suggests that firms should pick one of four possible strategies (fig. 15.2). Once again it is possible to suggest some examples of firms following these broad strategies.

Figure 15.2: Miles and Snow typology

	Definition	Examples
Prospector	Constantly seeking out new markets and opportunities; is oriented towards risk-taking	Seán Quinn Group
Defender	Concentrates on defending its present markets, maintaining stable growth, and serving present customers	Clery's department store
Analyser	Maintains market share and seeks to be innovative, but not as innovative as the prospector	HB ice cream
Reactor	No consistent strategic approach; drifts with environmental events, and is only able to react to them	Possibly some public service organisations; many small enterprises

Sources of competitive advantage

There are two possible sources of competitive advantage: skills and resources. If a business is assessing which strategy to pursue, it will find that its skills and resources will be a major determinant.

Skills

Skills cover a wide variety of expertise and applications. They include:

- specialised knowledge of segment needs
- customer service orientation
- design expertise
- applications expertise
- trade relationships
- the ability to use relevant technologies
- systems design capability.

Marketing is obviously an essential business skill. The ability to employ the skills of research, communication and planning, for example, will be critical to success.

Skills are people-based, and therefore there are implications for recruitment, training, and development; individual managers or individuals with particular skills or experience will be in demand.

Resources

Organisational resources will also determine strategic choice, as they have a significant bearing on the ability to use the skills described above. Resources could include:

- distribution coverage
- financial structure and access to capital
- shared experience with a related business
- low-cost manufacturing and distribution
- production capacity
- ownership of sources of raw material or long-term supply contracts
- brands
- corporate identity.

Strategy selection

Which strategy to select will depend on a number of considerations. An assessment of the rewards and risks associated with a particular strategy will be made. The strategy will also have to fit in with the general objectives of the business, and the firm will have to have the resources to devote to it.

The implications of a particular strategy will therefore need to be assessed in terms of sales and profits, and the firm's operations. If the business has particular objectives—for example if it is following a differentiation strategy—this will determine what it is feasible to consider. Porter, for example, warned against companies attempting to implement more than one generic strategy.

Sometimes large companies will have different strategies for different businesses. In its hand-cut, higher priced crystal business, Waterford Wedgwood has maintained a differentiation strategy. It has also produced a separate range, under the Marquis brand, designed to compete in more price-sensitive segments of the higher priced market. British Airways launched a low-cost airline, Go, in 1998, which pursued a cost leadership strategy, while British Airways continued to follow a differentiation strategy.

Implementation

The implementation of strategy will require a detailed programme or plan. This will be accompanied by cost and revenue budgets. The programmes will include all the marketing, operational, financial, and human resource requirements. From the marketing viewpoint, a marketing plan will form the basis of the marketing programme.

The marketing plan

The marketing plan is a written document containing details of how the firm's marketing will be undertaken. It will include the assumptions the management has made about its environment and details of the objectives and activities in which the company will engage. The plan will be set in the context of the general corporate mission. Plans may be quite detailed documents: they are usually prepared for at least one year and probably two or three years ahead.

Contents of the marketing plan

1. Management or executive summary
2. Marketing objectives
    (a) Company mission statement
    (b) Detailed company objectives
    (c) Product group goals
3. Product or market background
    (a) Product range and explanation
    (b) Market overview and sales summary
4. Marketing analyses
    (a) Marketing environment and trends
    (b) Customer needs and segments
    (c) Competition and competitors' strategy
    (d) SWOT analysis
5. Marketing strategies
    (a) Core target markets (segments)
    (b) Basis for competing or differential advantage
    (c) Desired product or brand positioning
6. Statement of expected sales forecasts and results
7. Marketing programmes for implementation
    (a) Marketing mixes
    (b) Tasks and responsibilities
8. Controls and evaluation: monitoring of performance
9. Financial implications or required budgets
    (a) Delineation of costs
    (b) Expected returns on investment for implementing the marketing plan
10. Operational considerations
    (a) Personnel and internal communications
    (b) Research and development and production needs
    (c) Marketing information system
11. Appendixes
    (a) SWOT analysis details
    (b) Background data and information
    (c) Marketing research findings

Source: S. Dibb, L. Simkin, W. Pride, and O. Ferrell, 1997.

Analysis of strategic situations and alternatives

Having assessed the environmental forces, the marketer has to evaluate possible courses of action. This is facilitated by a number of planning concepts and techniques and analytical planning methods. Two of these—the BCG matrix and the General Electric business screen—are considered in the following sections.

The BCG matrix

The Boston Consulting Group matrix (1970) evaluates businesses or products relative to the growth rate of their market and the firms' share of the market (fig. 15.3). It provides a framework for evaluating the relative performance of businesses or products within a portfolio.

The BCG matrix may therefore be useful for companies that market several products or have several different businesses. Many larger companies, such as Guinness, Lever Brothers, or Procter & Gamble, will have products or brands that could be evaluated on the basis of their market share relative to growth in the market. Strategies may be developed on the basis of the product or brand position in the matrix. *Star* products will require marketing investment in the form of positioning, communication, and distribution; while *cash cows* will need to be managed to continue the cash surplus required for investment in other products.

Question mark and *dog* products pose a challenge. For a product to be classified as a 'question mark' it must not be meeting customers' needs, relative to competitors. If the product is not changed or repositioned, it may become a drain on the company's resources. Dog products generally do not have much of a future; they may, however, have a small loyal user base, which the marketer may wish to hold on to. On the other hand, if possible, they may be sold off.

Figure 15.3: The BCG matrix

		Market share	
		High	Low
Market growth	High	**Star** High growth, high market share. Will require marketing investment for more growth.	**Question mark** Low market share in a high-growth market. Product may need to be redeveloped or changed.
	Low	**Cash cow** Holds significant market share in a low-growth market. Generates cash for investment in other products, especially 'stars'.	**Dog** May not have a very long future. Could be sold or allowed to fade away.

The General Electric business screen

The General Electric 'business screen' (fig. 15.4) was developed to assess business performance on the basis of industry attractiveness and competitive position (Hofer and Schendel, 1978). *Competitive position* is determined by a number of factors, including market share, technological know-how, product quality, service network, price competitiveness, and operating costs. *Industry attractiveness* is determined by market growth, market size, capital requirements, and competitive intensity. Just as with the BCG matrix, the position of the business in the matrix will determine the strategy the firm should pursue.

Figure 15.4: The General Electric business screen

Industry attractiveness	Competitive position		
	Good	*Medium*	*Poor*
High	Winner	Winner	Question mark
Medium	Winner	Average business	Loser
Low	Profit-producer	Loser	Loser

Commitment to action

A commitment to action means that the firm is prepared to take action on its plans. Strategy implies action. The company will have to ensure that managers and those who will be required to implement the strategy are aware of and understand what the strategy is about.

There is therefore a need for top-down and bottom-up dialogue. In other words, strategies will usually be developed by senior management; these should be communicated to managers and other staff at lower levels, who should have an opportunity to provide feedback. If, for example, a strategy had implications for product sales strategy, the views of the sales staff should be sought. Their reaction, questions or observations would be useful in assessing how the strategy would be implemented.

All operational managers must understand why a strategic direction was chosen. Strategies will have implications not just for marketing but for production, personnel, and finance.

DEFINING THE BUSINESS

Central to the concept of strategy is the business definition, as this specifies the arena in which the business will compete. As we have seen, the business definition is a fundamental determinant of the company's plans. It should direct attention to the true function of the business, establish the boundaries of the business, and provide a basis for detailed strategy analysis.

Multi-dimensional business definition

The scope of the business can be defined as *multi-dimensional*. There are three principal dimensions: *customer function*, *technology*, and *segments*. These act as parameters within which the business can be defined.

Customer function

Customer function describes what benefits the product provides to customers: for example, the customer buying detergent is obviously looking for the benefit of cleanliness but may also look for other benefits, such as value for money or a product that can get rid of stubborn stains, that leaves a pleasant fragrance, or that does not damage clothes.

Most products and services can provide several benefits. Research and product development can show where additional benefits can be added. The Swiss manufacturer of the Swatch watch, for example, realised that the benefit the customer was looking for was a bit more than something that told the time: watches were fashion accessories and could be offered in different shapes and styles and for different occasions.

Technology dimension

The *technology dimension* describes the alternative ways in which the particular function can be performed. A courier service, for example, can provide delivery using bicycles, motorcycles, vans, ships, or aircraft. In other words, there are several ways in which to carry out the service; the technology used will depend on customers' requirements and the company's ability to meet them.

Customer segments

As we saw in chapter 5, customers' needs can differ. Marketers will therefore divide the market into *segments*, or groups of customers sharing particular characteristics and looking for similar benefits. A courier company, for example, might segment its market geographically and by different business or organisational types. Companies such as Federal Express, UPS, and DHL emphasise the fact that they can provide a worldwide service using different technologies. Smaller courier operations may operate within the confines of the main business or commercial districts in a particular city or may specialise in providing a service to particular customers, for example delivering legal documents.

The multi-dimensional definition can be illustrated graphically, as shown in the following panel.

MULTIDIMENSIONAL DEFINITION FOR PET FOOD

The market for pet food in Ireland is estimated to be worth €63.5 million. The Irish have the highest dog ownership per capita in Europe: 45 per cent of households own a dog. Cat ownership is lower, at 22 per cent of households.

The standard of pet care, however, has been low. Until recent years the majority of domestic animals were fed scraps. An examination of the pet food business reveals a number of customer segments, several technologies employed to produce products, and a number of benefits sought by pet owners.

Consumers have, however, become more educated about the importance of animal nutrition and diet. Manufacturers have eagerly assisted in the process by providing feeding guides and pet care information on their packaging.

With regard to market segments, an obvious basis for segmentation is between dog owners and cat owners. Within each of these are the owners of dogs and cats of different sizes and ages. Foods are therefore formulated for dogs or cats, with variations for puppies and kittens, growing animals, and even the mature animal. The benefits sought by pet owners include basic nutrition, a balanced diet, and treats. Different formulations are available, from basic low-price ranges to higher-priced ranges of complete meals. Treats are catered for by a variety of products, ranging from dog biscuits to cat snacks.

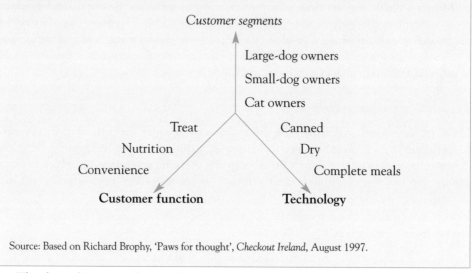

Source: Based on Richard Brophy, 'Paws for thought', *Checkout Ireland*, August 1997.

The three-dimensional definition emphasises the importance of the customer in the definition of the business. In the case of the pet food market it also shows where new functions, segments, and technologies can be applied. As pets play a central role in many people's lives, and pet ownership has been linked to the alleviation of stress and loneliness, the importance of pet nutrition has increased. By using the multi-dimensional definition, the marketer of pet foods can assess how they perform on these criteria and where opportunities may exist to develop new segments, serve new needs, or employ new technologies—possibly the market may become more segmented by animal age; new benefits sought might include low-cholesterol products; and technology might be employed to provide chilled or frozen pet food.

Understanding what drives the business

Marketing theory suggests that businesses are driven by customers' needs and by profit. There are many ways to achieve these objectives, and different firms can place a different emphasis on the means of doing so. A number of possible driving forces can be considered (Day, 1984).

- **Products offered:** The business continues to produce similar products but continually seeks new markets for these products, for example small Irish crystal companies. Few have the resources to compete in overseas markets, so companies concentrate on serving niches, such as the corporate market.
- **Market-needs-driven:** The business continually seeks alternative ways of satisfying market needs, for example Superquinn. The company is needs-focused and has developed its reputation for customer service on this basis.
- **Technology-driven:** The company produces only products that can apply the firm's technological capabilities, for example Iona Technologies, which specialises in the creation of specialist software.
- **Production capability:** This involves concentrating on production efficiency, process and systems, for example Guinness. Over the past 20 years the company has developed its brewing production process, using new technology to replace older, more labour-intensive methods.
- **Method of distribution:** The business promotes products that suit its method of distribution, for example HB ice cream. The company has paid particular attention to its marketing channels, which involved it in a seven-year court battle.
- **Control of raw materials:** The business concentrates on controlling and conserving resources as a means of increasing their value, for example Smurfit. A significant strategy for Smurfit has been backwards integration. The company owns thousands of acres of forest in Scandinavia, as well as the factories that can convert the raw material into paper and cardboard. In addition, Smurfit has engaged in forward integration by owning a number of printing companies.

Competitive advantage

In the long run the company's best interests are served if it does only what it can do better than its competitors. This is the nature of competitive advantage. The business must have skills and resources that make it unique and that mean it can be differentiated from competitors. Think of any product or service; the first ones that come to mind will usually have some characteristic that separates them from competing products.

Sometimes companies can achieve a competitive edge by challenging the conventional wisdom in the market. This has been referred to as 'disruption theory' (*Marketing*, 13 February 1997). In other words, every assumption about a market should be questioned. In some industries it was considered that being large and enjoying economies of scale would be a significant barrier to entry, deterring competitors from entering the industry. In the cement market, Irish Cement dominated sales until the arrival of the Seán Quinn Group, as the next panel illustrates. Care needs to be exercised: disruption theory does not mean making reckless or foolish decisions.

CHALLENGING THE CONVENTIONAL WISDOM

The Seán Quinn Group planned to open a new glassmaking factory in County Fermanagh in 1998. Employing 330 people, it would compete principally with Irish Glass Bottle, which had a significant share of the Irish market. The group's entry into glassmaking is almost a carbon copy of its entry into the cement market in the early 1990s. Then, also from a plant in County Fermanagh, it took on the market leader in that sector, Irish Cement. The company successfully launched its product and established a strong presence in the cement market.

Source: 'Quinn creates 330 jobs', *Times*, 3 March 1998.

Sustaining competitive advantage

Competitive advantage can be rather transient. The business may introduce a new product or develop a market segment, as Ballygowan did (see page 399); but there will be many imitations. Whether a competitive advantage endures depends on how the marketer reacts to environmental or competitive forces. The resources, skills and strategies of the competitors and the ease with which they can copy or improve on the product will be significant factors.

In attempting to ensure that the competitive advantage survives, the marketer may consider a number of issues. *Patent protection* should be considered, especially in the case of innovative products. Patents provide legal protection and may slow down the process of imitation or ensure that competitors can enter the market only with difficulty. Similarly, the development of brands and registering them as trade-marks can also provide protection. Brands are a source of competitive advantage; well-established brands can have a strong buyer franchise, and this should be sustained.

RESEARCH AND DEVELOPMENT IN ORAL HYGIENE

The first toothpastes were developed in the 19th century. Colgate toothpaste (in a jar) was introduced in the United States in 1873 and in Ireland shortly after the First World War. Toothpaste remained something of a niche product until the 1960s, when fluoride was added. Subsequent innovations included reformulations that added the ability to resist decay and gum disease and had cosmetic qualities, such as giving fresh breath and whitening teeth. Mouthwashes were also developed, which also had protective and cosmetic qualities.

The ergonomics of toothbrushes have been extensively researched, resulting in new shapes, designs, and sizes.

The market for oral care products in Ireland is valued at €51 million per year. It can be divided into a number of product categories, including toothpaste, toothbrushes, mouthwash, and dental floss. The toothpaste sector is valued at €30 million per year. The sector is dominated by the Colgate brand, which has an estimated market share of 54 per cent. The market has been growing as people become more concerned with dental care, although, in spite of the best efforts of toothbrush designers and marketers alike, the average Irish person gets through only 1.1 toothbrushes per year; a change of toothbrush every three months is generally held to be the ideal.

Source: *Checkout Ireland*, March and April 1997; *Retail News*, April 2002.

Another way of sustaining competitive advantage is keeping up to date with the changing needs and requirements of customers. This goes back to the fundamental principle of what marketing is about.

Investment may be required, for example in new technology, to maintain the advantage. This may be in production, communication, pricing, or distribution. Many soft-drinks manufacturers have invested in new-product development but also in the use of vending machines, which can provide the consumer with a chilled drink in an instant.

Research and development into new or existing products or processes may be required. In the oral hygiene market, the leading competitors have all invested in research and development on toothpaste, mouthwashes, and toothbrush design.

Organisational mission and objectives

The mission statement should indicate what the company's purpose is. It has a dual communication role, to both staff and customers (Child, 1997). Mission statements give an insight into what makes the company tick; they also provide an indication of what the company can be expected to do, as the following examples illustrate.

MISSION STATEMENTS

Consider the following examples of mission statements from Unilever, the Body Shop and the Kerry Group.

Unilever
Unilever's mission is to add vitality to life. We meet everyday needs for nutrition, hygiene and personal care with brands that help people feel good, look good and get more out of life.

Unilever will build its business by focusing on bringing vitality to life, meeting the growing consumer needs for:

- healthy life-style
- convenience, time being an increasingly precious commodity
- indulgence, with products offering more variety, sensuality, and enjoyment.

Source: www.unilever.com.

Body Shop
We consider testing products on animals to be morally and scientifically indefensible. We support small producer communities around the world who supply us with accessories and natural ingredients.
We know that you're unique and we'll always treat you like an individual. We like you just the way you are.
We believe that it is the responsibility of every individual to actively support those who have human rights denied them.
We believe that a business has the responsibility to protect the environment in which it operates, locally and globally.

Source: www.thebodyshop.com.

Kerry Group

Kerry Group will be:

* a major international specialist food ingredients corporation
* a leading international flavour technology company
* a leading supplier of added value brands and customer branded foods to the Irish and UK markets.

Source: www.kerrygroup.com.

We will be leaders in our selected markets—excelling in product quality, technical and marketing creativity and service to our customers—through the skills and wholehearted commitment of our employees.

We are committed to the highest standards of business and ethical behaviour, to fulfilling our responsibilities to the communities which we serve and to the creation of long-term value for all stakeholders on a socially and environmentally sustainable basis.

Strategic goals and objectives

Strategic goals and objectives will emphasise the specific aspects of strategy that will be concentrated on. They should provide guidance and a unified direction for the company, facilitate planning, motivate, and inspire, and be an aid in evaluation and control. Typical examples include statements about:

* market share leadership
* innovation
* productivity
* financial resources
* profitability
* workers' performance and attitude
* social responsibility.

Tactical goals and objectives

Tactical goals and objectives follow from the strategic goals. For example, a tactical goal might be to scan markets in Europe or the United States for acquisition opportunities or potential contracts. Tactical goals might also include new-product development, positioning strategy, and brand development.

Operational goals and objectives

Operational goals and objectives will be specific to individual departments. For example, if a company plans to sell more of a product, the sales or marketing department will receive specific targets. Targets will also be set for production or operations departments to make sure the sales targets can be met.

Strategic co-operation

Strategic marketing does not mean that the firm has to go it alone. In the 1990s much emphasis was placed on the concept of strategic alliances and the development of strategies based on the relationship that firms had developed together. Strategic alliances typically involve horizontal co-operation between competitors or firms engaged in similar activities, while strategies based on relationship marketing are more likely to involve vertical co-operation, for example between manufacturers and retailers.

Strategic alliances

Strategic alliances or partnerships between independent firms are entered into for a number of reasons. As trade barriers have been gradually eroded, competition in the global market has become a reality for many businesses. Environmental changes, keeping up with developments in technology and the lack of skills or resources for going it alone have also been motivations.

The move towards strategic alliances was spurred by globalisation and a desire by companies to compete on a wider world stage. It became common in the 1990s among airlines: consider the examples of Star Alliance, established by United, Air Canada, Thai, Varig, SAS, and Lufthansa, or Oneworld, established by British Airways, American Airlines, Canadian Airlines, Cathay Pacific, and Qantas.

Relationship marketing and strategy

As described in chapter 1, relationship marketing is an important concept in the company's general approach to marketing and in the management of the value-added chain. The development of mutually beneficial relationships will usually be a significant aspect of marketing strategy. Consider the example of the relationship between Boyne Valley Foods and the Superquinn supermarket chain; this proved to be extremely beneficial for both companies, and shows that co-operation in the market can yield positive results.

Strategic brand alliances involve one brand name being joined with another as part of a promotional campaign (Rao, 1997). The motivations for entering such alliances include cost-effectiveness, competitive market conditions, and customers' needs. Certainly if companies are pursuing strategies of enhancing product attributes or improved market credibility, a strategic alliance may be helpful. Strategic brand alliances have been entered into by various marketers, including washing-machine manufacturers and detergent companies. Joint advertising can be engaged in, resulting in further economies. In some cases the alliance has translated into new-product development, as when the electrical manufacturer Black & Decker and the paint manufacturer Dulux developed an electronic painter.

Marketing organisation and control

One of the generally accepted functions of a manager is organisation. The marketing function needs to be organised so that the company's plans and marketing activities can be effectively carried out.

Some companies organise their marketing function on the basis of their products. Product management structures imply that managers are assigned to specific products or brands, and they look after the marketing and development of these. Product management was originally implemented by Procter & Gamble in the 1960s, and it tends to suit companies with a range of products.

If there is a small number of customers, as in many business-to-business markets, the company may organise its marketing function on the basis of customers. Companies like the shipbuilders Harland and Wolffe may organise on this basis, such as passenger vessels, cargo or tanker vessels, military or patrol vessels, and oil or gas exploration platforms. Another possibility is geographical organisation: this would apply where the company markets its products in international or regional markets and the marketing function is organised to serve these.

The marketing audit

Firms need to evaluate their marketing ability and performance. Environmental changes and the need to ensure that the firm's competitive advantage is sustained and developed imply a need for an objective assessment. A useful tool for doing this is the *marketing audit*. This is an assessment of the effectiveness and efficiency of the firm's marketing policies, strategies and procedures compared with its opportunities, objectives, and resources. It is a comprehensive, systematic, independent, and periodic examination of the company's or business unit's marketing environment, objectives, strategies, and activities, with a view to determining problem areas and opportunities and recommending a plan of action to improve marketing performance.

An audit should be broad rather than narrow in focus and should cover all aspects of the company's marketing. Ideally it should be conducted by someone who is independent of the firm, which should ensure a greater degree of objectivity. The audit should be systematic: in other words, it should follow a prescribed form. It should be conducted periodically and should not just be a once-off event.

COMPONENTS OF THE MARKETING AUDIT

Marketing environment audit
The marketing environment audit should be a comprehensive overview of the forces in the firm's macro and micro environment (these are described in chapter 3). The person conducting the audit should question the assumptions the company has made about its environment.

Marketing strategy audit
The marketing objectives and strategies should be assessed in the light of the opportunities or problems facing the company.

Marketing organisation audit
This involves an examination of the way in which marketing is organised as a function and how it interacts with other functions in the business. The marketing function may be headed by a marketing manager, to whom a number of product managers or

marketing executives may report. On the other hand, in smaller firms there may be only one person who has responsibility for marketing.

Marketing systems audit
'Marketing systems' describes four broad areas: the marketing information system, the marketing planning system, the marketing control system, and the new-product development system. It is important that the company has systems that support its marketing activities.

Marketing productivity audit
The result of the company's marketing activities can be measured in a number of ways. Satisfied customers who have provided a profit for the business will be an important measure. Research should provide an indication of customer satisfaction; the critical financial measure will be the profits made. Profitability analysis will concentrate on the profits of the product, product lines, or individual brands. An assessment will also be made of the cost-effectiveness of the company's marketing activities.

The marketing functions audit
The marketing functions audit will involve an assessment of each aspect of the company's marketing mix. This will be assessed to ensure that they are integrated and that clear strategies exist for the products, pricing, promotion and place elements.

Source: P. Kotler, W. Gregor, and W. Rodgers, 'The marketing audit comes of age', *Sloan Management Review*, Winter 1977.

FURTHER READING

Day, G., *Strategic Market Planning: The Pursuit of Competitive Advantage*, St Paul (MN): West 1984.
Mullins, J., Walker, O., Boyd, H., and Larréché, J.-C., *Marketing Management* (fifth edition), New York: McGraw-Hill 2005.
Porter, M., *Competitive Strategy*, New York: Free Press 1980.

DISCUSSION QUESTIONS

1. Describe the implications of the four distinguishing features of strategic planning for each of the following:
   —Irish Biscuits
   —the Educational Building Society
   —a third-level college
   —the Abbey Theatre.
2. Comment on the relationship between goals and planning. Are they symbiotic?
3. Explain the importance of establishing a competitive advantage. How does competitive advantage affect the design and implementation of strategy?
4. Describe what competitive advantage you perceive the following firms to have:

—Nike
—Abrakebabra
—Murphy's stout.
5. Select a firm and carry out a marketing audit on it. If you cannot get access to a firm directly, conduct your audit using secondary sources of information.

REFERENCES

Boston Consulting Group, *The Product Portfolio Matrix*, Boston (MA): BCG 1970.
Child, L., 'Mission statements: an inspiration for us all?', *Admap*, January 1997.
Day, G., *Strategic Market Planning: The Pursuit of Competitive Advantage*, St Paul (MN): West 1984.
Dibb, S., Simkin, L., Pride, W., and Farrell, O., *Marketing: Concepts and Strategies* (third European edition), Boston (MA): Houghton-Mifflin 1997.
Hofer, C. and Schendel, D., *Strategy Formulation: Analytical Concepts*, St Paul (MN): West 1978.
Miles, R. and Snow, C., *Organisational Strategy, Structure and Process*, New York: McGraw-Hill 1978.
Porter, M., *Competitive Strategy*, New York: Free Press 1980.
Rao, A., 'Strategic brand alliances', *Journal of Brand Management*, November 1997.

NEWBRIDGE SILVERWARE

Introduction

> Newbridge Silverware is an outstanding Irish company that stands for all that is best in Irish business. In the past 10 years it has repositioned its brand and through innovative marketing has made the Newbridge Silverware brand one of the best known and respected, at home and abroad.
>
> *Joe Higgins, executive director, Bank of Scotland (Ireland) and Chairman of the judging panel, speaking as Newbridge Silverware was awarded the Best in Business Award, 2005.*

Operating in a mature market, Newbridge Silverware had indeed sought to develop its brand and extend its range of products and the Best in Business award was testimony to that. For William Doyle, the company chief executive, it was also proof that his brand extension strategy, which began in the 1990s, had yielded dividends. Jewellery, glassware, and several giftware items complemented the company's cutlery in retail outlets. The brand has been associated with many events, including Miss Ireland, the Rose of Tralee, and the Special Olympics. A successful visitor centre attracts tourists and shoppers to the company premises in Newbridge, County Kildare, where in addition to viewing the company's product range, they could also visit the museum of style icons—a gallery incorporating clothing and other items that had belonged to stars, such as Marilyn Monroe, Michael Jackson, and Audrey Hepburn.

In 2008, Newbridge had been enjoying a successful decade, but it began to feel the impact of an economic recession. Faced with more price-sensitive consumers and increased competition, especially from non-traditional sources, Doyle knew that the company faced further challenges, not least with decisions on how to develop a strategy to weather the economic storm ahead successfully. As he considered his strategic plans, he reflected on how the company had survived previous difficult environments. In the 1970s and 1980s it had downsized and concentrated on high-quality cutlery manufacture. In the 1990s it had diversified its product range to include jewellery, giftware, and household goods. In the early 2000s the manufacturing facility had been transformed into a visitor centre and the company had become more visible through high-profile sponsorships. Doyle knew a new strategy would be required to guide the firm through the difficult times ahead.

Company history

Established in 1934 as Newbridge Cutlery in part of a disused cavalry barracks, Newbridge Silverware are manufacturers of cutlery, tableware, and jewellery. The company thrived until the 1970s when, in common with many other Irish businesses, it found itself increasingly non-competitive in a free-trade environment. The company was taken over by Dominic Doyle, William's father, and a successful rationalisation programme was implemented, which enabled the company survive so that, by the 1990s, it was the only producer of cutlery in the Irish Republic. William Doyle succeeded his father in 1991, the company is still very much a family concern, his mother Mona created the showroom facility and his sister Oonagh is responsible for wholesale and retail sales. The company employs 80 people and its products are sold in a wide range of outlets in Ireland, and in a small number of outlets in the UK, the US, and Australia.

The cutlery industry

Cutlery is classified as a mature manufacturing industry; it is an industry that has become especially susceptible to low-cost import competition. The result, in common with other mature industries, have been large-scale closures and job losses. In most developed countries it is an industry in decline as characterised by Grant (1989), who identified four different categories of declining manufacturing industry (fig.15.6).

Competition in the cutlery industry, especially from Asian producers, intensified from the 1960s onwards. In addition, changing fashions and new product developments meant that demand for some cutlery products declined. The growth in sales of sliced breads, for example, affected demand for bread knives, and the development of plastic cutlery also had an impact, especially in the catering market. Changes in house design meant that many new homes did not have formal dining rooms, which affected demand for sets of higher priced silverware.

Figure 15.6: Classification of mature industry strategic environments

		Source of decline	
		Declining demand	**Low-cost foreign competition**
Levels of seller concentration	Concentrated	Tyres Steel Cigarettes Rayon Babyfoods	Domestic appliances Construction equipment Consumer electronics Shipbuilding
	Fragmented	Fragmented Acetylene Electric coffee percolators Cigars	Textiles Clothing Footwear Fasteners Hand tools Cutlery

The output of the cutlery industry includes household tableware, surgical steel products, and cutting tools used in industry. In relation to household tableware, by 2010 China accounted for 65 per cent of all stainless-steel cutlery sales in Europe and 25 per cent of world sales. In volume terms, the British Cutlers and Silverware Association estimated the world market for cutlery to be 80,000 tonnes per year.

Globally, the industry is characterised by increased competition between manufacturers from Asia and South America and surviving manufacturers in the United States and Europe. US and European cutlery output has been declining, for example between 1995 and 2005 cutlery output in the US declined by 20 per cent. Employment dropped by 25 per cent to 7,000 employees. US and European manufacturers such as Oneida and WMF now tend to concentrate on premium-quality products, product specialisation, and design. The German brand Wuesthof, for example, specialised in knife production and design. It co-operated with Le Cordon Bleu, one of the world's leading cooking academies, to produce a lightweight design that became popular with leading chefs.

In Ireland Newbridge Cutlery was not immune to the changes that had taken place in the international industry. New cutlery designs were introduced and a successful diversification strategy into glass, giftware, and household goods has been developed. In carrying out his assessment of the company's future William Doyle considered each of his product categories, beginning with cutlery. He often travelled to Sheffield, the centre of cutlery manufacture in the UK, to meet with producers there, who were facing similar difficulties.

The United Kingdom Experience

The city of Sheffield in England is generally synonymous with the cutlery industry in the United Kingdom, it is thought that manufacture began over 700 years ago. A Cutlers Company or Guild was founded in Sheffield in 1624 to regulate the trade and prevent deception. When Newbridge Cutlery was founded in the 1930s, five Sheffield cutlers came over to help establish production and train craftsmen.

Many developments in cutlery design and manufacture originated in Sheffield. One company, Elkingtons, developed electro-plating technology in 1840, which enabled base-metal pieces to be plated with a silver coating, thus creating a more affordable new product range. These products were known as EPNS (electro-plated nickel silver). In the 1920s, a Sheffield metallurgist developed stainless steel, which is now the standard material used in most cutlery manufacture.

In the late 1990s employment in cutlery production in Sheffield had dropped to 2,000, where once there were 300 cutlery companies, this had reduced to 12 (*Yorkshire Post*, 29 May 1988). While the industry is a fraction of its former size, the 'Made in Sheffield' origin endures, indeed the importance of the Sheffield name, albeit at a niche level, has ensured that the industry has not completely disappear (Wolffe, 1997). By 2009 the industry in Sheffield had declined further, and some manufacturers like Jessop and Smith had closed down (*Yorkshire Post*, 13 March 2009), while Richardsons, another of the city's oldest manufacturers, had been taken over by the Dutch company Amefa, saving the jobs of the remaining 51 employees (*Yorkshire Post*, 10 October 2007).

Some Sheffield producers have diversified successfully, for example 60 per cent of the UK's demand for medical scalpels are produced by Sheffield manufacturers. The Harrison Fisher company, a producer of knives that has been in production since 1838, invested in product design. This gave it an advantage over Asian competitors and meant that it was no longer a reactor to the powerful buyers in department stores and other retail outlets (*Strategic Direction*, 2007). Arthur Price, another long-established brand, became to world's first producer of 'anti-terror' stainless-steel cutlery. This passed the increased security requirements for airlines, which, following the terror attacks in the United States in 2001, had been forced to use plastic cutlery for in-flight meals.

Other producers had not, however, been involved in any significant product development and most concentrated on the production and marketing of designs and ranges, some of which had their origins several hundred years ago.

The Irish cutlery market

Newbridge was the only producer of cutlery in the Irish Republic and concentrated production on silver-plate products that were targeted at the premium price end of the market. The market in Ireland was dominated by imports, which accounted for 95 per cent of cutlery sold. The Irish retail market for household cutlery, also known as flatware, was estimated to be worth €25 million (company estimates). In volume terms, stainless-steel products comprised 90 per cent of the market, with silver plate or other precious metals accounted for the remainder. In value terms, silver plate was worth 25–30 per cent of the market.

The market for cutlery consists of the consumer market and the catering market. Stainless steel products, which were generally for everyday use and came in different quality grades, cater for the sales of up to 90 per cent in both markets. Newbridge supplies a range of stainless steel products mainly in the 18/10 category (the highest quality grade of stainless steel cutlery). High-grade stainless steel pieces such as table knives retail at up to €7 per piece; whereas low-grade knives could retail at less than €0.25 each. At the premium-priced end of the market were silver plate or EPNS products, which are often purchased as gifts, especially as wedding presents. A boxed set of silver cutlery could cost between €300–€1,000 depending on the number of pieces and the design. Newbridge is the market leader in the silver cutlery market in Ireland.

The catering market includes hotels, restaurants, hospitals, canteens, and airlines. These purchase mainly stainless steel cutlery, although some of the more prestigious companies use silverware. Cutlery tended to be purchased in bulk and infrequently. In some cases, such as the airlines, smaller sized pieces are required and these are usually stamped with the airline's logo. Newbridge does not actively target the catering market.

STAINLESS STEEL

Some of the more traditional silver-plate patterns and styles have tended to be copied in the different grades of stainless steel while other plain, non-patterned styles had also been developed. The trend towards less formal dining has resulted in many variations. Many stainless-steel producers offered cutlery with various shapes and designs, while many retail chains—such as Ikea, Habitat, Laura Ashley, and Marks and Spencer—have commissioned their own ranges of cutlery.

Newbridge sells a range of stainless steel cutlery that was available in high-quality grades of stainless steel, which are produced in a variety of traditional and contemporary patterns. Newbridge out-sources all its stainless-steel products, as it was no longer viable to manufacture them in its own plant. Some stainless steel cutlery is sourced in Sheffield, the rest from Asia.

Competition

Direct competitors to Newbridge include Sheffield companies such as Arthur Price and Viners, who offer ranges of silver-plate and stainless-steel cutlery. Similarly, Oneida is also a significant competitor. In retail outlets in Ireland, such as department stores and gift shops, Newbridge products are often displayed in competition with these brands. Most Sheffield producers concentrate on the premium end of the market, producing ranges of solid silver, gold or silver-plated cutlery, which are principally sold in the gift market. The development of the internet has prompted some, such as United Cutlers and Elkingtons, to develop websites for direct selling. Other companies, such as Richardsons, have concentrated on mass-market, stainless-steel products. Newbridge were market leaders in the silver-plated (EPNS) market in Ireland with an estimated share of 90 per cent (retail estimates).

The premium tableware and gift market

Since the 1990s, Irish consumers have been spending more money on premium tableware, including glassware, ceramics, china, and pottery, as well as cutlery. The market has been responsive to changing styles and designs, and manufacturers ranging from Waterford-Wedgwood, Denby, Villeroy and Boch, and Nicholas Mosse, have increased their ranges. Some manufacturers have introduced designer-inspired ranges, such as the John Rocha range of glassware produced by Waterford, or the Louise Kennedy range from Tipperary Crystal. William Doyle approached Paul Costelloe, one of Ireland's leading fashion designers, with a view to him designing and endorsing a new range of premium-priced cutlery and the range was launched in 1997. In describing the range, Costelloe said, 'I do believe it reflects my own taste for understated elegance and casual dining with style.' The product largely appeals to younger ABC1 consumers who place a lot of emphasis on style and design. The collection has proved very popular and, by 2000, was the company's single most successful line.

Another trend has been for manufacturers to extend product ranges with related items, for example Waterford-Wedgwood has commissioned one of its subsidiaries, the German tableware manufacturer Rosenthal, to produce a range of cutlery using the Wedgwood brand name (Daly, 1998). This represents a continuation of Waterford's brand licensing strategy that was being used to extend the brand across different related products. The Waterford name has already appeared on a range of Wedgwood chinaware produced in the UK and a range of table linen produced in the Philippines, China, and Belgium. Waterford's strategy is to enhance the brand in what was referred to as a 'table-top' initiative.

In Newbridge's case, the successful Paul Costelloe cutlery range was extended with the addition of a collection of glassware. Doyle also introduced a new range of silver-plated giftware and a range of cast tableware. Particularly successful items in the Irish market include silver-plated photograph frames, clocks, and candlesticks.

The Newbridge giftware range also expanded the distribution base, with an increased number of gift and craft shops, such as Kilkenny Design, Blarney Woollen Mills, and Quills, stocking the Newbridge range of cutlery, jewellery, and giftware. In 2008 the company had approximately 300 retail customers in Ireland.

The Newbridge name is associated with quality in the retail trade. In consumer markets the name is readily recognised. The typical Newbridge customer is 35 plus and bought cutlery in the high-price/premium category for their own use or as a gift. Newbridge competes in this segment with its EPNS range. The market is traditional in taste and when a particular pattern has been selected, there is a high probability that further ancillary items will be added. Cutlery is sold in department stores, gift shops, houseware shops, and in some jewellers. In addition, as sales have increased exclusive outlets, for example in the Square Shopping Centre in Tallaght , have been established.

Jewellery

In 1994 one of the company's craftsmen was experimenting with scrap pieces of sterling silver left over from the production of other products. The scrap silver was a valuable commodity and some pieces were made into pendants and bracelets. These were shown to a few jewellery retailers, but the response was negative. The jewellery did, however, catch the eye of one of the presenters of an RTÉ fashion programme, who was visiting the company's showroom. She decided to devote a segment to the jewellery in one of the shows and the response took Doyle by surprise—viewers liked what they saw and people began to enquire at the showrooms about buying the items they had seen. Production of the jewellery began, and sales increased rapidly so that, by 2010, they represented one of the company's most successful lines.

Difficult times

Brand extension initiatives have been successful for many luxury-goods manufacturers; however in the period between 2001 and 2010, there were two significant periods of global economic slowdown. Following terrorist attacks in the US in 2001 there was a period of economic downturn when sales of luxury goods were especially affected. In 2008 the world experienced an economic recession following the collapse of a number of large financial institutions.

Towards the end of the decade, in February 2009, the Waterford-Wedgwood company, which had been experiencing declining sales and increased competitive pressure across its range of luxury goods, went into receivership. In addition to the loss of almost 1,000 jobs, it was a significant blow for Ireland's manufacturing industry.

Newbridge has a strong brand presence in the Irish market and is weathering the recession. Doyle has always been aware of the value of publicity. Initially this involved presenting company products to celebrities or visitors to Ireland, all the time emphasising the unique Irish characteristics of the brand. Later the strategy evolved to the selection of events the company sponsors, such as the Special Olympics in 2003 and the Rose of Tralee from 2004 onwards. These photo opportunities and sponsorships have all helped to build awareness and have generated a significant amount of positive press coverage.

The opening of the Museum of Style Icons in 2009 at the company's headquarters also generated much attention. Various items that had belonged to stars of stage and screen such as Audrey Hepburn, Marilyn Monroe, Michael Jackson, and The Beatles were put on display. The museum was dedicated to design and style excellence and in addition to the items belonging to stars and celebrities, also featured examples of the work of leading Irish fashion designers. Admission to the museum is free and also brought visitors to the company's showroom and restaurant.

The future

Waterford Crystal has dominated the Irish premium glassware and table-top market and its demise created significant uncertainty in the industry. While the company reopened a small production and showroom facility in Waterford in 2010, it is a fraction of its former self. All luxury goods manufacturers faced difficult times as the economic recession that began in 2008 took hold. In 2009 and 2010 consumer spending dropped, especially for luxury goods.

The 2000s had seen the successful introduction of new ranges and products, and Newbridge's sales increased. Ireland's economic growth in the same period created a very buoyant giftware market and consumers who were, according to Doyle, much more interested and appreciative of modern, elegant designs.

By 2010 these consumers were much less certain of the future. Unemployment had risen from 4 per cent of the working population to almost 15 per cent. Earnings and salaries were also in steady decline, with economic commentators warning that it would take several

years before a recovery would begin. This period also coincided with Newbridge's new strategic plan with Doyle wondering what lessons he could learn from the way the company has responded to challenges in the past.

FURTHER READING

Boston Consulting Group, *The Product Portfolio Matrix*, BCG Inc 1970.

Day, G. S., *Strategic Marketing Planning: The Pursuit of Competitive Advantage*, St Paul (MN): West 1984.

Ennis, S., 'Marketing Planning in the Smaller Evolving Firm: empirical evidence and reflections', *Irish Marketing Review*, vol. 11 (1998), no. 2, 49–61.

Hamel, G. and Prahalad, C. K., 'The Core competences of the corporation', *Harvard Business Review*, May–June 1990.

DISCUSSION QUESTIONS

1. Elaborate on the challenges faced by marketers as they attempt to market in a recession.
2. What are the strategic lessons that Newbridge learned?
3. Develop a strategic marketing plan for Newbridge.

REFERENCES

Daly, G., 'Waterford spreads its name around', *Sunday Business Post*, 5 July 1998.

Grant, Robert M., 'Competing against low cost cutlery imports', *Long Range Planning*, vol. 22 (1989), no. 5, 59–69.

Strategic Direction, vol. 23 (2007), no. 7.

Wolffe, R., 'Sheffield: A comfort zone built on branding', *Financial Times*, 27 February 1997.

Index